The Conquest of Mental Retardation

Publisher's Note

Dr. Burton Blatt was dedicated to establishing a more accepting society for people with disabilities. His vita lists 291 published contributions to the field of special education. *The Conquest of Mental Retardation* is his final and most ambitious work. In January 1985 Dr. Blatt died following a brief illness.

The evolution of this special project began in 1982 when Dr. Michael Begab, Senior Editor at University Park Press, convinced Dr. Blatt to write a textbook containing his collective thoughts on the subject of mental retardation. Dr. Blatt accepted the challenge and began what was to become his finest work.

In June 1984 PRO-ED acquired the complete human services line of University Park Press; included among the books to be published was Dr. Blatt's first draft of this book. The enormous scope and nature of the work called for a second, more condensed draft. In the fall of 1984, I visited Dr. Blatt in Syracuse and discussed revisions, and in December 1984 the author's second draft reached us.

Early in 1985 we asked two eminent scholars in the field of mental retardation to serve as guardians of the project's integrity. Drs. Edward Polloway and David Smith of Lynchburg College graciously accepted roles as editors and saw the project through to completion. Their contribution helped to create a volume that meets with Dr. Blatt's greatest hope for the book—that it be suitable not only as a textbook in special education courses but that it also stimulate thought and action among all professionals working in the field of mental retardation.

Dr. Blatt did not provide a preface with his original manuscript; the one contained herein was written by the editors and makes a special statement about a special book. The acknowledgments page in this text is the one originally prepared by the author; in a final version Dr. Blatt would no doubt have included the names of many other friends and colleagues who contributed to this effort. For him, we thank you all.

Donald D. Hammill
PRO-ED, Inc.

The Conquest of Mental Retardation
BURTON BLATT

Foreword by Seymour Sarason
Preface by Edward A. Polloway and J. David Smith

5341 Industrial Oaks Boulevard
Austin, Texas 78735

Copyright 1987 by PRO-ED, Inc.

All rights reserved. No part of this book
may be reproduced in any form or by any means
without the prior written permission of the publisher.

Printed in the United States of America

Library of Congress Cataloging in Publication Data

Blatt, Burton, 1927–1985.
    The conquest of mental retardation.

    Bibliography: p.
    Includes index.
    1. Mental retardation.   I. Title.   [DNLM: 1. Mental
Retardation. WM 300 B644c]
RC570.B528 1987   616.85'88   86-15129
ISBN 0-89079-140-6

5341 Industrial Oaks Boulevard
Austin, Texas

10 9 8 7 6 5 4 3 2   88 89 90 91

To Ethel

With love, and for having faith

in me and in us together

Contents

Foreword ix
by Seymour Sarason

Preface xiii
by Edward A. Polloway and J. David Smith

Acknowledgments xv

Part 1 *Beginnings* 1

1. About This Textbook 5
2. What We Can Know Before Studying the Field 13
3. Historical Survey of Mental Retardation 27

Part 2 *People Who Are Mentally Retarded: Who Are They?* 61

4. Defining and Counting Mentally Retarded Persons 65
5. Perspectives on Mental Retardation Through the Eyes of Different Beholders 81
6. Formal Classification Schemes: The Search for Causes and Effects 115

7. Explanations of Mental Retardation   137
8. The Controversies   149

Part 3   *The Conquest of Mental Retardation: The Dream, the Illusion, and the Reality*   171

9. The Expansion of Services: 1950s to 1970s   175

Part 4   *The Politics of Mental Retardation: Monopolies and Monoliths*   191

10. The Industries   195
11. Social, Cultural, and Political Forces   219
12. Aspirations and Values   235

Part 5   *Social Change and the Professions*   251

13. Ideals, Practices, and Declarations   255
14. Practitioners and Scholars   269

Part 6   *Beyond the Science Fantasy: Perspectives on Where We Have Been, What We Have Become, Why It Is Important*   293

15. Banishment: The Creation of Monsters   297
16. Intelligence   309
17. Life, Eugenics, Euthanasia, and Sterilization   319
18. Mental Retardation and Mentality   333
19. Living Well Together is the Best Revenge for the Past   349

References   373

Index   383

Foreword

OF ALL THE TEXTBOOKS I have ever read, this is the first in which the author seriously asks: What are the criteria for calling something a textbook? That is a very subversive question. How appropriately subversive the question is can only be appreciated by sampling introductory texts for a discipline or for a set of conditions or for a line of inquiry. Such comparisons will reveal overlaps, but it will be hard to avoid the impression that the differences have more impact on the reader than the overlaps. It would be surprising if that were not the case because each writer has a somewhat (and many times it is more than just somewhat) different conception of what a beginner in the field should gain as a foundation for making decisions about more advanced inquiry. Some textbooks are written explicitly for students who are unlikely ever to take another course in the field. Most textbooks, I would guess, are written in the hope of attracting students to the field. And if that hope is not one of the author, it certainly is that of the instructor.

The important point is that the writers of textbooks differ about the number of facets of the field the beginner ought to know as well as about the scope and depth with which any one facet is treated. Put in another way: However much the textbook writer achieves anonymity through the editorial "we," and however much the writer strives to give an "objective" picture of the field, what is between the hard covers derives from a particular point of view that is time, place, and era bound and, more important for my present purposes, rests on considerations of values—the "shoulds and the oughts," the opinions about what is more and what is less worthy, and those quite subjective conclusions about where a field is heading.

As one would expect from Professor Blatt, he does not shrink from asking and trying to answer difficult questions. He takes the issues seriously, far more seriously than he takes himself. That does not mean, of course, that he is not passionate about what he believes—his passion is apparent on almost every page of this book. But Professor Blatt knows, quite exquisitely, how much of what we think and say are as much expressions of belief as they are of fact. But that knowledge—far from intimidating him or causing him to hide it from the reader—parades throughout this book. So what we get in this book are the serious problems seriously stated and discussed in a personally honest and open way. You will learn where Professor Blatt stands on each of the issues; you will also learn that he does not oversimplify them or unreflectively derogate those who take a different stand. If this book is not modest in size it is in large part because Professor Blatt believes that without history, biography, philosophy, morality, and ethics, a textbook in mental retardation is guilty of ignoring a past that is still in the present, of distorting some of the most bedeviling problems of the present, and of painting a picture of the future that is as unrealistic as it is uninteresting.

This is a text that borders on the encyclopedic, but as we have come to learn about Professor Blatt, he knows how to hold our interest—not by pictures that characterize so many textbooks or by catchy, Madison-Avenue-like headings or by many other eye-catching stratagems; but rather by the force of both the rationale of his argument and his passion. But there is another factor, as subtle as it is persuasive, as unusual as it is refreshing. Professor Blatt *respects* the reader. He expects him or her to be motivated to learn, to be capable of examining his or her preconceptions and to be treated like someone who can and wants to see the larger picture, and to rise to and not flee from the challenge of the complexity of the issues. We are used to hearing that young people today are rarely highly motivated to grapple with issues, that they want the terrain simply described (leaving out the conceptual valleys and mountains), and, besides, that they do not take kindly to serious reading. Maybe, but I would bet and give odds that the large majority of students will find themselves engaged with Professor Blatt in a joint quest for an enlarged understanding of the major scientific, philosophic, and historic issues in the field of mental retardation.

This is, I must emphasize, a textbook on the issues that illuminate the nature of our society from the perspective of a field long a challenge (usually an irritating, thorny, "we wish it would go away" challenge) to our major institutions. Consequently, this book is literally a unique blend of sociology, psychology, education, philosophy, history, and science. It is heroically ambitious, not because Professor Blatt is ambitious in any traditional sense but because the field of mental retardation, if it is to be seen whole, requires ambitiousness in scope. This is not a put down of other textbooks but rather a way of saying that there has never been a text that has covered so many of the issues so deeply and interestingly. Candor requires that I state that unlike many of the existing texts this one is devoid of trivial details (i.e., the kind of details that appear to be factual but in their isolation effectively obscure important truths).

I must confess that when Professor Blatt told me he was writing a textbook, I was both surprised and disappointed—surprised that he would even consider writing a textbook and disappointed that he was not playing to his considerable strengths as observer, advocate, policy analyst, intellectual leader, and goad to our moral conscience (amongst other things). My reaction, of course, reflected my knowledge of traditional textbooks, especially those in the field of special education. What I should have counted on, but did not, was Professor Blatt's steadfastness of view and boldness of purpose and conception. I should have known that he could not write a traditional textbook if he tried. So, as he has done many times before, he has presented a challenge to those who have the responsibility for teaching those who are entering the field.

This is not a textbook only for beginners. I learned much from it even though I have read almost everything Professor Blatt has ever written. In this book he has brought it all together creatively, instructively, and compellingly. Neither the field nor the readers of this book will ever be the same. That is the highest praise one can give to a textbook.

Seymour B. Sarason
Yale University

Postscript

Dr. Blatt died in January 1985. The response to his death was predictable: deep, boundless grief that a unique individual who almost singlehandedly transformed the field of mental retardation was no longer with us. The history of the field in the post–World War II era would have been quite different without Dr. Blatt's research, exposés, and intellectual-moral leadership. The contents of this book reflect well the sources and substance of his contribution and impact. It is part of a legacy for which, as individuals and a society, we are grateful. If he is no longer with us, his contributions are and will be for a very long time.

Preface

THE CONQUEST OF MENTAL RETARDATION is a textbook and yet it is more than a text. Many of the topics explored here are consistent with those that textbooks often address. This book, however, deals with themes that transcend the typical content of which textbooks in general and certainly those on mental retardation are made.

Conquest is clearly about mental retardation but at the same time it is not about mental retardation. This apparent paradox may be puzzling for the reader until Dr. Blatt's key message comes through:

> In this book, I have tried to say that the field of mental retardation is, itself, unimportant. But it offers opportunities to examine the most important issues facing the human race. It isn't that secluding retarded people is wrong, but that secluding people is wrong. Or sterilizing them. Or ending their life. In that sense, mental retardation is both the most trivial and the most important field.

Thus the paradox. As Dr. Blatt has indicated, mental retardation is a most narrow field of study, but at the same time it is one of the most encompassing fields. The information to be learned about this field can easily become just so much encyclopedic minutiae. Much more importantly, though, this same information can be addressed in a manner that reveals its relevance to many of the most critical social issues of our time. Burton Blatt has addressed mental retardation in such a context.

The book is a scholarly and philosophical rendering of a complex topic, yet it also stands as a personal statement of a life view. It is a perspective on life offered by a person who served as a mentor, friend, colleague, and inspiration to so many people in this field. Dr. Blatt lived what he wrote. His professional and personal concerns for retarded persons were intricately linked. He seems to have resisted compartmentalization of his life at every juncture. Thus he has argued that understanding more about the field of mental retardation provides a vehicle through which we may come to understand more about ourselves.

The book is focused and yet visionary. The direction in which it takes us is apparent but challenging. The interrelationships of complex issues presented here require the active involvement of the reader. To do justice to this work requires becoming a committed participant in it. We hope that our efforts have contributed in some small way to the book's resonance. We hope that we have assisted in bringing the poetry of his voice and the acuity of his mind to the reader.

Finally we must consider the question — what is the conquest of mental retardation? Dr. Blatt's answer is neither brief nor direct. He has made it clear, however, where we must look for the answer. The conquest will not come solely with the efforts of researchers or the expertise of specialists. The more crucial ground of conquest lies within all of us — in our hearts and minds.

Edward A. Polloway
J. David Smith
Lynchburg College

Acknowledgments

I HAVE WRITTEN many books. None took as long to write as this one, yet none gave me more pleasure to write. In a way, this book is "late," in that the field may now have more books than it knows what to do with. But if the proverbial worm had been "late," the bird would never have caught him. In a way, I put all my intellectual eggs in this "basket." But didn't Mark Twain give exactly that advice, just so long as I will remember to take good care of the basket? I hope that the people who mean the most to me will feel that the long wait was worthwhile.

I think about all of the wonderful ideas that have been given to me, gifts from more brilliant and generous friends. Not that I deserve to be in such company, but in a sense it's usually less the case of the great writer than the good listener with brilliant friends and opportunities for interesting observations. My cup runs over; I have enjoyed more than my share of exhilarating experiences, marvelous books, and especially loving friends. Among those no longer here are Dick Hungerford, Margeret Neuber, my father, my mother, and my father-in-law. And then there are Andrejs Ozolins (who in infinite ways contributed useful ideas to this particular work), Seymour Sarason, Frank Garfunkel, Bob Bogdan, Doug Biklen, Jim Winschel, Steve Taylor, Wolf Wolfensberger, Tom Szasz, Hank Mann, Herbert Schneiderman, Gunnar Dybwad, Linda Davern, (my bright graduate assistant, who not only read every word and comma here, but who worked with me for uncountable hours during the tedious weeks when we reduced the manuscript to something at least portable), Pat Bean (my secretary at the University, who in her off hours typed this manuscript, and who is both a superb collaborator and a loyal colleague), Mary Kishman (a faithful friend and secretary), Mike Begab (the editor at University Park Press, who knows how and when to cut, but more importantly, who first encouraged me with this book when others wouldn't, and who saw the need for a text with a context, for a book that strives to be more than simple and brief, for a book that expects the reader to be motivated), Don Hammill, my new publisher and my old friend, and to Ethel Blatt.

This book is dedicated to all of them, but especially to Ethel—my wife, my love, my friend. They lived it with me. I wrote it for them. It may appear as if the book is only Burton Blatt's, but they are my platonic (spiritual) coauthors. Engagement with books can be more than educational; it can also be emotional and socializing—for author as well as reader. Some people think of writing as a work requiring courage; others as something needing a large ego. But always, it is a collaboration—of the writer and everyone who touches him, and all things that he notices. So much for authorship!

Burton Blatt
Jamesville, New York
December 1, 1984

Part 1

BEGINNINGS

'tis the good reader that
makes the good book.

Ralph Waldo Emerson

1.

About This Textbook

THIS IS A TEXTBOOK about mental retardation—not simply about genes, chromosomes, schooling, psychology, or science. It seeks to explain this puzzling condition through recourse to facts but also through metaphor and analogy, stories and examples. It draws parallels between this problem and others, between our concerns about mentally retarded persons and issues facing society at large. I wrote the book for people new to this work, or not yet in it. But I also wrote it for my colleagues, my friends, who have been asking me to set down on paper my understanding of mental retardation and my vision of how we might better deal with it—how it might yet be conquered. I write as an essayist and struggling poet, but hope that my facts are straight and my science is tolerable.

My main purpose is to arouse if not disturb you, to force you to examine not only the dilemmas in *their* lives, but also those in *your* life, to help you understand better that if aspects of our work seem unresolvable, it is because they are—if only for the moment—unresolvable. So I will encourage you to endure, to work, to understand all you can understand. Then you will have succeeded. I will encourage you to consider the recurring themes of the book—they are not unnecessary redundancies because people never learn them well enough: the idea that all human beings are valuable, the idea that capability is educable, but also the idea that freedom is more precious to a person than even competency, and the idea that people are people—not only are we our brother's keeper, we are also not unlike him. The overriding belief connecting these themes is implied in the book's title— that mental retardation *can* be conquered. Total victory, however, will not be achieved until people learn to live with each other, until segregation of all forms is eliminated, until people who deserve to be free are free, and until there is widespread agreement that *all* human beings are precious and valuable to society. Total victory would not be achieved if only retarded persons were to change, or if retardation were to be more effectively prevented — as desirable as these possibilities are. All the rest of us must change as well.

If this book succeeds, it will be because it is more than a textbook. That is, it is more than an introduction to the field and more than a recounting of discrete "facts." If it succeeds, it is because it weaves the basic facts — certain known aspects of our work — with that which yet seeks resolution.

What is a textbook supposed to do? There is seeming agreement that it is flawed if it *only* transmits facts. Yet, this is essentially what most textbooks accomplish, regardless of the authors' intentions. There is consensus that a textbook is very flawed if it transmits inaccurate facts; yet there exist numerous textbooks which, although factual, are inaccurate. There is little agreement on much else of what should go into a textbook. Of course, publishers have for the most part agreed that textbooks must be readable for students, pleasing to the eye, competitively priced, and attractively packaged. Most publishers would also agree that textbooks must include enough (roughly 85%) material that is like that contained in all other textbooks on the subject to encourage professors to adopt the book for required reading. But beyond the wish to transmit facts and avoid inaccuracies, there is almost total disagreement about the real purpose of a textbook.

From my perspective, the main purpose of a textbook is to encourage students to consider a field more deeply and thus to stimulate their interest to go beyond the facts of a subject. Encouraging students to juxtapose one fact with another, one hypothesis with another, one generalization with another, is more important than simply transmitting facts. Gaining an understanding of the material and correlating a multitude of facts leads to what might be called "reasoning." And as thoughtfulness and reasoning capability develop, there is less need to accumulate and remember facts. The purpose of this textbook is thus not to force facts onto students, but to enliven curiosity and stimulate intellectual interest; to engage the reader in ways that will encourage learning and understanding.

As I have stated, while this book is for beginning students, it's also written for those who have mastered their share of the standard textbooks in the field but who nevertheless remain dissatisfied with what they know and with its relevancy to their work. Not all first textbooks need be only for "first readers." Textbooks on mental retardation have been expected to provide a comprehensive introduction to the field, and to do it in terms of the "hard" knowledge of scientific specialties. Beyond the introductory core, students are given clear bearings for their professional development, either to engage more deeply in a specialty or to broaden into adjacent specialties such as social work, nursing, rehabilitation, psychology, genetics, education, or neurology. Today, this comprehensive approach to introducing the field is no longer desirable if, in fact, it is possible at all; the field has grown too big and too broad. Mental retardation has become a complex network of numerous interrelated specialties, as well as an international social issue involving moral, political, and economic questions. Before we realized these broader implications, clinicians could practice their skills in a cultural vacuum. Today, they must navigate the less tranquil waters of dynamic communities, encountering such nonclinical matters as zoning laws and other legal and political realities. By the same token, public servants, school board members, urban planners, and other citizens can no longer go about their work without considering the presence among them of people who are mentally retarded; indeed, retarded people today vote for or against those same public officials.

One of the emerging conclusions about mental retardation is that the data of the clinical field are inextricably bound to the values and beliefs of society as a whole. This bond is something that a contemporary textbook on mental retardation must deal with and illuminate. And because we can no longer conceive of facts apart from beliefs, the demand for objectivity becomes the demand to identify those beliefs through which we filter our facts.

The central belief embedded in approaching mental retardation as a social problem is that *all people are valuable*. Seymour Sarason (1985, p. 3) has written about according *all people* (all those discussed in this book) "the status of *persons* and *personhood*, emphasizing our similarities as thinking and feeling people and trying to counter the dominant view that they are incomplete, damaged semi-empty vessels." One's value as a human being does not have to be deserved. In a way, the quality of nobility itself may be measured by the degree to which one practices this belief. In maintaining this perspective, I have attempted to develop a textbook that anyone — people of all careers and from all walks of life — might read. Indeed, ultimate solutions of our *social* problems will come as everyone becomes more like the specialists. That is the specialists may remain specialists, but the general public must become knowledgeable and involved participants.

The central belief through which I view mental retardation as a specialized field is that all people are educable. The educability hypothesis is an open question and remains a legitimate subject for speculation and research, and that is how I approach it in this book. What I am saying is that the outcome of such examinations cannot be permitted to have any bearing on decisions that must be made regarding mentally retarded persons. The orientation of those who would help a retarded person must be to *find* ways of teaching and bringing about growth — not to determine *whether* it is possible. This fundamentally moral stance is one that cannot be verified among the scientific or technical discoveries of the field. The specialist must discover this stance through an awareness of his or her kinship with all other human beings. This is the sense in which I have identified these two beliefs — that all people are *valuable* and that all people are *educable* — as central to my understanding of mental retardation. I hasten to point out, though, that these beliefs do not exhaust my biases. Cutting across the social and scientific aspects of the field of mental retardation, I have other beliefs that will emerge throughout the book. For example, I believe that integration is preferable to segregation, community living to institutional residence, and help to treatment — preferences that seem absurdly platitudinous in the abstract, yet can engender serious controversy in certain contexts.

The beliefs that all people are valuable and all people are educable are especially important because they engender a conceptualization of the field as a whole rather than as the sum of the particular problems that arise within it. In that they are both universal statements ("all people") and essentially moral statements, they confront us rather directly with a field that goes beyond the domain of "expertise" to involve "everyone." Better solutions to the problems of retarded people will emerge as clinical service becomes not only more skilled but also as it becomes a natural part of the continuum of human relationships — that is, as the boundaries of specialization become diffused.

The understandable, though unfortunate, outcome of specialization in this field has been the differentiation of people. One trained in any specialty becomes "different" by virtue of possessing unique skills or knowledge. At the same time, for each specialization there emerges a target population with the dovetailing "difference": They appear to need or want the unique skills or knowledge of the specialist. In many cases, this can mean efficiency and a desirable state of affairs. People learn to seek the specialist appropriate to their needs or wants in order to satisfy them and, thus, shed the "differences" that interrupted the course of their lives. With mentally retarded people, however, there can be pernicious consequences to such differentiation (as there can be for mentally ill patients and old people as well as several other groups). The "difference" of being labeled mentally retarded tends to *engulf* the person's whole identity. By definition, mental retardation is not temporary interruption of an ordinary life; it is characteristic of a total life. And, to the extent that only a specialist can understand the "difference," only a specialist can understand *anything* about a mentally retarded person. Thus, by a certain logical inevitability, the mentally retarded person loses the understanding of ordinary citizens and neighbors. In my judgment, this isolation causes far greater and more widespread problems than the very "difference" that sets the isolating mechanisms in motion.

What we are left with, then, is a dilemma: There are people who need help, some of which only qualified specialists in mental retardation can provide; yet, the offer of such help, or even the mere identification of someone who needs it, tends to remove a person from the human flock.

Until recently, the response to this dilemma was to try to overcome it by ever more powerful applications of specialized techniques. However, there are many reasons why such a response has been unsuccessful and will not succeed in the future. The concern is, therefore, with counteracting the isolating forces by offering an approach to specialized training that emphasizes what people have in common rather than what separates them, and by considering ways in which more acceptance and understanding of mentally retarded people can be disseminated outside the boundaries of specialization.

The discussion so far has presupposed that the nature of mental retardation, though complex, is defined and understandable. This, however, is not an entirely warranted presupposition. Scientific definitions are no longer acceptable; they leave too much unaccounted for. They could form the basis of a diatribe on what mental retardation *isn't*. But I can marshal no comparably confident statement of what it *is*. Partly, this is because until more of the implications of the new paradigm emerge, definitions must be tentative. We must be prepared for implications we didn't expect or didn't want. But in even larger part, the difficulty of producing an alternative definition stems from the fact that what has happened in the field of mental retardation is not merely a loss of confidence in standard definitions. Rather, there has been a loss of confidence in definitions *as such*. A manifestation of this can be seen in the realm of IQ testing. Until recently, the important questions concerned how such tests could be improved. Today it has become a question of whether these tests should be used at all. I believe neither that IQ tests are useless nor that definitions of mental retardation (or intelligence) are impossible. What I am urging is that these issues represent the emergence of very serious and fundamental questions in the field that cannot be answered simply by producing new facts. There is an analogy here with the Copernican revolution, which brought a new understanding of what everyone had "seen" all along. Likewise, the field of mental retardation needs a new understanding through which to view well-known facts.

Where can we begin in developing this understanding? For several reasons, it wouldn't help to look for the "real" historical beginning in order to understand today's pressing issues. For one thing, the real beginning is inaccessible to us, buried in an irretrievable past. The search for a history is seriously misleading if we suppose that there was some discrete point in time at which the problem of mental retardation *began*. Rather, mental retardation is a concept that developed *with* history. It has changed through time in its nature and in its significance. This flux is part of what we must learn to understand. What we need is a way to grasp and understand the perpetually recurring and changing beginning — a way that may be less like what we call science than it is like the myths and dramas of the ancient Greeks. Plato used the myth of the cave to help understand what it is to know, what is the shadow and what is the genuine figure. Through his story of a man who had lived in a dark cave, passing into the full light of the sun — from seeing faint shadows of things by firelight to seeing them in full brilliance and dimension — we come not only to understand what Plato means by "full knowledge"; we can even appreciate what it would be like to have such knowledge. We are taken beyond the facts of knowledge to a glimpse of the experience of knowing. Perhaps the field of mental retardation today needs a comparable myth to understand what it is to *not* know.

I am raising, of course, the rather heretical (but compelling) notion that science does not reveal everything needed to understand mental retardation. We live in an age when every schoolchild learns that myths were laid to rest long ago by science, and never so decisively as in the last few decades. The "Great Leap for Mankind" in modern times has not been a great stride in literature or philosophy; rather, the "Leap" has taken the very literal form of a man stepping from his flying machine. We don't like to seem entirely barbaric, so we do teach the schoolchild that Einstein played the violin and concerned himself with the meaning (not only the structure) of the universe. Perhaps the achievements of science and technology are just too spectacular for us to remember that scientific advances are merely the answers to specific questions — and that our questions are determined by our view of the world, by what we believe is good or important. Science follows rather than leads the dominant beliefs of an age. It fulfills rather than banishes our myths.

One of the most important myths that contributed to the origin of the field of mental retardation in the eighteenth century was Rousseau's "noble savage." Just as the ancient Greeks "explained" the world they knew through stories of figures like Prometheus or Odysseus, the noble savage constituted an "explanatory myth." But because few people have been as wise as the wisest Greeks, Rousseau and many other thinkers of the period didn't grasp that it really was a myth. They didn't understand that the *myth* of Prometheus could tell us far more than any actual Prometheus we could hope to find. The discovery of Victor, the "Wild Boy of Aveyron," helped to set this error in motion. Victor did not reveal the secrets of human nature. His story didn't even reveal very much about pedagogy or mental retardation — or, rather, if he revealed anything it was because the world was (and is) paying attention to Victor and his teacher, Jean Itard, far more than to the thousands of other pupils and teachers who could have revealed the same things. The meaning of the *myth,* however, could reveal a great deal. What we can find in the myth of the noble savage or the wild child is not that savages are noble and educable but that *all* people are noble and educable. It is not an anthropological fact but an affirmation of the kinship of all human beings.

Yet, we can't dwell forever with our myths and affirmations. There are real problems that real people suffer, and we must try to understand and ameliorate them. How can we begin? We need to understand what these problems are. At first we need to make them plausible, understandable, rather than to explain them. We have to clarify what we know about the problems people call the "mentally retarded" experience. What makes them problems? How do they arise? What are people saying or thinking when they perceive a problem as being one of mental retardation? It should become clear that we have to unearth not only information about retarded people, but also information about the world in which they live, about the demands that are or must be placed on them, about the elasticity of the social fabric in which they can or can't fit. And this requires us to examine most closely our own "intuitive" response to retarded people. We are the creators of the conditions without which there are neither problems nor solutions. Hence, the preoccupation of much of this textbook is that *we will conquer mental retardation not only by better science, but by a better way of life.* My aim is not to diminish what science *can* do; specialties from education and psychology to neurology and surgery can offer a great deal, often life itself. My aim is to make it clear to the student that these specialties reveal little that teaches us how to live with people who are mentally retarded.

This approach to studying mental retardation cannot produce a conventional textbook on the field. I cannot offer students the prospect of a clear, comfortable, and circumscribed professional specialty; first, because there is little that is clear or circumscribed; and second, because I view the idea of a "comfortable profession" as a dangerous oversimplification. The point is that increasingly specialized knowledge about mental retardation will, in itself, do relatively little to ameliorate the problems faced by mentally retarded people. This book focuses on the whole fabric of society: us. In order to understand and respond to the voices of mentally retarded people, we must understand ourselves, our society, our institutions (in the broader sense), our values and our traditions. Thus, I will consider this textbook successful if some students who had intended to make a career in the field change their minds—not because their intentions of helping mentally retarded people eroded, but because they recognized different ways to apply their dedication. On the other hand, I hope that those who do pursue careers in the field will better appreciate that their goals involve immersion in a broad social-cultural context. *In order to succeed in these ways, this textbook must preserve and illuminate the relevance of mental retardation to the fundamental problems of our society and, thus, to students of all disciplines.* To succeed, this book must deal with elementary principles, not merely of a field but of our lives.

As plainly as possible, I will try to lay out the elementary principles, basic problems, and understandings of this field. And wherever possible, these principles, problems, and understandings will be discussed in terms of the larger society, common understandings, and fundamental human needs. A writer must not be an island. It is not good to write a book for people who will not read it. A writer publishes not to be different from but to be a part of people. If there is a skill, it shouldn't be wasted. The need for a textbook focusing on the grammar (the structure and principles) of mental retardation rather than, for example, the grammar of life, is to me simple enough. It may be pretentious to think I can offer wisdom about a field, but unthinkable to believe I have something relevant to say about life itself. People get things done when they focus on their specific problems and solutions (not only because the individual is always the beginning context, but also because that's the simplest place to begin). I am better acquainted with the details of the problem called "mental retardation" than the details of life. The paradox is that I too am a specialist, and I too am intimidated when speaking beyond the safety of my specialization. So, I have struggled to create a textbook (a basic statement) on the elementary principles of mental retardation, a field I have been connected with for almost four decades. I hope this book will not be simply more academic baggage but that it will be a useful companion to the other books, papers, and ideas you find to be valuable as you engage yourself in this work. And more as confession than as bragging, I hope my penchant for the obscure scholar, the recondite idea, the unpopular belief, or the fugitive reference does not discourage you.

And lastly, as I try to offer an introduction to this book — a work that has suffered through more surgery than the author, more cutting than my barber, and even more anxiety than students — it is imperative to warn you that this is a different textbook — a very long and different essay on a very old and complex problem.

2.

What We Can Know Before Studying the Field

WHAT DO YOU KNOW about mental retardation? Make no mistake; you know a great deal. At this point, you may not be familiar with the various technical definitions of mental retardation — either the traditional ones that cast the condition as incurable, or the newer ones that are grounded in a functional perspective (if you behave retarded, you are retarded). But you know more than you think, if not more than you will know after formal study of this common yet complex problem. Although formal definitions will be discussed later, this chapter will engage you in (a) the *idea* of mental retardation (its ancient lineage), (b) the hypothesis of educability (its neglect by those who conceive of the problem as irremediable), and (c) the notion that every judgment has an historical context (even those concerning the heros and supposed villains in this field). Thus, this chapter begins to examine what the field is all about, illustrating the major points with biographical vignettes on the lives of Helen Keller, Alfred Binet, Richard Hungerford, Martin Luther, Jean Jacques Rousseau, and with brief mention of others who have influenced this field, intentionally or not.

Imagine living in a community that has no doctors, no psychologists, no teachers, no social workers — a community of individuals who are *neither* professionally trained *nor* in communication with the technical-academic world. Here in the United States 100 years ago, most people did not have ready access to special services; 400 years ago, hardly anyone on the face of the earth had doctors to treat them, professional teachers to teach them, or nurses to medicate them. And while it can be said that each of the traditional professions has roots that go back to ancient times, it must also be said that these professions became visible in the Industrial Revolution and flowered in the atomic age. The future may not be clear, but it *is* clear that most of today's professionalized human services — care of elderly and sick people, delivery of babies, childrearing, marriage counseling, financial planning, and vocational training — were once provided exclusively by family and friends. It is equally clear that the specialized field of mental retardation is of relatively recent formation.

How is it, then, that Plato and Aristotle, Martin Luther, Moses, and probably Noah knew something about mental retardation? There are many instances in the Old Testament (the Torah) and the Talmud (the oral law) in which "fools," "simpletons," and other "handicapped" people are discussed. Indeed, people with "blemishes" — peculiar heads and other anomalies — were judged unfit for certain duties. And it was Jesus who taught his followers that those who are the least among *us* are the greatest in His eyes; what is done to them is done to Him. In a sense, "mental retardation" was discovered long before it was invented. This is another way of saying that before there was a *field* of mental retardation — before it had its own terminology and explanations, before there was an interest in studying the problem professionally and scientifically, before there was a will to do something about the problem — there *was* a problem. And while the problem was formalized for all sorts of reasons, and by all sorts of people, we have always known that individuals differ intellectually and we have been driven to note and comment upon these differences.

Before the evolution of the sciences and professions, when a village would endure by its wits and its good luck with rain, wind, and sun, it knew exactly who in its midst was defective, strange, and different. The villagers didn't then, and we don't now, need scientists to point out our "different" people. Scientists explain reality, sometimes hide reality, may even alter reality, but they can't forever prevent its discovery. The reality of a severely mentally retarded child predates science.

What about the parents of this child? What is there about a retarded child that may make it unbearable for parents to live with him or her? Parents had severely handicapped children long before there were places to take them for treatment or for institutionalization. What did *those* parents think? How did they know what to think? How were they guided? While some animals *do* kill their defective young, humans typically do not. But while we don't know whether other animals have aspirations for their offspring, we do know that human parents not only have dreams for their children but they are even sustained by these aspirations. Children are supposed to grow up, to sit, to speak, and to walk at certain ages. They are supposed to mature to independence. Parents (and teachers) are supposed to become unnecessary as children mature. When children are very young, they should learn to speak and use the toilet and dress themselves. When they are a bit older, they should be able to master certain skills—in the home, at school, at work, in public places.

"Mental retardation" is one explanation when the dreams or expectations are not realized. Problems occur when parents have dreams that conflict with what they know about their child. Parents long for their child to be a valuable member of society, and parents need to believe that all people, especially their children, have value.

The Idea of Mental Retardation

Mental retardation can be defined in many ways. We discuss the concept in terms of educability. We understand it in terms of causes (etiology). We particularize it in terms of the intelligence quotient (IQ). We examine it in terms of consequences. We do something about it in terms of treatments. Scientists study it, clinicians treat it, administrators deal with it, parents anguish over it, extended families contend with it, and many citizens ignore it. And while it's called a metaphor by some, and something "real" by others (because it's a puzzle or a serious problem), behind all of the ways we think about and respond to mental retardation is the *idea* of it. Indeed, in a rational world there is an idea behind every phenomenon. But what is an idea? It is an image, either shared or personal. It's knowledge, either general or idiosyncratic. It differentiates one thing from other things; but it also stipulates the relationships between that thing and other things. An idea about a person is a story that explains that person. An idea about a phenomenon is a hypothesis that explains the phenomenon. An idea about the future is a prophecy, while an idea about the past is a history. Physicists have ideas about the physical world, biologists about the biological world, theologians about God, and psychologists about the mind. To the degree that ideas persuade people to act on them, they are very powerful and, consequently, can be very dangerous. But in another sense, ideas themselves have no power and present no danger. But because people do act on them, and because we don't know very much about the process of their creation—in spite of the fact that we write and talk an awful lot about ideas and how they are created and nurtured—there is nothing that is more important than some ideas nor less important than others. And so, in spite of the fact that ideas have no power just as unused tools have no power, ideas can be powerful because they can change the course of events.

To an historian, the interesting thing about an idea is its history. To a philosopher, its philosophy. The theologian may look to ideas for help in comprehending the incomprehensible. To an educator, the interesting thing about ideas is that people can learn them. To educators and others committed to helping people, the power of ideas lies in the possibility that people will understand them and will use them to change themselves and the world.

The idea of mental retardation has an ancient lineage; as we have seen, the idea of mental retardation goes back to the Old Testament. The beautiful and inspiring story of the Exodus of the Children of Israel from Egypt as told in the *Haggadah* also deals with the idea of mental retardation (Shahn, 1965). The father is taught how to tell his children the story of the exodus from Egypt in a manner appropriate to the character and capabilities of each child. To the wise son who seeks to understand the meaning of the testimonies, statutes, and judgments that God commanded the people to obey, the father must carefully explain the laws. But the wicked son deserves no such explanation. Since he has repudiated God, the father must make it clear that what the law prescribes for the parent is proscribed for the son. While the learned son is given all of the details of the Passover celebration, the wicked son is given none, because his repudiation of God must be acknowledged with even sterner repudiation by the father. And the simple son? He can only ask what is happening, so he is given a simple reply, one he can understand. As for the baby, the son who is not yet capable of asking questions, he must be told the story of the Exodus without having to ask. For him, the story must be told as if he did ask; thus, some day he will ask.

The idea of educability, the conviction that human beings can learn, that things can be done to bring out an infant's capability for changing—that is, for learning—is embedded in that section from the *Haggadah*. And the idea that the essence of human rights is the belief that even the mentally retarded individual, the simple son, must be given opportunities to develop, is also contained in the *Haggadah,* written long before there were such people as certified teachers and licensed psychologists. The idea of mental retardation has always been, and is today, a conception about people who are demonstrably different from most others, yet cannot be denied membership in the human family. Even in the worst of times, even when differentiation is most severe and human bonding is most tenuous, there is never a serious denial of that membership.

Mental retardation is an old idea, and its permutations are usually not traceable to specific events or people. Even today, we only speculate about the meanings of mental retardation and deviancy, and—conversely—capability and normality. But throughout history, the one constant is that mental retardation is accompanied by pain and disillusionment.

On Seeing Important Points When Making Judgments About People

In addition to understanding the power of ideas, one should also understand the shortcomings of history before studying the field of mental retardation. Histories are "inconvenient" in the sense that they do not so perfectly reduce the events of an era to unambiguously explain to later generations what occurred. Certainly, no history can recreate *all* actual events. Indeed, a major goal of the historian is to bring together and analyze what is judged to be most relevant. But in pursuing that purpose, much is lost; and some of what is lost causes confusion in the minds of those who weren't there. These unavoidable omissions and distortions lead to historical contradictions and erroneous understandings.

The world often doesn't know its great people, even when it thinks it knows them well. In our field, Helen Keller, Itard, Binet, and occasionally even Rousseau have been cited as seminal thinkers. Furthermore, our published histories have not been considered complete without reference to Martin Luther and Plato. Unfortunately, the reader who is satisfied with second- and third-hand iterations and interpretations of history faces the likelihood that important points will be missed, unimportant ones magnified, and too many points distorted. *Any* major history includes second-hand accounts of those who weren't present and aren't now available to tell the story; but most histories in mental retardation include third- or fourth-hand accounts; and the errors increase as the historian is distanced from the actual events. Consequently, virtually all histories in our field are dangerously incomplete, which leads to two kinds of problems: That which is preserved may be less relevant than that which is unknown; and the "facts," however pertinent, are to a degree divorced from the social-psychological context of the period. That is to say, all events—and, indeed, all words and ideas—have antecedents. To understand what actually occurred (and why) requires one to know what the times were like. Without such understanding, the people involved become uni-dimensional caricatures of their real selves, and events are made to appear as if each event occurred in a smooth, logically sequential and unambiguous unfolding. We all know that our own lives don't always progress smoothly and rationally, yet we read and understand history as if we expect the past to have been less surprising and puzzling to our ancestors than the present is to us. An important point is missed when we insist on closure on every historical issue. For to so insist is to *force* history and, thus, to *distort* whatever we might be able to learn and profit from it. The life of Helen Keller may serve well to illustrate this commentary.

Helen Keller

Stricken by disease as an infant, the deaf and blind child Helen Keller became one of the world's great public figures, a brilliant and inspiring advocate for the humane treatment of handicapped people and *others in need* (Keller, 1903). But before she became that brilliant world leader, she was considered to be seriously mentally defective. Before she met Anne Sullivan, she was a child shut off from all stimuli, all hope. Before the age of seven, Helen Keller was a half-wild "animal," untutored, unsocialized, unable to perform the simplest tasks expected of children. At the age of 19 months, disease had left her without sight or hearing, and according to the best advice available, without any hope for a normal life. She was thought to be a helpless "idiot."

Today, most people know the story of the miracle wrought by Helen Keller and Anne Sullivan. We know that the teacher and pupil developed a system for communicating, first by connecting objects with letters through spelling the object by manual alphabet in the child's hand, and next by connecting the word and the object with function or concept. To be sure, Helen Keller was a very bright child to progress so quickly from "idiocy" to Radcliffe College student. But we must remember that, before Radcliffe and before Anne Sullivan, there was only the perceived defective. Decades later, students continue to be thrilled and inspired by the life of Helen Keller. But what is often missed is that she and her teacher(s) had their own lives— beyond their concerns for each other and their common victory over the cruel accident of Helen's infirmity. To be sure, Helen lived with Anne Sullivan, who devoted herself to Helen, but Helen Keller wasn't the whole of Anne Sullivan's life. And Anne Sullivan wasn't the whole of Helen Keller's life. From 1914 until she died in 1960, Miss Polly Thompson lived and worked with Helen Keller. And there were other family members and colleagues who worked with and encouraged this remarkable woman. Furthermore, to think of Helen Keller as only an advocate for the blind and deaf is like thinking of Franklin Delano Roosevelt as only an advocate for the victims of polio. As true as such designations may be, they conceal as much or more than they reveal about the individuals concerned. Not to know that may be to miss what the lives of historical figures might have truly taught us about our own lives, had we been willing to explore beyond the obvious.

For a time, Helen Keller was an important figure in the American Socialist Movement, advocating for the working class in its struggles against capitalist exploitation, militarism, and sexism (Foner, 1967). Certainly influenced by her own disability and the blocks in overcoming it, Helen Keller's examination of industrial greed, slum life, and child labor led her to escape preoccupation with her special sightless and soundless existence.

As she strove to free herself from the disabilities that disease had created in her, she more and more sought to understand the disabilities that society had created for society's downtrodden multitudes. Seeing with her hands and her soul while others could see only with their eyes, she was led to the idea of a new social order, a world free of worker exploitation, free of preventable disease, free of sexism, free of all forms of human oppression. And although she spoke about her deafness and blindness, it was to remind us that only *we* seemed to want to remember that fact, that *she* remembered her infirmity only when we insisted that it was important.

What we must remember while studying about the field of mental retardation is that the people who influence it live that part of their lives in the context of much larger and more complex relationships. Historical contradictions often result from efforts to simplify lives and events. But that which prevents us from compressing history into a convenient, neatly comprehensible package is exactly what makes good history. Good history is necessarily uncertain and inconvenient. You may find in your study of the history of mental retardation that what is purported to be clearest turns out to be least believable—which leads us to the "good guy-bad guy" dilemma, one of the truly persistent phenomena in our field.

Alfred Binet and Richard Hungerford were hailed as "good guys" in their time, and although some historians have since reversed that judgment, these two educators were clearly positive forces in the history of mental retardation. The similarities of and differences between the two may be instructive. Both were unusually well known during their lives and both played a part in the entrenchment of the nativist (hereditarian) movement in the United States. Both were misunderstood during their lives and each is even more misunderstood today (although Hungerford is misunderstood only by the few who know he even existed, while Binet continues to be misunderstood by throngs). For the differences: As Binet's fame grew with the ever more widespread use of his test, Hungerford became virtually unknown by his contemporary mental retardation professionals. And while Binet developed a procedure to "educate" an inferior intelligence, Hungerford developed a curriculum to contend with the consequences of intellectual inferiority. The aforementioned notwithstanding, important points about their lives can easily be missed if care isn't taken to understand these men in the context of their times.

Alfred Binet

Alfred Binet's 1909 book, *Les Idées Modernes sur les Enfants (Modern Ideas About Children)*, described his system for "educating intelligence." So, although he and Theodore Simon are usually associated with developing the first systematic, widely used instrument to identify mental defects, Binet's major interest was in discovering *interventions* that might effectively ameliorate the problem of intellectual limitation. And although Binet is best known today for his contribution to the quantification of intellect, he was also interested in developing educational programs that examined the hypothesis that an important aspect of intellectual ability is attributable to training and practice (Blatt & Garfunkel, 1969). Ironically, Binet — who gave the technical inspiration for Goddard's (1912) work with the Kallikaks (a study of "family retardation") as well as for a host of nativists from Cyril Burt to Arthur Jensen — was in a profound sense himself an environmentalist (one who believes that environment plays an important role in human development). In fact, Binet once developed an intervention technique (called "Mental Orthopedics"). It was designed to increase the intellectual ability of the mentally retarded child through a deliberate curriculum attending to the cultivation of attention, memory, perception, judgment, and motivation of the child. Binet set out to create a powerful environment that would reduce the inability of mentally retarded children to comprehend and profit from schooling. That he was not more successful in ameliorating or preventing mental retardation does not make him any less an environmentalist. Likewise, Martin Luther King was no less an integrationist because he died before realizing his objectives. If Alfred Binet exhibited any bias vis-à-vis the nature-nurture issue, it was in the direction of nurture, the environmentalist point of view. But through its silence on this aspect of Binet's life and work, the written history leaves the impression that the man who created *the tool* — the intelligence test — would approve of the ways in which it is used today. Consequently, the written history leaves the erroneous impression that Binet believed that (1) the intelligence test measures innate capability, (2) that ability is fixed, and (3) hence, mental retardation is essentially incurable. In fact, his beliefs were the opposite of these. If little else, the relative silence in the literature concerning Binet's beliefs (and prejudices) may leave the reader with the impression that scientists don't have prejudices, which simply is not true. If nothing else, silence about a scientist's prejudices leaves the impression that there is no room in science for prejudice. It's good form, if bad science (which "everyone" knows is supposed to be honest, even about that which is embarrassing) for scientists to conceal their irrationalities.

Richard Hungerford

Like Binet, Hungerford was a man whose work is susceptible to misunderstanding when viewed apart from its historical context. He represented what many of his contemporaries considered to be the "best" thinking of mental retardation leaders of the post-World War II period. It is difficult to unravel that history not just because his biography hasn't been written, but rather because Hungerford himself wrote very little.

Hungerford directed the largest and most widely recognized special education program for mentally retarded students in the United States — perhaps in the world. He was also president of the American Association on Mental Deficiency, editor-in-chief of the *American Journal of Mental Deficiency,* publisher of *Occupational Education* (a now-defunct influential journal for special educators), director of a city special education program, and creator of the Occupational Education curriculum — which became the model for virtually every major curricula developed for mildly mentally retarded people during the 1950s and 1960s.

In a sense, Hungerford was the most prominent proponent of segregated programs for mildly mentally retarded students in the nation. He had direct responsibility for an enormous public school program that was completely segregated by measured intelligence. He was president of the oldest and most prestigious professional organization in the field, which primarily represented institutions and their leadership. And he was a committed nativist, a believer in the idea that much of human variance is genetically determined — that most mildy retarded children inherited their inferior capabilities from their inferior parents. On every score save one, Dick Hungerford would be judged by today's standard as one of the "bad guys" of American special education. He viewed mainstreaming more as drowning the victim than saving the child. He viewed the placement of mildly retarded children in regular classes as an abrogation of the school's responsibility. He viewed anything other than a different developmental curriculum for mildy retarded children as pandering to those who didn't know the difference between a genuine curriculum and its watered down and bastardized versions. But to conclude that Dick Hungerford was one of the "bad guys" of the last generation would be to miss the point; the fact is that he was truly one of the great men of the field.

Special education and, for that matter, our residential institutions, were not created by mendacious and foul-minded people. Among the developers of segregated programs of the late 1800s and early 1900s were great and inspiring humanitarians. Not all of them, of course, *but it is crucial to recognize that there were relatively as many great humanitarians then as there are now, in the era of integration.* Why did Hungerford believe that retarded children needed separate special classes and programs? Why did Samuel Gridley Howe create the first American institution? Their argument was plain enough: Retarded children were more often than not excluded or exempted from attending public schools; those who did attend regular classes were ignored or, worse, abused and ridiculed. Households were ill-equipped to serve the needs of severely retarded family members who were more often than not left in a back room. The segregated special class and institutional system were created out of humanitarian outrage that this nation, which claimed to care so much for the immigrant, the weak, the fragile, and the poor, cared so little for its special children. In the current generation, a similar outrage spawned mainstreaming, the proponents of which look with horror toward the past. Hungerford, possibly as much as anyone else, built and powered the segregation movement, which became the most popular bandwagon of that generation, and which continues to live in the present. But he, unlike many others who jumped onto the bandwagon, knew what he was doing, why he was doing it, and for whom; and he even knew what the trade-offs were. People always should know much more about the bandwagon they jump on than the tune that it's playing, for when the conductor signals the last stop it may be the cemetery rather than the Mardi Gras (Blatt, 1979a, 1979b).

Hungerford's rationale for the educational philosophy of segregation may not have been strong enough to hold up in an era pressing for more and more freedom for all people in normalized environments. But if we truly want to learn from the historical eras led by Hungerford, Binet, Montessori, or Itard, then we must work at understanding what those people were trying to achieve, where they got their ideas, and why they held to them. To pigeonhole Richard Hungerford as a segregator, or Alfred Binet as a psychometrician, misses this important aspect of history: Ideas emerge from a context, which we must understand in order to understand the ideas. Asking the "What if . . ?" question is one means of illuminating historical context. For example, what if Dick Hungerford had been given the responsibility to create a completely integrated special education program in New York City? What if New York Mayor LaGuardia, having brought Hungerford to salvage a corrupt and inefficient program, had insisted that rather than reform, educational revolution was needed? What if Hungerford had been at the pinnacle of his influence during the 1960s? It is quite possible that the genius who created the special class model would have created, instead, a way for society to vigorously and intentionally enlarge its tolerance of variation. After all, while it is true that Dick Hungerford fostered a segregated educational system for handicapped people, he also wrote, preached, and lived the idea that life is enriched through our associations with those who are different, and that every life can be dignified and meaningful.

Brief excerpts from three of Hungerford's essays follow. Hungerford's essays are relatively unknown, despite the belief held by some people that they are among the best and most inspiring ever written in our field. These three essays represent almost the entire corpus of his published work (Blatt, 1975). Notwithstanding the modest quantity of Hungerford's writing, some of you may be puzzled about why you never heard about him before:

It is so hard to say your child may grow up to be a dishwasher—to work with him day after day for only slight gain in order that he may learn by sweat and tears what others pick up casually or pass by with disdain. It is so hard neither to demand more of him than that which he can do nor less than that of which he is capable. It is so hard to be without rancor toward God or envy toward the more fortunate and yet train your son, who has been so "sinned against," to guard in drudgery the health of those who have so much. It is so hard to accept for one's son the ministry of dishwater. We could accept it so much more easily if it came only to us. . . . (Hungerford, 1950, p. 32).

The retarded do not care, we have been told. Yet we, who are considered unhandicapped, have had moments of shock when we could only sit down while the world whirled around us. We have laughed without much meaning; we have done cruel or cowardly things. How then can we be sure that the retarded do not care? Perhaps they merely fail to find their way through that first shock. (Hungerford, 1946, p. 51)

Nothing on earth is so near to heaven as brotherhood. It is the one ideal which is older than memory and stronger than pain. And to paraphrase Voltaire, if there were no brotherhood, men would have to invent it. Yet by that very fact it is forever changing; and when we seem almost to have grasped it, it has sped to a new height. The long, painful trek of society forward is the product, not only of brothers, but also of brotherhood. Man has been guided both by what he has experienced and by what he has dared to desire. (Hungerford, 1949, p. 125)

Martin Luther

Was Martin Luther a "bad guy"? Such an historical indictment might be traced to Kanner's (1964) *The History of the Care and Study of the Mentally Retarded*. Kanner took on the heroic task of bringing together important scattered data, much of it buried in obscure and inaccessible journals and pamphlets. His goal was to lay by the heels unsubstantiated legends and fragmentary accounts, to present an objective, scientific history of mental retardation. In spite of the most worthwhile motives, a real question remains as to whether Kanner succeeded in setting straight the history of mental retardation. For example, he concluded that the Enlightenment was one of the worst historical epochs for mentally retarded people, and furthermore, that Martin Luther spread the idea that the feebleminded are Godless. Kanner made that judgment at least in part from the following commentary, quoted from Luther's famous "Table Talk":

Eight years ago, there was one at Dessau whom I, Martinus Luther, saw and grappled with. He was twelve years old, had the use of his eyes and all his senses, so that one might think that he was a normal child. But he did nothing but gorge himself as much as four peasants and threshers. He ate, defecated and drooled and, if anyone tackled him, he screamed. If things didn't go well, he wept. So I said to the Prince of Anhalt: "If I were the Prince, I should take this child to the Moldau River which flows near Dessau and drown him." But the Prince of Anhalt and the Prince of Saxony, who happened to be present, refused to follow my advice. Thereupon, I said: "Well, then the Christians shall order the Lord's Prayer to be said in church and pray that the dear Lord take the Devil away." This was done daily in Dessau and the changeling died in the following year. When Luther [sic] was asked why he had made such a recommendation, he replied that he was firmly of the opinion that such changelings were merely a mass of flesh, a *massa carnis*, with no soul. For it is in the Devil's power that he corrupts people who have reason and souls when he possesses them. The Devil sits in such changelings where their soul should have been. (Kanner, 1964, p. 7)

Kanner's is not the only version of that story, which, as recorded by Mathesius in 1540, is sufficiently different to raise questions concerning the accuracy of the rendition quoted above:

In Dessau there was a twelve-year-old boy like this: he devoured as much as four farmers did, and he did nothing else than eat and excrete. Luther suggested that he be suffocated.
   Somebody asked, "For what reason?"
   He (Luther) replied, "Because I think he's simply a mass of flesh without a soul. Couldn't the devil have done this, inasmuch as he gives such shape to the body and mind even of those who have reason that in their obsession they hear, see, and feel nothing? The devil is himself their soul. The power of the devil is great when in this way he holds the minds of all men captive, but he doesn't dare give full vent to the power on account of the angels." (Luther, 1967, pp. 396-397)

During a 20-year period, about a dozen men took irregular turns recording Luther's "Table Talk," usually after the evening meal (Luther, 1959, p. 1623). There were times when two or more recorders took down the same remarks. At other times, nobody recorded what was said. Sometimes, the recordings were made during an actual discussion, but at other times they were written up later. All of the original records have been lost. Compounding these inconsistencies were the inconsistencies that arose from frequently hurried notetaking, summarizations condensed to the point of obscurity, and the considerable lag between the actual table discussion and its publication, at least 20 years after the death of the great reformer. What did Luther mean to convey with his reputed comment that the idiot is a "mass of flesh without a soul"? Should the second-hand or private opinion of a person, however important Luther was, be held up as public opinion, much less formal notice to the world? Not only our field itself, but even Luther and his reputation as a great theologian might have been bet-

Jean Jacques Rousseau

And Rousseau? How should history judge him? As a philosopher, as a human being, as a father? Jean Jacques Rousseau was born in Geneva in 1712 and died in 1778. In his great work *Emile* (Rousseau, 1762/1961) he put forth his ideas for fostering a child's development. A great and enduring work, *Emile* changed society's conception of the child. Rousseau's (1762/1961, p. 1) purpose was to "give pleasure to a good mother who thinks for herself." Rousseau worried that we don't know very much about childhood and that we erroneously focus on what the adult should learn about the child. Rather, he said, we should ask what the child is capable of knowing. But *Emile* is not free of paradox. At the outset, Rousseau (1762/1961, p. 5) states that "God makes all things good; man meddles with them and they become evil." The same Rousseau, however, says that "to preserve a useless life you are wasting the time which should be spent in increasing its value, you risk the sight of the despairing mother reproaching you for the death of her child, who ought to have died long ago" (p. 21). Rousseau begins his work by asserting that "under existing conditions a man left to himself from birth would be more of a monster than the rest" (p. 5); but later, Rousseau says:

> I would not undertake the care of the feeble, sickly child, should he live to four score years. I want no pupil who is useless . . . to himself and others, one whose sole business is to keep himself alive, one whose body is always a hindrance to the training of his mind. If I vainly lavish my care upon him, what can I do but double the loss to society by robbing it of two men, instead of one? Let another tend to this weakling for me; I am quite willing, I approve his charity, but I myself have no gift for such a task; I could never teach the art of living to one who needs all his strength to keep himself alive. (p. 21)

Rousseau's life itself, as well as his work, provides the historian with contradictions and puzzlements that may never be settled. He admitted to fathering five illegitimate children, all of whom were placed in a foundling hospital (Lemaitie, 1907). Whether or not he actually was the father of the children or a cuckold who resigned himself to "paternity" to escape public scandal defies resolution, but Rousseau did say that "in abandoning his children he acted in their best interests since the only alternative was to have let them be brought up by Thérèse and her family, who would have made 'monsters' of them. 'I would do it again,' he asserts, 'with fewer doubts, if it had to be done'" (Green, 1955, p. 93).

The same man who could deposit each of his five children to the care of a foundling home could also write a book that extolled the goodness of children and encouraged their education. It is out of such contradictions that the ever-present question emerges: What will we choose to learn from history? It may not be sufficient for one to claim that Rousseau was, after all, simply a human being, great but nevertheless imperfect. But whatever genius he had, it is important to be mindful that people cannot be explained as simply good or evil, right or wrong.

As these brief vignettes illustrate, there is no resolution to the question of who is good and who is bad if the determination is made on the basis of what someone is called, or where he or she works, or whether he or she *did* something good or bad. The only way to make such a determination is on a person by person basis, taking into consideration not only an individual's actions, but also motives and goals. And even then people should be judged — if they must be judged — on the whole of their lives and not the parts. But it's risky business to judge character, especially the character of a person long gone and only imperfectly remembered.

As imperfect as histories may be, in many ways the history of a field is exceedingly important. One of the things most people *don't* know before studying a field is its history. History informs us about the problems experienced by our ideological predecessors. It informs us about how they went about solving problems. It informs us about the right tracks they traveled and the wrong ones. (It seems that only in recent times have our mythic heroes been criticized. Only today is there perceived freedom to discuss Newton's alchemy, Goddard's racism, or Henry Ford's and Luther's anti-Semitism.) History gives us a feeling for the ethos of a time and the worries of a society.

I conclude this chapter with a familiar theme in my work. The individual — you and I — represents the beginning, the end, the involvement, our accomplishments. Before we can attempt to comprehend the world, we must comprehend ourselves. Before we attempt to achieve some form of mastery in this complex society, we must know and master ourselves. Before we attempt to enjoin others to right wrongs, we must change *our* ways. While we may blame an evil or stupid system for the abuses we see everywhere, if *we* do not change, we too contribute to the evil.

3.

Historical Survey of Mental Retardation

WORKERS SERVED OR LIVED with disabled people long before there was a field of mental retardation. There were also people who, through their books and talks, informed professionals centuries later about solutions to problems in dealing with clients. Indeed, modern philosophy of treatment has its roots in the works of these ideological ancestors. In this chapter, you are asked to see the parallels of Socrates' dilemmas and ours. Similarly, Plato, the early Christians, and the later pioneers in Europe and North America, contributed great ideas to our evolving comprehension of the field, its clients, and workers. The discussion includes Itard—possibly the first "official" teacher of a mentally retarded child—and Seguin, his student who came to the United States and profoundly changed the shape and purpose of practice in mental retardation. It also discusses Howe, Wilbur, Montessori, Binet, Terman, Goddard, Wallin, Skeels, Kirk, and others who have so changed the conception of this vexing problem. Embedded in this chapter is a recurring theme—EDUCABILITY—the idea that capability is a function of preparation and motivation, the idea that all people can change for the better.

When does a field begin? This is an irresolvable question. Did the "field" begin with Itard, or Montessori? Where does a circle begin or end? When is water warm and when is it lukewarm?

Before the Field

Here, we seek to propose a plausible conceptual beginning of the field of mental retardation. It will be more heuristic and explanatory than it will be encyclopedic. It will treat myth as seriously as fact—not that myth is fact, but rather, it can serve a similar purpose; it too can reveal aspects of truth. This history will also strive to connect known facts to myths, and to what is understood about the psychological and social structures of a particular time. Theories and definitions come and go. Professional and political controversies rage and then dissipate. But something at the bottom of those debates triggers them. There are specific if imprecise social, cultural, and human feelings connected to what the controversy is about. There are in each generation "prehistoric" (i.e., unself-conscious) responses or prejudices that emerge into visible intellectual or political issues. Those "prehistoric" features are shared by us all and, indeed, may dominate and blind us when we don't try to uncover and deal with them carefully. If, on the other hand, we reveal them to ourselves, they may help keep us honest and may even give us a sense of genuine problems rather than popular shibboleths. Thus, in order to unravel the meaning of mental retardation, we must try to explain the known facts and events in such a way as to comprehend why people saw so little need to explain—or even mention—certain mores. That is the explicit work of historians. What everyone once knew, no one needed to mention. And in a later generation, what no one *now* knows gets to be the puzzle that in the future will unhinge historians in their attempts to piece together into coherent commentary the bits and pieces of past life. Sometimes it is necessary for even the most diligent worker to reinvent what only on hindsight was a memorable beginning, that which today is looked back on as a brave and wonderful event—but once was ignored.

Socrates

For "corrupting the youth by his teaching," Socrates was killed in 399 B.C. (Perkinson, 1980). In his "Apology," laid out by his student, Plato, Socrates tried to describe his life's mission. Although he was unlike other teachers known in Athens, he sought to improve the youth, not to corrupt them. To Socrates, the main difficulty seemed to be with the Athenians, who were not so much concerned with human improvement as with developing in their young the traditional skills of the world and of their particular society. Put another way (and somewhat simplistically, because life isn't as dichotomous as we make it appear in order to drive home a point), while

Socrates strived to uncover what he and others didn't know, the leaders of Athens sought to have taught that which was already known and accepted, what had *always been* rather than what might some day have been perceived. In some quarters of ancient Athens it was felt that everything worth knowing was known.

The core of Socratic philosophy may be illuminated by this instructive story from his "Apology"—in which he defended himself against a charge punishable by death. A friend of Socrates, Chaerephon, asked the Delphic Oracle if anyone was wiser than Socrates. No one was wiser, came the reply. But Socrates himself would not believe that assessment, knowing more than anyone how little he knew. So he sought out people who would refute the Oracle's claim—that is, who would demonstrate their greater wisdom. He spoke with politicians, poets, people of all stations. But what he discovered was that they were not genuinely wise, though that's how many of them regarded themselves and were regarded by others. Reluctantly, Socrates concluded that he was wiser than those reputed wise men because he, more than the others, knew how little he knew. Of course, Socrates *knew* that he was intelligent and educated; but much of his intellectual strength was powered by the *awareness* of what was yet to be learned, of his own ignorance. For example, his curriculum and role as a teacher were informed by his idea of the incompleteness and fallibility of human beings, who intend to do good but fail to do good, who intend to improve but fail to change. His "device" was founded on the conviction that errors can be discovered, that while wise people know a great deal, they must use logical analysis to progress beyond current knowledge, that there *are* fundamental laws of thought that can reveal confused thinking.

What can we, in the field of mental retardation, learn from Socrates? The temptation is to find out what he might have said about retarded persons, but this course diverts us from virtually everything Socrates stood for as a teacher and as an educational reformer. Probably, what we can better learn from Socrates is not what he thought about mentally retarded people but what he would think about us and others who deal with those who are mentally retarded. And probably if he were here now he would be pressing us to reveal not only what has been learned since Socratic times but also what we do not perceive in our own time. Another lesson we might learn from an examination of Socratic history is the seriousness with which the ancient Athenians dealt with educational issues compared to today. In his attempt to create a new curriculum—to shift the emphasis away from gymnastics and military education to an emphasis on the increasing of knowledge by revealing ignorance—Socrates not only incurred the wrath of the Athenians but paid for their discomfort with his life. It is important to note that in ancient Athens, the pupils were not on trial but the curriculum and the teachers were. In ancient Athens, the professionals did not monitor and evaluate the curriculum; the citizens themselves did. What about Socrates' idea that human improvement can take place only because humans are imperfect? What about the idea that every human being is fragile, mortal, error-ridden? Is it true, as Socrates claimed, that such skepticism is indeed an optimistic way of viewing the human condition? Is it true that only the incomplete human being has room to improve? Then isn't it also true that, in such a society, mentally retarded people offer a great and noble challenge to those who would seek to help another human being improve? Socrates was a teacher who did not "teach," a teacher who did not inform his students what was good or true, a teacher who looked especially for what was wrong and misguided. Today, where is there a curriculum based on what Richard Hungerford once called the three R's of special education for mentally retarded students: Relatedness, Reality, and Responsibility? Moreover, even in Hungerford's day, did such a curriculum actually exist, except in the mind of its creator and in the hearts and fantasies of its very few true adherents? Today, who would die to defend his or her teaching and curriculum? Today, who would die for the right of children to learn? Socrates comes to mind. Maybe there are others in history who have, or would have, so died. But the list is short.

Plato

The Athenians appeared to show little remorse for the death of Socrates, in spite of Plato's efforts to reestablish his reputation (Perkinson, 1980). In fact, Plato's differing views of the educative process solidified the antagonism. While Socrates viewed education as a process of making people aware, Plato tried to help people uncover the truth. While Socrates was content to permit the student to learn out of a sense of inadequacy, Plato was persuaded that an educational authority can teach the truth to those capable of learning it. The Socratic idea of an open and heuristic society was replaced by the Platonic philosophy of an infallible political authority, which rejected democracy in favor of a disciplined and educated intellectual elite. In this manner, Plato avoided the role of social critic, a dangerous role that had led to Socrates' downfall.

Rather than play the critic's vulnerable role for citizens of the city-state, Plato sought to select the very best students, train them, and place in their hands the power to rule the people. Plato believed that the wise person knows the truth, knows what is just, and knows what is good. And furthermore, people can be taught to be wise, and the teacher can impart wisdom, even virtue. While Socrates thought that improvement obtained from the discovery and elimination of mistakes, Plato believed that improvement resulted from learning the truth. The Socratic curriculum was by nature incomplete, and completion could never be realized, while the Platonic curriculum had a goal — the possession of knowledge. While Socrates could not work toward a definable society, Plato claimed to work toward the realization of a perfect society.

Augustine

St. Augustine may well have been the earliest advocate of the "modern" notion of educability. After converting to Christianity, he established a monastery in his hometown of Pagaste (Northern Africa) in 388 and was ordained a priest in 392. Throughout his life, Augustine continued to develop and refine Socratic and Platonic ideas of the imperfection of the human condition. But Augustine taught that humans — unlike other beings — can approach perfection through the teachings of Jesus Christ. Implicit in this theology of Christianity is the belief that man's behavior is modifiable. Thus, the theology of St. Augustine expresses the *idea* of educability, the hypothesis that capability is educable, that intelligence and other aspects of human development are modifiable as a result of practice, training, and motivation.

To be sure, there have always been, and continue to be, currents antithetical to the belief that capability is educable. While Plato looked to a secular education grounded in idealism and Augustine to a religion grounded in reason and faith as the force to improve man's behavior, Aristotle, who lived from 384-322 B.C., concluded that the ability to reason logically and practically differentiated human beings from the other animals. The human being without skills in inductive reasoning, Aristotle believed, is incapable of serious education, and, thus, of approaching perfection. It has even been claimed that while Augustine would have sought to humanize the individual with an inadequate mind, Aristotle would have concluded that such a person was not actually human, and consequently could not be humanized, could not be educated (Kolstoe, 1972).

This discussion of the perspective of philosophers who have shaped the thinking of Western civilization also underscores the longstanding argument of nature versus nurture. Throughout the centuries, the tensions between *environmentalists* (those who believe in the modifiability of behavior through significant shaping experiences) and *nativists* (those who believe that people are what they inherit — that once established by genetic endowment, capability unfolds from a relatively invariant genetic plan) has not abated.

The Birth of the Field

At the very least, the historical record concerning how the ancients treated mentally handicapped persons is ambiguous. Although Plato was virtually silent regarding the place of handicapped people in his Republic, he nevertheless elaborated on a philosophy of education that recognized human fallibility and the role of education in improvement. And while St. Paul exhorted early Christians to "comfort the feebleminded," during many periods in early Christian history, and certainly during the reformation, such people were treated with loathing and were vilified as "filled with Satan" (Rosen, Clark, & Kivitz, 1976, p. viii). The period commencing with the revolutions in France and the United States is somewhat clearer concerning what was attempted on behalf of handicapped people, what was achieved, and who powered the movements.

By the time its great revolution was still personally remembered by its oldest citizens, France was a vibrant, dynamic, and creative society. Its authors were writing about injustices to God, to human beings, to nature. Its philosophers were idealizing human beings, convinced that people deserved a better way of life; philosophers envisioned what that life might be like. Voltaire was attacking intolerance of the clergy, Pereire was advocating the treatment of deaf-mutes, and Rousseau — among others — was anxious about how government is formed. The French Revolution was surely engineered by a relatively few individuals, but embedded in their discontent was the widespread anger of throngs. The angriest was the large and well-educated middle class, who worried that too few people had genuine rights and participation in government, that French law denied trial by jury and freedoms of the press and religion, and that the gap between the rich and the poor was widening while the nobility lavishly indulged their every whim, fancy, and fantasy. Louis XVI and too many of his predecessors were tyrannical and inefficient kings, which fueled this anger. At the same time, a kindred spirit from the other side of the Atlantic provided additional fuel to the antimonarchy efforts in France. Indeed, the flames of the American Revolution, lighted in part by French dollars and soldiers, heated the passions of French patriots to revolt against the overprivileged indolent nobility which, with the clergy, held one-third of all the wealth of France, and who, to add insult to despair, were also exempt from paying taxes.

In France, the successful Revolution brought to an end special privileges for clergy and nobility. Peasants were given the land to farm. The ideas of Locke and Rousseau were articulated as the guiding philosophy of the new government. With unambiguous enunciation of the rights of each citizen, France experienced a wave of patriotic fervor and a will for self-improvement that perhaps no nation has ever experienced before or since. And what occurred in France had its analogue in the United States.

Jacob Rodrigues Pereire

It was in the context of this period that Pereire demonstrated success in the instruction of deaf-mutes — a feat that others had not even attempted (Kanner, 1964). On June 11, 1749, at the Academy of Science in Paris, he showed that with certain training a deaf person could read and speak. His work caught the attention of Rousseau, and eventually Jean-Marc-Gaspard Itard and Edouard Seguin. And although Pereire himself never worked with retarded persons, his compassion and his ingenious teaching methods served as an inspirational model for Itard and others.

Jean-Marc-Gaspard Itard

Itard is widely cited as the "first teacher of the mentally retarded," which, loosely translated, means that he was the first *recognized* teacher. Why Itard? And how did it all happen? It was the right time, a strange boy was discoverd, Itard was in the vicinity, he was a doctor, he did treat him, and he wrote about it. Writing about Victor, as much or more than treating him, made Itard forever important in the annals of the field, because his was the first published account of the educational treatment of a mentally retarded person. Hence, this is an important story.

In their introduction to Itard's (1932/1962) *The Wild Boy of Aveyron*, translators George and Muriel Humphrey portrayed post-revolutionary France as a questing, dynamic, and enlightened culture. Implicit faith was placed in the science of Lavoisier, Galvani, and others. The enlightened philosphers — Voltaire, Montesquieu, and Rousseau — held sway: Human beings were not only noble, but improvable, and the world was not only good, but would get better. This faith suffused French society. There was not only hope, but demonstration for the first time that deaf people would speak and blind people would, if not see, learn ways to circumvent their handicap. Even mental illness was no longer thought to be hopeless and incurable. What better time for a young doctor, already engaged in work with deaf-mutes, to claim that with a civilizing experience even a retarded child could become normal?

And the child himself? Victor was seized in the forests of Aveyron when he was (possibly) 11 or 12 years of age, naked, scarred, unable to speak or presumably to hear. Was this Rousseau's "noble savage" or merely an idiot deserted by his family? The boy squatted for hours on the ground, or rocked back and forth like a wild animal, always indifferent to movement, rain, cold, filth. The child was turned over to the care of the naturalist, Bonaterre, and from him to Itard. Some people declared the boy a fake, and Pinel, the great psychiatrist, concluded he was an incurable idiot. Itard disagreed with the great physician; he concluded that Victor had been greatly neglected, and that with deliberate training and encouragement, the boy could change from savage to civilized person. Believing that Victor's apparent retardation was due to his lack of experience and opportunity for training, he undertook a program to help the boy acquire what he had missed through his years of isolation from civilization. By finding ways for Victor to interact with people, creating situations for the child to imitate speech, and bombarding his senses with strong and increasingly discriminating stimuli, a great deal was accomplished. Victor learned to recognize letters, arrange them in words, form sentences, and even write. But there were such puzzling and frustrating aspects to the program! For example, if the key to his door was so much as touched, the child tensed, ready to escape; he surely heard, but he never learned to speak more than a few words. And while some thought he changed remarkably, he never changed so much that he was ever other than an exceptionally disabled person. Indeed, after repeated discouragements, Itard concluded that he did not achieve his goal to civilize Victor, and he withdrew as the child's teacher and custodian, leaving him in the care of his housekeeper. However, the French Academy of Science encouraged Itard to publish his memoirs of his work with Victor. Itard did, which not only made Itard very famous, but may have been the single most important event in the creation of what is now viewed as a genuine field.

The question of whether Victor was born deficient or psychotic (Silberstein & Irwin, 1962), or was made defective by an incredibly aversive environment, will never be precisely answered. Furthermore, that question is not nearly as important as the evidence Itard provided that even very severely impaired people can be improved through educational intervention. On several accounts, Itard's work provides important documentation. It was the first of its kind, and all "firsts" of important movements are especially important. Further, it was a significant demonstration of the philosophy of the early "sensationalists" (advocates of learning through the senses). Finally, Itard was the scientific progenitor of Seguin, who probably more than anyone else was responsible for the creation and development of institutions for mentally retarded persons in the United States.

Edouard Seguin

Plato wrote in his *Dialogues* of "disorders of the soul," and Maimonides in his *Ethics* wrote about "Diseases of the Soul." Edouard Seguin conceived of mental retardation in a somewhat similar way and was convinced that mentally retarded persons should be treated through "Moral Treatment" (Goshen, 1967). After he immigrated to the United States on the heels of the French Revolution of 1848, Seguin became the greatest European influence on the development of educational programs for retarded persons in this country. He was strongly influenced by the work of Itard, with whom he worked briefly before Itard's death in 1838.

In *Idiocy, and Its Treatment by the Physiological Method*, Seguin (1864/1976) recounted the story of Victor (who, incidentally, Seguin said was about 17 years old, not 11 or 12). Although Seguin agreed with Pinel's diagnosis of incurable idiocy, he remained sympathetic to Itard who, although he never "cured" Victor, so devoted himself to another human being as well as to the science of educational treatment that he inspired other teachers, including Seguin. And so, when in 1837 Itard invited Seguin to take responsibility for another child at the Children's Hospital in Paris, Seguin agreed. Consulting with Itard on the details of his earlier work with Victor and others, the young physician developed a program grounded in his sponsor's work. Like Itard, Seguin advocated sensory training, elaborating on Itard's theories by dividing his pupils into two types: "a superficial type in which the peripheral nervous system has been damaged or weakened and profound type in which the central nervous system has always been defective" (Robinson & Robinson, 1976, p. 458).

Although Seguin consulted Esquirol, "The Oracle of the Mental Medicine," he said that Esquirol "had nothing to teach me" (Seguin, 1864/1976, p. 156). Despite Esquirol's pessimism concerning the prognosis for Seguin's efforts, the latter credited Esquirol for "exquisite tact." Furthermore, Esquirol's doubts goaded Seguin to prove the more experienced and famous doctor wrong. Eighteen months later, Seguin's young pupil was much improved; he could speak, write, and even count.

Esquirol's reaction has become all too familiar to teachers and clinicians today. While he agreed that Sequin's pupil had changed significantly, and while he gave full credit to him for the change, Esquirol concluded that the child had *resembled* but had not *truly* been an idiot. To this day, when an individual who has been diagnosed as mentally retarded later performs normally, most clinicians remain wont to conclude *ex post facto* that the original diagnosis was erroneous, that the person must have been pseudo-mentally retarded, because mental retardation is incurable and irremediable. That resistance to the idea of mental retardation as a functional designation is reflected in the evolving definitions of this condition, which, until recent years, precluded any possibility for cure, remediation, or even amelioration. And while the newer definitions allow for remediation and— dare I say?—cure, professionals in the field have not been singlemindedly driven to embrace that concept.

In spite of Esquirol's reluctance to endorse Seguin's "cure," he nevertheless encouraged him to continue development of his educational program for such people. Consequently, Seguin accepted responsibility for other children at the Hospice des Incurables Bicêtre. In 1844 a committee appointed by the Paris Academy of Sciences examined 10 of his pupils and concluded that he "had definitely solved the problem of idiot education" (Kanner, 1964). If only their words could have been founded more on substance than on wish! Combining psycho-physiological training (see especially, "Psycho-physiological Training of an Idiot Hand," 1864/1976, and "Psycho-physiological Training of an Idiot Eye," 1864/1976), Seguin nevertheless concluded that "none but God can do anything of himself alone" (Rosen et al., 1976, p. 153). Consequently, Seguin was after God Himself to intervene on behalf of these defectives who for so long had been ignored by their brothers. He was exceedingly impressed with the work of several generations of Spanish monks who had demonstrated success with many types of mental patients, which they accomplished through moral training rather than drugs and other medical regimens (Goshen, 1967).

The irony of Seguin's professional life is in the contrast between his moral treatment program and what eventually became of the several institutions with which he was associated—environments he either created or supported during his long and distinguished career in the United States. He was probably more responsible than anyone else for the development of what later became America's large, dehumanizing, and unmanageable institutions. Virtually everything that triggered the institutional scandals of the 1960s and 1970s was certainly foreign to Seguin's ideas of how institutionalized people should be treated and educated. Seguin warned against just about all of the evils revealed during the past two decades—usually in the name of training, management, or inevitability—a century earlier. Yet, in the name of Seguin's educational precepts, America's institutions developed programs that not only ignored but were precisely contrary to those very precepts.

Combining physiological and moral treatment, Seguin advised the workers of the day that "psychical correction is useless unless blended with the eradication of the wrong. Punishment is to be avoided . . . till it be certain that the understanding of the wrong preceded its commission" (Goshen, 1967, p. 167). Seguin's pedagogy demanded anchoring behavior to understanding—the child's behavior, the teacher's behavior, the interaction of child and teacher in an environment that can be described and explained. And, just as punishment is useless unless the person comprehends the reason behind it, so reward is useless without such understanding. Otherwise, the teacher's moral sensibility does not monitor and does not enhance development, but rather, it may confuse the child and pervert development.

As noted, Seguin was pivotal in the development of residential programs for mentally retarded persons in America; this was especially so in Massachusetts, New York, and Pennsylvania, where, ironically, our most serious institutional scandals were revealed in recent years. Before he died on October 28, 1880, Seguin wrote several enduring works. Neither his contributions nor his philosophy should be judged by what institutions became during much of this century. In Seguin's case, fairness dictates that we evaluate the man by *his* works in *his* time, and not by those of his misguided ideological progeny.

Johann Jakob Guggenbühl

Johann Jakob Guggenbühl was born on August 16, 1816, near Lake Zurich, Switzerland (Kanner, 1964). Two well-known stories are connected with his work in the field of mental retardation, one famous and the other infamous. The famous and inspiring story concerns an experience he had in 1836 while he was a student of medicine. While passing through a Swiss village in the Canton of Uri, he was attracted to a crippled and dwarfish cretin (the historical term for a person with congenital hypothyroidism, which can result in severe mental retardation). The man was praying near a roadside cross. As Kanner recounted the story, Guggenbühl followed the man home, where the young medical student met the man's mother, who told him that she had taught her son the Lord's Prayer and, since that time, he had prayed every day at that cross. Because she couldn't afford schooling for him, he had never received any formal education. That incident purportedly encouraged Guggenbühl to embark upon the study of cretinism; thus an accidental encounter became the work of a lifetime. Similarly, many of our leaders in the field, up to the present day, came into this work quite accidentally. Indeed, until relatively recently, it was almost impossible for most professionals to *plan* careers in mental retardation. People were trained as doctors, psychologists, teachers, and only later—sometimes years later—stumbled into this vocation accidentally.

The second story connected with Guggenbühl's work is less pleasant, but possibly more familiar, especially to people today who are responsible for administering institutions. After two years of intensive observation of many cretins in Switzerland, Guggenbühl became a physician in an asylum near Berne, and soon after established his own colony 4,000 feet above sea level on the Abendberg, near Interlaken (Wallin, 1917). He carefully selected that site for two reasons: the belief that colonies enhance development more than prisons and almshouses, and his accurate observation that, while cretinism was common in the valley below, it was unknown at the higher elevations. He further believed that residents would benefit from the regimen of pure air, sunshine, clear water, exercise, baths, massages, and dieting, and to physiological training per Seguin's methods (Wallin, 1917). To be sure, even though Guggenbühl did not know about modern methods of treating hypothyroidism, it did appear that many of his residents improved greatly. The more they improved, the more attention was given to his institution; and the more attention was given to his institutiton, the more Guggenbühl was asked to lecture in Switzerland and eventually throughout Europe. Within a decade, similar institutions were founded in Germany, the United States, England, and other countries.

Embedded in Guggenbühl's program was his unshakable conviction that God had chosen him for this work, and that he must seek to do no less than to save the immortal soul of every cretin entrusted to him. It was a spectacularly successful experiment, noteworthy for the creativeness of its approach and the success of its results. Moreover, even by the standards of today, Guggenbühl's experiment was an incredibly accurate prophecy of what was to be "invented" in the twentieth century. For example, Guggenbühl placed in his colony two perfectly normal, albeit neglected, children in order to bring a sense of normalcy into the institution (Kanner, 1964). Who knows where Harold Skeels got his inspiration to make a similar decision for similar reasons a century later? Certainly, Guggenbühl had something to teach Skeels; whether Skeels was directly influenced or not is immaterial; the point is that Skeels learned somewhere what Guggenbühl had known generations before. And surely, Guggenbühl and many others have things to teach *us* today.

Unfortunately, the Abendberg (and Guggenbühl's world) caved in. Quite simply, while he was away from his institution teaching others about its good work, those left in charge were not up to so demanding a responsibility. Scandal followed on the heels of a visit to the institution by the British Minister in Berne. His indignant complaints about the neglect and disorder he observed opened a Pandora's box of investigations that eventually led to the closing of Abendberg just when it was enjoying its greatest influence in encouraging the creation of similar institutions everywhere else in the Western world. Guggenbühl died on February 2, 1863, at the age of 47, disillusioned but still insisting that he had been misunderstood, that his institution had deserved to continue, that without him and the Abendberg the cretins would again suffer. And whether he was right or wrong about other matters, he was indeed right about the cretins. They would again suffer.

American Association on Mental Deficiency

The influence of Seguin and Guggenbühl on practices related to institutions in the United States can be seen in the efforts of this country's first professional organization in the field of mental retardation. In early June, 1876, seven men met in Media, Pennsylvania, to create The Association of Medical Officers of American Institutions for Idiots and Feebleminded

Persons, now called the American Association on Mental Deficiency (Sloan & Stevens, 1976). They were called together by I. N. Kerlin, Superintendent of the Pennsylvania Training School, to create a forum for discussion of questions relating to causes, statistics, and management of retarded persons who were then called feebleminded. It was also hoped that, through the influence of those established leaders, the development of new institutions would be fostered across the country. Those present included Edouard Seguin, then running the Seguin School in New York City; Hervey W. Wilbur, superintendent of the New York Asylum for Idiots in Syracuse; G. A. Doren, superintendent of the Institution for Feebleminded Youths at Columbus, Ohio; Charles T. Wilbur, superintendent of the State Institution for the Feebleminded in Jacksonville, Illinois; H. M. Knight, superintendent of the Connecticut School of Imbeciles in Lakeville; and George W. Brown, superintendent of a private institution for feebleminded children in Barre, Massachusetts. All founding members were physicians, a fact of considerable historical significance and a characteristic of leadership in mental retardation that went unchallenged until decades later. Seguin was elected as first president. Although Kerlin did not become president until 1892, he—probably more than anyone else—was the guiding strength that powered the Association during its early fragile years (Sloan & Stevens, 1976).

The original goal of the Association, to stimulate the development of institutions, was plainly achieved. In 1876, seven states supported such institutions, and by 1885, 20 states had created institutions (Sloan & Stevens, 1976). Who were some of those early leaders? Where did they come from, and what were they trying to accomplish? In part for the sake of convenience, but also because these particular individuals provide provocative connections between the past and the present, I have selected Samuel Gridley Howe, Hervey Wilbur, and H. M. Knight for further discussion.

Samuel Gridley Howe

For sure, Howe is inexorably linked to Guggenbühl, whose work he saw firsthand on a visit to the Abendberg. But it wasn't until 1848 that Howe was able to persuade Massachusetts officials to create in South Boston the first publicly supported school for mentally retarded persons in North America. That same year Hervey Wilbur took a few retarded children into his home, and, thus, this country began its long, volatile, and essentially unhappy affair with institutionalization. A physician, Howe was in every sense a splendid human being. Philanthropist, egalitarian, advocate for handicapped and other unwanted people, Howe stands out as the first genuine American statesman in the field. But at the beginning, he was a statesman almost literally without a state, until Howe and Wilbur's efforts to establish programs for mentally retarded persons. The closest approximation to such an idea in North America may have been the inclusion of a few retarded children in the program at the Asylum for the Deaf and Dumb in Hartford, Connecticut, in 1818 (Kanner, 1964). Howe, who had been a courier for Polish revolutionaries and had been caught and actually imprisoned for those activities, who had served for six years as a surgeon in one of the Greek wars, who had distributed relief supplies to refugees, who had created what is now the Perkins Institution for the Blind, possessed exactly the stamina and fortitude necessary for the task of building something where there was no analogue, no tradition, and essentially no interest. Howe had also advocated emancipation of the slaves long before it was a popular idea — much less a political issue — so it was not surprising that he associated with Dorothea Dix, Horace Mann, and other reformers of the day.

Howe's first large success was with three blind children, diagnosed as "idiots." From that experience he concluded that if *they* could make such progress, much more could be accomplished on behalf of idiots who were not blind, that "there is not one of any age who may not be made more of a man and less of a brute by patience and kindness directed by energy and skill" (Kanner, 1964, p. 42). The legislature was, if not entirely convinced, willing to appropriate $2,500 for each of three years for training 10 idiotic children in a wing opened at the Perkins Institution on October 1, 1848. James B. Richards was appointed first teacher and, indeed, was the first officially recognized teacher of mentally retarded children in North America.

Hervey Wilbur

At approximately the same time, Hervey Wilbur developed and administered a school for mentally retarded persons at the other end of Massachusetts. It enjoyed such success and recognition that when the New York State legislature decided to develop such a school in Albany, Wilbur was asked to be its first superintendent (Graney, 1979). The school was relocated to Syracuse in 1854, and Wilbur continued on as superintendent until his death in 1883.

What were these people like, Howe and Wilbur? What did they want to accomplish? What guided and goaded and inspired them? One clue to a man is his associates, and early on both Howe and Wilbur connected themselves to Edouard Seguin. Consequently, it was natural for Wilbur to invite Seguin to deliver the dedicatory address at the laying of the cornerstone of the new Syracuse institution. His words reveal not only something more about Seguin, but also something about his colleague, Wilbur:

> God has scattered among us — rare as the possessors of genius — the idiot, the blind, the deaf-mute, in order to bind the rich to the needy, the talented to the incapable, all men to each other, by a tie of indissoluble solidarity. The old bonds are dissolving; man is already unwilling to continue to contribute money or palaces for the support of the indolent nobility; but he is every day more ready to build palaces and give annuities for the indigent or infirm — the chosen friends of our Lord Jesus.
> See that stone — the token of a new alliance between humanity and the class hitherto neglected — that, ladies and gentlemen, is your pride; it is the greatest joy of my life, for I, too, have laboured for the poor idiot. (Seguin, 1855, p. 43)

Further Evolution of Institutions

What was the purpose of the work of Seguin, Howe, and Wilbur? Wolfensberger succinctly characterized it as "making deviant individuals undeviant" (1975, p. 24). Nothwithstanding the fact that virtually all the first superintendents of state schools were physicians, the particular institutions of these three men were governed by educational principles and objectives, a thrust it must be added, that rarely took hold in the institutions of the late nineteenth and early twentieth centuries. The notion then was not to "cure" mental retardation, but it surely was to enhance adaptive behavior so that those people would then be able to function in society (Wolfensberger, 1975). Further, those early institutions were viewed as temporary boarding schools, and after the child had sufficiently mastered adaptive skills, he or she was to be returned to his or her family, to ordinary schools, to ordinary society. The first institutions in Massachusetts and Syracuse were never meant to become permanent residences for incurables. Those early institutions were not intended for severely and multiply handicapped people. Selecting candidates for admission was a serious responsibility that required careful screening and evaluation. Although those early leaders did not express the belief that they could make idiots normal, each had faith — and evidence — that the retarded person could be educated. Truly, they created, and while they were alive, directed genuine schools.

It is not difficult to determine that something went wrong with the conceptualization of the institution as a place to *educate* the mentally retarded person. There is evidence today in almost every traditional institution that this is not the case, in spite of massive institutional reforms during the past two decades.

Let us look at some of the reasons why Howe's vision of a school rather than an institution for "incurables," and Wilbur's vision of an institution so small that it might be organized on a "family plan," did not persist for long in the twentieth century. Let us examine why the intent to locate institutions in "the very heart of the community" (Wolfensberger, 1975, p. 26) and the idea of making the deviant undeviant are ideas that have seen better days. As Wolfensberger noted, the problem *wasn't* that Howe, Wilbur, and the other early leaders failed in returning significant numbers of their residents to the community. Many did return, although some of course could not. After all, these were all people with significant problems, and, of course, there had to be failures. There were others who might have been able to return to the community if there had been community placements available. But few placements were available and, as the years rolled on, more and more of the "failures" and difficult-to-place residents collected as an intractable group. As that group enlarged, so too did the asylum-like character of those once-schools, which evolved into true asylums. The more those places became asylums the less they were schools, and the less they were schools the more reluctant society became to place the so-called "improvables" with the "incurables." Therefore, by the turn of the century, the populations in these institutions were much different from those first gathered by Howe and Wilbur. The character of the institution changed, too. New terminology — from educational remediation to chronic hospitalization — reflected this change. Even the names of these facilities changed from "school" to "hospital" or "asylum." The passage of universal education laws and, later, provisions for special education programs in the public schools, hastened the conversion from school to asylum. And of course, as population density increased in the city, real estate there became more expensive, and as pupils were replaced by "asylum inmates," it made prudent fiscal sense and good program sense to build the newer institutions in the country where land was cheaper, neighbors fewer, and where the trees and grass could soften if not entirely obliterate the impact of seeing the *new* vision of care — the back ward, that invention of mental health professionals which has yet to be equaled for its perpetration of undiluted punishment (by those trained to heal), inflicted on defenseless people (designated as patients).

Clearly, people knew what kinds of problems existed in institutions. But knowledge does not constitute true awareness or concern. Encouraged by Howe himself, Dorothea Dix brought these problems to the public in her now-famous 1843 Memorial to the Legislature of Massachusetts (Blatt, 1973). Her indictment of the Commonwealth's barbaric almshouse and jail systems caused an enormous sensation, moving the legislature to refer the matter to a committee chaired by Howe. People in cages, chained, living in filth and degradation, beaten and lashed, untreated, neglected, and tortured; these were the vivid observations Dix recorded during visits to those terrible places across the Commonwealth. She did not blame the jailer or the almshouse keepers; she saw them too, as victims. They were ordinary men and women who didn't have the skills, knowledge, or resources to provide decent and humane care for mentally ill and mentally defective persons (Wilson, 1975). It was the system that had gone wrong, not the keepers. Most of all, Dix subjected to glaring, critical light the general conception ordinary people held concerning handicapped and other devalued people; they were not considered quite deserving, quite human. To a degree, that conception exists today and is a foundation of the system.

To a great extent, the "bad guy" has always been the *system,* even today. And the responses to such indictments have always been the same. While the legislature expressed dismay, and while "uninvolved" humanitarians everywhere expressed shock, the jailkeepers, the almshouse masters, and the town politicians who oversaw those pestholes were shocked too. But their outrage was directed at the messenger, not the message. Dix was vilified as a slanderer and a meddler, as others have been vilified in recent years for delivering similar bad news to the mental health-mental retardation community (Blatt, 1970b, 1973). Little more than a century after Dorothea Dix's Memorial to the Massachusetts Legislature, the present author spoke to that same body on precisely the same problem, and was accorded virtually the same reactions—dismay from the legislature, incomprehension from the uninvolved, and venom from the involved (Blatt, 1973). The more things change, the more they stay the same.

Evolvement of the Connecticut Philosophy

Itard, Seguin, Howe, and Wilbur represented the link between the first special programs for mentally retarded people in Europe and the United States; it could be argued that Henry M. Knight represented the link between the traditional large asylum and innovative, diffuse contemporary regional programs. A Connecticut state legislator himself, Knight gave up his medical practice in 1858 and opened up his home in Lakeville, Connecticut, for the care and education of mentally retarded people (Kanner, 1964). Within three years, sufficient public interest encouraged the state legislature to support the program, and Knight was appointed the first superintendent of the Connecticut School of Imbeciles. The school grew considerably through the years, but it could not keep up with the ever-increasing demand for institutionalization. It was closed in 1917, when the state opened a new institution in Mansfield Depot, a small rural area in the southeastern part of Connecticut. Although many times larger than the Lakeville facility, Mansfield, too, struggled to meet the demand for institutionalization, which reached alarming proportions in the years just prior to World War II. When in 1941 the state created its second large institution, the Southbury Training School, it was hoped that the waiting list at

Mansfield, which by then was at least 1,000, would be substantially reduced. As we have since learned, such was wishful if not altogether illogical thinking. By 1961, both Mansfield and Southbury each had a waiting list of 1,000, with little or no hope of alleviating that and other problems. From this apparently irresolvable disaster emerged the fragile beginnings of a regional, community-based approach to providing care and treatment for mentally retarded people. That part of the story brings us to the present day, and, consequently, will await its completion in the next section. In the meantime, however, Sarason, Zitnay, and Grossman (1971) can provide us with a fascinating and instructive historical account of the antecedents of what later emerged as the post-World War II solution to the problem of mental retardation, the modern regional center:

> Until 1941 the Mansfield Training School was the sole state residential facility for the mentally retarded. Like all such facilities in the nation, it had a waiting list of pathetic and overwhelming length. In addition to the complications resulting from the fact that it was the only state facility for mentally retarded children, there was the fact that the school was almost inaccessible by public transportation. Just as in the public schools the special class would often be in the least desirable location, the state schools across the nation tended to be "out there someplace." It was still a time when society isolated its deviants—psychologically, socially, and geographically—from the natural community. Again like all other state schools, the Mansfield Training School housed its residents in large units: scores of children slept together and marched together to eat in central dining halls.
>
> The pressures from the waiting list were ever present and growing, and the inequities of there being only one state facility became increasingly apparent. Finally, a board of trustees was appointed by the governor and given the task of planning, building, and staffing a new residential facility. . . .
>
> There were three major goals governing the development of the Southbury Training School:
>
> 1. Southbury was to be an *educational setting*, rather than a hospital or the typical custodial institution.
>
> 2. One of the most frequent statements about Southbury was "that it would have two doors: one to come in and one to go out." Behind this statement was *the aim of avoiding the tragedy of long waiting lists*. To the extent that it truly became an educational institution having two ever-moving, swinging doors, it would avoid the long waiting-list problem.
>
> 3. The children were to be housed in as homelike a setting as possible. There were to be no large living facilities or large, centralized dining halls. (As it turned out, there were small cottages, each of which had a house mother and father who lived in-house in an apartment, and each cottage had its own kitchen, cook, and dining room.)[1]

---

[1]From *The Creation of a Community Setting* (p. 10) by S. Sarason, B. Zitnay, and F.K. Grossman, 1971, Syracuse, New York: Syracuse University, Division of Special Education and Rehabilitation. Reprinted by permission.

It is possible that without the great Connecticut experiment in regional center development, there might not be today the nationwide emphasis on deinstitutionalization and normalized community services. While its reputation for innovative contributions may have seen better days, the Connecticut story plays an extraordinarily important role in the evolution from the large, paternalistic, custodial institutions of the early twentieth century to today's progressive community and family support systems. The Connecticut experiment should be recognized for its pioneering efforts in the field.

The Growth of the Field

Lurking not far beneath the surface of plans for retarded persons, even today, are the "danger" questions: How dangerous are these people to themselves, to others, to future society? Since before there was an identifiable field, and to this day, society has vacillated in its conception of and approach to the "danger" questions. These questions have not, however, disappeared. In fact, there is little evidence to suggest that these questions persist with any less intensity today than they did a hundred or a thousand years ago, enlightened modern protestations notwithstanding.

The ancient societies that monitored the goings on of their defective citizens viewed them with contempt and often treated them cruelly (Wallin, 1917). They were cursed as peculiar, so different, so "within themselves" (i.e., withdrawn) that they were called "idiots," which literally translated from the Greek means "private person," and which today means severely mentally retarded person. These were people who were viewed as so incapable of human interaction that it was once believed they could rightfully be regarded as outside of the human family. As we learned from the Nazi experience, persecution and extermination inevitably follow group declassification of human beings. There is a connection between the reputed abandonment of deformed infants by the ancient Greeks, the hanging of witches in Salem, Massachusetts, and the extermination of Jews and others by the Nazis. These were people who, it was believed, either couldn't take care of themselves, were dangerous to others, and/or would contribute to the degeneration of the race. To understand what happened in Salem is to understand, though not forgive, what happened in Germany. The witches were hanged not because they had strange visions, not because they gave birth to four-legged animals, not because they cast spells, but *because* they were witches! The Jews were exterminated *because* they were Jews, and mental defectives today are institutionalized *because* they are mental defectives.

Our conception about a particular group of people develops, a way to deal with them is regularized, and the treatment becomes the justification for the treatment—evidence aside, decency aside, otherwise meticulously upheld laws aside. The anchoring of treatment to characterization of labeled people is the enduring burden of the unlucky millions whom we tag with "mental retardation." So it is not surprising that criminologist Benedict Augustin Morel's theory—that mental retardation left unchecked will lead to the propagation of a race of sterile degenerates—was not discredited until long after he had exerted enormous infuence on French psychiatry (Kraepelin, 1962). Furthermore, more than a hundred years after Morel's mischief, his ideas have strong appeal to the "man in the street." And while Dugdale's (1877) study of the Jukes family and Goddard's (1912) study of the Kallikaks, which both claimed strong hereditary ties to mental retardation, were discredited generations ago, they remain part of the "common wisdom," if not a part of the scholarly literature in psychology and genetics.

The eugenics movement was the dark side of mental retardation, and sterilization and colonization were its consequences. In contrast, people such as Maria Montessori were the light, and community living and public schooling were the consequences of their contributions.

Maria Montessori

An ideological disciple of Itard and Seguin, Maria Montessori became involved in the treatment of retarded children at the turn of the last century (Wallin, 1917). She viewed mental retardation much more as an educational than a medical problem, a view that was then both idiosyncratic and puzzling. Her view was idiosyncratic in that the common understanding connected the condition to the world of medicine, its classification to the terminology of diseases, and its prognosis to the category of incurability. Her view was puzzling because she herself was trained as a doctor and believed she was doing the work of a doctor. She must have been on the right track, because her work had enormous influence on the field of mental retardation in Italy in her time. Today, it yet enjoys significant influence throughout the world in the broader field of education.

Montessori conceived of development as the unfolding of latent impulses, and she stressed the primacy of the individual. In this sense, she was influenced by Locke, Rousseau, Froebel, and Seguin (Wallin, 1917, p. 23). Montessori placed great emphasis on studying the individual child through scientific observation, especially of spontaneous behavior and interests. She believed that young children need the liberty to express themselves. She also insisted, however, on carefully developed and specified physical and sensory training, methods strongly influenced by Seguin's "physiological education." Many of her teaching materials were designed to maximize independent use. The child could set the pace as well as gauge how well he or she was using the materials. This method of "auto-education" (self-teaching) was created to deliberately train the various senses: visual memory and discrimination, auditory memory and discrimination, and the other sensory areas involving touch, smell, taste. Further, this method was designed to train—for want of a better term—kinesthetics, which refers to the use of a variety of sensory functions to foster the child's conscious perception of his or her own muscular movements (Blatt & Garfunkel, 1969).

Montessori's career is especially noteworthy in the field of mental retardation for two reasons. First, she became famous as an educator because of her stunning work with teaching retarded children to read and write well beyond any reasonable expectations of that time. Second, she was one of the first "disciples" in the field who became more famous than the master, Seguin. In retrospect, it is possible to see that Montessori's career foretold the emergence of mental retardation as an established field of sufficient interest and consequence that people could go into it as a profession, and, just possibly, even change the world. But of course, such a conclusion was hardly recognized a decade or two ago, and not at all during Montessori's time.

In spite of great success and public acceptance of Montesori's program with retarded pupils, and eventually of the school she created in 1907 for young children of average ability—the Casa del Bambini—Montessori did not escape criticism on this side of the Atlantic. Possibly the most influential of her critics was Professor William H. Kilpatrick, the great psychologist at Teachers College, Columbia University. In large measure, Kilpatrick was responsible for the slow and noticeably reluctant acceptance of her philosophy in the United States (Kilpatrick, 1914). Montessori's greatest programmatic influence in this country probably did not begin to occur until after World War II. Today, there are many so-called Montessori schools dotting America's educational landscape, most of them for nonhandicapped and bright children, but a few devoted to the education of children with special needs. In the following excerpt, Montessori (1964), whose work has been so truly influential on educational policy and practice, discusses some of her ideas as well as the sources of her motivation.

> I succeeded in teaching a number of the idiots from the asylums both to read and to write so well that I was able to present them at a public school for an examination together with normal children. And they passed the examination successfully.
>
> These results seemed almost miraculous to those who saw them. To me, however, the boys from the asylums had been able to compete with the normal children only because they had been taught in a different way. They had been helped in their psychic development, and the normal children had, instead, been suffocated, held back. I found myself thinking that if, some day, the special education which had developed these idiot children in such a marvellous fashion, could

be applied to the development of normal children, the "miracle" of which my friends talked would no longer be possible.

Having through actual experiences justified my faith in Séguin's method, I withdrew from active work among deficients, and began a more thorough study of the works of Itard and Séguin.

The voice of Séguin seemed to be like the voice of the forerunner crying in the wilderness, and my thoughts were filled with the immensity and importance of a work which should be able to reform the school and education.[2]

Although she used the term differently than current workers, Montessori's discussion of "normalisation" offers significant insights into her philosophy of learning. Certainly, she warned about the fragile nature of curative therapies that are reinforced in environments alien to those to which the children must eventually return. She also made important distinctions between what we would call freedom to make responsible choices and anarchy:

What is still needed is a general understanding that if work and freedom can cure defects of growth, it means that work and freedom are normally needed for the child's development.

In fact, it often happens that when children, after being cured or improved, go back to live in conditions that have not been altered, and which were the original causes of their "deviations from normality," they lack the power, or the opportunities, needed to remain normalised, and their improvement is purely temporary.

Freedom is understood in a very elementary fashion, as an immediate release from oppressive bonds; as a cessation of corrections and of submission to authority. This conception is plainly negative, that is to say, it means only the elimination of coercion. From this comes, often enough, a very simple "reaction": a disorderly pouring out of impulses no longer controlled because they were previously controlled by the adult's will. "To let the child do as he likes," when he has not yet developed any powers of control, is to betray the idea of freedom.

Real freedom, instead, is a consequence of development; it is the development of latent guides, aided by education. Development is active. It is the construction of the personality, reached by effort and one's own experiences; it is the long road which every child must travel to attain maturity.

Normalisation comes about through "concentration" on a piece of work. For this we must provide "motives for activity" so well adapted to the child's interests that they provoke his deep attention.[3]

---

[2]From *The Montessori Method* (pp. 41-42) by M. Montessori, 1964, New York: Schocken Books. Copyright 1964 by Schocken Books. Reprinted by permission.

[3]From *The Absorbent Mind* (pp.204-206) by M. Montessori, 1967, Madras, India: Kalakshetia Publications. Reprinted by permission.

Alfred Binet

Like Montessori, Alfred Binet established himself by solving a problem in the field of mental retardation, and only later generalized that work to the larger society. Binet came to be regarded as the father of the "Measurement Era," but he may have had hopes that his work would lead to another achievement, one that always eluded him, as it has eluded virtually everyone else with a similar vision. Binet's scholarship provides a centerpiece for the examination of efforts to educate intelligence. "Educating intelligence" refers to the development of procedures and conditions that bring out capacities for change in the individual (Blatt & Garfunkel, 1969). The term implies that change occurs in both rate and complexity of learning, especially as far as school-related problems are concerned. The term emphasizes the Latin origin of the word "education"—leading forth, bringing out, eliciting. This approach to education focuses on increasing the individual's capability to change—that is, to learn. How is change (learning) measured? Standardized intelligence tests as well as more informal tests measure an individual's capability for certain types of learning. On a more pragmatic level, a person's ability to learn is reflected in how he or she handles everyday problems. One appealing hypothesis holds that an individual's capacity for learning is enhanced to the degree that the person (a) needs to change, (b) aspires to change, (c) is optimistic about the possibility of changing. That is, "educating intelligence refers to more than hypothetical mental faculties or abilities. It also refers to attitudes about self, learning, and abilities without which the phenomenon of change cannot be comprehended" (Blatt & Garfunkel, 1969, p. 6).

Many modern-day conceptions concerning the hypothesis that a significant portion of capability is a function of practice, training, and motivation derive from the work of Alfred Binet. (See his *Les Idées Modernes sur les Enfants*, 1909.) Through his "Mental Orthopedics" he sought to strengthen the faculties of attention, memory, perception, judgment, and will, and by doing so enhance the retarded child's capabilities. This effort was contrary to the admonitions of Kilpatrick and others who claimed that the senses could *not* be improved by training (Kilpatrick, 1914). The key individual in Binet's program was the teacher—an astute observer, a person who knew each child well and who had the skills to adapt instruction to meet the individual needs of each child. To avoid discouragement and bad work habits, the teacher would insure that instruction was on the child's level of ability and then would proceed from the known to the unknown. The teacher would not take for granted that every child in the class came to school with a background of experiences conducive to successful learning, so the teacher would deliberately set out to assess what the child knew, what he or she was ready to learn, and what the child would need in the weeks and months ahead. The teacher would be less interested in teaching pupils ideas that seemed the most useful to them at the time than in providing them with opportunities to *learn how to learn* as active discoverers of an unfolding and revealing environment. In modern parlance, Binet utilized what we today term the "discovery method" — reliance on a child's natural curiosity and capability for exploring the environment, for coming to grips with the meaning of it, and for developing his or her faculties for learning through such experiences.

It is not by accident that Binet concentrated so much of his energies on mentally retarded children. His driving interest was in exploiting his idea that the study of retarded children serves all children, that the pedagogy that could educate their intelligence might also educate the capabilities of nonhandicapped and gifted children, an idea that had not escaped Montessori's imagination. What influences powered this remarkable man's remarkable conceptions?

Alfred Binet was born in Nice on July 11, 1857; he died in Paris on October 18, 1911. Contrary to popular belief, Binet never became a physician, and was one of the few early leaders in the field not so prepared (Wolf, 1973). By present-day American standards, he came into the field of psychology in a curious manner, first finding it by himself, and then by beginning a self-instructional reading program. During the ensuing years, he developed wide interests, ranging from work in evolution, mental retardation, psycho-pathology, free will and determinism, and heredity, to comparative psychology, experimental psychology, learning, and — of course — the measurement of intelligence. He was a philosopher, experimentalist, clinician, writer, editor, and professor. And although he was considered shy and retiring, he knew and worked with Babinski, Charcot, Fere, Balbiani (his father-in-law), Cyril Burt, Henry Goddard, Lewis Terman, and, of course, Theodore Simon. He surely was aware of the work of Cattell, who coined the term "mental test" and who was the first American to urge the use of such tests (Robinson & Robinson, 1976). He was also aware of Galton's work in systematically observing development. But rather than concentrating on the measurement of elementary capacities through simple procedures, as Cattell had been attempting, Binet felt it would be necessary to examine more precisely the continuum of reasoning, judgment, memory, and abstract capability in order to form a global understanding of intelligence. The Society for the Psychological Study of the Child invited him to search for ways to differentiate those children who could learn normally from those who could not. Through that work, begun in 1904, he and Simon developed the first genuine scale of intelligence — 30 tests organized by order of difficulty and purporting to sample those complex mental functions that the authors were certain contributed much of what we think of as "intelligence." Possibly because he himself vacillated so much on the educability issue (Sarason, 1981), and certainly because he was much misunderstood, especially by American psychologists, Binet's scholarly career was marked by a series of contradictions and ironies. Many of the conceptualizations that led to the development of the Binet scales obtained from the traditions of environmentalism. Much of his work, however, was appropriated by nativists. A great deal of his work in pedagogy was based on the hypothesis that people can change and that intelligence is educable. Ironically, however, the rationale behind "training" classes (as opposed to "developmental" or "educational" classes) for mentally retarded persons is in large part based on the concept of the stability of the intelligence quotient. Indeed, the hopelessness generally pervading the field vis-à-vis amelioration, or reversibility of defect, can be traced to this concept. Binet's work presaged the work of environmentalists such as Skeels (and his collaborators), Kirk, Sarason, Weikart, and others. Thus it is ironic that nativists from Goddard to Jensen and Herrnstein found evidence in Binet's scales for their ideas concerning the irreversibility of mental defect. It would be exceedingly provocative to hear Binet himself comment on today's discussion of the long-standing nature-nurture controversy.

Louis William Stern

Where did the IQ come from? Of course, it derives from Binet and Simon's mental age scales, but the IQ itself wasn't their invention; Louis William Stern (1914) is usually credited with its creation. Stern was born in Berlin in 1871 and was educated at Friedrich Wilhelm University in Berlin, earning the PhD in 1893. He eventually attained full professorship at the University in Breslau, but only on condition that he convert to Christianity. So he left in 1916 to head the faculty of philosophy and psychology at the Colonial Institute in Hamburg. After expulsion from Germany in 1933, he went to Holland for a year and then to the United States, where he taught at Duke, Harvard, Columbia, and Brown. There is a William Stern archive at the Jewish National and Hebrew University Library in Jerusalem; and, although he has an extensive bibliography, much of his work remains untranslated from the original German (Stern, 1971). While Binet and Simon used the absolute difference between mental and chronological age as an index of retardation, Stern observed that this system would necessarily lead to different conclusions at different ages. Consequently, in 1912 he recommended the utilization of a ratio of mental to chronological age, thus obtaining a "constant" mental quotient: the IQ. His contribution to a better understanding of mental development caused some misunderstandings because, while simplifying the meaning of the relationship between mental and chronological age, he also unwittingly encouraged the simplification of the extraordinarily complex concept of intelligence.

The work of Binet and Simon was transported to the United States by Henry Goddard and others, and it was made more "practical" by Stern. The idea of quantitative measurement of intelligence was embraced with a vengeance here, becoming the scientific toy of the then-infant mental measurement movement. Once an inexpensive, reliable, and "painless" test of intelligence became available, there was no way to impede, much less halt, its usage. It seemed that an intelligence test that was both inexpensive and accurate (i.e., reliable) would soon become for social scientists what the thermometer was to physicians. Consequently, a sea of studies accrued purporting to examine questions connected with *changes* in levels of tested intelligence, *comparisons* of various racial and other groups, and *correlates* of intelligence. For purposes of such studies, it was assumed that the intelligence quotient was analagous to, if not synonymous with, native intelligence.

J. E. Wallace Wallin

J. E. Wallace Wallin was a contemporary of Montessori, Binet, and Goddard as well as of Harold Skeels and Sam Kirk. He was also my contemporary. His career spanned the inauguration of the first psychology program at Clark University at the beginning of this century and the establishment of several psycho-educational clinics and programs to prepare teachers of mentally retarded students before, during, and after World War II. A teacher for more than seven decades, Wallin deserves credit as the originator of the American concept of the psycho-educational model. He implemented the first traveling psycho-educational clinic, drafted the first public school regulations for severely retarded children, and wrote two of the first American textbooks on the education of handicapped children and on clinical psychology. He is also the individual probably most responsible in America for some semblance of a history of this field (Blatt, 1968).

Wallin's career exemplifies the hard going of the early pioneers in the field of mental retardation. While he was known as a scholar, administrator, clinician, and author (32 books and over 350 articles, monographs, reviews, and essays), Wallin was also known as a controversial figure, a man who had several dozen positions, from most of which he either resigned or was terminated—with acrimony on both sides. To have known Wallin or to have read his many papers, which attempted to set the historical record straight, might give the specialist in this field a much deeper sense and appreciation of its rich history. A person I and my contemporaries in the field knew well, Wallin was a student of Scripture and Ladd (pioneer psychologists) at Yale. He was G. Stanley Hall's (founder of the American Psychological Association) post-doctoral assistant at Clark. He was also once a young instructor who was supervised by Woodrow Wilson at Princeton, and for a time he was a teacher educator at the Old Vineland Training School where Sam Kirk, the great special educator, was enrolled as one of his *students*.

This is an old, yet young, field. Here was a man who lived through 75 tumultuous years as a teacher and leader in this field. His works not only illuminate history, but his life made history. Nevertheless, with all of his accomplishments, fame, and prestige, he was also the man who more often than not told school boards and superintendents that they were derelict in their duties toward handicapped children. He was the man who told colleges and universities that they weren't doing well enough in preparing teachers and psychologists. He was the man who showed scientists and scholars in the field how they could do better, and clinicians how they must do better. Today, if not altogether forgotten, he may be most remembered as a cranky old man (Blatt, 1968). He should be remembered and honored for his creation of the psycho-educational movement in special education as well as for his considerable influence as a teacher of teachers and scholars.

Nowhere in the social sciences has there been more controversy, more battle, more acrimony, more scandal than in the mental retardation research connected with intelligence, its meaning, and its modifiability. In a sense, the concept of intelligence is the quintessential social science battlefield, and the IQ is the battle cry that goads people who otherwise know better to assume extreme and untenable positions as well as to engage in foolish, unseemly, and sometimes dishonest behavior. It's a commentary on that unfortunate state of affairs, as well as a reflection of the general pessimism concerning the possibility that capability is educable, that there exists a shadow upon the work and the persons—unfortunately, also the many honest and competent persons—involved in efforts to enhance educability.

Harold Skeels

Harold Skeels' work in the 1930s and 1940s in the areas of psychology and mental retardation came at a time when the assumptions of inflexible IQ and genetic determinism clearly held sway. However, even though he became much respected and ultimately was the recipient of a Kennedy Scientific Award, he and his colleagues did not escape the shadow.

In 1939, he and Dye reported that the IQs of two young children went up significantly after transfer from an unstimulating orphanage. During infancy, these children, who were both illegitimate and of feebleminded mothers, were placed in the state institution in the hope that they would find a nurturing environment in the company of the older women residents of the facility. Skeels and Dye were surprised to learn that six months later, the IQs of the children had increased remarkably, and that a year later their measured IQs were found to be in the normal range. Furthermore, the children maintained normal intelligence past their third year. What had occurred? Not only were the older retarded women in constant attendance to these babies—they being the only young children in the entire institution—but many staff members were also very attentive to the needs of these children. For example, on their days off, attendants took the children for car rides or on shopping trips. They bought them toys, books, and other play materials. Eventually, administrators at the institution could no longer justify keeping the children, and so more suitable foster homes were found for these children, where they continued to thrive normally.

Building on that experience, Skeels and his colleagues developed a series of programs that included the transfer of one- and two-year-old functionally retarded children from the state orphanage nursery to the state school. Skeels and his associates conducted other studies to examine the mental development of children from inferior social and intellectual backgrounds who were placed in foster homes during infancy; the results confirmed earlier observations that children placed in stimulating and nurturing environments at a young age will develop better than those who are placed in adverse or sterile environments (Skeels & Harms, 1948; Skodak & Skeels, 1949). Still other studies by Skeels' Iowa group found that children who attended nursery school showed gains in IQ (Coffey & Wellman, 1936) and that those who did not attend nursery schools showed decreases in IQ (Skeels & Harms, 1948; Skodak & Skeels, 1949).

It is well known that the kinds of field research conducted by Skeels and his associates use measures that are lacking in reliability and make methodological compromises that are never desirable. In the context of the debate over modifiability, the work of Skeels and his colleagues was attacked particularly vehemently on scientific grounds (Goodenough & Maurer, 1940/1961). Suffice it to say that while much of the scientific criticism of their work was valid, their conceptualizations concerning the nature and correlates of educability stimulated to a great extent the creation of Head Start and other early education movements of the sixties and seventies. Furthermore, many of their innovative stimulation programs have been "reinvented" in recent years. Without doubt, Skeels' Iowa group served as the ideological progenitor of the later works of Sam Kirk, Ira Gordon, and many others. And while in past decades Skeels and the others of his group were perceived as academic pariahs, in more recent years they have been recognized and honored for their contributions to the study of educability, and, particularly, to the service of mentally retarded and disadvantaged children. Skeels' (1966) last study before his death was a 30-year follow-up of his original group of 25 infants. Thirteen infants were placed in stimulating environments, and a control group of 12 remained for a prolonged period of time in a relatively unstimulating orphanage. He (Skeels, 1966) found that

> the two groups have maintained their divergent patterns of competency into adulthood. All 13 children in the experimental group were self-supporting, and none was the ward of any institution, public or private. In the contrast group of 12 children, one had died in adolescence following continued residence in a state institution for the mentally retarded, and four were still in wards of institutions, one in a mental hospital, and the other three in institutions for the mentally retarded. (pp. 54-55)

The most negative appraisal that seems reasonable with regard to the work of the Iowa group is that they were unable to make a scientific case in support of their hypothesis that intelligence is educable. They were unable to control treatment variables, they relied on *ex post facto* data, and they (necessarily) studied people in a catch-as-catch-can manner—*in their natural environments*. These methodological factors weakened their ability to establish persuasive scientific evidence to support their conclusions. In spite of the methodological difficulties, however, they were superb creators of intellectually stimulating environments, superb observers of natural settings, and tenacious professionals who were able to recognize an important idea when they stumbled on it and courageous enough to follow it in spite of years of discouragement and widespread hostility from both academics and practitioners. These were very wise people for the manner in which, as Seymour Sarason might have commented, "they took the obvious seriously."

Cyril Burt

For certain, there exists an enormous uncharted chasm between what is known (what is true) and what is believed (what people want to know) concerning the relative influence of heredity and environment in shaping human intelligence. The sad case of Sir Cyril Burt is instructive, although probably not typical of the excesses and duplicity surrounding the nature-nurture (heredity-environment) controversy. Sir Cyril Burt died in 1971, after a long and influential career as a British psychologist. At the time of his death, he was acknowledged as a pioneer in the scientific study of intelligence testing whose intellectual disciples included Arthur Jensen and others on both sides of the Atlantic. Shortly after Burt's death, Leon Kamin, of Princeton University, and others in England, raised serious questions about Burt's data and integrity. In L. S. Hearnshaw's book, published in 1980, the sordid story was revealed in its entirety, or at least as much of its entirety as could be deduced from Hearnshaw's reconstruction of Burt's life from thorough examination of his papers, personal journal, and the *British Journal of Statistical Psychology,* which he edited for almost 20 years. Burt's once widely quoted studies of identical twins separated early in life, which led to his conclusion that genetic endowment was much more significant than environment, were found to be fraudulent. There is even a question of whether some of his reputed coworkers on those studies actually existed. By any reasonable assessment, this man — who gave authority to the idea in Western society that blacks are inferior to whites and that they deserve their impoverishment by virtue of their intellectual inadequacies — was a faker. It can also cross the reader's mind that more than by chance, scandal and academic treachery have been associated with the nature-nurture debate. This is an issue that gets at the very core of human existence, to the very question of human perfectability; it also gets at the real political war between the proletariat and the governing elite. Exactly because capability is in part inherited and in part environmentally determined, and exactly because the problem is not amenable to easy — or, for the most part, any — genuine scientific study, the "debate" will continue. And unfortunately, we will probably continue to find more than our share of charlatans, careerists, and thoughtless zealots in control of some aspects of that examination and dissemination of the obtained "wisdom."

The "good news" is that, since Kirk's 1958 study of the educability hypothesis, there has been a steady stream of investigators concerned with the issue. And while it remains an open question whether practice and training can have significant influence on intellectual and social development, this is clearly an era in which the idea is not unthinkable and, indeed, is on the minds of many academics and clinicians.

The Kennedy Influence

On February 5, 1963, President John Kennedy delivered a message to Congress calling for a national effort to deal with problems of mental illness and mental retardation. In some respects, this was the apex, if not the beginning, of his massively popular War on Poverty (Blatt, 1970a). In his remarks to Congress, he asserted that there was evidence to suggest that cultural and educational deprivation that led to mental retardation could be prevented. He noted a well-established literature indicating that, if appropriate opportunities are provided early enough, many deprived children would learn as well as children from more favored economic environments, and that without early attention, even in the absence of organic impairment, the cumulative effect of prolonged neglect would, for some children, lead to retarded development.

The President's message, while not the first call for federal involvement in the education of handicapped people, may have been the most influential to that time. That message continues to remain important, if for no other reason than that it serves as a conceptual link between Itard and his pioneering colleagues and Public Law 94-142, which seems to be one of the ideological maps for the future.

The Educability Hypothesis

As I remarked earlier, the educability issue seems to permeate the literature as a nagging, unresolved major question. A great deal of importance has been assigned to it by the most distinguished scholars in the field, indeed, by society in general. It may be that an additional reason it may hold such importance is because it gets at the most fundamental theological question: free will versus predestination. Think about the human being as a machine — an automobile, a ship, an airplane, a dynamic machine. Machines shift gears, but they don't change radically; that is, machines don't change their shapes, their habits, their purposes, their appearances, their character. And so, when one hears about machines — or people — shifting gears, one isn't surprised or disbelieving. It's normal for machines and people to shift gears. The life of the machine is destined to hold a certain place in a certain manner; by its nature, the machine is predictable and reassuring. Machines don't have free wills. Machines can't reconstitute themselves, start all over again, change remarkably.

But what about people? There is a debate here. The atheist will point out the wars, the holocausts, the plagues, and other terrors as evidence for the denial of God's existence. The theologian will point to those phenomena, and others even more terrible, as the affirmation of God's design for human beings. What the atheist claims there was no God to prevent, the theologian claims is the expression of God's unique gift to human beings: our free will, our freedom to determine our destiny, our control of the earth's forces. In a sense, the nature-nurture argument is the same as the one involving predestination and free will. It's one thing for a human being to shift gears, it's another thing to change vessels. It's one thing to learn and grow in predictable ways, it's another to become a *different* person. It's one thing to have an opportunity to be educated and, thus, to make the most of what you have, but it's another thing to be stupid now but bright later. It's one thing to be mentally retarded, to be in a good special education program, to learn to read a little, to do a job, to make your way independently, to be able to live with your disabilities. It's quite another thing to *have been* mentally retarded, and to *now be* perfectly normal, to *now be* very different from what you *had once been*. It isn't any wonder that the nature-nurture argument inflames adherents on either side.

The educability hypothesis has suffered both at the hands of those who would not consider it (in spite of any evidence), and by those who insist on propagating it (in spite of a paucity of evidence). Like the ideas of normalization, deinstitutionalization, conservatism or liberalism, the educability hypothesis is powered (or dismissed) by the conception one has of what human beings ought to be like and what opportunities they ought to have. Whether the educability hypothesis is true or not must await further and better examination. But what may be even more important is the idea that people should be treated—in schools, in developmental facilities, by their families, by society—*as if* they can change, *as if* careful systematic interventions on their behalf will make a difference. Whether you accept that notion is in large measure determined by what you see as the responsibility of the clinician and the citizen, on the one hand, and the agency and society, on the other.

Discussion

During ancient times (and to a degree, to this day), people whom we now call mentally retarded were treated with contempt, ridicule, and they were even exterminated. From the beginning of known history, such people have been abandoned or abused, cursed because they were different, and feared because they were different. "Idiot" was defined by the ancient Greeks as someone who is either so lacking in training or so disinterested as to be incapable of human interaction. To the Hebrews of the Old Testament, it referred to a selfish person. The term persists today with vestiges of its ancient meanings—to refer to the person so locked within the self that he or she is unable to experience and enjoy the world in human ways. Since ancient times, mentally retarded and other disabled people have been assigned status outside of what is thought to be the human race. And yet, everyone since ancient times—including the Spartans, who abandoned their physically deformed, and the Nazis, who slew those "without value"—knew for certain that these were indeed human beings. The historical conspiracy against retarded people has not been thoughtless but quite deliberate, and it is based not on the belief that these aren't human beings but, rather, on the will to deal with these people *as if* they aren't human beings. In part, the science of eugenics was probably created out of the Greeks' need to legally exterminate their defective members. Even in ancient times, science may have been called upon to do dirty work "on behalf of" the society.

There is evidence that the Hebrews, the ancient Christians, and those who followed the Koran assumed more tolerant attitudes toward mentally retarded people, although, as Kanner (1964) warned us, our knowledge on this subject is quite limited:

> It has been customary to cite a few sporadic passages from Greek and Roman literature, from the Bible, the Talmud, and the Koran. . . . The sum total of all those quotations, however, amounts to little beyond the fact that the existence of such persons was known and that occasionally friendliness toward them was advocated. (p. 3)

It's difficult to make very much out of the stories handed down from century to century concerning, for example, Luther's attitudes toward these people. Were they possessed by demons, and, thus, did they deserve to be loathed? Or were they God's innocent children, to be comforted and pitied, to be clothed and sheltered? Centuries ago, was the prevailing attitude, "As you do this to these the least of my brothers you do it to Me"? or "I should take this child to the Moldau River which flows near Dessau and drown him"? As there are today, there were many attitudes—official attitudes of the church and its priests, and unofficial attitudes of the people. What is known is that the Old Testament, the New Testament, and the Koran speak about people's relationships not only to God but to each other; each of these Books enjoins us to practice the Golden Rule, each extols the nobility of the human being, all human beings. While there's a great deal we'll never know about the particular ways mentally retarded people were treated in ancient times, we do know that, with the creation of our modern theistic religions, the idea of all men in God's image became widely shared, and we want to believe that this truly new conception made people better—not only in the eyes of God but in each other's eyes.

Possibly, Wallin (1917) accurately reported the reenactment of ancient cruelties during the Renaissance and Reformation. Possibly, Luther and the other religious leaders of the time preached on behalf of the cruelest treatments to "cure" the feebleminded so as to purge them of the disease inflicted by Satan himself. But if we should give credence to that version of history, there isn't an obvious explanation of the fact that in the seventeenth century humane institutions were created by clerics to serve those whom their theological forebears had once tortured. Enlightenment is a comprehensible metaphor. But the idea of an "Age of Darkness" followed by an "Age of Light" is as comprehensible as a world that's black *or* white, night *or* day. It has been said that, at any precise instant, it is difficult to distinguish the dawn from the dusk. And while it has also been said that "We are our brother's keepers," even when those noble words were *first* uttered, the idea of it had seen better days. From the volume of ancient history with regard to treatment and care of mentally retarded persons, we have learned that (1) even then, people were designated as "different"; (2) even then, people were admonished to remember that they too are strangers in the land of Canaan; they too are weak, fragile, and interdependent; (3) even then, there were those whose vision of humanity could not admit to inclusion of mentally retarded persons among its members; (4) even then, special training of workers did not guarantee that mentally retarded people would be treated like people, much less like brothers; (5) even then, as today, some mentally retarded people fared better than others, some were luckier than others.

We live in the age of normalization, deinstitutionalization, advocacy, and Public Law 94-142, an age in which hundreds of thousands of citizens are members of a national association dedicated to the welfare of mentally retarded persons, an age in which virtually everyone in the society has been informed about who these people are, what they have, and what they need. It is probable that we have been right about some things and wrong about others. It is certain that in a century, or perhaps in a decade, we will be ridiculed for the ideas we hold today. All human beings behave at the moment as if they are never going to change—not that they believe they know everything that's needed to be known. Rather, they believe that that which they know to be true *is* true. Two thousand years ago, Socrates challenged that conception. His fellow citizens didn't listen then. We don't listen today. Never mind the history of mental retardation; the history of the human race has taught us that, for certain, people's ideas change, and, also for certain, they change in unexpected ways, in ways that make us look foolish in retrospect. And we don't like it. That's what we've learned from history. But the one thing we've learned from history is that we don't learn very much from history. We have confused ourselves, and we confuse those who grope to understand us. What were once the pompous "megatrend visions" of the futurists have often become the "implausible nightmares" of those entrusted with official explanations—the historians. Possibly, why we don't learn from history is because we rarely get it straight. And when we do, we rarely know what to make of it. It's not always difficult for us to miss the point. In the history curriculum of the field, there is little of consequence. While we revere Rousseau, we also remember that Buddha tried to teach more than 2,000 years earlier that the man who has pity on every living thing is truly noble. We have yet to learn the important lessons for living. We have yet to learn well enough from history. Or, as a forgotten pundit once remarked, "There is nothing new except what is forgotten."

Part 2

PEOPLE WHO ARE MENTALLY RETARDED: WHO ARE THEY?

The Pariahs' Preacher

All is vanity everywhere,
    Except among the pariahs,
Who are, because all is vanity,
    Everywhere.

The sun also rises, while one reads Ecclesiastes,
But it goes down, yet the Book remains,
As Willowbrook State School is created,
And Willowbrook Developmental Center is destroyed.

    Rivers run to the sea,
As dayroom crud moves to the sewer.
    Samuel Gridley Howe is invented,
Walter E. Fernald dies.

Rivers run, but the sea doesn't fill,
    Abuse pushes in, but there's room for more.
        The Ladd State School sounds bright and lively,
            But it's exactly Ladd, so dark and deadly.

For everything there is a season,
A time to be born, and a time to die.
    We inhabit Wrentham,
    We evacuate Wrentham.

    I remember oppressions that do not leave my head,
        So I praise those gone, for now they are dead.
Posey belt, posey belt, wrap yourself around,
Tie up that retard, grind him in the ground.

Better is a poor person, than a powerful king
    who can't accept admonition.

Better the underling than the boss, Wyatt than Stickney,
    Hobson than Hansen.
Better not to vow than to vow,
    and not deliver.
Better not to have a year, than to have
    "A Year of the Child."

    A good name is better than precious oil,
as the patient in spirit is better than the proud.
    Belchertown, Letchworth, Partlow,
Rosewood, Cloverbottom, Cambridge.
    Some righteous men perish in their
righteousness, and there are the wicked who prosper.
    v. Stickney, v. Greenblatt,
v. Pennsylvania, v. Board of Education.

    Folly is found everywhere.
    But to oppress is the greatest folly,
    For it turns wise people foolish,
AND IT EXISTS BECAUSE ALL IS VANITY.

Burton Blatt

4.

Defining and Counting Mentally Retarded Persons

SOME THINGS ARE easy to count, such as the number of children in a family or in a particular grade of a school. Other things are more difficult to count, such as infinity or — for more ordinary mortals — even the number of pupils in a city. In the former instances, the task is "merely" to tally the names of the children in a home or of those enrolled in a particular class. But even here, there can be ambiguity. What about the foster child? What about the child who is officially on the class roll, but doesn't attend school, is informally assigned to another class, or is in the hospital? Such anomalies are generally dealt with by the functional definitions of "family," "pupil," and "class."

Because the class is sufficiently small to examine first-hand, one can be reasonably accurate in reporting how many boys and girls are enrolled in a particular classroom. When it comes to counting pupils in a city, however, a degree of precision is lost. Families are always moving; thus children are always moving. Some children are excluded from school, others are exempted from school, still others are suspended from school, and there are some who don't attend school but remain on official registers. But all such counting, be it of children in the home, in the class, in the school, or in the city, proceeds from functional definitions — that is, definitions that permit explicit categorical assignments.

We count some things that are even more problematic than the aforementioned examples. To count how many people are impoverished (or how many are wealthy) requires definitions and categorizations that are not only difficult to achieve but are difficult to justify. Often, it's simply impossible to verify data supporting the assignment of individuals to one or the other category. That is, there are "facts" and "values"; *much of the counting in mental retardation is connected to values*. For example, who's gifted or who's dull are judgments based on definitions that are subject to disagreement; indeed, such definitions may not even stand up when employed by the very people who developed them. Thus, much of the counting we do is error-ridden; the definitions we employ require judgments to be made in the face of ambiguous evidence. And here lies an essential problem: If those who categorize and count people use judgment in making such assignments, they will not get a reliable, repeatable count. If they don't use judgment, they will get an inexplicable count. Either way, when counting certain kinds of people (e.g., mentally retarded), it is almost impossible to claim much more than the proposition that, in the judgment of those who did the counting, these are the people who met a particular (hopefully stipulated) *a priori* operational definition. That's why in the final analysis, "mental retardation" is an "administrative" term. People so labeled *are* mentally retarded, and people not so labeled *aren't* mentally retarded. In the same fashion that the label "college student" is based on one's attendance at a college, the label "mental retardation" is based on one's identification and placement (or denial of placement) because of that condition.

There are other reasons why counting mentally retarded people is, at best, uncertain, and, most probably, results in inaccurate data. Tredgold and Soddy (1956, p. 10) succinctly summarized these further complications:

> The enumeration of the mentally deficient section of any community is a very difficult matter for many reasons, and the figures concerning this class ascertained by the official census are so notoriously inaccurate as to be not worth quoting. For one thing, even if parents realize that their offspring is definitely defective, they are not unnaturally reluctant to proclaim the fact on a census paper. In many cases, however, particularly of the milder degrees of defect, which are by far the most numerous, although parents may recognize that their children are in some way abnormal, they do not realize that mental defect is present. It follows, that if an approximately accurate enumeration is to be made, it can only be by means of a special investigation; although it is practically certain that even by this the ascertainment will still be imperfect.

Bogdan and Ksander (1980) developed a provocative perspective on "enumerology", or what we might think of as the "science of counting." They lay out a series of assumptions designed to engender reflection on what we do when we count various types of people in various situations. Bogdan and Ksander defined this idea of "enumerology" as "the study of social processes by which numbers are generated, and the effect of these processes on behavior and thought" (p. 302). They thus provided us with an interesting way to conceptualize mental retardation, its extent, and its impact on society. Here is their admonition:

> The process of counting produces rates and measures. Counting is an attitude we take toward people, objects, and events. Phenomena only appear as rates and measures after an attitude is developed toward them which acknowledges them as existing, important to count, and susceptible to counting procedures.
>
> The perspective that counting is a disposition toward things ties enumerology to the study of language and classification, but enumerology is not the same as these fields. The concept of *alcoholic,* for example, has to exist before a count of alcoholics can be made, and the concept of *cure* has to be present to have cure rates, but having these concepts does not necessarily lead to counting alcoholics and deriving how many have been cured as the result of a particular program. To use another example, although the concept *feebleminded* was in use in the United States before 1830, it was not until that time that a rate of feeblemindedness was produced as part of the national census. (Bogdan & Ksander, 1980, p. 303)

This chapter examines such questions as: How is mental retardation defined? How are mentally retarded people counted? What is the relationship between intelligence and social justice? What is the relationship between the definitions of mental retardation and the interests of professionals, consumers, and the larger society? Implied is the idea that counting, as an activity, has saliency to the degree that there sometimes isn't anything else of consequence one can do about the problem. That is, when all else fails, the activity involved in counting people may seem better than doing *nothing* to help those people.

Definitions of Mental Retardation

Humankind has recreated Babel; much of the confusion comes from the work of scientists and other specialists. And unclear, imprecise language is hardly more common anywhere than in the field of mental retardation. In the Genesis 11:6-9 account of Babel (Hertz, 1964) God said:

> Behold, they are one people, and they have all one language; this is what they begin to do; and now nothing will be withholden from them, which they propose to do. Come, let us go down, and there confound their language that they may not understand one another's speech. (p. 39)

Szasz (1973) interpreted this "second sin" as the human attempt to encroach on God's territory. When all human beings spoke one language and used words precisely, they came to believe that the people could accomplish anything, with or without a god. Hence, they would no longer need God, nor would they need to mind His command to disperse themselves across the earth. This affront against God — their sin of perfect communication — caused Him to create differences of language everywhere and for all time to come. Of course, there are other explanations of the parable of the "second sin," but as Szasz pointed out, authorities in the name of religion, the state, and the professions honor those who displace common sense and ordinary language with obfuscation, technical jargon, and other attempts at thwarting easy discourse by those outside the annointed ranks. In our day, speaking and writing clearly on issues with which only professionals are supposed to deal remains an affront to higher authority. And while it may no longer be called a sin against God Himself, there is little doubt that mixing too deeply into the business of mental retardation causes the layman to eventually be labeled a troublemaker if not, indeed, a quack and a charlatan.

Not only have entire books been written on terminology and classification in the field (e.g., Grossman, 1977), but virtually every textbook in the field has at least a chapter on terms and their definitions; furthermore, thousands of papers have been written that have sought to clarify those terms and definitions, add new ones, delete old ones, make a case that mental retardation is "this" rather than "that," or is "that" rather than "this." It is questionable how helpful our preoccupation with terminology has been — either for the clients and their families, or for the scholars and other specialists in the field. On the other hand, given the realities of how public policy is implemented, mental retardation must, if such people are to be served, be defined. People must be identified and counted. Mindful of the pitfalls inherent in the re-creation of Babel, let us turn to the definitions.

Officially, the generic term used by the American Association on Mental Deficiency to refer to this population is "mental retardation." But as exemplified by that organization's very name, other terms are used, such as: mental deficiency, mental subnormality, feeblemindedness, mental handicap, slow learner, moron, idiot, imbecile, familial, garden-variety, clinical, aclinical, educable, trainable, and custodial; the list can go on and on. In the public schools, mental retardation is generally defined as having an IQ less than approximately 70 and not doing well in and out of school. In the institution, mental retardation is more often than not defined by IQ, but also in terms of etiological factors (causes), severity of defect (mild, moderate, severe, or profound), or stigmata (identifying characteristics such as those associated with Down syndrome, cerebral palsy, microcephaly). In ordinary society, mentally retarded persons are often referred to idiomatically (e.g., stupid, retard, mongoloid, special, idiot, slow, feebleminded). The American Association on Mental Deficiency most recently defined mental retardation as significantly subaverage general intellectual functioning (less than approximately 70 IQ), resulting in or associated with concurrent impairments in adaptive behavior (problems associated with early development, learning, or social adjustment), and manifested during the developmental period (between birth and 18 years) (Grossman, 1977, p. 11).

You will find that there are many definitions of mental retardation and many specific and generic terms to identify those so defined. It is impossible to comprehend what a particular author is driving at by merely reading the terms used. You must read beyond the labels and the classifications in order to understand whether the author is discussing people who are mildly mentally retarded or severely mentally retarded, for example. Because mental retardation is in the most fundamental and important ways a metaphor (people make of it what they want to, people interpret it in light of their own understandings and prejudices), the definition "mental retardation" and the terms used to denote the condition represent a hodgepodge of (sometimes irreconcilable) values, words, and ideas. It's not possible to achieve a useful taxonomy of the condition or of definitions when such a situation exists. The most we can do is to seek to know what's going on here, what we can rely on, what agreements and disagreements we have, and to realize that in spite of good intentions, it will sometimes be difficult to communicate with others in the field about this "thing" we're dealing with. It is possible that those in the field who claim to use more precise language are either abiding optimists or pretentious. Or, they simply underestimate the difficulty inherent in generating precise definitions of something when consensus has not been reached concerning who the people are, how they acquire the condition, how (or if) they can be "cured," what the consequences of the condition are, and what the condition even means.

How, then, is it possible to arrive at a useful definition of mental retardation? For one thing—keeping in mind that we cannot pretend to a high degree of precision—we can look at how several definitional dichotomies have evolved. Historically, this "thing" we term "mental retardation" has been defined in two ways: metaphorically and functionally. The metaphorical definition usually makes extensive use of analogies (mental retardation is like this, or that) or relationships and associations (people who are mentally retarded behave like these people but not like those people). A functional definition, in contrast, doesn't attempt to draw such comparisons and doesn't attempt to justify its scheme. Further, it is more like a photograph and might include such terminology as "mentally retarded people have IQs no higher than X," or "at maturity they have mental ages no greater than Y," or "they function Z years below the chronological age on such and such tasks."

There is another important definitional dichotomy: the traditional and the administrative. Traditional definitional criteria require that the condition be constitutional (biologically based), be present at birth or early age, and be incurable. Since the person is irreversibly "different," he or she will always be in need of special treatment and consideration.

Conversely, the administrative definition makes it plain that no judgments need to be made concerning the origin or the future course of the condition. The burden is to uncover sufficient evidence to conclude that the individual is mentally retarded *at the time of diagnosis*. Furthermore, that conclusion is based on the *fact* that the person has been identified and dealt with administratively because he or she is mentally retarded. Given these basic dichotomies, let's take a closer look at some of the more prominent definitional schemes.

Tredgold offered one of the classic metaphorical definitions (Tredgold & Soddy, 1956). First, he divided abnormalities of the mind into three groups: mental disorder, mental decay, and incomplete development. "Mental deficiency" (or mental retardation) could be applied to all groups. While the neurotic and the psychotic may have problems that are retardation-like, however, such people suffer from a loss of capability rather than an absence of capability. And while even the psychotic person may recover his or her mind, the retarded person would be seen as permanently afflicted. Mental retardation corresponds to the term "amentia" (without a mind, never having had a mind), while mental illness corresponds to the term "dementia" (loss of mind). To Tredgold, the metaphor "mental retardation" includes: incomplete development, scholastic ineducability, inability to profit from ordinary schools, low IQ, inability to maintain an independent life, and general maladaptive behavior. There are several connotations associated with Tredgold's concept of mental retardation that are similar to those associated with other traditional definitions: (1) the condition involves arrested or incomplete mental development that arose very early in life (certainly before the age of 18 years); (2) the etiology of the condition may be found in either inherited factors or pre-, peri-, or postnatal disease or injury; (3) the locus of insult is primarily in the brain; (4) the condition is essentially incurable and without hope for substantial amelioration; (5) the condition is invariably hopeless insofar as significant change of the individual is concerned. Undergirding the metaphor is the belief that deficient behavior results from a deficient brain.

In more recent years, there have been other conceptions of the condition. In the main, these newer ideas have been powered by problems that arose with the traditional concept, such as: the inability of either neurological scientists or medical, psychological, and educational clinicians to demonstrate central nervous system differentiation between mildly mentally retarded persons and nonhandicapped persons; the inability of researchers to locate infant and preschool mildly retarded children; the inability of epidemiologists to explain sufficiently the significantly different prevalence rates for mental retardation among very young, school-age, and older people; the inability of social scientists to differentiate between the effects of mental ability and those of social class; and the inability of learning theorists to reconcile the traditional definition to the fact that most children who are diagnosed in school as mildly mentally retarded *were not* so diagnosed as preschoolers and *will not* be so diagnosed as adults. Regarding the last point, there exists a clear discrepancy between what some learning theorists call "school" as contrasted to "out-of-school" intelligence. Relative to the criteria of early onset, permanence, inability to profit from ordinary schooling, and postschool maladjustment, traditional definitions such as Tredgold's simply do not hold up for all people diagnosed as mentally retarded, especially those subclassified as cultural-familial, mildly mentally retarded.

Beginning in 1959, when its terminology manual broke significantly from past definitions, the American Association on Mental Deficiency began to search for a so-called functional definition, one designed to obviate the inconsistencies and dilemmas associated with the traditional metaphor. Its efforts may eventually lead to general acceptance of a reasonable and defensible definition that would not pretend to be more than it is: an "administrative" category. A review of this shift from a traditional to a functional definition is in order because of its great importance.

Prior to 1959, mental retardation was almost universally defined in the United States as a constitutional condition of the central nervous system, existing from birth or early age, incurable and irremediable, resulting in the inability of the individual to profit from ordinary schooling. This traditional definition was anchored to a classification system that utilized arbitrarily determined IQ scores to fix levels of capacity. For example, people with IQs from 50 to 75 were once categorized as "moron" (and later as "educable"), those with IQs from 25 to 50 as "imbecile" (and later as "trainable"), and those with less than 25 IQ were categorized as "idiot" (and later as "custodial"). In 1959, the AAMD *Manual on Terminology and Classification in Mental Retardation* (Heber, 1959) defined mental retardation as subaverage general intellectual functioning, originating during the developmental period (0-16 years) and associated with impairment in adaptive behavior. The definition did not assume that constitutionality is a requirement for mental retardation and it referred to current functioning rather than, as was traditional, to time of onset. Furthermore, the definition did not rule out the possibility of prevention, cure, or amelioration of mental retardation and its associated consequences.

During subsequent years, the definition underwent several changes. The change usually referred to as most important was the requirement that mental retardation refer to *significantly* subaverage general intellectual functioning (Grossman, 1977). As a result, the psychometric ceiling shifted from one standard deviation below average, approximately 85 IQ, to two standard deviations below average, approximately 70 IQ. Further, the theoretical incidence of psychometric retardation in the general population shifted from approximately 16% to less than 3% of the general population.

The implications of such definitional changes have not escaped those concerned with counting mentally retarded persons. The incidence and prevalence of mental retardation are directly related to its definition. It is one thing to determine deficits in adaptive behavior from individuals representing 16% of the general population, and another thing to determine deficits in adaptive behavior from a pool of just under 3%. But, as will be discussed in the next sections, most incidence studies uncover not much more than 1% of the general population who have been dealt with in some fashion because of presumed mental retardation. Hence, we return to the functional-administrative definition. Simply stated, someone is mentally retarded when he or she is "officially" identified as such. In that sense, mental retardation is as useful (or useless) a label with which to understand a human being as any number of other labels, such as rich man, poor man, Democrat, Republican, saint, sinner. Mental retardation is merely another administrative label; it is probably one that leads to more serious consequences than most other labels, but, in principle, it is no less functional a designation than the others.

Incidence and Prevalence

Prevalence can be defined as the number of persons in any given population who exhibit a characteristic at a specific point in time. Often, prevalence is reported as X per 1,000 or X per 100,000. Incidence refers to the number of new cases of a condition that have been identified within a specific period of time. For example, the prevalence rate of measles would refer to the number of persons sick or diagnosed with the condition at the end of a particular day or week. The incidence rate would be the total number of *new* cases of measles reported during a certain period. Discussion of incidence and prevalence with respect to mental retardation, however, requires clarification.

Because mental retardation is very often a chronic condition (especially in its moderate and severe forms), and because virtually all new cases persist for many years if not for lifetimes, the incidence of mental retardation referes to the *total* number of peole who are retarded in all age categories at any given time. Conversely, the prevalence of mental retardation refers to the number of retarded persons in a given category (e.g., preschool, school age, adult) at a given time. Prevalence estimates can be higher for one subset of the total group of mentally retarded people than for another; for example, it is probable that the preschool prevalence of mental retardation is significantly lower than school-age prevalence. It is also probable that, in this country, the prevalence of severe mental retardation among young children is higher than the prevalence of mild retardation among young children. To put this in still another way, the incidence of mental retardation (possibly 1% of the total population) is smaller than the prevalence of mental retardation among school-age children (possibly 2%) but greater than the prevalence of mental retardation among preschool children (possibly .5%). In absolute numbers rather than percentages, the "true" incidence of mental retardation is always the sum of the "true" prevalences.

It is worth examining these terms in detail — too often, presentations of this topic are not sufficiently clear about the way incidence estimates are used in this field. For example, for many years the common belief was that approximately 3% of the population is mentally retarded; thus, in the United States, a country of approximately 200 million people, we should find six million retarded people. In fact, the prestigious President's Committee on Mental Retardation once proclaimed on spot radio and television ads as well as in its official publications that there were six million retarded people in the United States. Of course, this gives the public the impression that someone had actually identified and counted those ten million mentally retarded people. Yet, you would be hard-pressed to locate any major study that concluded that the 3% rate is accurate (Blatt, 1973). This discrepancy between psychometric mental retardation, which is based purely on IQ scores, and a definition of mental retardation that demands an assessment of adaptive behavior, has led us to much confusion as to the characteristics of mentally retarded people, what can be prognosticated about such people, and how many there are.

The monograph by Birch et al. (Birch, Richardson, Baird, & Illsley, 1970) on the epidemiology of mental retardation represents one of the better attempts to bring order and thoughtfulness to the incidence-prevalence problem in dealing with what is, on the one hand, a metaphor, and what is, on the other hand, a concrete, administratively contrived designation — "mental retardation." The best part of the book "is that the authors make epidemiology no more unmanageable than any other uncommon twelve-letter word. The weakest part may be attributed to the fact that epidemiology is, after all, more complex than we pretend" (Blatt, 1972, p. 439). Epidemiological research seeks to define, describe, and clarify conditions that are associated with specified disorders. It analyzes the incidence, characteristics, and distribution of such disorders, thereby seeking to correlate the demographic variables associated with the condition with the etiological factors. Birch and his colleagues examined the prevalence of mental retardation, its subtypes, associations, and antecedents among a group of children in Aberdeen, Scotland. Their study ranges through such diverse problems as the correlates of social class and intelligence, general etiological factors, and the incidence and character of this heterogeneous group labeled in Scotland as "mentally subnormal," a group analagous to that which we in the United States call "mentally retarded." The research team confirmed a consistent finding of earlier studies that the prevalence and characteristics of mental retardation depend significantly on such influences as definition and criteria, program supports, broad cultural values, social class, and other factors that support the idea that retardation has as much to do with political and administrative matters as it does with biological, psychological, and other scientific matters.

Birch and his associates found that the incidence of known mental retardation among a group of children between 8 and 10 was 12.6 per thousand, far less than the presumed incidence suggested by the normal probability curve. Further, they found another population of children, not *administratively* defined as retarded, but nevertheless *psychometrically* retarded. That is, there are children who have low measured intelligence, but who, nevertheless, had neither previously been designated as mentally retarded nor placed in special schools or special residential settings. *Such children should not be labeled mentally retarded.* This difference between psychometric and administrative mental retardation is enormously important to understand if program planning and service delivery are to proceed beyond the realm of superficial suggestions, and worse, unnecessary placements.

Aside from the study conducted by the Birch team, the literature is extremely scant in this area. Of course, there are many epidemiological studies of discrete conditions such as Down syndrome or PKU; but there have been very few examinations of incidence and prevalence of *all* categories and etiologies of mental retardation. Added to my own modest work in southeastern Connecticut (Blatt, 1973), the few available studies in this area include one of handicapped children on the Isle of Wight (Rutter, Tizard, & Whitmore, 1970), the Baltimore, Maryland study (Lemkau, Teitze, & Cooper, 1941, 1942a, 1942b, 1943), and the Onondaga County study (New York State Department of Mental Hygiene, 1955). In a sense, the relative neglect of epidemiological study reveals a great deal about what *is* studied. For example, insofar as the law is concerned, statutes that cover the activities of the affluent are so much more precise than those that are concerned with disadvantaged or handicapped persons. In my opinion this is hardly an accidental circumstance. Similarly, you can understand the paucity of epidemiological study of mental retardation by looking at the frequency and quality of epidemiological research in other areas.

After all is counted and analyzed, the prepotent lesson here is that there is a difference — a political, pragmatic, legal, and scientific difference — yet a hardly known and less understood difference between psychometric and administrative mental retardation. Newer definitions stipulate this difference, discuss it, and quote it; but it is hardly believed, especially when decisions are made that change lives and that sometimes prevent lives—especially when decisions are made that have the potential for doing good or mischief.

Intelligence and Social Justice

There is an impressive array of studies correlating IQ to delinquency, criminality, incarceration, and other forms of maladaptive behavior, and there are many studies describing society's treatment of adjudicated retarded people. Essentially, the literature informs us that the IQs of delinquents are, on the average, about one standard deviation (approximately 15 points) lower than the IQs of children in general. There is also sufficient evidence to conclude that, as a group, adults in penal institutions have lower IQs than those living free. And so it goes; people who run afoul of the law and end up imprisoned are not as bright, not as well educated, not as accomplished as those who do not run afoul of the law. Nevertheless, there is little if any evidence indicating that mentally retarded people are especially amoral, immoral, criminal, delinquent, degenerate, or dangerous. This is a case in which counting one way (delinquents tend to have lower IQs) may lead to facts—ambiguous facts, to be sure—but nonetheless facts. But counting the other way (people with lower IQs tend to be delinquent) leads to lies, and the worst kind—those that destroy reputations, and, thus, lives.

Heat and Light

In that spectacular chasm between passion and evidence, every now and then we are able to squeeze thoughtfullness (if not truth) and things that are helpful (rather than harmful) out of the debris strewn along the mental retardation landscape.

Who gets arrested? Viewing the six o'clock news commentator describing the riot-torn penitentiary, it doesn't require much perception to notice that most prisoners these days are black. And a little investigation reveals that most of the others are poor, uneducated, "unimportant" people. Imporant people don't go to jail; and as witnessed by what happened to the "Watergate Fellowship," when they do go to jail, they go to special jails that are more or less reserved for the few among us who are caught in "white collar" types of crimes.

For whatever reasons, crimes committed by low income people are adjudicated more often than those committed by high income people, and the crimes of the former are more apt to lead to jail terms than those of the latter. There also seems to be little doubt that IQ is correlated significantly with social class. The inescapable conclusions to all of this are that (a) low income people have filled our jails; and (b) as a group, low income people have lower IQs than high income people. There is, therefore, a higher prevalence of mild mental retardation among the so-called "criminal element"; and, as a group, adjudicated delinquents and criminals have lower IQs than those who have never been so adjudicated. It's also quite clear that few moderately mentally retarded people, and virtually by definition, no severely retarded people, run afoul of the law, are ever adjudicated as delinquents or criminals, or ever spend time in jails. Consequently, while there may be a relationship between intelligence and criminality, the relationship is "J" shaped, that is, it is nonexistent insofar as severely mentally retarded persons are concerned (Blatt, 1960).

Several decades ago, it was common to read about "defective delinquents," that is, people who were delinquent because they were mentally defective. Although it is doubtful that there exists a demonstrated case of "defective delinquency," the idea nevertheless persists that low intelligence more often than not leads an individual to moral degeneracy. The works of Dugdale (1877), Goddard (1912), and more recent investigators described causal realtionships between intellect and morality. Why the insistence on such a relationship? First, there is relatively high prevalence of mild retardation among delinquents and criminals. Second, mental retardation has been considered a global condition by both laymen and experts for so long that it remains a convenient "explanation" of all and any behavior of individuals so identified, even when such an explanation does not hold up when dealing with people are are not retarded. For example, when a brilliant university student rapes or murders someone, it is inconceivable that the crime will be "explained" in terms of either his university status or brilliance. Indeed, when such an act occurs society is dismayed and puzzled that such an individual went so far astray. The "man in the street" is not willing to conclude that the brilliant student murdered someone because he was *too* smart. But he is also not quite ready to concede as overstatements that mentally retarded women are potential prostitutes and mentally retarded men are potential criminals. The "man in the street" misses the inconsistency of his prejudice, even when the ludicrousness of his claim is tested against the equally valid assertion that all university professors are *potential* criminals, and all presidents are *potential* criminals (as, indeed, one or two may have been).

I am somewhat afraid that it may seem as if this book was concocted in a hot and sweaty kitchen. Its purpose, though, is to shed light on the problem, not merely to make you hot under the collar. I make these remarks here because possibly nowhere else in your study of mental retardation will you, the reader, be required to work as hard at understanding the meaning of mental retardation than at this time, as you struggle to nail down a suitable definition—one that you will not only live with but live by.

So, again what is the meaning of mental retardation? I perseverate on that question because, quite literally, the answer is at the fundamental core of every understanding and decision concerning people so designated. Your definition of mental retardation is intimately linked to your philosophy, attitudes, prejudices, and—if you take the definition as seriously as you should—your practices. What is the meaning of mental retardation? Scratch under the surface of the question, and you may find lurking the most serious question: What is the meaning of life? What is the definition of mental retardation? Scratch at the surface of that question and you may get more than you bargained for, if, of course, you—the respondent—are as serious as the question itself.

Mental retardation *does* exist. Those who do not believe in its existence have never visited a state asylum, have never observed the tortured people, have never tried to minister to the lost souls. Mental retardation does exist. It can be defined psychologically, medically, educationally, or administratively. It is defined officially by the scientific and professional organizations such as the AAMD and the American Psychological Association. It is defined unofficially by the "man in the street," the neighbors next door, the school principal and teacher. Once upon a time, mental retardation may have been created to give asylum to the needy, offer companionship to the lonely, and bring peace to the troubled; but that was once upon a time. Once upon a time, mental retardation may have been a benevolent concept, but it is not benevolent today. In a fundamental sense, the arguments and scandals in the field can be traced directly to the fact that definitions vary so widely.

At the core of the controversies and scandals, at the core of much of our treatment practice, lies the fundamental question: What is the nature of human capability? Is it modifiable or invariant? Is stupidity learned and can it be cured? And so we argue about definition in terms of the question, What are the components of intellect? Or, we argue about what should be measured—current or potential behavior. Or, we argue about what is being demonstrated—a person's environment or inheritance. Or, we argue about the relationship of purely intellectual factors to emotional factors in contributing to either functional or potential intelligence. Then we apply those arguments to a discussion of definition—either to historic models such as those proposed by Tredgold and Soddy (1956), Doll (1935), Benda, Kanner (1964), Terman (1925), and others; or to more contemporary efforts at defining the condition, such as that of AAMD (Grossman, 1983). And after such deliberate examination, it would not surprise me if you, the reader, should decide to rely on the most functional approach to the definitional problem — an administrative definition (or contrivance, if you will): Mental retardation occurs when someone is identified as mentally retarded, and either placed in a program or activity, or denied placement, because he or she is so identified. I suspect that this particular approach brings more light to the problem than any of the other approaches, because it at least demystifies the concept of mental retardation.

Changing the Count: A Summary

Early on, Tredgold (Tredgold & Soddy, 1956) defined mental retardation as a state of incomplete mental development inevitably leading to the inability to maintain an independent life. Years later, the definition was modified to focus on *current* behavior, leaving open such questions as reversibility of defect and reversibility of social inadequacy. In a major change of the official definition about 25 years ago (Heber, 1959), practitioners were given a "green light" to plan programs which could enhance educability and social adjustment. Subsequent definitional modifications to this day (Grossman, 1983) have not significantly altered either philosophy or practice in the field.

Once upon a time it was thought that approximately 3% of the general population were mentally retarded. This estimate was based on an extrapolation of the normal distribution curve to the general population — with an IQ cutoff of approximately 75 serving as a ceiling below which were the people we commonly call mentally retarded. When the field appropriated a so-called functional definition during the late fifties and early sixties, the IQ cutoff shifted from 75 to 85, thus enlarging the pool of "psychometrically" retarded individuals from approximately 3% to approximately 16% of the general population. Subsequently that functional definition was again changed, returning the cutoff to 70, and so returning the theoretical incidence of psychometric retardation to 2% or 3%. Thus, changes in the definition of mental retardation have, during the past 25 or 30 years, caused dramatic shifts in the estimates of incidence and prevalence. Mental retardation was once considered to be incurable; that is now considered to be an open question. The incidence of mental retardation was once thought to be about 3% of the general population, then it was thought to be as high as 16%, and now the estimate is back again to 2% or 3% (notwithstanding the fact that few epidemiological surveys have found more than a 1% or 2% incidence).

The phenomenon of "changing the count" is not unique to the field of mental retardation, although this field is more prone to such changes than, say, the field of obstetrics, in which a baby born is a baby born. But the field does have company — for example, the field of learning disabilities. Once upon a time, what we now call learning disabilities and what was once called brain injury was thought to be a relatively rare condition affecting possibly 1% of the school population. Today, there are at least a few people writing in this field who claim that possibly 40% of the children in school are learning disabled (Brutten, Richardson, & Mangel, 1973). Obviously, the experts today in learning disabilities are not referring to the same children to whom the experts 30 or 40 years ago referred. To be sure, the experts today in mental retardation are not referring to the same people to whom the experts of 200 years ago referred — or, for that matter, 25 years ago.

I return again to the contention that, however mental retardation is defined, it remains essentially an administrative category. People are mentally retarded because, at this particular time, society has deemed it necessary to identify them as such and treat them (or not treat them) because they are so identified. Mental retardation is nothing more and nothing less. To the student attempting to compare counts across eras or disciplines, the "facts" are not necessarily illuminating: You must understand what has been counted — and how it has been counted — before you can begin to comprehend the data.

In the least generous light, think about those who count mentally retarded persons as you would think about the antique dealer making a market for carnival glass or baseball cards. Think about the analogy of the professional in the field of mental retardation and the stock dealer whose job is to create a demand for a certain stock. We use labels and wear them as we use neckties — except the former are not always as benign. Even more than ties, labels bespeak of the club, the class, and the culture — the person.

5.

Perspectives on Mental Retardation Through the Eyes of Different Beholders

EVERYTHING IS IN the eyes of the beholder! Ten people asked to react to the sight of a new Rolls Royce or the Grand Canyon, however, will probably offer commentaries more similar than if they were asked to react to the sight of an old man or a child with obvious physical and mental disability. Mental retardation can be understood in terms of measured intelligence, developmental skills, academic performance, vocational success, physical appearance, demeanor, speech—our understanding of the concept is filtered by our own proclivities, prejudices, and sympathies; experiences we had and those we should have had. Mental retardation can also be understood in terms of the metaphors we use, as well as those the larger society employs.

This chapter explores various perspectives on mental retardation, relying on reports that deal with diverse issues. Should services for mentally retarded persons be in the form of charity? Or do mentally retarded persons have a legal, social, and moral right to treatment? Are retarded people "blessed innocents"? Or do all people have potential to grow and contribute? This chapter will discuss retarded people as "surplus," as workers, as they cause pain, and as they bring joy.

Remaining focused on the implicit beliefs people have concerning mental retardation, together we will examine the views of the larger society, strangers, experts, the family, and the views of mentally retarded people themselves. Of course, roles shift: Strangers become parents, brothers, and sisters. Through firsthand experience, family members become "experts"; and while everyone is a member of the larger society, everyone at the same time occupies a particular niche and harbors some form of special prejudice or agenda. It's fair to say that *everyone* has understanding, if not of the technical term "mental retardation," then of its usage in the vernacular. This chapter gets at the substance of those vernacular views. No one is immune from holding a point of view, from dealing in metaphors. Even the experts—perhaps especially the experts—communicate by metaphor.

On Metaphors

In a sense, *all* metaphors are true and valid. But in another sense, they are true only in the eyes of the metaphor's creator, and valid only to those who share that perspective. The fact that some metaphors enjoy wide acceptance and usage is a normal part of the language of a culture. Robert Frost put it aptly when he suggested that a metaphor is a way of saying one thing in terms of another. Metaphors are those parts of our language that communicate by indirection; but, in spite of indirection— or maybe because of it—metaphors seem to get closer to the heart of things. And because metaphors seem to get to the heart of things, they can be powerful. This power, in turn, can be benevolent—or dangerous. Metaphors seem to have been "made" for the field of mental retardation. Or was it vice versa? Whichever way it is, metaphors *can be* fuzzy symbols that reflect the particular perspective of the people who believe in them more than they reflect the actual heart of things. Thus, the metaphor and the field of mental retardation is a "marriage that could have been made in heaven" (to use a metaphor).

The View of Society

Society is in a muddle, and one of the bigger unnoticed muddles has to do with handicapped persons. For at least two decades, federal, state, and county governments have promulgated and forcefully implemented programs on behalf of handicapped children and their families. For at least two or three decades, during a time when the economy was booming and the corporate tax structure made it appealing, big business in its own fashion supported handicapped persons. For all the years since World War II, the trend has been onward and upward on behalf of handicapped persons. Now things appear to be different. Never altogether clear about who deserves what, society is now at odds on whether certain groups of handicapped persons are indeed "deserving."

For sure, new questions have been raised concerning direct federal support of programs for handicapped persons. This is of critical importance for obvious reasons. It is not so obvious, though, why what happens in the White House and the Congress bears directly on the importance and meaning given to charity and volunteerism in our society.

Cuts in federal money for social services and related programs during the early eighties approximated $100 billion. We have heard terms like "safety net" and "the truly needy" to ease the anxiety of those who worry about the *truly*, truly needy. No matter what politicians may say, anyone who takes the trouble to poke around in shabby neighborhoods (but also in "silk stocking" areas), will find truly, truly needy people — sick people, handicapped people, old people, undereducated people, the unemployed, the hungry, fragile people, people who need help. One politician informs us that we shouldn't expect the government to provide services, that the government *isn't in the business to provide services*. (What, we may ask, *is* the government in the business to provide?) Another politician calls for an increase in voluntary support of programs for the needy, suggesting the creation of a Presidential Task Force on Private Sector Initiatives (Kemper, 1981). With a blue-ribbon group of corporate chief executive officers, leading industrialists, and other worthy citizens, the President believed that the people would come to the rescue, would bail out the federal government and provide programs and resources for those in need.

But that idea may not be what the people wanted, much less what big business and working people wanted. While President Reagan offered persuasive arguments as to why the federal government must dismantle much of its service business, Clark made an equally compelling case that "the business of business isn't in charity" (1982). Clark reported that giant corporations are not well equipped or especially good at dispersing charitable donations. Furthermore, they never have been especially interested in such work. Moreover, their stockholders will simply not stand for raids on their resources, however well-intentioned or excellent the charity may be.

Well, then, maybe the support will come from the public at large, the man and woman in the street. We shouldn't hold our breath. In the aggregate, United Funds, March of Dimes, and Jerry Lewis' telethons bring in big bucks, but they don't come close to the $100 billion (more or less) to be eliminated from federal support for social services. Well, if the business of government isn't service to the needy, and the business of business isn't charity, and we aren't our brothers' keepers, then some needy people will die before their time, and many needy people will suffer.

Beginning especially with the New Deal era, our government became increasingly committed to the philosophy that it has a responsibility to all of our citizens, especially those who are fragile, handicapped, and elderly — and this philosophy certainly influenced whatever common belief system exists concerning mentally retarded persons. We've heard of the "welfare state," "big brother," and the idea of a shared social conscience. Such beliefs have been discussed as if they will be the decline, if not the downfall, of what we think of as the American ethos. Such beliefs have also been perceived as expressions of a society that cares about all of its people, a society determined to guarantee the rights of all of its people. What one person terms "welfare," another person calls "opportunity." What one person calls "charity," another prefers to think of as "philanthropy." What's called "big brother" here is the "Golden Rule" somewhere else. What's viewed by some people with revulsion as an inhuman system of incarceration is viewed by others as living up to the belief that we were, we are, and we must always be our brothers' keepers. The polemical battles in mental retardation are quite heated when it comes to the examination of these ideas. What to the priest may be a "blessed innocent," to the economist is "surplus population," and to the administrator is "big business." Of course, it is possible to caricature problems in such a way as to minimize their seriousness or forestall their proper examination. And nowhere is the argument more heated than when it comes to questions connected with charity and welfare.

Biklen (1983) has argued that progress in mental retardation is betrayed by its intimate connection with the American propensity to give charity, suggesting that charity has always been a problem as well as a solution. According to him, charity is big business, with various donations in this country today approximating an annual total of at least $40 billion. The number of specific charities ranges from a mind-boggling one-half million to six million. And that may only be the tip of an enormous iceberg, especially when we consider the dollar value of millions of hours contributed by volunteers to various charitable organizations. With respect to handicapped persons, Biklen calls the "charity" compulsion a "betrayal." That's one side of the argument.

There's another side to the argument. To Biklen, it may seem indecent for handicapped children to have to depend upon good will (charity) to receive services. On the other hand, we are admonished countless times in the Bible to practice charity, to believe that we are our brothers' keepers. At one time, we were taught that through charity we might receive communion with God in expiation for sins against Him. There is a dilemma here. Biklen has bemoaned the multi-billion-dollar charity industry, powered as it is by the image of dependent handicapped people. On the other hand, strong Biblical tradition exhorts us to practice charity. It is possible that the problem does not lie in the concept of charity itself, but in *how* it is practiced. Perhaps dollars and slogans cannot substitute for attention to one another, for face-to-face involvement. It's one thing to donate money to the local geriatric program, and it's another thing to find a place in your home for an elderly parent. What is being raised here is the suggestion that the concept of charity may not be the culprit, but the way it is dispensed today is where we will encounter the mischief.

Society has many views of people who are mentally retarded. Some would place such people in the category of "blessed innocents," people who can live their entire lifetimes remaining as innocent as the day they were born and thus be assured of a place in heaven. That's a very special category, not reserved for the Pope; even he must justify to God his eternal existence although he is not required to justify to society his temporal existence.

Some regard people who are mentally retarded as surplus, not only as expendable in hard times but as unnecessary to begin with. On the other hand, mentally retarded persons are *never* surplus to professionals in the field. Indeed, for professionals they are absolutely essential, for without them there would be no field of mental retardation; there would be no need to write about them, to dose them, to study them, to serve them. And so, to one segment of the population, retarded people may be entirely unnecessary, yet to another segment they may be absolutely essential. Unfortunately, those who would treat mentally retarded people as surplus will probably never know enough about them—thus, they will never correct their erroneous and destructive prejudices. And the professionals who truly "need" mentally retarded persons often need them for the wrong reasons—perhaps in a thoughtless and selfish way. Moreover, the professionals often don't even realize how much they need the people who justify their existence.

Then there are those who have a sense of what mentally retarded people yearn for—habilitation, *freedom,* a chance to work and contribute to society, opportunities to live in the real world and take the risks that each of us must assume as the price for our freedom and opportunities. Unfortunately, it may be that this last group of individuals is in the minority. It may be that, if there truly are so few who would set retarded people free, it is because the Retardation Industry is powered by a coalition of charity, welfare, Big Brother, incarceration, and extermination interests.

Sometimes, we do the right things for the wrong reasons, sometimes the wrong things for the right reasons. Rarely in this field have we accomplished the right ends for the right reasons. For those of you who seek to accomplish something good on behalf of mentally retarded people, there is much work to be done. Some people can, by devoting their lives to this effort, benefit mentally retarded persons. A good way to begin is to take the obvious seriously. A good way to succeed is to do something *yourself* before you enjoin *others* to commit themselves.

The View of Strangers

In the Workplace

In 1966, Bernard Posner published an analysis of his week-long experience as a laundry worker masquerading as if he were mentally retarded. From his account, he was accepted as a retarded person, and reactions to him ranged from sympathy to scorn, from patience to impatience, from more attention than he wanted to studied neglect, and from easy association to clumsiness. As a member of the President's Committee on Employment of the Handicapped, he wanted to find out firsthand how it would be for a retarded person to work somewhere; how he would be treated by his bosses and fellow workers, and what problems a retarded worker would face. How a perfectly normal looking man could get away with such deception merely on the weight of a fabricated story told to the workers is an interesting question that deserves consideration. According to Posner, the only things he did to reinforce the lie were to wear a red knit stocking cap, speak as little as possible, and chew gum. Posner reported that he acted normally, because that's the only way he knew how to act. He also "indulged in the pleasant luxury of not comprehending too fast, of asking that things be explained over and over again until I was sure I had grasped them" (p. 64).

What happened? Some people spoke very loudly to him, as though shouting would enhance comprehension. Some people wouldn't look Posner in the eye. A black worker in his late teens didn't know quite how to deal with this white man in his late forties—first addressing him as "Sir," but knowing that this wasn't "correct," after a short time not addressing him at all. At lunch time the first day, Posner waited for someone to tell him it was time to eat, but nobody did. Nobody asked him to join the group for lunch. He ate alone. But that was the first day! Little by little, people drew him into their conversations, even those who originally would not look Posner in the eye. By the second day, people started encouraging him, saying that he would catch on to things, and that this was the way to do it. By the second day, somebody asked "the retarded new worker," to share her fried chicken. And one of the workers whispered that he, Bernard, had learned something new that day, and he should feel proud of himself. So it went. Day by day, people forgot the *mental retardation* condition and began to learn about the *man*. Of course, even by the end of that week, there were people who self-consciously turned away when Posner passed by. But with equal deliberation, others greeted him as if to say, "We know who you are, and it's OK." And after all, a week merely "seems" like a lifetime.

What did Bernard Posner conclude from his week as a retarded man? Those who worked with him seemed to accept him as a person much more quickly and genuinely than those at the top—the supervisors. Posner also had some things to say about the general dreariness of doing repetitive work, and even expressed sympathy for the burdens on the bosses to produce and meet schedules. What was most revealing to him was how quickly and naturally most people accepted a coworker who was willing to work. Posner constantly told people that he didn't learn so well and didn't catch on very fast, but his coworkers seemed to accept those admissions without letting them stand as barriers between them. Posner wasn't sure that he would have been accepted had his coworkers been reminded constantly that he was "mentally retarded." It seems that if a stereotype is readily at hand, such as the designation "mentally retarded," the stereotype itself fills in all the cracks in the relationship, thus providing answers to the common questions people have about each other. But when there isn't an official stereotype, when everyone is treated "normally," people can forget labels. Most of us are able to get on with the difficult enough job of treating each other on the basis of our actions and not our labels. Posner's experiences at least suggest that if people are not constantly reminded that someone is different, in typical situations people will judge each other on what they can see for themselves. In this case, Bernard Posner came off as someone who belonged in ordinary society, earning a living alongside other ordinary people. The only genuine problem that remained from the experience was dealing with his own guilt, created from his deception of those good human beings.

In the Community

What do ordinary people think about people who are mentally retarded? In order to study mental retardation as a social phenomenon in a community, a group of social scientists undertook a survey of more than 2,000 householders in a southern California city in 1963 (Lewis, 1973). Summary data from this large sample (reputed to be representative of the general population) indicated that the general community was not ready to accept the idea of retarded people living in their midst. What may be surprising is that the rejection was general, strong, and not confined to so-called severely retarded people but rather, it extended to *all* mentally retarded people, even so-called "educable children." Of course, some respondents indicated acceptance of retarded people within the community. Although a great deal of progress has been made since 1963 in "educating" the general public concerning the needs, capabilities, and rights of individuals who are mentally retarded, Lewis' work raises concern in terms of policy developments in recent years, when there has been a strong shift in the direction of deinstitutionalization and the promotion of normalized community settings for retarded people. In view of this shift, more community education seems warranted *now*, especially if the field continues to deinstitutionalize mentally retarded people. Whether Lewis' data would be as negative today as it was in 1963 would be important to know, but that's not the point. The fact is that, even today, there are those in the community who would segregate mentally retarded people, and the field must be clear in stressing the importance of guaranteeing the integration of such people.

Gottlieb (1975) reviewed the literature on the attitudes of the general public, peers, and professionals toward mentally retarded persons. Of the many studies he examined, those involving the attitudes of teachers predominated; but that's not at all surprising in view of the well-known fact that mental retardation (especially mild mental retardation) is usually first recognized when children are confronted with the school experience. His second general finding, also not surprising, was that while the relationship between proximity to people who are mentally retarded and attitudes about them is not terribly clear, whatever evidence does exist indicates that proximity is associated with *increased* rejection. Of course, as the author made clear, all of these data must be interpreted from the standpoint of the severity of retardation of the subjects examined, their chronological ages, and, quite probably, their social status and sex. There is such a range within the broad category, "mental retardation," that any generalizations can become absurdities, misleading at best, and probably detrimental to gaining an understanding of problems and issues. As Gottlieb pointed out, "It may also be possible that the public may not be aware that the condition of mild mental retardation even exists" (p. 103). If that is true, then it could also be reasonably concluded that mildly mentally retarded people are not only integrated into society but also that they do not actually exist as an identifiable clinical entity, except in the minds of professionals whose very jobs depend on their identification and "treatment." And if that is true, such categorization can be considered to be forced and unproductive. All conjecture, but also very serious stuff to be examined.

Of course, how people view mental retardation (or any disability) is strongly influenced by a host of complex psychological and social factors. One of the more helpful discussions of the meaning of "mental retardation" — indeed, the meaning of "handicap" — was provided by Lee Meyerson many years ago (Cruickshank, 1971). Meyerson characterized disability as any impairment in a particular social and/or psychological context. According to Meyerson, while variations in physique exist — that is the objective observation — only certain of those variations are disabilities; and, furthermore, only certain disabilities should be seen as "handicaps." Disabilities exist when variations lead to limitations of physical ability, or limitations imposed by society, or limitations individuals ascribe to themselves. For someone to have a handicap: (a) The individual must have some form of disability (or limitation), (b) society must devalue the person for this limitation, and (c) the individual must accept society's judgment.

By this logic, people who are thin to the point of physical limitation—but who live in a culture that values thinness, would not necessarily be categorized as "handicapped." By the same token, people who are heavy to the point of being prone to heart disease and physical limitations—but who live in a culture that values girth, are also not handicapped. In some cultures, being black is a handicap, while in other cultures it is a strength, a protection. In some cultures, being female is a handicap, while in others it is an asset. A facial mole on Elizabeth Taylor is a mark of beauty; but when it appears on the face of a worried teenager, it can cause the most serious depression. Helen Keller did not consider herself to be handicapped, but there are people with mild hearing problems, or moderate visual problems, who are handicapped. The important point to remember is that "handicap" requires the individual to accept society's devaluation of their "difference." As my colleague Steven Taylor (personal communication) related, it has been said that "if Itard had become lost in a deep forest and stumbled upon Victor there, who would be dependent upon whom. . .who would be the 'idiot' and who the 'teacher'?"

In the Schools

Ashmore (1975) has argued that one of the places to begin to make people more aware of "differences" among us is in the schools and with children. What is needed, he said, is for the schools to go beyond merely socializing children to be sympathetic to physically and intellectually handicapped peers and to deliberately create environments where children learn to be comfortable with those who are "different." He provocatively suggested that "attitude change procedures involving forced compliance and self-confrontation seem to offer more promise than mass media campaigns" (p. 173). In essence, he argued for the creation of a school culture that would require children (and presumably teachers) to confront "difference," learn about "different" people, and eventually gain appreciation of their place in the community.

The majority of ordinary citizens with no ties to social services may be viewed as the most important and least considered group to influence in terms of enhancing positive views of mentally retarded persons. All too often, the prepotent question has been how to get the people already committed or already involved to be *more* committed and *more* involved. All too often, the emphasis on community education has been on parents and other consumers, public leaders, and the very professionals and other staff who are paid to provide services to retarded persons. In a way, this is like treating the cancer specialist for the disease, or treating the cancer patient to think more positively about people with the disease. Of course, sometimes the cancer patient does need such treatment, but it's also true that those who are least involved with an illness are most ignorant about it; those more closely connected generally find a way to learn what they need to know.

In sum, the views of strangers are central to changing society's views toward mentally retarded persons. Prestigious professionals in human services make little significant ideological impact on the world around them. By their nature, professionals think differently about these concerns than the average man or woman on the street. Not only are their views incompatible with the mainstream, but the combination of their economic self-interest, their very training, and their intent to remain psychologically distant from both their clients and the larger society, limit their potential as change agents. Stated another way, while professionals may be able to create and foster an ideology, they are most often unable to make it actually happen. For that reason, the National Recovery Act needed a Roosevelt, Emancipation needed a Lincoln, and the 13 Colonies needed a Jefferson—leaders who could engage and rouse the citizens. Such movements would have failed had they been left to the professors and specialists.

The View of Experts

For the professional, mental retardation is a mixed "curse." To be sure, anyone of good will wants to see the people happier, and does not wish for anyone to be mentally retarded. Experts do not inflict mental retardation on the people they serve, nor do they want such burdens for their clients. It must also be said, however, that the expert—the professional—is one of the few people who has something to "gain" from all the suffering. Even as experts attempt to deal with the problem as skillfully and sympathetically as they can, even as scientists attempt to eradicate the problem, without the problem the experts have nowhere to go, nothing to do, no opportunity to ply their profession. Willingly or not, with the best of intentions or not, altruistically or not, the expert in mental retardation has a conflict of interest that few people have to face. It is altogether to the benefit of the afflicted person and his or her parents to eradicate mental retardation. It is altogether to the benefit of the taxpayer to eradicate mental retardation. It is not altogether to the benefit of the expert to purge the condition from society.

The irony is that while the expert has been trained and has every intention to deal with mental retardation objectively, from an informed position and with professional skill, the expert will continue to reap professional rewards only as long as the condition exists. Conversely, a parent or uninvolved citizen is neither trained in the field nor expected to be objective, but they would have everything to gain and nothing to lose if the condition did not exist. We can view the expert in mental retardation in the same way we view the general who hates war, but who nevertheless could not have become a general without war. But even here, the comparison is invidious insofar as the retardation expert is concerned; the soldier can make a career in the army even without a war, while the mental retardation expert can have his or her career only in the presence of mental retardation.

Perhaps it is not surprising or inconsistent, then, that some experts in mental retardation gravitate strongly to the notion that mental retardation is a "disease" that always leads to "incompetence." To these experts, those who don't believe such hard realities are "deluded." Perhaps it is not difficult to understand, then, why school systems have been known to organize "head hunters" to search for mentally retarded pupils, especially in this era when funding is intimately connected to prevalence and treatment rates. The ranks of professionals that constitute the field of mental retardation form a monolith, a single block of ideological "stone" from which society is informed what the condition is (the official definition), what the client needs (special education, special institutions, special services), who should work with such people (specially prepared experts), and who shall determine policy on behalf of these people (the American Association on Mental Deficiency, the Council for Exceptional Children, and other such organizations). The field is defined by the monolith, its activities are stipulated by the monolith, its policies are translated into county, state, and federal laws, and its work is evaluated by that same monolith.

So, too, the view of the expert in mental retardation is molded by the monolith. Yet, this does not mean that the expert has nothing to offer. You, the student should carefully consider that the view of experts is to some degree thoughtful, and much of it is based on long experience; almost all of it is grounded in the very best of intentions. Notwithstanding, you should not necessarily accept without question or criticism the view of the experts, which to a great extent is passed on by a monolith that is not without the instinct of self-preservation.

The View of the Family

To repeat an earlier claim, metaphors are always true and valid. And while metaphors about mental retardation vary widely among people, certain identifiable groups hold common metaphors. Suffice it to say, families think differently about their retarded children, brothers, and sisters, than do outsiders. And furthermore, when a member of the family is retarded, the people in the family generally think differently not only about their loved ones but also about the problem in general. Relatively little work has been published on the family view, although there is some literature available. Here, the work of several researchers is presented. These researchers represent varied perspectives on the issue of how a retarded person may impact on the family.

Typically, the unfolding of a literature review proceeds chronologically. I've taken liberties here in order to juxtapose studies that are relevant (if chronologically discontinuous) to each other because of either the nature of the substance or the relationship of the settings.

Carver and Carver

One of the first important studies of families was the Carver and Carver research, published in 1972 though completed more than a decade earlier. Their research was designed to examine families that had a severely retarded child. It should be noted that their work was done at a time when options other than institutional placement were limited for most such families. There were virtually no preschool programs available for severely retarded children during the 1950s and very limited public school opportunities, alternative day-care programs, sheltered training environments, summer camps, specialist consultation, parent education, governmental or other third party reimbursements for specialized private care or education, or relief other than that offered by the institution. It should also be noted that John and Nellie Carver were themselves parents of a severely retarded child and at the time of this study they had already elected to institutionalize him.

In the early 1950s, John Carver was a junior professor of sociology at what was then New Haven State Teachers College (now Southern Connecticut State College), and he was also a doctoral student in sociology at Yale University. With the help of his wife, he began a dissertation that eventually became an academic landmark on the topic, in spite of the fact that for many years it was essentially unavailable to the scholarly community. It was not published until years later—after John Carver died in a tragic automobile accident, and after Nellie Carver became convinced that the guarantees of anonymity they had once made to the families who participated in their study could be honored. After all, these families were now much older, and many of the participants were either dead or no longer worried about protecting themselves from society's accusations and innuendos concerning their retarded son or daughter. Also, times had changed, in extraordinary and profound ways, and community attitudes had become more positive. And so, a book was finally published by Syracuse University Press in 1972, titled *The Family of the Retarded Child*. Some today may question the capability of *any* state school to offer decent habilitation and education, and consequently they may question the value of the Carvers' contribution. But that would be to miss the essence of this remarkable contribution, the richness of the data, and the singular honesty of those families who opened their hearts to these authors.

Using an elaborate interview schedule that dealt with parents' activities and relationships within the immediate family, with close friends, the extended family, and neighbors and acquaintances in the community, the Carvers located 37 families who had institutionalized their children not more than five years earlier, were maintaining a home together, and were living in the greater New Haven area, where the research was done. Of those families who met study criteria, 30 were actually interviewed. Suffice it to say that these families approximated the ethnic and cultural norms of New Haven at that time, with several of the parents being college graduates, most high school graduates, none retarded themselves, and most of them more or less middle class.

What did the Carvers find? The average set of parents noticed that their child was "different" before he or she was one year old. They realized that the child was "retarded" at about two years old. And while they accepted the doctors' diagnoses, most couples initially decided to keep their child at home. That decision brought great "strain" (a word the Carvers used with frequency and precision) to the family, to relationships between parents themselves, and furthermore, between parents and the extended family and friends. In some cases, close relatives provided moral support, but most parents did not find substantive help and understanding coming from those relatives. Indeed, there was a marked decrease in contacts with extended family after the problem was nailed down as serious mental retardation, and more than likely "permanent." A few parents actually suffered overt hostility from unsympathetic in-laws. A number of them experienced serious problems with neighbors who were unable to understand what was going on, and, for whatever reasons, chose to "blame" the affected parents, sometimes because their children were creating annoyances in the neighborhood. These families also suffered financial hardships during the period when their children were at home, often because of the heavy costs of necessry medical treatment, other times because they placed their children in one private facility or another with the hope that they would "come out of it." Indirect costs also appeared to be very heavy. Mothers who wanted to work could not because they had to stay at home to take care of their children. Fathers who might have been able to accept promotions that meant transfers were unable to progress at work because they were anchored to the community where there were at least a few people who "understood," who made their lives a bit less arduous. Still other fathers immersed themselves in their work, possibly to forget their troubles at home. Siblings, too, were burdened with responsibilities and tensions beyond what was ordinarily expected of children. They were required to assume responsibilities and demonstrate a sensitivity and compassion that few adults are asked to assume.

There were *so many* upsets, *so many* catastrophies in the lives of each of these families. For example, one upper class father described one evening meal (typically set for a time after his child was usually in bed) during which the child did not go to sleep, but rather found a way to cascade burning logs from an upstairs fireplace down a flight of stairs. Another father ruefully admitted that his house was stripped to the essentials, with handles removed from refrigerator and stove so that his daughter would not hurt herself or the house while the family was attending to other matters. Families spoke of their children with love, but they also spoke with despair. Their children broke so many things—hearts, fragile dreams, relationships.

The Carvers found that the strains were removed from families and the children themselves after institutionalization. In fact, many parents found that in spite of (or because of) institutionalization, they had *better* relationships with their retarded children. During weekly visits to the institution, during vacations, or at other times of limited contact, interactions were richer, healthier, and more satisfying to everyone. Of course, things are different today, but we should not forget the immense difficulties that face such families, especially when there is no relief in sight. Those who are crafting the newer policies aimed at deinstitutionalization should recall the Carvers—their experience and their work with families. It isn't enough to convince families that their retarded children should remain at home— without also convincing society that *it* must exert deliberate efforts to provide the help such families need. Human beings should never feel utterly alone. People with these problems must not feel they are alone, if for no other reason than the plain fact that every family at some time, in some way, experiences serious problems. Some scholars have predicted that we will someday conquer death itself (Silverstein, 1982). But we will never conquer the need for sympathy and support in times of trouble and unhappiness.

Did the Carvers or the families they interviewed experience *anything* positive before deinstitutionalization? Did any good come from those family experiences? Based on their extensive interviews, the Carvers concluded that when families have integrity—when there is love and commitment to one another—an event such as the birth of a severely retarded child often brings a family closer together, strengthens bonds, develops both individual as well as family character. On the other hand, when the family has already been troubled by matters not connected with the birth of a retarded child— even when those families might have endured for years without formal and devastating breakup—the instrusion of a problem so global often seems to be the straw that breaks the family's back. Such families then become even more troubled and unwilling to live and work together as a unit.

This discussion opened with brief mention of what things were like "then" — services in the community were unavailable, residential settings other than the state institution were unavailable. It is also true that the Carvers themselves had made the decision to institutionalize their son before they embarked on their study, which may have biased them. If their study had been conducted by researchers who were less personally involved, would the study have yielded different results? Would researchers who were less involved have concluded that the institution has a valid place in a decent and humane society? This question gets at the very core of the institution-community argument. This question also gets at the core of the problem of the capability of the social scientist to engage in value-free research. Caveats aside, this work by John and Nellie Carver remains as a profound illumination of what it means to have a severely retarded child in one's home.

Frances Grossman

For one of the few times in history, the Carvers raised questions concerning the effects of a mentally retarded child on nonhandicapped siblings. Frances Grossman later examined these effects in depth. As a junior faculty member at Yale, Grossman (1972) came into association with a sibling of a retarded child. Arising from that relationship with Cindy, she and another colleague developed a discussion group for young adolescent siblings of retarded children. From those modest beginnings, a five-year examination of college students with retarded siblings was undertaken. As Seymour Sarason said in the foreword to Grossman's book, her work should not be considered relevant only to the field of mental retardation. Rather, it has importance for those who are interested in how families are organized, how they maintain their stability in the face of catastrophe, and how they endure under unusual psychological (and often material) hardships.

What did Grossman and her colleagues find? A surprising number of siblings seemed to have benefited from the experiences of growing up with a handicapped brother or sister, a conclusion similar to the Carvers' observation that strong families grow stronger when faced with problems of this kind. These young men and women appeared to be more tolerant, more compassionate, more aware of the nature of prejudice than other young people. Of course, the study also found that some siblings seemed genuinely damaged and were resentful of the family situation in which they found themselves, guilty about their anger at parents or their retarded siblings, and fearful that they too might be flawed or "tainted." At times, they felt deprived of the attention and support that they might have otherwise rightfully expected from parents, of "luxuries" their parents were unable to provide because of overwhelming concerns they had for the retarded child. And while Grossman and her colleagues found about as many college students who had benefited as were harmed, they speculated that, because this particular sample was biased toward families who had successfully coped with the problems of retardation, a more representative sample might have revealed a greater number of siblings who had not particularly profited by having retarded brothers or sisters or who had even been damaged in some psychological or social way.

Overall, this provocative work suggests that mental retardation represents a major source of aggravation, disharmony, and trauma for any family faced with the problem. And while some families cope incredibly well, *all* such families have problems. And while some siblings are strengthened by the experience, *all* siblings have some problems and seem to need help in wrestling with them. *For sure,* mental retardation in a family creates psychological as well as material problems, more on the order of the death of a loved one than when someone has a curable illness, however severe, or loses a job, however disappointing that loss. The presence of a mentally retarded child in a family changes the lives of each of its members, and, collectively, changes the character of the family itself—for better or for worse, or both.

Bernard Farber

Bernard Farber (1959, 1960) examined siblings of children who were severely retarded. Possibly because his studies were conducted at a time when far fewer community programs were available, one of his significant observations concerned the strong relationship between the severity of a child's retardation and its effects on nonhandicapped siblings—noting that burdens increase to the degree that retarded brothers or sisters are less able to assume responsibilities for their own lives and relationships. This was in contrast to Grossman's report that the severity of a child's handicap alone did not have a significant effect on siblings. As Grossman (1972) remarked "it is not the handicap itself, but the way in which it is interpreted and responded to, that determines the impact on the involved individuals" (p. 181). Of course, it is quite possible that sufficient time had elapsed between Farber's and Grossman's (1972) work, or that there was something about the subject sampling, that would account for this difference. Otherwise, much of Grossman's work confirmed Farber's reports of a decade earlier.

G. Saenger

One of the earliest sociological examinations of retarded persons in the context of their families was Saenger's (1957) now-classic research. His basic purpose was to evaluate the adjustment of people who had once been enrolled in the New York City classes for pupils who would now be termed trainable mentally retarded. Of a total group of 2,640 former pupils, parents of 520 were chosen to be interviewed. The study focused on such matters as parental attitudes and opinions, institutionalization, family adjustment, and work. Consistent with the Carvers' research, Saenger reported that when there was tension and rejection in the family, retarded individuals experienced much greater adjustment problems than when there was cohesion and integrity. Saenger's data also seemed to reflect the theme that mental retardation, in and of itself, is not the only—maybe not even the major—variable connected with maladjustment of retarded people in the community. It is noteworthy, too, that at a time when institutionalization was about the only option parents had for specialized services for their adult moderately or severely retarded children—two-thirds of the Saenger sample *were living in the community* and, furthermore, many were (unexpectedly) earning some sort of a living. This, of course, was an era when there were few sheltered workshops, job training programs, or other opportunities created for people who could not easily place themselves in the competitive job market.

The results of Schonell and Watts' (1956) survey of the effects of a retarded child on the family seem consistent with the Saenger findings. And Gordon and Ullman (1956), in examining the reactions of parents to their children's retardation, found that there are many who were able to cope effectively with the most excessive stresses, and, of course, there were those who appeared totally unable to deal with such a problem, again raising the question of whether mental retardation is the predisposing factor or only the straw that broke the family's back.

One other book deserves special comment—because it represents a genre noticeably absent in the professional literature until the past few years, and because it provides perspectives that are not generally possible from "uninvolved objective professionals." It is written by a father about his son.

Josh Greenfield

Josh Greenfield (1972) is the father of a severely disabled child. His book, *A Child Called Noah: A Family Journal,* is essentially a portion of that professional writer's journal, covering the first five years of Noah's life. On July 1, 1966, Greenfield wrote in his journal:

> I'm a father. I'm drunk. I have another son. His name is Noah Jiro. He was born this evening a few minutes after seven and weighed 7 pounds, 10 ounces. And whereas Karl seemed to look like me at birth, Noah is luckier. He looks like his Japanese mother, Foumi. (p. 16)

The beautiful second son could not turn over by himself at one year, couldn't walk at two years, and at the age of four was not toilet trained and he did not feed himself. Although at age two he spoke in complete sentences and had a vocabulary of over 150 words, at age four he hardly spoke at all. The parents were puzzled and discouraged, and more and more "the rhythm of our lives, the good fortune of our marriage, seems to have dissipated. It is hard for Foumi to believe in me and for me to believe in Foumi any more" (p. 64). At nine months, Noah's doctor expressed concern, but it was "strictly a gut reaction," because Noah was otherwise healthy. Before too long, the child was taken to a pediatrician who specialized in neurology. Since Noah now was talking a bit, there was not too much cause for anxiety. "He's hypertonic and a slow developer, time will correct the delayed development" was the pronouncement. This brought relief to the family, but a week later there was another consultation with a pediatric neurologist who, not nearly as reassuring, concluded that Noah's slow development might be symptomatic of retardation. Another pediatric neurologist saw Noah at age three, and delivered his verdict: "classical retardation." But that was later changed upon learning that Noah was talking at the age of one but had stopped talking about two and a half. At age three, Noah was said to have "autistic" tendencies. A little later, the label was "degenerative brain disease." Other diagnoses made at various times concluded that Noah was either emotionally disturbed, trainable mentally retarded, brain damaged, organically retarded, educable mentally retarded, or schizophrenic. Greenfield's book, however, isn't merely a morbid catalog of etiological profundities. The nomenclature and terminology discussed in the book speak more about professional prejudices than diagnosis and evaluation. And with each such diagnosis, there was hope or despair, recriminations or affirmation of love—and always visits to new centers, new panaceas, new treatments and therapies. The family considered the Doman and Delacato programs at the Institutes for the Achievement of Human Potential in Philadelphia, Bruno Bettleheim's Orthogenic School, chiropractors, special schools for retarded persons, megavitamin therapy, and the operant conditioning program pioneered at the University of California-Los Angeles by Dr. Ivar Lovaas. The megavitamin therapy, Lovaas and his associates, and Dr. Bernard Rimland offered the greatest help and support to the family.

Nevertheless, discouragement remained, and disillusionment deepened and continued unremittingly. On November 1, 1970, Greenfield recorded:

> Our lives must come first. Yet institutions mean cold, slow death to me, a surrender of a life to an organism that does not really care. Hospitals just as surely as they can heal and enhance life can wound and openly destroy it. (p. 120)

Despite valuable efforts of professionals to help the family, there was never enough professional support or public understanding. Greenfield wrote in April of 1971:

> Noah had one of his classic days—frequent toilet accidents, constant shrieks and then a beaut of a night. I don't think he ever closed his eyes—or allowed us to. This morning found Foumi going to the closet, packing her suitcase: "I can't go on, my hair is turning white, my eyes can't focus. I'm losing my voice. I'm not painting. I feel I'm simply throwing my life away because of this crazy kid." All I could do was agree. There was no solving the problem, there was only the deferring of it. Meanwhile, I guess I have to share more of the unpleasant labors. (p. 168)

There is no happy conclusion to this journal, or this family. Entries became private again when the book ended, but Noah's life continues as an enigma and as a source of both love and frustration. Greenfield finished the book, yet continues to have his diary *and tomorrow*. But of those fragments made public, what beautiful and provocative prose is in store for those who would seek the experience.

> I've taken a job, ending my precarious free-lance writer existence. I've had to; a family makes a realist out of any man. I can skimp on meals; my two sons can't. I have dreams to sustain me, while they only live ferociously in the present. They must cry boisterously whenever they are denied, while I, of course, can merely shrug wistfully. (p. 21)

Time and good judgment will decide if Noah's life will illuminate our own lives in ways that Victor, The Wild Boy, influenced earlier generations.

The Views of Mentally Retarded People

Mentally retarded people have things on their minds, important things which, unfortunately, rarely find expression. More than a decade ago, Bengt Nirje had already figured out that the most direct and often the most satisfying way to find out what is on people's minds is to ask them.

Malmö Conference

What follows are brief excerpts from Nirje's minutes of a meeting held in Malmö, Sweden, in May 1970, where a group of 50 mentally retarded young adults reviewed their lives and conceptualized their unmet needs:

Leisure time activities

We found that:
We want to be together in small groups during our leisure time
Dance evenings ought not to be for more than fourteen to sixteen persons
Under no circumstances do we want to walk in large groups in town
There should be more possibilities for sports and exercises
There should be more evening courses in, among other things, alcohol and narcotics

Vacation

We found that:
We all think one should decide oneself what to do during vacations.
We think travel abroad is good, but one should travel with other nonretarded young adults of the same age
Travel should be prepared with courses in the language, manners, and habits of the countries we visit
We have all agreed that summer camps for adults should be banished (This refers to segregated camps for both retarded adults and children)

Living conditions

We found that:
We wish to have an apartment of our own and not be coddled by personnel; therefore, we want courses in cooking, budgeting, etc.
We want to have a right to our own apartment but without priority in the waiting list (in Sweden, one may have to sign up for an apartment well in advance)
We want the right to move together with the other sex when we feel ready for it, and we also want the right to marry when we ourselves find the time is right

We who live in institutions and boarding homes have found that:
The homes should be small
We want to choose our own furniture, and have our own furniture in the room
We will absolutely not have specific hours to follow in terms of going out, returning, etc.
We want to have more personal freedom, and not as it is now in certain institutions and boarding homes where you have to ask for permission to shop for fruit, newspapers, tobacco, etc.

We who live at home have found that:
It is largely good, but one ought to move out when the time is right to

a sheltered apartment or hostel; one cannot for his whole life be dependent on his parents

We want, however, to have our own key when we live at home

Education

We think ten years of separate (special) school is good enough, but there should be more courses in languages, math, contemporary events orientation, social orientation, handwriting, social training, etc.

We think that the name "separate school" is degrading

There should be student councils which can take part in decisions about the curriculum, the choice of books, leisure-time activities in school, etc. The same goes for vocational schools.

Vocational schools

We think that one should attend the vocational school for three years, but that the possibility for an extra year should be available (This is according to Swedish law)

We demand more training in a wider range of vocational fields so that we can have larger freedom of choice in determining our vocations

We want to choose our vocations ourselves and have influence over our education

Adult education

We ask for adult education in daytime, either in study circles a few days a week, or during a longer continuous period

To compensate the salary one loses during the study period, we ask for study grants (stipends)

Questions concerning work

We demand more interesting jobs

We do not want to be used on our jobs by doing the worst and the most boring tasks we do at present

We demand that our capacity for work should not be underestimated

We want that when we are working in the open market, our fellow workers should be informed about our handicap

We want employee councils at the place where we work (sheltered workshops)

We think that we should be present when our situation is discussed by doctors, teachers, welfare workers, foremen, etc. Now it feels as if they talk behind our backs

We demand to have more information about our handicap, and the possibilities we have to enter the open market

Last day of discussion

Today we have talked about what to do to improve the bad conditions we have found during the discussions Friday and Saturday:
We demand that continuous information should be given to the counties and communities, schools, sheltered workshops, and other institutions for our handicapped group about the prevailing bad conditions
We demand also that much stronger information be given to people in general through newspapers, radio, and TV

Autobiographies

Paul Scott/May Seagoe. Once upon a time a child kept such a beautiful and provocative diary that nobody believed he had written it. His name was Paul and he was called "Mongoloid," for that's what the condition (now termed Down syndrome) was labeled in those days. The common wisdom was that so-called Mongoloids didn't read, much less keep diaries. A publisher asked me to examine the manuscript, which, while intriguing, presented several problems, not the least being that its conclusions were contrary to the professional wisdom of the time. Indeed, to this day its conclusions defy professional wisdom. The manuscript, then titled *Diary of a Mongoloid,* was published two years later under the title *Yesterday was Tuesday, All Day and All Night: The Story of a Unique Education* (Seagoe, 1964), but not without many discouragements to Seagoe, the author-editor, and not without her tremendous efforts to overcome disbelief in its authenticity. Why? May Seagoe wrote about a Mongoloid child who *learned* to be normal. I read the manuscript and reported several observations to the editor. First I applied a readability formula to the child's work when he was 13 years old. His written ability was at least fourth-grade level, and as he got older this ability increased in a spectacular manner for one with his "condition." In view of Paul's unusual language ability, I thought it imperative to establish the authenticity of the diary.

Why was it that someone like me — someone engaged in the study of educability, someone who hypothesized that capability is educable — would find it difficult to believe that such a work could elicit anything but serious reservations if not outright disbelief? The answer to that question perhaps lies in the deeply embedded hopelessness associated with virtually everything connected with mental retardation. In a letter to me in 1963, Professor Seagoe — still without a publisher for her book — remarked that "as the book is written, it is slanted toward the intelligent layman." But she may have been wrong. The intelligent layman, in particular, has been convinced (by science, professionals, and the media) that the mentally retarded person must remain chronically disabled. The intelligent layman could understand how a gifted teacher like Anne Sullivan could help Helen Keller to grow, to learn, to be influenced, because Helen had capability waiting to unfold. The intelligent layman's idea about deaf, blind, or deaf-blind persons is that an educational treatment can help the child overcome or circumvent the handicap. The same person's conception of "Mongolism" is that it is permanent, a condition immutable and forever destructive. Thus, how could Paul—or any "Mongoloid"—not only read at grade level, not only write at grade level, but think at grade level, and beyond?

Paul was an unusual case. In some ways, his achievement equaled Helen Keller's. In some ways, Seagoe's book deserves the prominence of Itard's *Wild Boy,* and Rousseau's *Emile.* Those books, too, are in the tradition that illuminates the idea that *all* people can learn and that *all* humankind is noble. Paul Scott seemed in some ways to have been the "typical Mongoloid"—short, quick and agile, double-jointed, with broad hands, stumpy fingers, small head, short neck, flat nose, thick lips, large protruding tongue, harsh and explosive voice (Seagoe, 1964, p. 3). Of course, in other ways he wasn't typical at all. He was one of four children. His older brother died in a tragic summer camp drowning before Paul was born. This death left Paul's parents grief stricken, especially his father, who blamed himself for the unnecessary tragedy. With the birth of Paul Clinton Scott III, the parents would now have another son to carry on the family name and tradition, and possibly, to ease the unremitting pain. But God, who may deal cards but never plays the hand, gave these parents a Mongoloid. During his first few years, he was slow at everything—in sitting, in walking, in speaking, in feeding himself, in learning. And when Paul was six, his parents' marriage ended. Paul's two older sisters were placed in the custody of the mother, and Paul remained with his father.

The Scotts were very wealthy, descended from one of America's oldest Southern families. After the family breakup, Paul's father resigned from his father-in-law's business and gave up active involvement in his own business activities. He moved to California, and spent the rest of his life almost single-mindedly devoted to Paul's development and education. The results were so astonishing that they were hard for anyone to believe, and thus publishers were reluctant to publish them; and even after publication of the book, not much attention was paid to it. It was almost as if the story were so powerful it defied acceptance as valid.

Paul's teacher, Helen Bass Keller (not related to Helen Keller of Keller-Sullivan fame), taught remedial reading at the campus demonstration school of UCLA. She devoted her life to the education of children and the training of teachers. The early work she accomplished with Paul may have been her greatest contribution. Literally in desperation—having spent two years taking Paul from Johns Hopkins, to the University of Chicago, the University of California at Berkeley, to other clinics, rejected by each and with nowhere else to turn — Paul's father was led to Mrs. Keller, a woman with widespread reputation for remedial work with purportedly intractable children. Like the others, Mrs. Keller was initially put off by the challenge. At the age of 6, Paul had no intelligible speech and made few efforts to talk at all. Although charming in many ways, he was also willful, spoiled, and difficult to manage. He grabbed at what he wanted, made scenes when he couldn't get his way, and caused disturbances in restaurants and other public places. He was essentially a child without any obvious training, and, more seriously, without seeming potential for other than the most rudimentary instruction. In every way, young Paul was a complete opposite of his handsome, educated, urbane father — an incoherent and uneducable child. Mrs. Keller tried to express to the father as sympathetically as she could that she "did not teach children like Paul."

The father made it plain that Paul could learn, that he was not mentally retarded. Out of sympathy or out of the desire to forestall the disagreeable task of rejecting the child, Mrs. Keller agreed to see Paul again. And she saw him again, and again — many times. And the child learned — to speak, to read, to write, to express himself with thoughts, to think. When Mrs. Keller was unable to continue working with Paul because of her responsibilities at the University, Paul's father arranged for Miss Grace Hill to continue work with the child. Miss Hill, an art student who had recently completed a program in occupational therapy at the University, was initially appointed to supplement Mrs. Keller's work with Paul. More and more, however, Miss Hill took on the major educational effort on Paul's behalf, eventually not only serving as his tutor but also living with the family and accompanying Paul and his father on their several trips to Alaska, the Panama Canal, Cuba, and throughout the United States.

When Miss Hill was forced to resign in order to take care of her aging mother, Miss Alida Chipman became Paul's tutor. From that time, when Paul was 11, until he died at the age of 47 in a private residential school, Miss Chipman remained his constant companion, teacher, and substitute mother.

The Scotts and Miss Chipman traveled the globe, to Peking, the Fiji Islands, Capri, the Sahara Desert, Kashmir, from the Taj Mahal to the Pyramids, from the tomb of Lenin to interview Haile Selassie in Jerusalem. The trio traveled everywhere, saw "everything," discussed "everything," and Paul wrote it "all" down — as he saw it, experienced it, and felt it. Throughout the years, almost from the time he began instruction with Mrs. Keller until his death, Paul kept a diary, a document which should be as valuable to the field of mental retardation as Lord Byron's was to letters.

In 1937, when Paul was 21 years old, father, son, and teacher traveled through Europe, taking in the coronation of King George VI of England, visiting Denmark, Norway, Sweden, Finland, and Russia, spending time in Vienna, and returning home through Holland, Belgium, and France. That trip, just one of many, provided experiences for the young man which were dutifully recorded. The following are a few of Paul's diary notations (uncorrected):

> *June 13.* About 12 miles from Amsterdam is the home of the famous Edam Cheese: we went to the factory in Edam but it is a poor outfit: I put on wooden shoes and dutch trousers for a picture with dutch gals: I was in Dutch: our guide was a lad about 20 who had 7 brothers and 3 sisters: he spoke very fair English picked up from tourists: a remarkable individual and most likeable. . . .
>
> *June 18.* Paris is mobbed prices in hotels high and merchandise is about on the same level with U.S.A.: the great and historic boulevards and squares are still beautiful illuminated at night: . . . .
>
> *June 21.* A strange development of the Soviet five day week was reflected today: no markets open: the French farmers took their five day week also: hence no produce since Friday: the help situation in Paris seems as bad as Russia: this morning we visited the Notre Dame Cathedral and after Tiffin we went to the exposition and took a boat ride through the fair on the Seine River. It was enjoyable.
>
> *June 22.* This morning we visited the large department stores: after Tiffin we went to the zoo and it was splendid: the layouts of grounds and quarters for the animals were extraordinary: we said aloha to the exposition and sightseeing generally on this European trip and began packing to leave Paris for New York City New York U:S:A:
>
> The French are clever deceivers: they make the impression because the franc is cheap: but prices are boosted up: the exposition is a fraud: it is natural yet surprising to see the war wounded in all the European countries: they operated hotel lifts with one arm guide services and so on: Aloha Europe: (Seagoe, 1964, pp. 106-109)

Virtually all Western children are educated about foreign lands and customs vicariously—that is, making do with dioramas in place of real Eskimo villages and old fur coats in place of live arctic seals. They are told about King John and the Magna Carta and that lovely day on the field of Runnymede when the English people were guaranteed their freedom forever. But Paul *went to* the Arctic, and *stood* on that hallowed field in Britain. Paul Scott's life was a living example of John Dewey's educational philosophy.

After Paul's father died, he stayed on with Miss Chipman for a while, grief stricken, lonely. Eventually, he was placed in a residential school and died during his middle years, still testing as mentally retarded. But his diary, this autobiographical record, belies those tests. It may be that the case of Paul represents one of the few documented successful efforts to educate intelligence.

Bogdan and Taylor. The work of Robert Bogdan and his associates has been particularly significant in the development of autobiographies of people with special needs. Bogdan is one of few people who have not underestimated the revealing stories that many mentally retarded people have and would be willing to contribute, but whose voices are essentially silent because there aren't many who are willing to listen.

In his foreword to Bogdan and Taylor's (1982) recent work, *Inside Out: The Social Meaning of Mental Retardation,* Seymour Sarason asked, "Is it not strange that this may be the first book in which the phenomenology of 'mentally retarded' individuals is given to us by those individuals and not by 'investigators'?" (p. vii). What Bogdan and Taylor offer in this work is the unfoldment of two life stories, expressed by two people who have been labeled "mentally retarded" by their families, by their teachers, by everyone in their lives. Ed Murphy was put in a state school at age 15, where he lived for four years. He then lived in a series of family care homes. Pattie Burt lived in many homes and institutions before eventually gaining the opportunity to live in her own apartment. Their stories are told from *their* perspectives in their own words. Each story illuminates the life of that individual without the distorting filter of the biographer. The stories recount daily hurts and triumphs. They illustrate the indomitable will of individuals who have to more than endure, to more than live, but to conquer their environment — in order to succeed.

Ed Murphy's prologue prepares the reader for a sensitivity — indeed, for an intelligence — which is unexpected from someone who has been officially labeled "mentally retarded":

> There is discrimination against the retarded. There are people out of ignorance who have hurt retarded children. It really doesn't help a person's character the way the system treats you. One thing that's hard is that once you're in it, you can't convince them how smart you are. And you're so weak you can't convince them how smart you are. And you're so weak you can't really fight back. Some of the help you get isn't help. Like the way they talk to you, 'I'll help little Eddie . . . you're so nice.' Not that I'm saying that they intentionally treat you that way.
>
> I'm talking like an expert. I had to live it. Shit, I'm just another person out there. I have to pay taxes. I'm not really different. I only had different experiences in my life than you. I can tell you about them. When you are talking about state schools you need experts. Experts are people who have lived it. I'm not taking anything away from scholars who have sat for years in offices and know the problem. But I know the problem too. (Bogdan & Taylor, 1982, pp. 29-30)

Like Edgerton (1967), Farber (1959), and the Carvers (1972), Bogdan and Taylor have learned and shared with us the critically important insight that mentally retarded people, themselves, "know the problem too." And had we listened to retarded people themselves, we too would have learned long ago not only that they know the problem but that they know it in profound ways. Indeed, had we listened to retarded people years ago, we might have learned then about institutional abuses, labeling psychology, "blaming the victim" sociology, and "abusing the different" pathology. What Bogdan and Taylor—and others who listen to the voices of handicapped people—teach us are the most important lessons to be learned about mental retardation.

Marian Rose White. Most people have the idea that only the educated have wisdom, and that unlettered people have little that's valuable for academics to know. I *don't* like *that* idea one bit—I don't believe it. Everyone has something valuable to say, if we're smart enough to listen and to look in the right places.

In the fall of 1980 I received a tape recording in the mail from a woman who had been institutionalized more than 50 years ago by her mother. What follows is a brief unedited portion of the transcript of Marian Rose White's autobiography. She asked me to share this story with others. She also asked me not to delete or fictionalize her name, the names of other people, or where she had resided all those long years. Too much of her life had already been concealed, distorted, and fictionalized for her to aid tht kind of conspiracy. In fact, as this book was nearing completion, Marian Rose White's "biography" was presented on commercial television. The televised account, depicted by professional actors, is not in precise accord with what follows. I have confidence in this version. I also have confidence that, while Ms. White was institutionalized the greater part of her life, she isn't mentally retarded. Then why the inclusion of this material here? That's the whole point. Society once judged her to be mentally retarded. So she *was* mentally retarded. Today, she is normal. So much for invariance of capability.

There aren't many stories like this around. There aren't many people like Marian Rose White around. If you read this carefully, I suspect that you won't regret it:

> I was born March 1, 1920, in San Francisco. I lived with my father and mother until the age of nine years. My father, who refereed in the prize fights in San Francisco was known to the world. His brother was the manager of Young Corbett. When I was nine years old my mother placed me in Sonoma State Hospital for the mentally retarded, for the doctor had told her I was retarded.
>
> The nurse said to my mother, "What is your little girl's name?"
>
> My mother did not answer for a minute and I looked up and I said, "My name is Marian Rose."

"I am talking to your mother."

I says, "I know my name."

They asked my mother how old I was. I told them I was nine years old. They got mad at me and told me to sit in a chair, and them and my mother went into the office.

The next Monday I came back to Sonoma where I started my life as a resident at Sonoma State Hospital. In those days you did the work. We were taught to make beds, undress little children, bathe them and put them to bed. I helped with the children though I could not bathe them yet, for I was yet too young. We had to get up very early. We got up at five o'clock in the morning, got dressed, made our beds, polished the floor, and went into the day hall to wait for technicians to come on at seven. When the technicians arrived we all lined up and marched downstairs to eat our breakfast. The girls sat on one side of the dining room and the men on the other. In the dining room you were not allowed to open your mouth or speak a word, or you would get scolded. Every morning we would have prunes and mush. Prunes and mush was the menu. It is the menu till this day.

We would get done with breakfast and go upstairs. Us older girls would comb the younger girls' hair and get them ready for school or to go out to play. We would line up two by two and go on a big porch. We would march around that porch with our arms folded while technicians stood behind us with a stick. Anyone dare make a move, you would get hit in the leg. Things were rough. I should say they were. They would give us cold baths, and put pillowcases over our heads, and duck [sic] us into a cold bath of water. For little things, they would punish us that way; that was their way of teaching us good behavior. To some people, they gave dope medicine for bad behavior. They put me on phenobarb one time, but they had to get me off in a hurry for I was seeing things that were not in my room or around the ward. They took me off. I got along fine after that and learned to work more with the children and learned to love the work I did.

One time, as a girl, I worked at Finnerty Cottage with cerebral palsied children. One Sunday afternoon I came over extra early and was playing records. We went into the day hall because it started to rain. A mother brought her little girl back to us and put her into my lap. One of the new technicians came in to me and took the little girl and said, "I'll stop her crying."

I said, "Leave her with me please, for she will not cry no more."

But she said, "I do not take orders from the residents." (In those days she said patients.) She took her into the bathroom and put her in the bathtub full of cold water. That evening the little girl passed away.

Things like that went on behind closed doors for many years. I was a victim of a cold bath myself. We were playing hospital in the yard one time and I did something I shouldn't. The technician took me upstairs and put a pillowcase over my head and gave me a cold bath. We were in the bathroom — the funniest thing — my mother walked into the bathroom and said, "I could have you fired if it wasn't for Marian Rose."

"Don't do it," I said. "She only did it because she thought she was doing what was right and what was required of her on paper."

One of the technicians, named Nell Brice — I'm not afraid to name her; she's dead, and will not hurt anybody — she used to beat us girls for no reason at all.

One day she gave me such a beating that I ran away from the ward and hid behind the church. I could not get anyone to help me against that woman and that was my only escape, so I ran behind the schoolhouse near the church. When they caught me they brought me back, shaved my hair, put a rope on me and marched me around the auditorium and around the grounds, like a horse. My mother was pretty angry about my hair and told them never to do that again. But you know, they don't listen to your mother. In those days if your mother told on them, you were severely punished.

Lux was one of the worst wards on the grounds. People would dirty themselves. People would not keep their clothes on. We had people who did not care to be talked to. They would sit in a corner by themselves, next to the wall, and you could not get through to them. We had people who would not walk or talk, who were treated very badly. I know some of the children were left to die in cribs. But in my day there was nothing else they could do. Today they have all the modern science and modern things to work with. Yet, we do not have decent teachers.

In those days though we had children and people who could speak for themselves and stand up for themselves. Now they have more severely handicapped children who cannot speak, nor hear, and some of them could never speak for themselves. They have to have people like me and other people to stick up for them. I hope that by the grace of God that I have done right by these people for I would never harm a hair on any of them.

In your book, *Christmas in Purgatory,* I looked at those pictures and thought to myself, "Were there really such torture chambers?" When I saw the people locked in the cells, I knew what it meant. In Lux they had a big black girl—oh, that I will always remember! When they punished us they would put us in the ward with her the first day we were punished and let her beat the hell out of us. She had great big feet—I could see her feet till the day I die—and she would step on us or hit us. When they put me into the cell with her, she knew I played records.

She said to me, "You play records for me tomorrow when you get out of my room?"

"Yes, I will." I said to her.

She hit me but not hard. I made a scream so they thought she gave me a good one. The next day I took the records down into the corridor and played for her.

The technicians never did know what we pulled. But we pulled a hot one that day or I would have been crippled or dead, for many a girl met her death by her. Heaven only knows what happened to her. Whatever did, I hope it's for the best. I feel sorry for her for she was *made* the beater of the institution. If they would let her beat us up, the technicians could not be blamed for what happened. That was one of the big cover-ups at Lux Cottage.

Another one was that they would take the girls out into the big corridor on the cement blocks and hose them down when they were full of shit. They would get it so caked onto them there was nothing else to do and they had to hose them down. It probably hurt. I know it hurt when it hit me when I was trying to get one of the kids up off the floor. The technicians down there, some of them were real witches.

Oh, I pray to God that someday no matter what happened, there will be better homes for some of these children in other places. Some of them were locked backwards into cells as I told you about that black girl. Some had shock treatment as a lot of people know. It was a very bad thing in those days; it blew many a brain. Some were tied to poles and given a whipping many times a day with a switch or a counter brush. I remember one time when we were very young children. I was so full I didn't want to eat my apple in the dining room so I brought it upstairs. Well, we were taken over a small chair and given "one, two, three, applesauce" with a counter brush. My butt hurt for two days. I guess that's the way life is anyway, you get in trouble for everything.

They used to sit us on the toilet and give us a great big round mush bowl full of epsom salts, and we'd have to eat the epsom salts for punishment. Well, it was the worst thing to eat in your life, if you ever ate it. Don't try it, it ain't that good. Well, one time they put five of us on the toilet and gave us epsom salts because I said I didn't want to bathe this one girl because she was too hard to get in and out of the tub. She was twice my size, and I was a pretty big woman at that time. We said, "Let's dump it in. Let's dump it in!" The toilet would flush every few minutes so we timed just about the time that toilet would flush and we dumped all the epsom salts in. When the technician came, she thought we ate them. Well, she wondered why some of us didn't have a b.m. right away. Oh, I tell you, some of the things we went through you would never believe! You'd never believe it. And I'm telling you, I don't believe it yet.

But you know, maybe that's the way life is. Maybe it was to show me something. But whatever it showed me, I can't answer you because, it's a funny thing, I don't know.

And so many things happened in my life too. I've met a lot of nice people. I'm back at the hospital now, working as a foster grandparent in the hospital and as a teacher in the classroom with the children. I cannot be a teacher yet until I can find a way to get a diploma so that I can pass the examination and become a teacher at the hospital. I hope to do it some day before I die. I would like to be able to work until I am 73 years old, then retire and say I retired from the job I loved the most.

I am on the People First Committee program, because one of the cerebral palsied boys has asked me to be. It breaks my heart when I sit out meetings to know it is the same group of men and women that were my children in the classroom. It is a wonderful thing when they get up at a meeting, though some of them can hardly speak, and speak up for what their rights are; to see the smile of their face and the joy in their heart when they say, "We have our rights." It is so beautiful to me, and I am very happy to know it.

I know I sound like a funny person to you, but my feelings are very deep. Deeper than a lot of others' because I walked in their shoes.

Mentally retarded people have viewpoints about their condition and also about the world in general. We are not mentally retarded and, consequently, can't present those viewpoints with any authority. For that you have to go directly to these people themselves — or to their published words which are beginning to amount to quite a body of literature. What we have learned confirms a few generalizations: (a) People do not regard themselves as hopeless and terminal; (b) people do not regard themselves as anything but human; and (c) people do not regard themselves as deserving to be alone, unwanted, and without friends. And those beliefs are exactly correct. We are all equal as human beings, and to live well we must believe that about everyone, especially ourselves.

Discussion

Possibly the most provocative metaphors we create are about ourselves, our lives, where we come from, what we do on earth, and what will be after we leave this "vale of tears." Possibly, our most deeply important metaphors have been those concerned with our freedoms. *Freedom,* in the last analysis, is the prepotent issue — insofar as how we see retarded persons, insofar as how they see themselves. That's why I keep coming back to it — as the goal each human being lives for, would die for. If we could only think about retarded people as we think about ourselves, most of their problems with society would be ameliorated — as would most of society's with them.

A beginning understanding of the concept of freedom has to do with coming to grips with the idea of free will. Dubos said: "The greater the freedom of a particular organism to select where it goes, what it does and how it responds to stimuli, the more complex and more creative is the living experience" (1981, p. 38). Human beings have the greatest degree of freedom — we change enormously in appearance and behavior as our environment changes. As Dubos further said, we can't prove scientifically that human beings are innately endowed to be free. But, because we are constantly making choices about our lives, and making decisions about ourselves, isn't it reasonable to simply take for granted that people have free will? It has even been said that free will is God's "excuse" for wars, pestilence, hunger, and other human suffering. We, among all the animals, are free to go and come as we choose. We alone plan futures; we alone explore new worlds and climb highest mountains simply because they're there. Unraveling the meaning of metaphors about people must not be far from the meaning of human freedom. And so too, the metaphors of mental retardation must be first understood through a perspective of free will, and then through the perspectives of political and social freedom.

Again and again, we are confronted with the therapy-freedom issue when we deliberate on such matters as institutionalization versus deinstitutionalization, specialized schools versus integrated schools, specialized treatments versus general treatments, specialist care versus generic care, official intervention versus family responsibility. Your metaphors about mental retardation will surely be shaped by how you respond to the question of whether the delivery of "therapy" is the primary objective in serving mentally retarded persons. There are many in the field who believe just that. I believe that it is crucial to realize the prepotence of a more fundamental responsibility: to respect the human quest for freedom. If freedom is the higher goal to which people aspire, is there room in our metaphors on mental retardation for that same goal for these people? People are willing to die to preserve or restore their freedom. Is anyone willing to die, does anyone truly sacrifice, to read another grade or two higher, spell a bit better, add a few points to an IQ score? Possibly, that is another way of explaining why liberty is like crabgrass; the more it's cut the quicker it grows.

People are ambivalent about mentally retarded persons, and indeed, about anyone who is perceived to be "different." They are ambivalent, uncomfortable, embarrassed, angry, guilty, everything (anything) but certain. Retarded people themselves are ambivalent, angry, uncertain. People who are "different" pay a price, despite the irony that the wish to be "different" powers much of our energy, most of our ambition, and nearly all of our foolishness. Each of us *wants* to be "different," to stand out, to be apart from the mob, to lead the throng. Notwithstanding, none of us want to be so "different" as to embarrassingly stand out — not as the leader, but as the freak, not as someone to be admired, but as someone to be loathed.

And so we find news articles heralding the astonishing decision of five Nobel laureates to give sperm that eventually will be matched with the "right" women, hopefully to produce exceptional — "gifted" — children. This is not an idea out of the mind of someone who has never had a good idea, but the conception of people like Stanford University's William B. Shockley — an old man now himself, but not too old to contribute his sperm to improving the breed. Shockley, winner of the 1956 Nobel prize in physics, a staunch advocate of the view that blacks are genetically inferior to whites, joined this "club" of sperm contributors, not because he regards himself as a perfect human being or even the ideal candidate, not because he is proposing to make supermen, but because he believes that we need more "people at the top of the population." Who really knows what's in another man's head? But whatever it is that drives Shockley — who is glorified by one segment of the population and vilified by another — it is clear that he does not want to suffer with mental retardation if he can help it. But who does? That is the unthinkable question which pollsters and other social scientists have not been able to truly probe.

Notwithstanding, we have some clues. Every once in a while there is an outcry in the newspapers that state institutions for mentally retarded persons, or a state department of mental health, or some official organization, endorsed, proposed, or perpetrated involuntary sterilization. A couple of years ago the headlines came out of Virginia, but many states for many years have overtly or tacitly endorsed involuntary sterilization — even states heavily populated by Catholics, such as Connecticut and Massachusetts. What does it mean? Quite simply, the citizens — the voting public — do not want mentally retarded people to spawn mentally retarded children, who will spawn other mentally retarded children. In some deep sense, it's probable that almost everyone in our culture would agree that — everything being equal — we want our children to be born with two normal arms and two normal legs, with good minds and pleasing personalities. Who can object to that? Nobody! Again, a prepotent question: What are people entitled to as human beings? Is the culture driven for the common good or the individual good? If you ask a politician that question, you may get one answer. If you ask a scientist that question, you may get another answer. If you ask a theologian, you might hear yet another.

The ambivalence continues. As noted earlier, Biklen (1983) has written a most provocative commentary on charity in *Community Organizing*. His conclusion is intriguing — handicapped people are betrayed by the very charity that is offered them. At one time, citizens helped other people not with money but with love and attention and time. As I remarked earlier in this chapter, maybe the sordid business Biklen decried is not the result of a bad concept — charity — but perhaps people do not know how to give affection and support and attention to one another. That is, people no longer genuinely know how to give charity. We substitute dollars and slogans for time and care. So, of course, I raise the question with my good colleague, Douglas Biklen, that there may be another culprit, not charity, but how it is dispensed today.

As James F. Beré remarked in a *New York Times* article (October 3, 1981): "Corporations feel an obligation both to help the underprivileged and to aid a wide range of activities that we hope will advance our society" (p. 27). This chief executive officer of one of America's multi-billion dollar, multi-national organizations justified responsibility not only on the basis that it is the *right* thing to do but also on the basis that the survival of American capitalism depends on the collective strength of the society. Here is the motivation that made America great, that conquered its wilderness, its prior inhabitants, the very elements that make this so rich a land — *purposeful charity,* doing good for others to do good for oneself. In fairness, Beré also concluded:

> We all need what only private philanthropy can offer. We need its understanding of human frailty, its availability in times of stress, of danger and of deprivation. We need its concern for the poor, the weak, the uncertain, the frightened. (p. 27)

This is what corporate philanthropy is all about. (Not everyone agrees that "the business of business isn't charity.") This is probably what much of America's charity is all about. Whether this conception of charity is right or wrong, Beré appears to have hit the nail on the head: Charity may not begin at home, but for it to be sustained in our culture it must come home. In one way or another, those who give must be given something in return.

Yes, charity today is big business, and Biklen may be right that the poor don't get very much out of it and that, in too many cases, it does more harm than good. But if we are going to truly wrestle with the concept of mental retardation, with the problems that people have because they are so designated, then we must also wrestle with the idea of charity. We cannot discard the idea; we must grope to find what has been fine and decent (and even religious) about extending help to another human being — whether extending your hand or sharing your loaf of bread. Examining the concept of charity, like examining what propels people to contribute sperm to create a better, if not master, race, and what propels other people (or are these the same people?) to advocate sterilizations and even euthanasia, may provide us with new and sharper visions of both what people are like now and what they can become. We can gain a perspective on mental retardation by asking someone what he or she thinks about retarded people. We can gain another perspective on mental retardation by asking someone what he or she thinks about sterilization. And we can gain still another perspective on mental retardation by studying the people (the strangers, the families, retarded people themselves) and their behavior (what they do). Then, we must try to come to grips with their values (what charity means to them, what life means to them). What we will find is one giant puzzle — where each piece is related to some other piece, and where our job for a lifetime is to try and put the pieces together. Some day, there will be people who will have put all the pieces together, who will have solved the giant puzzle. That is, some day the metaphors of mental retardation will be commonly understood, even if there may never be a day when they are commonly shared.

6.

Formal Classification Schemes: The Search for Causes and Effects

THE DEMAND TO communicate quickly sometimes causes us to label people. Our insensitivity at times causes us to label with cruel effect, and at times we do not seem to profit from the mistakes we make. For example consider a recent edition of the *Good Housekeeping Family Health & Medical Guide* (1980), surely found in more homes than our most advanced textbooks in mental retardation and more influential in shaping the minds of the general public than the combined influence of the best scholars in the field. What does *Good Housekeeping* say about mental retardation? "Morons have IQs of approximately 50 to 70 and constitute the largest class of mental defectives" (p. 417). This source also informs its readers that these "morons" are usually the children of intellectually dull parents. The reader may be astonished to learn from *Good Housekeeping* that "morons" are not detected as handicapped until they go to school, because as young children they tend to lack curiosity, are quiet, and are well behaved. If they do not receive special training, *Good Housekeeping* predicts, many will drift into unemployment and crime. The "experts" who work for *Good Housekeeping* may have prepared for their "study" of mental retardation by reading the historic works of Henry Goddard and Walter E. Fernald (although even Fernald reconsidered his conclusion that all mentally retarded men are potential criminals). The guide continues by defining imbeciles as having IQs of approximately 20 to 50. Those people, the guide states, are incapable of independence; their parents usually have normal intelligence. Finally, idiots constitute the lowest grade of mental handicap and are estimated to have an IQ below 20 (p. 417). They require constant protection, with the majority stunted in growth, bedridden, without speech, and often not surviving childhood. Knowing what you now know about mental retardation, would you award *Good Housekeeping* its own seal of approval? Unfortunately, citizens look to such publications for informed discourse, and professionals not only write such nonsense but other professionals read it and believe it. Who actually knows where the doctors and teachers learn about mental retardation? Professionals are not immune from using language and classification schemes that confuse rather than clarify.

This chapter reviews the various ways professionals classify people designated as mentally retarded—by etiology (causes), by educational attainment, by intelligence quotient, and by special characteristics. This chapter will emphasize the relation between the phenomenology of mental retardation and broad social problems. This approach is based on the premise that phenomenology—the actual classification schemes—tells us less about mental retardation than do the social forces underlying the labels. From this point of view, the labels represent the "trees" of the problem. Here, I am much more concerned with the "forest," which involves understanding major social problems as they relate to the phenomenology of mental retardation.

Before I begin the discussion of etiology, an important caveat is in order. First, consider the insight offered by Dubos (1981), whose examination of human capabilities forces an inescapable conclusion, that each of us is born with a great range of potential that enables us—at least in theory—to develop an almost limitless diversity of characteristics. But in fact we

> develop only those aspects of our nature that are compatible not only with the conditions to which we are exposed, but even more with the choices we make in the course of our lives. The marvel is that nature and nurture can become so completely integrated that they generate a unique socialized entity, the human person, out of the biological organism, *Homo sapiens.* (p. 28)

Each person is unique—even "identical twins"—yet, there is an invariance among human beings. Although we differ profoundly from one another, all human beings have in common many important characteristics and needs. These Dubos calls "the biological and behavioral invariants of humankind." These invariants are found throughout the world, regardless of race, social class, religion, or other significant influences on human behavior. For example, while the nutritional habits of vegetarians appear to be far different from those of people who eat meat, in the final analysis, all human beings—whether vegetarian or carnivorous—require more or less the same intake of calories, carbohydrates, fats, minerals, vitamins, and other primary nutrients. Thus, human life is both variant and invariant. Human characteristics derive from nature (our heredity) and nurture (our environment).

Therefore, as you consider the etiology of mental retardation, which is classified according to the broad categories of exogenous and endogenous, remember that heredity and environment are not dichotomous and can never be dichotomous. In any individual, genetic mechanisms mold—and are molded by—environment. As Dubos (1981) put it:

> The various human races exhibit obvious physical differences which have emerged as a result of exposure for many generations to different surroundings and ways of life. Some of these differences are hereditary because they have been encoded in the DNA molecules which determine the genetic constitution peculiar to each human race. This is the case for the skin pigmentation characteristic of racial groups, for the small size of the African pigmies and the Australian aborigines, and probably for a few minor anatomic differences between Japanese and Caucasians. . . .
>
> However, most of the physical and behavioral characteristics that are distinctive of ethnic groups are in reality not genetic but consequences of differences in socio-cultural conditions. For example, most immigrants from Sicily were of short stature when they landed in New York at the turn of the century, but their children and especially their grandchildren born and raised in the United States are now likely to be as tall as the descendants of the original settlers from northern Europe. . . .
>
> Human development is thus profoundly affected by environmental forces and ways of life which act so rapidly—within one or a very few generations—that their effect cannot possibly be due to genetic changes.[1]

Like Dubos, I believe that the anthropological, genetic, historical, and philosophical literature shows that the "cards" with which one starts life are replayed, shuffled, and changed many times during the "game of life." With this in mind, I present one perspective on the multiple metaphors connected with the study of etiology in mental retardation.

Classification by Etiology

Medical etiologies have obviously changed during the years. Down syndrome (formerly called Mongolism), for example, was once thought to be caused by a constellation of factors embedded in the mother's inability to properly nurture her fetus, but modern cytologic techniques have led

---

[1]From *Celebrations of Life* (pp. 47-48) by R. Dubos, 1981, New York: McGraw-Hill. Reprinted by permission.

to the identification of chromosomal abnormalities that appear to be connected with the etiology of this syndrome. Whereas once we did not know anything about mother-fetus incompatibility, today we not only know what happens when an Rh-negative mother carries an Rh-positive fetus, but we know what to do about it. Whereas once we did not know how two deleterious recessive genes cause Phenylketonuria (PKU), today we not only understand the cause of the disease but we can also mitigate its effects. Whereas once hydrocephalus almost always led to severe disorders, at least in certain instances proper corrective action can be taken and a child can grow up quite normally. Whereas infants once expired at birth because premature deliveries brought them into the world weighing less than two pounds, babies today who are no heavier are nursed to health, and eventually, go to waiting families—where many of them can live normal lives. Because we know so much more today about what certain genes and chromosomes do, and what certain insults to the fetus or the newborn do, and because we can now base treatments upon this knowledge, countless children are alive and well today who in the past would never have survived the rigors of the birth process. Countless others, however, are alive but *not well* today, and most of those would not have survived the birth process in the past. We understand more today about such matters, but we are also left with "problems" that did not exist as recently as a decade or two ago. While great gains have been made in preventing or ameliorating mental defect, and certainly great gains have been made in understanding the various causes of mental retardation, it must also be admitted that the overall etiological picture has not changed completely in the last 100 years. Many of the causes that led to mental defect then lead to mental defect today. There are not proven methods of prevention for many conditions and still fewer methods for cure. Whether a parent has a mentally retarded child or not remains in the purview of some of life's games of chance. Possibly, that is the most significant reason for you to come to grips with this material. *It could have happened to you.*

Exogenous Conditions

The *Manual on Terminology and Classification in Mental Retardation* (Grossman, 1977), published by the AAMD, noted that "exogenous" is an obsolete term. Be that as it may, this term seems to be suitable for presenting as simply as possible various causes of mental retardation. Exogenous mental retardation as used here refers to the various conditions that arise from prenatal, perinatal, and postnatal trauma, infection, blood incompatibility, and other causes, *except* those related to inheritance. As is now well known, things that happen to the developing fetus or to the newborn can lead to serious consequences.

In utero, the fetus is highly susceptible to insult, be it an infection contracted from the mother or the effects of otherwise benign medication that the mother might take during her pregnancy. This is especially true during the first three months of fetal life. Although less common, there are instances of mental retardation resulting from a serious trauma such as an automobile accident. More recently, evidence has been accumulating that suggests cause and effect relationships between mental retardation and a mother's smoking, drinking, and frequent use of other drugs. Included in the category of exogenous mental retardation is a range of mild to very serious disabilities arising from such causative factors as oxygen deprivation during delivery to lead poisoning of the young child who has eaten peelings from lead-based paints; indeed, lead from paint may be one of the most underestimated factors contributing to deficits, especially among lower socioeconomic groups. As you may have already noted, the origins of some of these conditions may go back almost to the point of conception, while on the other hand, two- or three-year-old children are vulnerable to brain damage as a result of accident, disease, or ingestion of poisonous substances.

To be sure, there is a serious gap between what is known about the causes of mental retardation and what is unknown. There is also a serious gap between what we do know and what society has been willing to implement in the way of prevention and amelioration. But it also can be said that we are making significant progress in unraveling the causes of heretofore puzzling conditions. Additionally, more of what is now known has been applied insofar as mandatory screening programs for certain conditons, easily available treatment programs for the few conditions that can be successfully treated, and such general services as Well Baby clinics, neonatal units in major hospital centers, and public education concerning the harmful effects of alcohol, tobacco, and certain other drugs.

What follows is a relatively simple and somewhat standard summary of the various exogenous causes of mental retardation, with brief comments on a few examples in each category. This discussion is not intended to encourage you to feel qualified either to make etiological diagnoses or to provide expert counsel to families. Rather, it should give you a greater appreciation for the fact that, after all is said and done, any one of these conditions *could have occurred in you*; further, it should remind you that professionals are not immune from the problems that concern clients.

Infection. During intrauterine life, the developing fetus is very vulnerable. If the expectant mother has syphilis, the fetus can contract the condition and be so damaged neurologically as to develop mental retardation and a host of other serious conditions. If the mother contracts rubella (German measles), especially during the first trimester of her pregnancy, the likelihood is strong that the fetus will be damaged and the newborn may have mental retardation, deafness, blindness, microcephaly (small head), or any combination of these and other neurologically caused conditions. If the pregnant woman is infected by the protozoan-like parasite, toxoplasmosis, the newborn can be burdened with a range of conditions from convulsions, microcephaly, hydrocephaly, to a motor deficit.

Postnatally, there are various forms of encephalitis (infection in the brain) that can give rise to mental retardation, emotional disorders, and other conditions. At times, encephalitis is so severe that it can be fatal.

Trauma. Many parents, especially those who have not been able to ascertain the specific causes that led to retardation in their children, have concluded for themselves that the retardation occurred as a result of some trauma—either during pregnancy, during delivery, or during the early life of their children. Usually trauma is *not* the cause, but in some cases trauma does lead to mental retardation. Especially during delivery, accidents that lead to retardation can occur. For example, a difficult labor has been known to cause mental retardation in the newborn. Or, in the case of a serious physical accident—such as a car accident or a fall—the natural protective attributes of the amniotic fluid may not be able to withstand the shock without neurological consequences for the fetus. Long before it was known that alcohol and drug abuse might lead to retardation in a newborn, the impaired behavior of an intoxicated pregnant woman was recognized as a threat to the viability of her fetus.

In general, postnatal trauma is much less often a cause of mental retardation than commonly believed. Of course, most readers have heard of children who fall from bassinettes or bicycles, or have concussions and fractured skulls as a result of some other accident or child abuse. Even when such an injury is quite noticeable (i.e., pronounced swelling on the head, a loss of consciousness, headache), it very rarely results in mental retardation. This is not to say that some children are not retarded because of child abuse or accidents. But many parents believe that their children's mild mental retardation resulted from a given incident. Destructive family guilt and recriminations may persist if the pediatrician does not stress to parents that most such injuries are innocuous. It is usually helpful for parents to be informed of the actual cause of the child's mental retardation if it is known, or to be informed that the cause is not known if that is the case.

Toxic Agents. Accidental ingestion of medication or poison by the young child can cause serious brain damage. Probably more common than postnatal accidental poisoning, however, is prenatal poisoning of the fetus from alcohol, medication, or addictive drugs such as heroin. It is possible not only for a mother's drug addiction to poison the fetus, but also for the addiction itself to be transmitted from mother to fetus. Certain otherwise mildly toxic drugs prescribed for pregnant women who exhibit anxiety, too, may be dangerous to the fetus. In general, obstetricians try to avoid prescribing any unnecessary drugs to pregnant women.

One of the most frequent, misunderstood, and preventable causes of neonatal anomalies is what is now called "fetal alcohol syndrome." Literature going back to biblical times attempted to call attention to the dangers of alcohol insofar as pregnant women are concerned. In their extensive review of the literature on this problem, Streissguth, Landesman-Dwyer, Martin, and Smith (1980) concluded that a safe level of alcohol use during pregnancy has not been established. Although there are many puzzling and unanswered questions concerning "fetal alcohol syndrome," the harmful effects of alcohol are clearly established. Prospective parents should be made aware of the harm that alcohol can cause their newborn.

Radiation poisoning constitutes another threat to the health of the fetus. It can cause mental retardation and other anomalies. The atomic attacks on Hiroshima and Nagasaki led to documented cases of unusually high levels of newborn anomalies in the years immediately subsequent to the bombings. In a 34-year follow-up of children born to the Hiroshima and Nagasaki survivors, Neel found "no clearly statistically significant effects of parental exposures on the offspring chracteristics which we studied, but the various indicators of possible genetic damage all are in the direction expected if an effect was indeed produced" (1981, p. 1205). Similarly, the literature is replete with case studies as well as epidemiological surveys of the general effects of radiation on health and intelligence. It has been known for many years that high levels of therapeutic radiation can cause various forms of cancer, cleft palate, microcephaly, and other serious conditions in children. In more recent years, concern has been expressed about even low-level doses of radiation, such as those obtained from diagnostic x-rays. Especially during the first three months of gestation, the fetus is vulnerable to such aversive intrusion.

Incompatible blood factors have, until relatively recently, been a frequent and extraordinarily potent factor in the causation of retardation, cerebral palsy, epilepsy, and other behavioral and physical disorders associated with central nervous system damage. No doubt, the most well known of the blood incompatibilities is the Rh factor, so named because it was first discovered in the Rhesus monkey. Prior to its identification in the 1940s, this blood incompatibility caused serious damage to the fetus. "Rh" refers to a factor in the blood. Incompatibility can result if the mother is Rh-negative and the father is Rh-positive. Approximately 15% of the

Caucasian population is Rh-negative. If the fetus of these parents is Rh-negative (like the mother), no problem occurs. If the fetus inherits the Rh-positive gene from the father, however, incompatibility results; the Rh-positive blood causes antibodies to develop during pregnancy. In each pregnancy for this Rh-negative mother, the strength of those antibodies will increase if the fetus is Rh-positive, so that in subsequent pregnancies the risk of damage to the fetus increases. Further, Rh-positive is the dominant gene, so the fetus is more likely to be Rh-positive.

Fortunately, what was once a catastrophic situation is today almost entirely avoidable. Originally, the standard treatment for Rh incompatibility was a complete change of the newborn's blood in order to prevent the antibodies from attacking and destroying the red blood cells and damaging the brain. Unfortunately, that procedure was only partially effective with many children, mainly because the damage may have already been done to the fetus in utero, and also because such large-scale blood transfusions are not without various side effects and mishaps. Today, prevention is possible by utilization of a blood extract called Rh-immune globulin, which acts to eliminate potentially antigenic fetal cells from maternal circulation, and thus stops the development of antibodies in the mother. This procedure greatly reduces serious consequences of Rh blood incompatibility. The extract can be given to the woman after each of her pregnancies, thus insuring a "clean" prenatal environment for a subsequent fetus.

Endocrine Disorders. Before modern science and medicine began to control the deleterious effects of endocrine disorders, these caused several serious anomalies; for example, in the circus sideshow, the giant, the symmetrical "midget," the fat lady, the dog-faced boy, and many of the other sideshow stars suffered from one or another endocrine disorder. Fortunately, most endocrine disorders do not lead to mental retardaion. Some do, however, and when not treated, the results can be disastrous. Hypothyroidism (underactive thyroid), for example, can cause what used to be called "cretinism," characterized by small stature, chalky complexion, and mental retardation. For many years, though, a simple test at birth and subsequent drug treatment have greatly diminished this serious problem in the Western world.

Prematurity/Gestational Disorders. Until relatively recently, a newborn weighing less than 1,500 grams (approximately 3 pounds) rarely survived. Today, newborns weighing 1,000 grams (approximately 2 pounds) often survive. Such infants, though, are more likely than full-term infants with normal body weight to exhibit various developmental disorders, including mental retardation. A combination of prematurity (a gestation period of less than approximately 37 weeks) and low birth weight (less than 2,500 grams) can be associated with chronic physical and/or mental problems. Increasingly, neonatal units are able to "deliver" to the family an infant who will thrive and develop normally. The science of neonatal care is changing rapidly, and definitions of prematurity vary from clinic to clinic. Notwithstanding, there is general agreement that "the immature infant is more susceptible to neurological insult, has a higher mortality rate, and is at greater risk of succumbing to sudden infant death syndrome" than the baby who is born at full term (MacMillan, 1977, p. 147).

Malnutrition. In two ways, malnutrition can cause mental retardation: when the pregnant woman suffers from prolonged emaciation and/or when the young child is chronically and severely undernourished. Birch and Richardson (no date) studied the long-term consequences of severe malnutrition during the first two years of life. Their subjects were school children who during the first 24 months of life were hospitalizied because of severe malnutrition. They were compared with two other groups of children who during the first 24 months of life were hospitalized because of severe malnutrition. They were compared with two other groups of classmates or neighbors, also closest in age to the subjects. At approximately 6 to 11 years old, the 74 subjects bore out the researchers' expectations that they would be significantly less well developed physically than their siblings and unrelated classmates. This expectation was especially significant insofar as comparisons with classmates were concerned. Similarly, the study population exhibited significantly lower intelligence (as measured by standard individual IQ tests) in comparison with both siblings and classmates. Not surprisingly, the study children were judged by their teachers to have poorer attention and memory and were more easily distracted and less spontaneous than their classmates. Essentially, on all measures of physical and intellectual development, the children who were subjected to severe malnourishment evidenced significant delays compared to children who escaped early severe malnourishment. Of course, as Richardson (no date) pointed out in a separate paper, non-nutritional factors also influence intellectual development. Despite the methodological difficulties in isolating the factor of nutrition from the complex array of variables that can contribute to intellect, there seems to be little doubt that early severe malnutrition has deleterious effects on physical and intellectual development of children. Robinson and Robinson (1976) put it this way:

> Within the range of nutritional deprivation likely to be encounterd in the developed nations, then, diet apparently plays a minor role in producing irreversible CSN [central nervous system] changes and consequent mental retardation. On the other hand, hunger itself probably has a depressing effect on the alertness, vitality, curiosity, and attention of children. (p. 132)

Emotional Factors or Deprivation. Before the 1960s, diagnosticians tried to distinguish between mental retardation and "pseudo-retardation." If a person originally diagnosed as mentally retarded was later found to be nonhandicapped, the initial diagnosis was thought to have been incorrect. In cases of "pseudo-retardation," the apparent retardation may have been misdiagnosed as a consequence of emotional disturbance. Today, such a distinction is no longer made because a person is determined to be mentally retarded on the basis of criteria connected with current behavior only. That is, if a person has a low IQ and exhibits an adaptive disorder, he or she is said to be mentally retarded, irrespective of past behavior or what may be predicted about the future course of behavior. We should not, however, lose sight of the fact that there are people who *become* mentally retarded because of certain emotional factors or deprivation. For example, children may have such severe emotional disorders or may have been so severely emotionally deprived that not only have their personalities been damaged by their environments, but their intellectual capabilities also have been seriously impaired. Such children may have been isolated for many years ("attic children") or severely deprived and cruelly treated in other ways (Clarke & Clarke, 1965).

Children with severe emotional disturbance may be called psychotic or autistic. Those terms have been used interchangeably, but they should be used discretely. An older child whose behavior changes suddenly from unexceptional to bizarre may eventually be diagnosed as psychotic. The term autism is usually reserved for the child who displays extremely deviant behavior soon after birth and for many years subsequently. The etiology of this condition is not well understood. Some theorists, such as Leo Kanner (1949), have posited that autism has its roots in the context of the early mother/child relationship. Others, such as Bernard Rimland (1964), have sought chemical and other physiological explanations of the condition. Essentially, infantile autism—its cause as well as its treatment and predicted course of the condition—remains a puzzle. Suffice it to say that autism—characterized by early onset, an aversion to other people, bizarre and often unpredictable behavior, deviant and delayed speech, obsessive interest in certain objects, and the occasional development of unusual (and generally useless) special skills—is often accompanied by functional retardation or, at the least, such bizarre behavior as to make specialized educational services mandatory.

Endogenous Conditions

Another term for endogenous as used here is "inherited." At birth, the human being is dealt a "hand" (inheritance). The infant is also in a "game" in which he or she actively participates with the environment. Some people draw very stong hands, but play a careless game. Others draw a mediocre hand, but play it so well, so wisely, that they win (i.e., they live a good life).

There is little we can do about the "hands" that are dealt us (although, more and more, society seems bent on developing technologies to intrude on the hereditary aspects of the game). But there is a great deal we can do about how we live our lives. There are critical "showdowns" in life—beginning at conception. (Exactly what chromosomes and genes do you draw from mother and father?) There are many more subsequent "showdowns"—the stimulation available to you in the home, in the community, the early schooling you receive, the friends you have, the opportunities you have, the luck you have. Each can be a critical point, but few are life threatening. And virtually all but the very first critical point (the hand you are dealt, your inheritance) cannot occur without your active involvement. To be sure, there are accidents you personally cannot avoid—in utero, or crossing the street—but those too are very rare. In any case, what you start with—your inheritance—cannot be trivialized. What follows is a traditional classification of the various genetic influences that may lead to mental retardation. Following that will be a brief discussion of a few chromosomal disorders connected with mental retardation.

Genetics. Since the dawn of time, there has not been anyone exactly like you. Until the end of time, there will never be anyone exactly like you. Notwithstanding, each of us carries genes that link us to the beginning of the species. Thus, while no two are exactly alike, everyone is related.

What is a gene? Genes are biological units that carry specific traits. They determine the structure and rate at which proteins in the body are formed. Many of those proteins act as enzymes or catalysts, which are basic substances that control the rate of most of the chemical reactions that take place in the living cell. The gene is real, but it is also ideational. It is invisible to the naked eye; and, until recently, it was not possible to detect even with our most sophisticated microscopic equipment (Kronenberg, 1982). Today, the possibility exists that certain genetic disorders will be identified not only by the abnormal genes learned about through genealogical studies, "but by detecting the results of the abnormal genes' actions" (Kronenberg, 1982, p. 50).

There are possibly 40,000 genes distributed unevenly among the 46 chromosomes in a human cell. Those genes are responsible for producing the thousands of enzymes which, in turn, are responsible for the rates of hundreds of different chemical processes that take place within cells. The chemical substance of the gene is known as deoxyribonucleic acid (DNA), a giant molecule containing a double spiral strand that represents the genetic code. The fascinating work of Watson and Crick, which led to the discovery of the double helix, may illuminate for the reader how science proceeds, as well as how it can lead to the degrading behavior of those who chase after the external prizes and tributes that society sometimes confers on the great discoverer. But that's another story, and another lesson.

How does life begin for the human being? A sperm cell (for the male, a germ cell containing 23 chromosomes) slithers among millions of others during copulation and penetrates an egg (the woman's germ cell) that is ready to be fertilized. At conception, the egg is the size of the period on this page, and the sperm is a thousand or more times smaller. The joining of sperm and egg can be the beginning of a human life, one that contains a shared inheritance of man and woman. In each normal sperm and egg there are 23 chromosomes, which represent half the number each parent could have contributed to the union, half the number in each body cell.

Each parent has 46 chromosomes, 23 matched pairs. Those chromosomes are found in two types of cells: soma (or body) cells containing 46 chromosomes, or 23 matched pairs; and the germ cells, containing 23 chromosomes, half the number of chromosomes a parent could have contributed. Those germ cells—male sperm and female eggs—are held waiting to be utilized at the time of conception. In terms of probability, each parent is capable of transmitting 16 million different chromosome combinations. In the union of sperm and egg, there are any one of 300 trillion chromosome combinations possible. Hence the assertion that with the exception of monozygotic (identical) twins, there never was, and never will be, anyone exactly like you. Of course, even identical twins do not have identical experiences.

What if parents want to insure that their child will not be burdened with their less desirable characteristics? What if the physically weak man engages in a program of weight lifting to build himself up so that his son will not suffer the indignities of the 90-pound weakling? What if the vain woman decides to have her nose altered so that her daughter will not suffer the embarrassment of an unlovely proboscis? None of that will work. Regardless of how the man or woman play their "hand," the newborn will inherit the genes and chromosomes of the parents. The newborn inherits genes and chromosomes from a sperm and an egg that are replicas of those the parents themselves received when they were conceived. With a few exceptions, discussed later, nothing that has happened to the parents throughout their lives has been communicated to their germ cells to alter their genes.

Each birth is a new opportunity, a new chance to play a different game than one's parents or grandparents. And while each birth is soon accompanied by a constellation of other people and a certain psychological, social, ethnic, and religous context, the newborn starts fresh with a set of genes and chromosomes that have not been altered by the games of the parents.

There is something very hopeful about that aspect of each newborn awakening. An exception to this "Rule of the Unprejudiced Beginning" is when a mutation occurs in the germ cells of mother or father; this will be discussed later.

Polygenic Inheritance. In one of the more cynical comments published during the first year of President Reagan's administration, Clarence Pendleton, the President's choice to head the U.S. Commission on Civil Rights, remarked that "the best way to help poor folks is not to be one" (Osborne, 1982, p. 25). Paradoxically, the way the so-called cultural familial mentally retarded person could best be helped would be if *everyone* were cultural familial mentally retarded. Then, one person's failings would be everyone's failings, one person's strengths would be everyone's strengths. Cultural familial mental retardation can only be determined from a comparison of the "haves" and the "have nots." Or as Kanner might have put it, the severely retarded child with microcephaly is mentally retarded in an absolute sense — any culture at any time. But the cultural familial child is retarded only in a relative sense — in a particular culture at a particular time, many other people are better educated, better situated, and better adjusted to life. It is perhaps a sign of progress that the AAMD (Grossman, 1977, p. 137) defines cultural familial as an

> obsolete term for a type of retardation, presumed to be polygenic, in which there is a family history of borderline intelligence or mild mental retardation and poor accomplishments in society, academic retardation, poor work history, and often found in combination with adverse postnatal environment, low birth weight, and premature deliveries.

In spite of the designation as obsolete, of course, there do remain related categories such as cultural deprivation, cultural disadvantage and others, to account for the large numbers of individuals who are identified as mentally retarded but who do not have organic impairment.

Dominant Inheritance. When either mother or father is carrying a single dominant deleterious gene, there is one chance in two their children will inherit that gene. When this parent has the gene but is unaffected, the retardation or other anomalies associated with the condition are not "expressed." The question of "expressivity" is always important in these situations. That is, some genes and gene combinations have variable expressivity. Indeed, despite the fact than an individual may have inherited a deleterious dominant gene, he or she may be quite "normal." In that case, the dominant gene is controlled by the actions of other minor gene pairs. For example, an individual may have a gene that can cause neurofibromatosis, but phenotypically (i.e., in terms of the expression of the condition) the person is quite unaffected.

Let's briefly examine neurofibromatosis, one of the most common single dominant gene-related conditions. It is characterized by mild to very grave physical deformity. Quasimodo, the Hunchback of Notre Dame, and John Merrick, the man whose life was so vividly and beautifully portrayed in the Broadway show "The Elephant Man" may have had it. It is not common though it is by no means rare, probably affecting upwards of 100,000 people in the United States alone. Usually in childhood, the victim begins to find ugly but usually benign skin tumors. Sometimes, the body is covered by thousands of these tumors, which may also develop in the brain. The face can be grotesque, the bones can be misshapen, the voice can be severely impaired; the whole can—as in the case of John Merrick—present a picture of the "ugliest man alive." Sometimes the disease is so mild that the neurofibromas (benign tumors) can be removed by surgery; and plastic surgery may ameliorate the cosmetic problem.

The fascinating life of the "elephant man" illustrates a lesson much more important than how much an individual can endure pain and suffering. It illustrates a life triumphant, a life that exemplified so much goodness and intelligence that there were people—indeed, "beautiful people"—of nineteenth century London who looked at John Merrick's grotesqueness and found it much less significant than his wisdom and beauty. There is a deep and fundamental lesson to be learned from the story of the "Elephant Man." Unfortunately, scholarly treatises that deal with etiological conditions rarely recognize the *human being* imprisoned in the superficially unattractive trappings of the condition.

Tuberous sclerosis is an example of single dominant (but it may also be recessive) gene-related mental retardation. It is characterized by seizures, facial as well as central nervous system tumors, and mental retardation. Detailed discussion of various other single dominant gene-related conditions, all rare and usually connected with severe retardation, can be found in medical textbooks.

Recessive Transmission. It has been estimated by various scientists that the average person carries within the genetic "baggage" approximately 8 or 9 severely deleterious recessive genes, plus many more recessive genes that may have harmful influences on the person's physical and/or mental development. To express itself (phenotypically) both the mother *and* father must contribute the same recessive deleterious gene to the newborn. The mother and father, each carriers (each genotypically involved), do not themselves have the condition (phenotypically, each of them is clean). There is also the possibility that the particular deleterious gene has what is termed low expressivity. That is, not all genes express themselves in an individual in a predictable way; expressivity refers to the severity of the trait. Some genes virtually always produce in everyone affected a clinically recognized abnormality, and those are said to have 100% penetrance; penetrance refers to the percentage of people exhibiting the trait. While we can describe the phenomena, the mechanisms involving expressivity and penetrance may merely be as Wolf Wolfensberger (personal communication) has remarked, *presumed* but essentially *unproven*. Other conditions require unusual combinations of genetic and environmental forces to express the disorder.

Tay-Sachs is an example of a condition caused by inherited deleterious recessive genes from both mother and father. It usually is restricted to Jewish people from Ashkenazic background. Why should that be? The answer to this sometimes puzzling question may reveal why people should not marry close relatives. The answer may also dispel certain myths about conditions connected with ethnic or racial identity. At some point in history, a mutation occurred to a Jewish person's previously normal gene. Of course, the person never knew the mutation occurred. He or she was not ill for an instant, and his or her fertility was unimpaired. Because long ago families traditionally intermarried, eventually two of this person's descendents — each carriers of the deleterious gene — married and had their own children. Consequently, what was once a single normal gene of no scientific consequence became a serious problem in the twentieth century. And, of course, such a scenario also explains why certain conditions are confined to specific racial, religious, or other groups that rarely marry outside of their ethnic-racial "families." Tay-Sachs is essentially an incurable condition that leads to early infant mortality. Babies so affected — babies who inherit the Tay-Sachs lethal gene from mother *and* father — develop normally at first, expressing symptomatology of the disorder at about six months of age. Mild muscular weakness leads to rapid mental and physical deterioration. The infant becomes blind and paralyzed, and death usually occurs between the ages of three and five. Various genetic screening procedures today that test Jewish men and women of reproductive age are able to at least indicate to parents whether they carry this or another of the few so-called "Jewish diseases." Fortunately, the test requires the drawing of a simple blood sample. Unfortunately, the decision of the family to have children or not is not as simple, since there remain three chances in four that their child will be born without the condition, although there is one in two chances that the child will be a carrier of the lethal gene. Genetic counseling is clearly indicated in such a case.

Phenylketonuria (PKU) is another of the recessive transmitted conditions that can lead to severe retardation and other physical and mental disorders. Prior to the development of reliable and quick tests to identify children with PKU, there was little if any treatment available for such victims. But in the 1950s, a relatively accurate test was developed to make that identification; and about a decade later, Dr. Robert Guthrie found a much more precise and inexpensive blood test that allowed for quick and accurate identification. Coinciding with the rapid development of programs to screen children for PKU has been the work by Linus Pauling and other scientists in creating a synthetic diet. The diet, low in the amino acids and high in protein, controls the absorption of phenylalanine in the child's metabolic system. In many cases, this prevents serious retardation and other anomalies. The diet has stimulated a great deal of controversy, and there remain doubts about the long-term effects of the diet and about when a child can go off the diet. Nevertheless, because of the diet, PKU appears to be an example of a type of mental retardation that gives hope for eventual amelioration and possible cure.

Vexing arguments have arisen in the wake of these strides in treatment. Some scientists have claimed that while a general screening and treatment policy for PKU victims may prevent the condition in an individual, it may also lead to increased frequency of this condition in later generations. The other side of this argument is that even if the PKU gene should double in the population in several thousand years, by that time there will probably be better methods of treatment. So the arguments go—arguments that reflect our values concerning the rights of each individual to live as good a life as possible, and furthermore, the value of each individual as a human being (even those individuals who carry deleterious genes). To state it another way, at what point does the "welfare" of society intrude upon the "welfare" of the individual, and vice versa?

Chromosomal Disorders. Down syndrome is the most common of the chromosomal disorders that lead to mental retardation. In 1866, Langdon Down described a condition he called Mongolism, so named because the individual appeared to have oriental features. Many other "stigmata" (physical characteristics) are often found among such people—flat occiput (back of the head), small nose, slanted eyes (epicanthic folds at the inside corners of the eyes), protruding tongue, short fingers and a transverse crease across the palm, dry skin, sparse fine hair, short stature, increased incidence of cardiac and other physical anomalies, and delayed or incomplete sexual development. Those and other physical signs may lead a diagnostician to conclude that an infant has Down syndrome.

Reuben Feurstein, a distinguished scholar in the field of mental retardation, has suggested that children with Down syndrome may profit from a series of minor plastic operations (Pines, August 31, 1982). Feurstein described the work of German plastic surgeons who operated on more than 250 children with Down syndrome, reducing the size of their protruding tongues, bringing their ears closer to their head, altering the axis of their eyelids, raising cheekbones, and in other ways cosmetically improving their appearances. Considering that the risks are small, the surgery inexpensive, the trauma insignificant, and the benefits are great, this appears to be a reasonable proposal. Of course, it would be better if individuals with Down syndrome were not judged on the basis of physical appearance in the first place. We can at least hope for a better world. In the meantime, Feurstein's suggestion seems to be reasonable.

While most children with Down syndrome have mental retardation, and while all have physical anomalies, few are severely mentally retarded. A few, indeed, have normal or near normal intelligence. While the condition still presents puzzling uncertainties, even to scholars who have devoted themselves to the study of Down syndrome, it is well known that there is a high correlation between maternal age (and to a lesser extent, paternal age) and Down syndrome. For example, while the risk of having a child with Down syndrome is approximately 1 in 1,500 for mothers under 30 years of age, the risk for women over 35 is five to ten times higher, and for women over 45 there is approximately 1 chance in 40.

Essentially, Down syndrome occurs when the chromosomes do not divide or reduce normally. Usually, this leads to what is called "trisomy 21," the presence of an extra chromosome in what is usually the 21st chromosome pair. Sometimes, this occurs during the cell division state (mitosis). In that case, one cell has too many chromosomes and one cell has too few, leading to the relatively rare condition, mosaicism. At other times, the abnormal chromosome condition occurs during the cell reduction state (meiosis), such as occurs when there is a nondysjunction (when two chromosomes do not split apart, resulting in an extra chromosome in the soma cells) or translocation (when one chromosome attaches itself to another during the reduction stage).

Amniocentesis, a diagnostic test developed relatively recently, has been utilized to screen for Down syndrome and other conditions. The procedure consists of drawing fluid from a pregnant woman by inserting a needle into the amniotic cavity. Analysis of that fluid can determine the fetal chromosomal structure as well as, for example, the sex of the organism. Utilization of this technique has prompted an increase in therapeutic abortions.

Such abortions raise the question of ethics, especially in the face of the uncertainty concerning the future course of the child's development as well as with respect to the question that continually arises: Are all human beings equally valuable as human beings? These vexing issues and quintessential questions are discussed at length later in this book (see Gould, 1982, for a fascinating account of the history of Down syndrome that combines the drama of science and politics, humanism and racism, great scientific achievement and common scientific misdirection).

Of course, there are other chromosome-related conditions that have been known to lead to mental retardation and other anomalies. XYY (Jacob's) syndrome involves the presence of an extra Y chromosome in the male. This condition has evoked great controversy and speculation concerning the relationship of abnormal chromosomal development to criminal and other antisocial behavior. Probably arising from nondysjunction of the sex chromosomes in normal parents, such abnormalities have been the center of widespread controversy concerning eugenic control, sterilization, and other societal measures to prevent procreation of people so afflicted (whether they have actually broken laws or not).

It is possible that, as more abnormal chromosomal conditions are identified — more than 60 such conditions have been discovered in recent years — we will witness an increase in amniocentesis and thus an increase in so-called therapeutic abortions. Now that amniocentesis has moved out of the realm of experimentation and into the realm of general obstetric care, such predictions seem warranted.

Educational and Psyochometric Classifications

After the establishment of IQ tests in the schools early in the twentieth century, mentally retarded children were classified by intelligence — that is, psychometrically. In general, so-called "idiots" had IQs that defied measurement — they were "untestable." Children with IQs between 20 and 50 were termed "imbeciles." "Morons" had IQs between 50 and 75. Children with "borderline" intelligence had IQs between 75 and 85.

Shortly after World War II, the nomenclature changed in the public schools. Children with serious mental retardation, especially with IQs lower than 25, were identified as "custodial." Children with IQs between 25 and 50 were called "trainable," and children with IQs between 50 and 75 were called "educable." Functionally, all children were categorized in two major ways — eligible or ineligible for public school placement and eligible or ineligible for special education. Traditionally, eligibility for public school placement was based on the following criteria: must not present a danger to themselves or others, must have clean bodily habits, and must be able to communicate sufficiently well with other people so as to understand simple directions and commands as well as to be sufficiently understood as to be able to communicate their needs and interests. Consequently, a child who suffered from uncontrolled seizures may have been excluded or exempted from school because there was insufficient assurance that he or she could be adequately protected in the school environment. A child who needed a wheelchair might have been excluded from school because he or she presented a danger to the teacher who might need to carry the child to a second-floor classroom; or the child might have been unable to exit the building with sufficient speed in case of fire or other emergency. A child who was not toilet trained could be excluded or exempted from instruction in a public school because it was felt that teachers should not be burdened with the consequences of soiled clothes. Finally, a child who could not understand ordinary speech or make his other needs known could have been prohibited from participation in a program.

Today, school systems are required to accept virtually every child for enrollment; these so-called zero reject policies are implemented by states and local communities. The formerly used criteria for school inclusion are no longer defensible. Notwithstanding, it is probable that schools continue to exclude or exempt (unofficially) children from public education exactly because they are seen as dangerous to themselves or others, are not sufficiently in control of their bodily functions, or lack sufficient language to meet the demands of the teacher or other school officials.

Today, the term mental retardation is no longer as universally accepted as it was, for example, 30 or 40 years ago. Some states use the term mentally handicapped or mentally impaired, and frequently disabled is used in lieu of retarded. Especially in more affluent communities, children labeled learning disabled include those who once might have been categorized as educable mentally retarded.

To be sure, even long before Shakespeare's observation that "a rose by any other name remains a rose," and certainly before Gertrude Stein's provocative comment that "a rose is a rose is a rose," human beings were wont to change the names of things and then were puzzled by what it all meant. In mental retardation, we have changed the names of things almost as frequently as the fashion designer changes hems and, possibly, with little more significant consequences.

Special Characteristics: Physical, Personality, Academic, Social, Vocational

There has been for years a virtual sea of studies on the characteristics of mentally retarded persons (Blatt, 1956). You will be very much misled by the literature on this topic if you do not carefully examine the context of such discussions. You will also be misled if you do not keep in mind that mentally retarded people, like all people, are not uniform, that mental retardation should not be viewed as a unitary pathological condition, that *all* people vary in traits, interests, and performance. Human variance exists on all dimensions.

From the plethora of studies, you will find that research on physical characteristics asserts that retarded people may be afflicted with very severe physical anomalies, or, conversely, they may look a relatively normal picture vis-à-vis height, weight, motor ability, strength, and other physical attributes. Why is this so? On the one hand, mental retardation can be a direct consequence of central nervous system impairment, such impairment causing not only retardation (usually severe or moderate), but also various other significant problems, such as cerebral palsy, seizures, physical stigma of one type or another, respiratory and cardiac disorders, hearing and visual disorders, and many other disorders. The damaged brain can cause retardation *and* visual disorders or hearing disorders. Damage to the motor areas of the brain can cause cerebral palsy or other motoric disorders.

On the other hand, the great majority of children who are identified as mildy mentally retarded — the so-called educable group — do not appear to have neurological impairment of any special consequence and, consequently, may be robust physically. The literature in mental retardation clearly indicates that there is a strong relationship between physical disabilities and mental retardation among those people who have neurological disorders. Conversely, there is a very weak relationship between physical disabilities and mental retardation among those people whose retardation is not associated with any demonstrable central nervous system impairment.

Insofar as personality characteristics are concerned, too, there is a sea of studies. Through the years, mentally retarded people have been often characterized as delinquency-prone. At the same time, research indicates that mildly retarded people are more likely to be from a low socioeconomic group. Low socioeconomic status, in turn, has been shown to be correlated with delinquency. Does retardation predispose the individual to delinquency, or does living in an environment where there are many delinquents predispose the individual to such behavior? I believe that the latter is more likely. Another common characterization is that mentally retarded people are unable to secure, keep, and successfully engage in employment in the "real world." It should be noted, however, that when everyone who can work is given an opportunity to work — such as World War II — mildly retarded people not only secured positions in war factories and in the military as well as elsewhere, but they were quite successful at their work. Yet another common assertion is that mentally retarded people may have more emotional disorders than other groups, but scholars have also observed that such behavioral problems are likely to be more a function of a hostile social environment than a function of mental retardation. Some scholars are surprised not by the fact that there is a higher incidence of emotional disorders among mentally retarded persons than among other groups, but by the fact that so many mentally retarded persons enjoy perfectly normal and happy lives, and exhibit perfectly normal and well-adjusted personalities.

The post-school success of some mentally retarded persons offers cautious optimism to those who would examine the research literature. Essentially, many mildly mentally retarded adults function reasonably well in the ordinary world. They may have been special as children, but they secure jobs, marry, have families, vote, and live relatively successfully in their communities. Particularly since World War II, moderately retarded persons have been able to secure and hold jobs when opportunities were there for them to work. Today, people who were once labeled "hopeless"—severely retarded individuals—are living in group homes and other community domiciles. Such people surprise us not by their global dependency on caretakers but by the relatively independent and semi-independent lives they have made for themselves. If all of this appears optimistic, it should be noted that the field of mental retardation has for too long been characterized by unusual pessimism. One form of hyperbole begets another.

7.

Explanations of Mental Retardation

HOW CAN WE EXPLAIN mental retardation? We can define it—not easily, to be sure, but we do it. We can classify by etiology, by intelligence quotient, by adaptive ability. We can worry about those people so affected. We can worry about our treatments and programs. But how do we explain it—to ourselves, to retarded persons themselves, to others?

One of the most common ways of explaining mental retardation is in terms of what is wrong with those who have it. Or mental retardation is explained by comparing it to other conditions.

This chapter discusses explanations of mental retardation that have been developed by several scholars. To some degree, scholars' explanations of mental retardation shape the popular conception in the home and the community. An understanding of what's wrong with retarded persons was articulated for the man in the street by those who, years before and in much more rarified atmospheres, created special language forms to satisfy scientists and other academics. Eventually, those understandings filter down to everyone. Histories are written, if not made, by scholars. And ideas and theories are developed if not implemented by them. Of course, the man in the street spreads the stories about people that scholars discover or invent. We're all implicated. Each of us has opportunities to do mischief or good.

An explanation always leads to something—a program, a treatment, or a decision to do nothing. And to a great degree, the controversies surrounding the explanations of mental retardation are much deeper, much more pervasive, more troubling, and seemingly more insoluble than the explanations themselves. Many of the controversies in the field of mental retardation arise from the excessive application of good ideas: If a principle applies in one case, it is assumed to apply in all cases. If an institution appears to be serving its clients adequately, then the institution is enlarged. If mainstreaming is good under carefully developed conditions and treatment programs, then "everyone" belongs in the mainstream — whether there are adequate programs available for those people or not. If certain mentally retarded people have brain damage and need very specialized medical, educational, and other professional attention, then *all* people designated as mentally retarded have demonstrable brain damage; if some need specialized services, then *all* mentally retarded people need the array of specialized programs and personnel that professionals seem determined to provide — sometimes whether needed or not.

Keep this in mind as you read the following sampling of explanations of mental retardation, which represents only a few of *many* explanations.

What's Wrong With Retarded People?

At no time is it more apparent that facts and data cannot be interpreted in isolation from the context of which they are a part than when we attempt to "explain" that thing we call "mental retardation." For sure, something is wrong, or there would not be the fuss, the anguish — the attention lavished on some, and the utter neglect of others. But it isn't that *one* thing is wrong, as is the case when someone breaks a leg. And it isn't that there is a shared understanding of what's wrong, as is the case when the dreaded news is cancer or a defective heart valve. The explanation of mental retardation *always* depends on who is doing the explaining, or who is receiving the explanation, on where the explanation is given and received, on when it is given and received. Mental retardation is a concept the significance of which approaches comprehension to the extent that the "beholder" comprehends. Perhaps the most basic shared comprehension about mental retardation is the widespread belief that, while mental retardation won't kill you, if you have it, you can *never* rid yourself of it.

Discussing "what's wrong" implies that there is or will be knowledge of what's right. Of course, that's not always the case. Sometimes a wrong is never rectified, either because we do not know it is wrong or we do not know how to make things right. If you pick up the wrong book, you need to make a simple judgment, requiring only that *you* do not appreciate the book. You throw the book away, or you give it away, or return it to the library, or return it to a shelf. No one is harmed, no one is penalized.

What's "wrong" with retarded persons can sometimes be corrected; but all too often society concludes that nothing can correct it. That widespread belief about mental retardation is one of the few enduring pessimisms in our society. And it causes mischief, especially in this our culture, where that uniquely New World belief endures: that every mistake can and should be corrected, and every problem can and should be solved.

Sometimes, the professional's diagnosis of the disease—that which is wrong with the patient—does not at all reflect the patient's (or client's or pupil's) idea of the problem. Suffering is a good analogy. Since ancient times, physicians have been obliged to relieve suffering (Cassell, 1982). Notwithstanding, suffering is not usually the prepotent issue on the mind of the doctor or the dentist. What is uppermost is the desire to cure the illness, fill the cavity, or set the broken bone. Yet, as Cassell pointed out, suffering is not found in the locus of the shattered limb or cancerous tumor. Those parts of the body may hurt, but suffering envelops the total person, not only the body but the mind and the soul. The dermatologist removes a mole that may be malignant, and the patient is cured. But the patient suffers—not because he or she is cured, but because there is a scar on a once-beautiful face. The disabled boy is placed in a special class to improve his reading, but he suffers each day it is confirmed that he is "different" and needs to be separated from the other children. So people suffer; their anguish is often not acknowledged and thus it is never validated. The disabled boy's solitary suffering causes him to wonder whether anyone cares about him, or whether he is sufficiently mature, or even sufficiently sane. After all, no one but *he* thinks about his plight; no one but *he* knows that he suffers. No one but *he* has such a depressing view of life. As Cassell reminded us, sickness can cause suffering, but the cure, too, can contribute to suffering. As he (1982) also asked, "How could it be otherwise, when medicine has concerned itself so little with the nature and causes of suffering?" (p. 644). Despite difficulty in communicating their feelings to others, retarded people themselves are probably the only ones who truly understand the almost infinite ways they suffer, and how society's reaction to them—rather than the retardation itself—is their greatest burden.

Explanation by Comparison

Mental retardation can be profitably illuminated when cast in relationship to other phenomena, particularly those which are susceptible to similar misunderstandings. Mental illness is a case in point. Szasz illuminated the idea of mental illness with an analogy to witchcraft:

> In the fifteenth century, men believed that some persons were witches, and that some acts were due to witchcraft. In the twentieth century, men believe that some

people are insane, that some acts are due to mental illness. Nearly a decade ago, I tried to show that the concept of mental illness has the same logical and empirical status as the concept of witchcraft; in short, that witchcraft and mental illness are imprecise and all-encompassing concepts freely adaptable to whatever uses the priest or physician (or lay "diagnostician") wishes to put them. (Szasz, 1970, p. xix)

Szasz (1970) also made an analogy between the mental health movement and the Inquisition. Similarly, there are connections among movements such as mental health, mental retardation, gerontology, and other "social welfare" movements, and religion in general, or a religious denomination or persecution in particular. Such analogues are not only fascinating, but they are also illuminating to those who are not so angered by them that they cannot see them. Quite possibly, Szasz' great contribution to society will be less the idea of the "myth of mental illness" than the idea that *all* religions — those connected with God and those connected with Science — are metaphors. And while it was Szasz who contributed the idea that mental illness is a myth (i.e., a metaphor), it was people such as Robert Frost and Robert Lowell, T. S. Eliot, James Joyce, Wallace Stevens, and others who have taught us that only the poet in a person can prevent victimization by either the doctor or the priest, the school or the institution. Thinking about the connections between mental retardation as an academic field and religion conjures up analogues: Priest and Doctor; Bishop and Distinguished Professor; the Pope and Sigmund Freud; the Reformation and Dorothea Dix; the Advocates and Upton Sinclair; the Thanksgiving Basket and "Meals on Wheels"; the Ten Commandments and the Canons of Science; the Bible and the Classic Textbook; the Biblical Commentaries and the Archival Journals.

There are further analogies between mental retardation (and related disciplines such as psychiatry) and religion. Like Christianity and Judaism, mental retardation and psychiatry teach people precepts for how to live. But the religion of psychiatry and the religion of mental retardation differ from Christianity and Judaism in at least one fundamental way. While the latter two religions attempt to teach us how to find eternal salvation, psychiatry and mental retardation attempt to teach us how to endure in the here and now. And while Christianity and Judaism measure us against an Almighty God's commandments, psychiatry measures us not against God's image or wishes, but against the norms prescribed by society. While Christianity and Judaism do not condemn us because we cannot fly, the fields connected with mental retardation directly or indirectly condemn us if we are not in "step" with society, or if we are out of "focus" with reality. The point of course is not that one should better be able to go to the state institution to "pray," or to the psychiatrist to be married or buried. The point is that orthodox religion and orthodox professional practice in mental retardation share certain underlying commonalities; both rely on theories concerning how people are created and developed; regard their leaders as (more or less) final authorities; have designated places in which to engage in their activities; record their histories in books and other documents of varying importance and durability; claim to recognize what is good and bad, right and wrong; advocate obedience to certain ideals and causes and self-sacrifice to certain missions; and make claims and predictions about the consequences of their endeavors.

How to Destroy Lives by Telling Stories

A controversy occurs when there is more than one story and each story claims to be the "truth." Everyone knows that one person's truth is another's poison; yet at a given moment people tend to think they have the "truth," elusive or nonexistent as it usually is, disillusioning as it always becomes. Jan Harold Brunvand (1981) collected a group of stories that have endured not because they are true, but because they serve a purpose; they have underlying messages. There is the story, for example, of giant alligators who live in a city's sewers, descendents of tiny inoffensive pets brought home from Florida vacations. There is the story of bathed dogs dried off in microwave ovens, and the one about the unlucky fellow served fried rodent in a franchise restaurant instead of the standard chicken fare. One after another, the stories are recounted, many familiar to us, stories that have made the rounds in groups everywhere. Why do these stories persist? Brunvand suggested that they are important. There is a moral embedded in each of them, lessons to be learned. As each story has something to teach us, each has a lesson to be learned. Every story can enhance a life or destroy it. Every story can lift us or depress us. Every story can make a hero or a scapegoat. Stories sustain if not make a person's world. And, thus, the storyteller holds a certain power (and responsibility), for the storyteller is usually safer than those about whom he or she spins tales.

In the field of mental retardation, there is the story of the diabetic woman who wanted to use the local Call-A-Bus service for handicapped, sick, and elderly people. She had an infection in her only remaining big toe and had to go to the hospital every day for treatment. She could not afford cab fare, so she phoned Call-A-Bus. They asked her if she was going to get better. She said she hoped so. "They told me that in that case, I wasn't eligible."

There is the story about the English pediatrician who gave a lethal drug to a newborn baby with Down syndrome because his parents did not want him to survive. Three days after his birth, the baby died. Similarly, there is the story of the hospital that did not contest the parent's decision to deny surgery to a Down syndrome newborn, thus sealing the baby's fate to die several days later at one of our great medical centers. There is the story about courses proliferating in state institutions for workers who need to know how to protect themselves from angry and hostile residents. If a client lunges at you with both arms from the front, do this. Or if a client attempts to hug you from the back, do that. On and on, there is a technique for each assault. A move to counter every violent lunge and thrust. In this story, the worker who is taught to expect "violent monsters" may eventually encounter or create them. There is even the story coming out of an elementary school in Rhode Island that describes the padded cells planned for children with behavior problems.

Some stories enhance life; others degrade it. So we must be careful about the stories we tell, about the ways we define ourselves and other people. Because beneath all explanations and controversies are at least two incompatible stories. We include in this chapter a set of "Rules for Telling Stories":

A. Those about whom stories are told have:
 1. The right to tell their *own* story. A man has the right to claim he is Napoleon. Children have the right to "explain" themselves with whatever fantasies they find useful. Even "madmen" have that right.
 2. The right to have *true* stories told. Every human being is entitled to the story that he is educable.
 3. The right to *good* stories. I am valuable. You are entitled to stories which confirm your value. Even criminals are entitled to stories which do not deny their value as human beings.
 4. The right to withhold participation in another's story about them and, thus, the right to stick to their own story. I am what I am!
 5. The obligation to live up to good stories. Parents try to live up to their stature as parents as children attempt to live up to parents' expectations.
B. Those who would tell stories about others must respect these rights. They have the obligation to:
 1. Listen to the stories of those about whom they tell stories. Professionals must be especially vigilant, because they *always* have their own versions to "sell."
 2. Tell good and helpful stories. Of course, there is always the question, "Help whom? And how?"
 3. Tell true stories. We must be vigilant because professional truths tend to be irrelevant and are usually sterile. More often than not, the injuries we inflict are by neglect and not by design.
 4. Take responsibility for the stories they tell. Professionals don't enjoy such responsibility. We blame "syndromes" or our victims.

C. Those who hear stories by or about others must:
1. Distrust bad or destructive stories.
2. Seek to *know* the *truth* of stories, and to *understand* the *good* of stories. Knowing and understanding can be entirely different matters.
3. Remember that they become (we become) the sum total of stories they (we) believe. It becomes their (our) story.
4. Dismiss *any* story presented as finished. Even dead peoples' stories are not ended. There are stories that need to be told about Hitler, about Sacco and Vanzetti, about Moses, and about the billions of all the "ordinary" people who left legacies and lessons to be learned. (Blatt, 1981, pp. 132-133)

Professional Attempts at Explanation

The question is insistent for a response: "What's wrong with retarded people?" The "ordinary life" perspective presses us to recount what all people need and what should be done when someone lacks what he or she needs. The "physiological" perspective seeks to discover something neurological, or biochemical, or anatomical to explain what is wrong. The "environmental" perspective seizes upon the quality of life in the city, for example, or the mother's intelligence, or the history of a family's stupidity, cupidity, or morbidity. The "sociological" perspective looks at deviance as a particular point in a particular historical phase, and at the retarded condition relative to the culture, the people who inhabit it, their aspirations, and their character. Other perspectives involve children and families who are "possessed by the devil," or children and families who are "neglected by the Lord."

Embedded in each of those perspectives, and others, is the question: Under what conditions would you change your mind that a person is mentally retarded? If we examine such a question and responses to it, we force ourselves to conclude that there is no empirical theory that "explains" satisfactorily what is wrong with retarded persons. Surely, we sometimes know how people become retarded, but we are unable to explain exactly what is wrong with them. One of the reasons why a question of the kind posed here is impossible to answer is that it is the type of question for which you can too easily get a "wrong answer"; consequently, you cannot be certain to get a "right answer." Traditional definitions of mental retardation, which demanded central nervous system impairment, incurability, and dependency, were based on a weak theoretical foundation and could not hold up in the face of overwhelming contradictory observations.

If there is such a thing as mental retardation—if there are people whose conditions cannot only be ascribed to certain causes, but whose conditions can also be discussed in terms of predicted consequences—a case can be built out of ordinary experiences that explains what is wrong with such people. If that is so, then the theoretical or technical explanation of retarded people would distinguish those people from others who are not mentally retarded. We don't have that capability, and it is not enough merely to say that this individual isn't very smart or doesn't understand. We do know that not *everyone* who fails to understand something is mentally retarded. Hence, the theoretical or technical explanation must permit a more *differential* explanation—an explanation that differentiates this individual from others not so afflicted, as well as one that differentiates the various strengths and weaknesses of the particular individual. An explanation of what is wrong with retarded people must account for how we talk about such people, short of calling them retarded. Related to this is the necessity to stipulate what it means to be retarded. The Stanford-Binet test can point out how a child succeeds and fails in the testing situation, but is the laboratory test as precise as the *in vivo* test? And if it isn't, the explanation is faulty. That is, the IQ test may be a wonderful instrument, for certain purposes, but to be valid as a measure of capability to deal with life's problems it must be able to assess and predict intelligence in real-life situations. It is not enough to say that a child with a low IQ is in a special class, or a special institution, when we know that the reason for the child being in the special class, or special institution, is in some fashion related to low IQ. The explanation must reveal for us how and why the mentally retarded person suffers with such serious chronic difficulties that he or she cannot deal with the complexities of ordinary life that other people (of perhaps equivalent intellectual abilities) deal with successfully.

What now follows are three very brief illustrative "explanations" of what is wrong with retarded persons:

Insufficient Learning in Early Childhood

Since 1952, Omar K. Moore and his colleagues have been working on understanding "human higher order problem solving" (Moore, 1982). Moore's work led to the development of procedures for studying cognitive processes of very young children (Anderson & Moore, 1960; Moore, 1960, 1961). The program they eventually developed—Responsive Environments (later "Clarifying Environments")—included the following characteristics of the learning environment:

   a. It is attuned to children's exploratory activities.
   b. It informs children immediately about the consequences of their own actions.
   c. It permits children to make extensive use of their capacities for discovering relations.

d. It is so arranged that children are likely to make a series of interconnected discoveries about some aspect of their physical, cultural, or social world. (Moore, 1960, p. 4)

Moore's hypothesis is that when human beings are comfortable, when their basic biological drives have been satisfied, and when they are afforded the leisure to do so, they will enagage in exploratory behavior. Furthermore, as their innate curiosity is being satisfied, there is an accompanying drive to manipulate the environment as well as a motive to be competent. The Responsive Environment permits the person to learn from such conditions; but it does not teach. It allows children to discover things for themselves much as they learn their native tongues. In Moore's special environment, learning is said to be "autotelic." That is, children choose the environment (either an ordinary typewriter or a specially designed automated instrument) for its own sake, and not in response to intrinsic rewards or punishments. The child can make errors or achieve without incurring other consequences. The opportunity to operate in this fashion is critical to Moore's method, for he feels strongly that anxiety and fear hamper free exploration, discovery, and consequently, learning.

Using three first-grade typical children as subjects in his earlier studies, and later involving disadvantaged and handicapped children, Moore examined the hypotheses that the young, typical, or even retarded child can learn basic intellectual and interactional skills such as typing, printing, reading, and dictation prior to first grade. The following description taken from my own work with young disadvantaged children who were members of families with high incidences of school failure may help you form a clearer picture of the program:

> Miss Smith enters Jimmy's classroom and, at a natural interval, asks him to go with her to the booth. If Jimmy does not want to go with her that day, she does not attempt to coax him but, again, suggests that it might be fun to play with the typewriter. If Jimmy decides to go, the teacher and the child go to a desk where Jimmy has his nails painted appropriate colors, corresponding with colors on the typewriter keys. This a good opportunity for the teacher to review the colors on the child's fingernails. The teacher notes the colors which Jimmy can name and any comments he makes in response to the colors, for example, "That's in my shirt."
>
> Both the teacher and Jimmy then enter the booth. (The teacher lets Jimmy take the lead.) Jimmy gets into his chair. He may need assistance, such as moving the chair closer to the typewriter. The teacher asks Jimmy if he would like to put the paper in the machine. Usually, he does this and turns the roller to an appropriate spot so he can begin to type. Jimmy switches on the machine without being asked to do so and also places in the typewriter a carbon and a second blank piece of paper. The second copy is later given to Jimmy to take home at the end of the day.

> Jimmy is beginning the first stage of training and is, at this point, exploring the keys on the typewriter. As Jimmy strikes a key, the teacher repeats each letter, number, or other symbol. She also gives the phonetic sound of each letter, with the exception of the vowels and "c-k-g-j". . . .
>
> Using her pencil, the teacher points to the letters on the paper which the child has typed. This usually draws the child's attention to the characters which he has typed and he begins to see the relationship between the keys he has typed and the characters that are immediately reproduced on the paper. The teacher asks Jimmy to repeat the letters which she is saying as he types. . . .
>
> The maximum length of time for which Jimmy may remain in the booth is 30 minutes per session. He may, however, leave whenever he desires before the time is up. When he asks to leave before the 30 minutes, the teacher suggests that he type some more to see if he really wants to leave. If he does wish to leave, the teacher asks him to switch off the machine and take the paper out. This he can do. The teacher and Jimmy leave the booth. She gives him a copy of the work he has typed in that session and accompanies him back to his classroom.[1]

Essentially, Moore's explanation of mental retardation is that the condition arises from inadequate or insufficient early learning. Hence, with an intensive enriched preschool environment, emphasizing language development, auditory and visual discrimination and memory, quantitative thinking, motor coordination, speech training, creative and imaginative thinking, and deliberate instruction in the tools of school (reading, writing, spelling), mental retardation can be prevented with some children, ameliorated with others, and possibly even reversed with still others (Blatt & Garfunkel, 1969).

Expectations

Related intimately to the work of such people as O. K. Moore, whose curricula might be thought of as technical exemplars of the educability hypothesis, is the even larger group of scientists who have studied and attempted to better control natural environments. Such work has led to speculations concerning the possibility that people can change, on the one hand, and that mental retardation might be explained in terms of insufficient opportunity to learn, on the other hand. For example, while Moore hypothesized that a specially crafted technical environment can prevent or remediate mental retardation, Jerome Kagan speculated that some cultures enhance learning while other cultures blunt intellectual development (Kagan,

---

[1] From *Intellectually Disenfranchised: Impoverished Learners and Their Teachers* (pp. 120-123) by B. Blatt, 1966, Boston: Commonwealth of Massachusetts, Division of Mental Hygiene. Reprinted by permission.

1972). Years ago, Kagan discovered a small village in Guatemala. There he found children who "broke the rules" of child development, but nevertheless eventually prospered. It is a compelling story. His initial impressions were of poor and exploited Indians. Their infant children appeared to live in the most impoverished and unstimulating environments—isolated in their homes, apathetic and passive, timid, deprived. But Kagan also observed extraordinary and, at first, inexplicable, disconfirming evidence. The older children in the community—the eleven-year olds—were active, stimulated, stimulating, and competent. How could all of this be explained? Kagan answered his own question with an analysis of the Guatemalan village culture—the beliefs of the people, their cultural morés, and their expectations for their children. Essentially, it is the practice in such villages to intentionally place children in what in our terms would be nonstimulating early environments. Those same children, however, are *expected* to assume eventually dominant and competent roles in society. The children are *expected* to become competent and, thus, they *become* competent. "Educability" can be examined and understood not only as a developmental process, but also as an expectation.

Inattention to Prosthetic Supports

B. F. Skinner and his collaborators and followers have explained mental retardation in terms of the lack of what Ogden Lindsley called "prosthesis" (Lindsley, 1958, 1960, 1964a). They and others involved in behavioral analysis research have identified various specific problems among retarded persons, and in a number of situations have developed ways to circumvent or mitigate those problems. Hence, there has been an extraordinary increase during the past 20 years of behavior modification or operant conditioning programs for retarded persons—especially for the more severely retarded and multiply handicapped individuals. Such programs have dealt primarily with toileting behavior, eating, dressing, aggressiveness, self-injurious behavior, and language. Basically, such work attempts to isolate the particular behaviors to be shaped, and then a program is constructed to enhance those behaviors through a process of reinforcing even the smallest incremental improvement. The work they have demonstrated has been impressive. While I would debate whether mental retardation is curable and/or preventable, there is little doubt that it is modifiable. In a sense, eyeglasses are to the eyes what behavior modification may be to the brain.

Of course, there are many other explanations and treatments of mental retardation. These range from psychoanalytic and sociological accounts of "what's wrong" to anatomical and physiological arguments. The "what to do" part of the puzzle has also witnessed many types of interventions—

some ludicrous, some ingenious, some actually palliative if not curative. Although the questions have been studied and pondered from myriad perspectives, they nevertheless remain.

8.

The Controversies

SOME CONTROVERSIES are settled by evidence and rules of discourse, others by statements of faith and values, still others by political considerations. In science, controversy is settled by evidence and laws of discourse. But religion, evidence and rational discourse usually have little to do with the settlement of arguments. Is the Sabbath on the sixth or the seventh day? And which is the seventh day? In such an argument, what counts as evidence? In order to settle any controversy, it is necessary to first agree on what counts as evidence. And while the "limiting case" can be illuminating, it can also be misleading. For every Helen Keller, there is one who did not have an Anne Sullivan, but nevertheless prospered. But for every Helen Keller, there are many who did have an Anne Sullivan, and perished. It is important to remember, too, that where controversy is concerned, every overstated admiration engenders an overstated malignment; every enthusiasm engenders a contervailing depression. Controversy begets ambiguity as well as heat.

In the field of mental retardation, scientific evidence rarely settles the most important arguments satisfactorily. Rather, those arguments — nature/nurture, cure/permanence — are usually settled by explication of a set of values. We can attempt to settle those controversies by science. We can also attempt to settle them politically, as has been the case, to some degree, in the United States (e.g., Head Start). The political settlement of an argument involves various factions wanting to know about the substance of the argument, so that they can either do something about it or not do something about it. That situation leads to a political controversy.

It is hoped that, out of a discussion such as this, you will be in a better position to place these "controversies" in a more comprehensible context. It is also hoped that, out of such reading, you will be able to view with greater honesty and equanimity the human condition — and accept the idea that you cannot truly look at yourself without disappointment, and that you cannot truly look at others without at least some disillusionment. Possibly, a person's greatest strength is long life; there is time for many starts, many corrections, many opportunities to settle controversies. What follows are commentaries on key issues facing the field of mental retardation.

Nature/Nurture

The nature/nurture argument will not be settled easily. Already, we have a glut of reasonable commentary on the problem. For example, during Walter Lippmann's years as chief editorial writer on the *New York World* and as a regular contributor to *The New Republic,* he wrote about many of the country's serious problems — such as freedom of the press, social injustice, world government, *and* the nature/nurture argument (Steel, 1980). In a series of six articles for *The New Republic,* Lippmann explored the value and potential mischief of the then relatively new intelligence test, the Stanford-Binet, touted at the time as a guaranteed measure of innate capacity. Lippmann was skeptical, and concluded that the test had been oversold, misinterpreted, and used by some to justify social segregation. His examination of the Stanford-Binet led him to the conclusion that the test simply did not measure innate capacity. He challenged the claims of scientists who were eager to show that they could measure innate capacity, and he also questioned the motives of at least some of them, and — if not the motives — at least the damage they were perpetrating with their pseudoscientific dogma. His articles set up a controversy then, and while the content of such a controversy would probably be different today, it would no doubt be stirred if those same articles were to be published in current issues of *The New Republic* (Steel, 1980).

Gould's (1981) discussion of the nature-nurture argument might have clarified the question somewhat had not the particular argument been so close to the core of the human experience.

There is hardly any other issue that can be counted on more to inflame, enrage, entice, or infect the human mind and spirit than the proposition that differences among human groups and individuals arise from inherited factors, or conversely, from environmental influences. Of course, even the most zealous nativist knows that environment plays a part in shaping character and behavior. On the other hand, even the most rabid environmentalist knows that there are such things as genes and chromosomes, and that what we inherit contributes to our capabilities, physical qualities, and behavior. Realistically, the argument should not be about *one* or the *other* (although some debate the issues in just that way). But in reality, the nature/nurture argument has always been much less concerned with whether heredity *or* environment is *the* significant factor in determining individual and group differences than it has been concerned with the progress science is making in achieving greater precision concerning the relative weight of such influences.

Gould (1981) suggested two fallacies that interfere with rational discourse on the question: reification and ranking. Everyone appreciates the significance of mentality in our lives. Consequently, we invent the word "intelligence" and assign it to this very complex array of human capabilities. In time, the symbol for mentality, "intelligence," reifies the concept of a contrived, unitary trait for which we have invented a name, and eventually, for which we have invented a way to quantify. This leads to the second fallacy, ranking. If we can take a set of complex, even independent, capabilities and join them under a newly minted label, "intelligence," then we can rank individuals and/or groups by that global attribute. Of course, to achieve an acceptable system of ranking, we must devise some method to assign status—hence, the IQ test.

Added to the impossibility from the outset in achieving a workable designation and measure of what we call "intelligence" are the many other problems associated with the nature/nurture question. Thus, there has been failure standing on the supposedly scientific shoulders of prior failures. Gould, as have others, questioned not only the wisdom of the early measurement pioneers, but in several cases, their academic honesty in the context of today's understanding of what is and isn't proper. Added to the already devastating attacks on the integrity of Cyril Burt is Gould's new information concerning the intellectual honesty of that early twentieth century leader in the field of mental retardation, Henry Goddard. Most of the academic scandals in the field of mental retardation during this century, it would seem, have been primarily connected with the examination of the nature/nurture problem. Is it a coincidence?

To this day, the nature/nurture controversy continues unabated, undiminished, and relatively uninformed. To this day, the controversy is dressed in "scientific" clothes, in spite of the fact that these scientific arguments are debated on grounds of faith rather than through the application of scientific methodologies to examine testable hypotheses. Never mind that any number of our greatest scientists have already concluded that the issue cannot be resolved scientifically—not when there are 40,000 genes, not when a gene can barely be seen much less understood, not when the argument is more religious and political than it could ever be scientific. But for the record, I seek here to summarize the issues.

Elsewhere in this book, I have discussed the nature/nurture controversy in terms of the history of the field, the metaphors of mental retardation, incidence and prevalence, classification schemes, and in various other contexts. Here, I will focus on what Gould (1981) identified as *The Mismeasure of Man*. Many of our great American heroes believed without doubt that the average white person is superior to the average black person. Essentially, the black/white controversy is not greatly different from the more general nature/nurture controversy, and, for that matter, with the narrower question of whether mildly mentally retarded people who exhibit no central nervous system organicity inherit mental retardaion or acquire it in some fashion. These kinds of debates have been with us for centuries, differing more about how such variance is measured and why it occurs than whether or not it exists. That is, we have "always" had arguments about ethnic, racial, and religious differences; in a sense, that is what wars are all about, or, to put it more positively, that is what we mean by "nationalism" or "religious conviction." It should also be remembered that the recent "Black is Beautiful" campaign may have been a strategy that is new to North American blacks, but that was necessitated by the overbearing and pervasive campaigns that whites have been conducting ever since landing on these shores. Campaigns informed Indians, blacks, and immigrants that "Caucasians are beautiful, whites in general are more capable, Western civilization is better, and Anglo-Saxon and Nordic whites are best." Fueling these debates, especially on the side of those who consistently found whites to be superior, were the data collected on virtually every possible anthropometric measure available. The data brought together the monogenists and the polygenists: the one explaining white superiority in terms of linear hierarchies of races that left blacks low on a phylogenic scale in comparison with whites; and the other admitting a common ancestry in prehistoric times but concluding that the races had been apart long enough to evolve significant differences in capability and intelligence (Gould, 1981). This is by way of saying that those who believed in "one Adam" and "one race" made their peace with those who believed that God had created many distinctly different peoples. What resulted was a "comprehensive evolutionism" that accommodated monogenists and racists and that, during the decades from approximately the Civil War era to World War II, was encouraged by the work of one prominent scientist after another.

For the reader interested in this fascinating history, one which includes the work of Broca, Lombroso, Galton, Binet, Goddard, Terman, and several of our contemporary scientists, you may not find a more informed source than Gould. Suffice it to summarize this section with several conclusions about the nature/nurture issue:

1. Our earliest statesmen, philosophers, and scientists were more often than not racists. That is, in whatever ways they achieved such a prejudice,

there was a fundamental belief that blacks are biologically inferior to whites, and that other nonwhites are also inferior to whites.

2. Since early in the American experience, various kinds of anthropometric data have been collected to "prove" not only the intellectual but also the physical, moral, and spiritual superiority of whites. It's inconclusive whether the "allure" to the scientists was with the problem—the nature/nuture argument—or the numbers themselves. It's enough to note that virtually "everything" was measured, everything compared, every possibility studied.

3. The intelligence test was embraced on these shores and sustained here with far more vigor and attention than it ever received in Europe. While not our invention, it became our love.

4. The hereditarian theory of intelligence, which grew out of the widespread measurement of intelligence, *was* an American invention, and persists to this day as almost singularly American. It isn't that the idea of inherited intelligence had not crossed the minds of people in the various European and, for that matter, Third World countries, but that such an idea never really sustained the interest or received the almost obsessive popularity that it enjoys to this day in the United States.

5. From Goddard to Burt to various proponents of special drugs and diets, lobotomies, lobectomies, and special educational or therapeutic programs, it seems that the major academic scandals in the broad fields of psychology and special education—and in the narrower field of mental retardation—have revolved around the nature/nurture argument. Unfortunately, scientists working in this area have at times been driven to distrust the data in order to prove a case—sometimes because the scientist was impatient to prove that intelligence is essentially inherited, and other times because the scientist was impatient to prove that intelligence is educable.

6. The controversy continues and probably will continue until we realize that while it is the legitimate task of scientists to examine the nature/nurture argument, the job of the clinician *is not* to make a determination whether people can or cannot change, but to make it come true that people can change. The nature/nurture argument may well remain of interest to scientists, but it is not useful—and is probably destructive—to those who should direct their efforts to the work of creating and implementing programs that help people to learn.

Throughout this book, I return again and again to the nature/nurture argument because it is an expression of the fundamental question in mental retardation. Can people change, can they learn, can they improve?

Moreover, irrespective of how much people can learn, what are they entitled to? Irrespective of how much people will achieve or how much they will contribute to society, what are they entitled to simply because they are human beings? The nature/nurture question is truly the beginning and the end for all fundamental discussions of this thing we call "mental retardation." All of this is by way of saying that the controversy will endure—unabated by evidence, and probably without genuine hope for final settlement during our lifetimes, at least.

This section concludes with a discussion of a paradox. The nature/nurture argument can be cast as one that will either lead to support of a "social selection" hypothesis or will lead to support of a "social stress" hypothesis. The "social selection" hypothesis posits that people inherit weak brains through weak genes, and they therefore find it difficult to do well—at first in school and later in the larger society. Those who would be sympathetic to such a hypothesis might term such afflicted individuals as "cultural familial mentally retarded," and they might consider themselves ideological progeny of Henry Goddard or disciples of Arthur Jensen.

On the other hand, there are those who support a "social stress" hypothesis. They believe that there are certain noxious environments that some people were unlucky enough to have been born into; and it's *those* influences that, from early life, blunt an individual's capability for developing normally. The cumulative effects of such a debilitating sociocultural environment may lead to mental retardation. Those sympathetic to such an explanation of how retardation occurs in otherwise physiologically normal people may have as their ideological models such early environmentalists as Itard, Montessori, and Binet. Their modern allies might include Skeels, Kirk, Gould, and Sarason.

The paradox of our contemporary society seems to be that, when all things are considered, environmentalism ("social stress") as a major factor in mental retardation appears to be an appealing explanation for the liberal; and conversely, nativism ("social selection") appears to be the inclination of the conservative. Insofar as questions concerning the mentally ill, however, it seems that the liberals have lined up in support of a "social selection" hypothesis while the conservatives tend to be counted among the "social stress" theorists. In mental health-mental illness, there is perhaps a reluctance among some people (possibly political and social liberals) to "blame the victims" for their own mental illness, or to blame parents for their children's autism. Thus, understanding of mental illness is sought in terms of metabolic disorders or other biological factors.

It may be that it's one thing (it *means* one thing!) to have a defective or weak gene, but quite another thing to have a defective or otherwise awry metabolic system—even if that damaged system obtains from a defective gene. It may be that, in mental retardation, blaming the victim means blaming genes; but in mental illness, blaming the victim means blaming the social-psychological environment. One's position regarding the nature/nurture argument, thus, depends not only on a particular moment in history and the political-social climate of the day, but it also depends on the particular disease or condition under discussion. What is a "conservative" position in one context is a "liberal" position in another. In mental retardation, it appears as if today's "good" guys were yesterday's "bad guys" and vice versa. There is not only paradox here, but the seeds for unremitting controversy. Some see truth in the "nature" evidence; others see it in the "nurture" evidence. So the arguments endure.

Cure/Permanence

Intimately related to the nature/nurture argument is the controversy concerning the curability of mental retardation. Before 1959, mental retardation was *defined* as incurable, irremedial, without hope for even amelioration. Today, the heretofore settled question is left open to discussion since retardation is defined functionally. That is, if a person "behaves retarded" (with low IQ and an adaptive deficit), he or she is retarded; possibilities concerning remediation are neither advanced *nor* discouraged in the definition. Notwithstanding, the very thing that the definition now permits, general practice continues to prohibit. To this day, there is the widespread understanding among many professionals, and among many parents and citizens as well, that mental retardation is essentially incurable, is essentially a chronic condition. To this day, cure is to many people unthinkable insofar as mental retardation is concerned. Is it any wonder that the cure/permanence controversy is so intimately bound to the nature/nurture controversy? The question again arises: Can people change, can they learn, can they improve?

There have been any number of small and large controversies surrounding the cure/permanence issue. The effort toward seeking a cure of Down syndrome, which involves several very distinguished scientists, including Clements Benda and Henry Turkel, has engendered controversy. The arguments concerning surgical procedures with retarded persons once snared such luminaries in the field as George Jervis and other prominent neurologists. The arguments concerning the etiology of infantile autism and possibilities for amelioration, a debate begun by the distinguished pediatrics professor Leo Kanner, is continued to this day by such prominent scholars as Bernard Rimland. And of course there have been many arguments about instructional techniques that are based on the cure/permanence issue—controversies about the desirability of special methods and procedures, special curricula, special *something* that have been designed to prevent, reverse, or ameliorate mental retardation. Although these efforts have proven to be largely unproductive, efforts have not ceased. Skeels and his associates, for example, studied the mental development of adopted or otherwise unwanted children with inferior social histories, influences on their development, and the correlates of intelligence. On the basis of a lifetime of studies, Skeels made a persuasive case in support of "educability." Twenty-five years later Jensen (1973) claimed that any reasonable and proper analysis of the Skeels data would lead to the conclusion that there are strong hereditary factors associated with mild mental retardation.

As the nature/nurture controversy is surrounded by prejudice and misinformation, the intimately connected controversy concerning curability is, if anything, hotter, deeper, and more passionate. In that chasm between rational argument and the goal for understanding lies wasted careers, chicanery, and even academic dishonesty. But amid the rubble dotting that woeful landscape are a few facts, a few good ideas, and many good intentions.

In his Bingham lecture before the American Psychological Association, Cyril Burt reviewed the history of the mental testing movement and its findings concerning the inheritance of capability (1957). He concluded:

> The child's innate endowment of intelligence sets an upper limit to the best he can possibly attain. No one would expect a mongolian imbecile, with the most skillful coaching in the world, to achieve the scholastic knowledge of an average child. In the same way, no one should expect a child who is innately dull to gain a scholarship to a grammar school, or one whose inborn ability is merely average to win first class honors at Oxford or Cambridge. No doubt, in any individual case the ascertainment of this upper limit can never be a matter of absolute certainty: an I.Q. derived from tests alone falls far short of a trustworthy indication. Hence education authorities, like life insurance companies, have to follow Butler's maxim, and take probability for their guide. They cannot, however, afford to risk a lavish expenditure on cases where there are fairly heavy odds against success. (p. 11)

Burt actually raised interesting questions in this paper, and left several important issues open and deserving of study. But in the last analysis, he was convinced that mental retardation is essentially incurable, essentially permanent. After all is said and done, Burt and throngs of others have decided that we can't make "silk purses out of sows' ears." While history may continue to denigrate Burt and those of similar beliefs, dismissing them as little more than footnotes to the literature (if even that), their skills with pen and voice swayed many, even convinced those in academia. The one sure lesson is that people are ready to believe, to be swayed. Thus, if Burt and his followers represent only a footnote, it is nonetheless a footnote that informs the field.

Pathology/Variance

Do mentally retarded people differ in kind or degree? In psychology, there's something known as "abnormal psychology." There appears to be a need for such a subfield in mental retardation because there is evidence that convinces psychologists that the behaviors of certain people cannot be explained by utilization of general theories of learning and personality. That is, it is believed that people with mental aberrations may best be understood through special psychological theories and hypotheses. Hence, the need for abnormal psychology.

The question before us is: Is there a legitimate psychology of mental retardation? That is, do mentally retarded children learn differently from other children? Are different personality theories required to explain their behavior? Are mentally retarded people not only intellectually slow but intellectually different? It is an important question, and one that has not generated sufficient attention among scholars in the field. Without a great deal of examination of the question, courses in many of our universities and colleges imply that the question has been resolved; that mentally retarded people (like mentally ill people) require a *different* psychology to be understood. Hence, we still find such course titles as "Psychology of Mental Retardation"; and we still find even more prevalent commentary in our literature testifying to or alluding to some sort of "subnormal" psychology.

Around this discussion of "degree" or "kind" are several interesting debates, the Milgram (1969) and Zigler (1969) argument being among the more interesting. These debates focus on whether mental retardation can be explained by developmental theories, motivational theories, cognitive theories, or theories relating to abnormality and pathology. The debate leads to questions such as: Is the root cause of mental retardation motivational? Intellectual? Is there a discrepancy between values and aspirations of children and their families as contrasted with those of the larger society? Or is there a difference—a pathology—contrasting one brain and another? Of course, some mentally retarded people have demonstrably "different" brains; but others seem to be neurologically similar to ordinary people. What else can be said, at least at this time, given what is known?

The literature on personality development, on in- and out-of-school behavior, on postschool adjustment, and other indices of adaptation to society suggests that, even those with significant intellectual weaknesses—those with moderate to severe mental retardation, and also those with associated disorders—are generally people who exhibit normal variations of the "human theme." While it is true that people who might be called severely or profoundly retarded often exhibit unusually maladaptive behavior, and are often disconcerting to others, they still follow patterns of conduct that can be identified and discussed in terms of general learning and behavior theories. Certainly, long-term study of mildly mentally retarded people inevitably leads to the conclusion that they are much more like than different from other people. It might even be claimed that, all things considered, most mentally retarded people differ from others on levels of intellectual attainment and not on the major criteria associated with adaptation to society. Furthermore, even when such differences occur, they seem to be normal variations rather than either abnormal instances of otherwise normal phenomena or attributable to a special subspecies of the human family.

In essence, I am asserting that, for the most part, mentally retarded people do not differ very significantly from other people, except for their mental retardation. Second, I am asserting that, except in rare cases — these associated with people who are also mentally ill or have other very severe disabilities — whatever differences there are among retarded persons and others are differences of degree and not of kind. Finally, I am asserting that there is little use for a special psychology of mental retardation, as there apparently is for mental illness.

Institutionalization/Communitization/ Normalization/Mainstreaming

In this section several related but distinct concepts are brought together, each of which has been many times defined, clarified, and distorted for mischievous as well as harmless purposes. What is "normal"? Isn't it normal to be "different"? What is "home-like"? Is it *like* a home, or more *like* an institution? What's the "normalization approach"? Hiding differences or capitalizing on them? Living with retarded people as a duty (a job), or as a preference (a joy)? Is it "normalizing" to foster: life or death, incarceration or freedom, to be alone or part of the throng, literacy at any price, conventionality at any price? Is it more normal to endure institutionalization or other forms of segregation than to revolt? Is it normal to want to live normally while there is enough life to live normally? Orwell called insincerity the great enemy of clear language. Let's be sincere.

Not only has mental retardation been known since "the beginning," but the very issues facing modern society about what to do with and for people with chronic mental disorders were problems generations ago. McCandless (1979) described a controversy in England more than a hundred years ago concerning the suitability of an institution to *treat* mentally ill persons, the efficacy of public asylums in contrast to community programs, and the argument between psychiatrists and other medical practitioners on what represents the treatment of choice:

In 1845 Parliament had responded by passing two acts which established the principle of state responsibility for the insane. . . .

Yet in less than 15 years many persons were expressing doubts about the efficacy of the public asylums. No one denied their advantages. Confining the insane in large central institutions made it easy to supervise their care and thus to protect both them and society from the consequences of their actions. These were important considerations and strong arguments in favor of the new system. But there was something else to be considered: did the asylums actually "cure" anybody?. . . . Statistics showed that patients seldom left the public asylums cured: indeed, they seldom left at all.

The lack of cures produced other problems, such as overcrowding. The new asylums hardly opened before they were filled with more or less permanent residents. (1979, pp. 553-554)

And the solution(s)? Again, McCandless:

"Radical" reformers demanded the implementation of some form of community care. They argued that a policy of general confinement did not cure the insane; it merely herded them together into one indiscriminate mass of misery. To subject chronic patients to the monotonous routine of asylum life was unjust and expensive, and robbed these institutions of any pretence to being curative. The best interests of the country, the patients, and the asylums would be served if the chronics were "dispersed" to the community.

The more "conservative" reformers, who included the majority of those directly engaged in the care of the insane, doubted that community care was feasible except on a very limited scale. They believed that the great majority of the insane would have to remain in some form of asylum under the supervision of the lunacy commissioners and the medical superintendents. As an alternative to the existing system, some of these reformers proposed that the asylums could become truly curative institutions if the chronic patients were separated from the curable and placed in other structures associated with the existing asylums.[1]

It is difficult to discuss institutions without engaging in controversy. After all, the Willowbrooks and Pennhursts of the world are famous for being infamous. On the other hand, one of the persistent criticisms of the deinstitutionalization movement has been the assertion that the effectiveness of community living has not been well documented. Nevertheless, the ineffectiveness of the institution has been more than adequately documented. I see no reason why vigorous examinations of community placement cannot be achieved in order to settle the question.

Within our inability to develop an adequate data base to speak to that

---

[1]From "'Build! Build!' The Controversy over the Care of the Chronically Insane in England, 1855-1870" by P. McCandless, 1979, *Bulletin of the History of Medicine, 53*(4), pp. 553-554, 556-557. Reprinted by permission.

question lies a paradox, one that may not only puzzle us but one that may offer illumination. The paradox can also be discussed in terms of another question (possibly, paradoxes are best discussed by indirection): Has there been a conclusive demonstration of the effectiveness of living in one's natural home? Some may think this is a silly question. After all, the overwhelming majority of people in our society live in ordinary homes. What does it mean to document the effectiveness of one's home? Some homes are good; some are not so good. Some homes are good according to so-called objective criteria, but nevertheless, there are people who do not like to live in them. And there are other homes that are not so good as measured against objective criteria, but people nonetheless seem to prefer living there. It is virtually impossible to implement a serious study of the effectiveness of ordinary homes, or ordinary communities, or society.

Of course, many informed people write compelling papers on home life in America (or elsewhere), or American culture. People describe home life in America, or in certain segments of our culture—and even try to do something about it. But where is there adequate *documentation* to speak to the hypothesis that home life in America is effective or ineffective? It is simply not an intelligible question. It is too large, and it is connected to an almost infinite array of other unanswerable questions. Hence the paradox.

To the degree that mentally retarded people live in ordinary homes and in ordinary neighborhoods, it becomes less and less possible to document the effectiveness of those environments. Of course, one can describe a home, or even a neighborhood, but no one can speak to whether a culture or a normal environment is good or bad. By the very fact that there is such a thing as a normal environment or an ordinary home, the question has been answered. That is what the people want. That is the regularity. Social scientists are infinitely better at describing, analyzing, and discussing variations from the norm than the norm itself. The only way to judge an ordinary or normal environment that is on both objective grounds and also has practical meaning would be to judge it—the home, the community—on institutional criteria. And who wants that? And what good would it do? Put another way, we will know that deinstitutionalization works when mentally retarded people "disappear" in the environment. In the end, that is the true test.

Basically, the institutionalization controversy has been argued in two ways: as a developmental issue, and as a freedom issue. If the advocates for deinstitutionalization have made any serious strategic blunder during the past decade or two, it may have been their insistent, almost perverse, devotion to the clinical (developmental) argument. This devotion generated debates at national and regional meetings, (more or less) scientific studies published in professional journals, and polemics published in newspapers and newsletters affirming or denying that the institution is a better place for people, that the segregated school is a better place for children, that the group home is better or that the mainstreamed class is better.

The "freedom" argument does not address the question of whether segregation or integration is "clinically better" for mentally retarded people. Rather, this argument is based on the conviction that people are entitled to live free in a natural setting, irrespective of what particular environment most enhances their reading capability or vocational aptitude. American slaves were not freed from bondage on the basis that such freedom would enhance their school capability or vocational viability. The slaves were freed on the basis of the belief that people deserve to live free. Historically, the question of freedom has been a perennial subject for discussion in religious and philosophical literature, as well as in poetry and novels. The concept of freedom is at once maddening and elusive for the individual to understand, yet either simple or impossible to achieve. That is, if one denies authority, one is free; if one accepts tyranny, one is imprisoned. It is of course dangerous to deny certain authority, but such denial always confirms one's freedom. Indeed, in the ultimate sense, if one wishes it to be, freedom is the final option. Hence, lives are laid down in its defense, and untold sacrifices are made to insure its continuance. In fact, we might think of freedom as the ultimate gift that can be conferred on the human being. In a way, a person needs to be free to maintain a personal sense of humanness. In a way, the concept of freedom is irrevocably connected to the definition of humanity. In a way, for many people freedom is a more precious gift than life itself.

Let's attempt to lay by the heels the issues surrounding the controversy over institutionalization verus community living and special classes versus mainstreaming. This preliminary discussion should lead the reader to the real debate — on freedom, and the current and future society.

Simply stated, the controversy is between those who believe that *all* children should live in ordinary communities and attend ordinary schools in ordinary classes, and those who contend that children with special needs are best served in specialized programs.

More than a decade ago, Smith and Arkans (1974) presented a persuasive case for segregated special classes for retarded children, especially for those who are moderately and more severely retarded. They summarized the literature both sympathetic and opposed to separate special classes for the handicapped and concluded that the evidence clearly is on the side of those who have resisted widespread mainstreaming of these groups. They acknowledged the various decisions handed down by the courts, the general mood of many professionals and lay people toward integration. They even acknowledged that certain "evidence" had predisposed professionals and legislators alike toward mainstreaming. Notwithstanding, they worried about children with serious problems. They found not only existing regular classes unsuitable for such children, but also various resource programs.

Why? Moderately and severely handicapped children tend to have multiple problems, and consequently they need large uncluttered environments for the specialized equipment and programming they need. Furthermore, moderately and severely handicapped children represent a relatively small proportion of those who require specialized services; and not every school has either the appropriate critical mass of children or the resources to provide suitable specialized programs. Smith and Arkans asserted that regular teachers, with their large classes and limited specialized skills, cannot give proper attention to children with serious, and often multiple, handicaps. However individualized regular classes are, they cannot meet such specialized needs. Nor were they convinced that the lifelong planning that each of these children requires can be accomplished during the school years through participation in ordinary school programs. In summary, Smith and Arkans made the serious assertion that moderately and severely retarded children require specialized personnel, specialized equipment and facilities, often specialized architectural arrangements, very small classes, and unusual auxiliary services that lessen, if they do not entirely obviate, the suitability of regular programs (or even modified mainstreaming programs) for such children.

The questions raised by Smith and Arkans bring to saliency the issue concerning an individual's right to treatment versus his or her right to be different. Such a discussion may get at the core of what it means to responsibly create and implement programs for handicapped persons. Is it more important to provide the very best clinical program possible or more important to ensure that the individual will be in a mainstreamed program? "Clinical opportunity" and "integration" are not necessarily antagonistic, but are also not necessarily compatible. That is, if "all" we must worry about is connected with providing the child with the best educational program possible, then Smith and Arkans' criticisms of mainstreaming are immeasurably strengthened. If the *primary* objective, however, is to provide that child a program in the most "normalized" environment possible, then their criticisms are weakened. Reliance on the "least restrictive environment" covenant is not always helpful in practice. That is, several courts have mandated that handicapped children should be educated in the environment that least restricts their freedom (i.e., that permits them to be most integrated). This environment must at the same time provide those individuals with the most suitable habilitative (i.e., educational) program. Those are fine sentiments, but they lack sufficiently strong or clear advice concerning *which* priority takes precedence — the need for appropriate clinical services or the need to be free in a normal setting. If the latter takes precedence, then we must necessarily compromise the clinical program. If the former takes precedence — then there must be compromises with an individual's right to be free, to be educated, and to live in a normal environment. This is the issue that must be addressed in any discussion of the treatment of handicapped people.

As noted earlier, there is no empirical documentation that supports the contention that home life is "effective." Nevertheless, an entire body of research is devoted to testing this hypothesis. Many people believe that there is no compelling research to support either approach, integration or segregation, or that the most that can be claimed is that some children fare better in separate special class programs while others do better in ordinary programs. In general, such research, sometimes called "efficacy studies," leads to the conclusion that current segregated programs—essentially special classes and special schools—are of no more observable benefit to mentally retarded persons (or, for that matter, to handicapped children in general) than are other types of class organizations and arrangements (Blatt, 1956, 1971a; Robinson & Robinson, 1976).

It is my position that integration is always preferable to segregation. I believe that, in general, people want to live with their families and friends in ordinary communities, and that most children want to go to ordinary schools. I believe that segregated settings are not good for other than temporary periods when a person needs some specific treatment. That is, I believe that it is reasonable to be in a hospital when you are sick, but it is not reasonable to *live* in the hospital. It is certainly reasonable to be alone when you want to be alone, but enforced solitude and expulsion from society is not reasonable.

As is the case in the debates over nature/nurture and cure/permanence, the debate over institutionalization seems to be unremitting. Those who argue vigorously against deinstitutionalization contend that

1. The idea of deinstitutionalization is not grounded in an empirical base—that is, there is no evidence that a retarded person's development will be enhanced in a normal community.
2. Some people are so severely retarded that they cannot benefit from any sort of educational programming—they are "custodial".
3. The community is not prepared to integrate profoundly and severely handicapped people.
4. There are both good and bad institutions and good and bad communities, with neither type of setting inherently good or bad.
5. Institutions are more economically efficient than other ways of providing services to people with severe handicaps.
6. The argument for deinstitutionalization is less "real" than political, less grounded in substance than sloganeering.

Proponents of deinstitutionalization counter that

1. It is probably true that deinstitutionalization is not grounded in an empirical base. There is sufficient face evidence, however, that normal environments are more humane.
2. The idea that some people are so profoundly retarded that they cannot benefit from any educational programming denies the real lesson to be learned from *The Wild Boy of Aveyron*: that all human beings can learn. It also denies the lesson to be learned from *Emile*: that all people are noble. It denies the lessons to be learned from the lives of Helen Keller and Anne Sullivan and thousands and thousands of other documented cases of individuals who have changed remarkably when placed in nurturing environments.
3. The idea that the community is not now prepared (or legally required) to accept profoundly retarded persons, and probably never will be, leaves us with moral paralysis. Does this mean that we are to perpetuate injustice? If it does, then what about the people who are incarcerated legally and dealt with according to the legal codes of corrupt governments?
4. The idea that there are good and bad institutions and good and bad community settings is beside the point. Variation in quality is not the issue in dispute. What is in dispute is the question of whether one approach is in principle better than the other.
5. The idea that institutions are more efficient and less expensive than community settings is truly unbelievable. The per capita expenditure for institutionalization in New York State was recently reported as at at least $53,200 a year (Slezak, 1981), and there are some state institutions in New York State that spend $100,000 a year per resident. Does anyone believe today that segregation is less expensive than normalization? I would assert that segregation is more expensive than integration both in terms of dollars and in terms of human resources. In this regard, money is less the issue than how we conceptualize the value and the potential of other human beings.
6. The contention that deinstitutionalization is little more than a slogan is puzzling in view of the fact that to this date, estimates made by federal judges, state commissioners, and even people who support continuing the practice of institutionalization indicate that thousands of people are unnecessarily institutionalized.

The institutionalization controversy has been both clarified and complicated by the intrusion of the "normalization concept." Despite its popularity, "normalization" is widely misunderstood and misused. A commonly accepted definition of the term as well as a summary of the basic concepts that constitute its foundation may help to clarify the subject.

> First, normalization means making available to all mentally retarded people patterns of life and conditions of everyday living which are as close as possible to the regular circumstances and ways of life of their society.
>
> Second, normalization means giving society a chance to know and respect mentally retarded persons in everyday life and to diminish the fears and myths that once caused society to segregate them. (Perske, 1977, p. 5)

Perske (1977) also has discussed the basic elements of normalization. What follows is an interpretive summary of that commentary.

1. The idea of a normal rhythm of the day: Retarded people wake up, dress, eat at regular intervals, and do other things people ordinarily do in the course of the day.
2. The idea of a normal rhythm of the week: People live at home, attend school or go to work, and have time for leisure and community activities.
3. The idea of a normal rhythm of the year: People take vacations, enjoy holidays together, visit sick people, attend celebrations.
4. The idea of a normal life experience: All people should have opportunities to live secure and nurturing lives, to have enriching early childhoods, to go to school, to be part of a family, to have friends through the growing years, to have lifetime friends, to work, to contribute, and to spend their later years in dignity and purposeful activities.
5. The idea that all people are entitled to respect from others: Retarded people should be paid attention to, should be in control of those aspects of their lives that they can reasonably handle (exactly as the rest of us want and need such freedoms).
6. The idea of living one's life in a heterosexual world: Boys should have the opportunity to participate in activities with girls, and men with women. Life becomes not only more colorful but more meaningful to the degree that one's life includes variety in terms of activities and people.
7. The idea that all people have economic needs: Mentally retarded people require the security, supports, and legal guarantees that the rest of us require—during our growing years, during our working years, and during our old age.
8. The idea that one's environment should be normal and should be judged on normal standards: People should live in ordinary homes and com-

munities, and the quality of those environments should be examined in light of the cultural mores and resources of society.

To the best of Wolfensberger's (1980) understanding, the current usage and original stimulation for the widespread popularity of normalization should be credited to the work of Bank-Mikkelsen, once head of the Danish Mental Retardation Service and a world leader in the field. About the same time that the concept enjoyed its beginning prominence in Denmark, it received strong endorsement and dissemination by Bengt Nirje and other Swedes. Of course, Wolfensberger himself is mainly responsible for the significant impact of the normalization concept in the United States. There doesn't seem to be much doubt that long before the actual term "normalization" gained popularity, other scholars in the field used it (Wolfensberger, 1980). But those earlier examples appear to be rather casual and tangential to the main purposes of those works. Wolfensberger found the earliest mention of the term itself in a 1966 edition of one of Maria Montessori's books. Tracking that clue to the original 1950 Italian edition, Wolfensberger was surprised to find that Montessori actually wrote about the normalization of children. Notwithstanding, even here its mention was quite tangential to the thrust of the main commentary. Wolfensberger also reported the use of the term in a Swiss journal in 1958, its presence in a Canadian journal in 1964, and its appearance in the United States in 1966 in an article by a well-known practitioner in mental retardation, Simon Olshansky.

As Lewis (1973) pointed out, throughout Western history there have been inconsistencies and vacillations insofar as attitudes and behaviors toward people perceived as mentally incompetent. We tend to be vague, uncertain, uncomfortable, threatened, and distraught in the presence of handicapped people. And when such people intrude intimately into our lives, we may even by destroyed by what we find to be intolerable relationships with them. This is not pleasant, but unfortunately it is more accurate than most of us will admit, even to ourselves. At best, there has been a social, economic, political, and psychological ambivalence toward mentally retarded persons. So it was good that Wolfensberger, Nirje and others here and abroad articulated and fostered the normalization philosophy. It implies attention to helping other people to better appreciate, better comprehend, and better understand the contributions all people (even handicapped people) can make to the quality of their own lives. It implies attention to individual differences—not merely by blurring or ignoring those differences, but by recognizing them and discovering how such differences can enrich our lives, enrich anyone's life. Normalization does not necessarily mean that the individual is to be placed in an ordinary environment without special provisions to meet his or her needs; nor does mainstreaming necessarily mean that every child is to be placed in an ordinary classroom. Normalization does not necessarily mean that a child can get along without special help; nor does mainstreaming necessarily mean that the child can always get along without special teachers, special materials, or special curricula. Mainstreaming has to do with the right each child has to a free and appropriate publicly supported education in an environment that is the least restrictive; but it does not suggest dumping the child in an untenable regular classroom, ignoring special needs, or discounting specialized teaching, equipment, and curricula.

In several profound ways, Vanier has articulated a philosophy that goes even beyond the concept of normalization (Wolfensberger, 1973). Scholar, teacher, activist, advocate, Jean Vanier saw to the establishment of commune-like residences for retarded adults—but not residences where there were "workers" and "clients." Possibly more than anyone else, Vanier was able to overcome what Sarason so eloquently described as "professional preciousness." With gladness, with joy, with the gift and need for sharing, Vanier, the international traveler, made his home with people who share his values of love and friendship—many of those mentally retarded. In an unpublished talk that he gave in Nairobi, Kenya, in 1974, Vanier remarked:

> I have had the grace and joy to live with mentally handicapped adults over the last 10 years. With friends, we have been able to create some 45 small homes for men and women who were either roaming the streets, locked up in asylums, or just living idly—though frequently in a state of aggression or depression—with families who did not know how to cope with them. These homes of l'Arche are in France, Canada, the United States, England, Scotland, Belgium, and Denmark, as well as in Calcutta and Bangalore in India; our first home in West Africa is just beginning in the Ivory Coast. Each of these homes welcomes and finds work for eight to ten handicapped men and women and for their helpers or assistants. They try to be communities of reconciliation where everyone can grow in activity, creativity, love and hope. Some of the handicapped people leave us and find total autonomy; others who are more severely handicapped, will stay with us always.
>
> It is this experience of daily living, working and sharing with my handicapped brothers and sisters that has made me so sensitive to the question of their contribution to the development of our world. A man or woman can only find peace of heart and grow in motivation and creativity if he or she finds a meaning to life.

What normalization has done for retarded persons, Jean Vanier has done for other people, seeking ways to share their lives meaningfully with those who might need them. What mainstreaming and normalization have done for special education, Jean Vanier has accomplished for humanity.

The normalization concept, possibly more than any other concept connected with deinstitutionalization, provides the fuel for the philosophical argument against institutionalization. In addition, the trends toward deinstitutionalization and mainstreaming are connected intimately with the concept of "least restrictive environment." They were fostered after the institutional scandals of the sixties and the Civil Rights movement of the seventies. They are connected with the consumer movement, citizen advocacy, and the generally heightened political activism of the public. Deinstitutionalization, normalization, mainstreaming, zero reject policy, Public Law 94-142 or any other permutation of what has almost become an Integration Revolution in the United States had been very much influenced by research concerning where people learn and grow best, what people want, and what people need. These particular arguments cannot satisfactorily be resolved by science, as they cannot be much better understood by what science uncovers. Stated another way, the integration controversy is not one of those dilemmas that presents us with a puzzle to solve as much as it is one that presents us with an opportunity to expose our values. The integration controversy has to do with how we want the shape of the future society to be rather than with what the evidence is that will dictate the future society. The integration controversy is one of those arguments that is almost completely in our hands. It has little if anything to do with what is "best" for people and virtually everything to do with what people want to make of their lives.

Notwithstanding the longevity of residents in institutions for mentally retarded people (and in the United States, mortality rates are commendably low), in a metaphorical sense there is more "killing" than "living." Here, of course, I refer to psychological killing and psychological living. At one time, people feared to go to hospitals because there was essentially one reason for going (or, at least, one consequence of going) — to die away from known people, to spare the living from the sight of death. In a way — at least metaphorically speaking — this remains the major role of the institution for retarded individuals. We spare from the living the sight of psychological death.

When there is nowhere to go but the ground which inevitably comes to each of us, one waits for death. That is what is wrong with the convalescent home. That is what was wrong with the old hospital for the "incurables." And there actually were hospitals with such names and purposes. There are hospitals today with similar names, but the names are embarrassments now, and are always explained as historical artifacts that do not reflect the character of the institutions they stand for. But even this embarrassment does not extend to the institution for mentally retarded people, which even today is called a "hospital for the incurable," a place to die, not a place to be cured (certainly), a place to be admitted, but rarely released. Just as the institution is today's version of the Hospital for Incurables, so the segregated class is a permutation of that same idea. At one time, the American institution was universally accepted, if not always admired. At best, today it is universally acknowledged as an inadequate temporary compromise with minimal standards. Likewise, the segregated special class and school used to be called the placements of choice, until newer standards and values adjusted the conception. *Aun apprendemos*; we are learning.

In the field of mental retardation, possibly more than in others, time should be spent grappling with our controversies. In that chasm between facts and rhetoric, we may find wisdom. But in our field, there are many issues where facts are not sufficient to discuss the truth. In our field, facts often become truth only when they are tested by articulated values. In closing this chapter, I should openly acknowledge — even if it is obvious — that my biases are explicitly shown. It is difficult if not impossible to discuss the fundamental controversies of the field without showing bias, and it is critical to air these major unresolved — yet insufficiently addressed — controversies.

Part 3

THE CONQUEST
OF MENTAL RETARDATION:
THE DREAM, THE ILLUSION,
AND THE REALITY

The Preacher's Lament

Bucko, this is a raw and dirty business we're in, wild and crazy. It makes you sweat too much and smell too much. It dulls your senses and hardens your sensibilities. Such work deludes us into believing we can recognize those with delusions, much less cure them. It misleads us to think we can measure thinking, when what we measure is the application of our values on thinking. And, it discourages us from attempts to improve thinking, because our metaphors about improvement preclude improvement. It sends us to dark areas for the illumination of problems, into Gehenna to find angels, in search of examples in places unexampled. Bucko, this is a pariah's business, a waste-a-human business, a disposable people business. It's evil work we're in, yet there are saints among us. It's dirty, yet there are those here who are the purest of the pure. It's dehumanizing, yet we seek a common bond for humanity. Some hate the work yet love the people. Some hate the people yet love the work. And, they do the public's work in secluded places, away from things and other people; the out-of-mind are out of sight. See what I mean? Bucko, this is a crazy business, this crazy business.

Burton Blatt

9.

The Expansion of Services: 1950s to 1970s

LIKE ANY OTHER field, like any other group, the "mental retardation culture" has a history and prehistory. We attempt to analyze and comprehend history from the works of our historians. We attempt to unravel the puzzles of prehistory from the works of our archeologists. Mental retardation too needs excavations and analyses of its early sites, people, and activities. We need such work in order to reconstruct as completely as possible the culture of our early workers, clients, and families, as well as those of the general population who observed their comings and goings and made judgments about what was done and why, and how valuable it all was to society. But despite even the best intentions, historians and archeologists never get it all exactly right. Being honest and precise may be good for soul and mind, but it's almost impossible for these people, whose main hopes are to tell plausible and interesting stories. Histories convey how we think the past may be understood, and how it actually may have unfolded. But we are also aware that, while nostalgics dream of days that can't be relived, histories unwittingly portray those that never occurred.

We may understand the archeology (the prehistory) of a culture in at least three ways: (a) analogy, (b) context, and (c) the "wear patterns" of the culture's tools, utensils, weapons, and other instruments. We can also seek to understand our prehistory from analyses of the "wear patterns" of our ideologies and practices. Then it's all further analyzed in the context of what we think we know (the history), which is interpreted and recorded in terms of facts, stories, and traditions. In this chapter, I lay out for the reader what may be a partial but plausible history of special education and the parents' movement, the press toward institutional reforms and deinstitutionalization, and the mobilization of the professions. Where there is insufficient history, I fall back on speculation, on prehistory. My assumption is that informed prehistory—albeit always unverified and probably not altogether "true"—will provide the contextual underpinnings for a more illuminating understanding of the "believed facts"—that is, of the history. Of course, there will be some people who will have little patience for history, much less that which is grounded on much speculation and academic meanderings. When one is sick, one doesn't want the doctor to tell him how much better off (if not better) he is today. When one is in pain, one wants an analgesic rather than a dissertation on anesthesia. While one suffers in the institution, one appreciates less the history of mental institutionalization than a ticket to freedom.

On the other hand, we must constantly remind ourselves that there can't be a proper prediction without a proper history. Those who fight to avoid history ultimately fight to avoid all that could be comprehended.

Special Education and the Parents' Movement

Public education has been a popular scapegoat for virtually everything known to be wrong with today's society. It is reputed to be the cause of the "sickness," as well as the deleterious side effect when it is employed as the "cure." Education is often extolled as the remedy of problems, but is also sometimes viewed as the inhibitor of measures that might genuinely relieve modern afflictions. Public education has been accused of *causing* school failures, violence and vandalism, disrespect for authority, the sexual revolution, and, ironically, the markedly reduced birth rate. It has also been accused by many as holding children unwillingly for its own selfish purposes, and, conversely, for not providing other children with proper doses of good educational medicine (and the antidotes to prevent bad education). And there are even those who contend that if the money we're putting into public education went into, for example, conservation camps, vocational training, business and industry, or defense, schoolchildren and the general society would be much better off. Notwithstanding, our unwieldy, and as some would say, monolithic, education system in the United States has produced a generally literate society—one in which 72% of all of our 15- to 19-year-olds are enrolled in school full time (in comparison with 66% in Canada, 51% in France, 51% in Germany, and 43% in the United Kingdom). Except for Japan, which reports a few percentage points higher full-time school enrollment, no country in the world has a greater percentage of its teenagers in school (Schultze & Williams, no date). Without exception, no country in the world has a greater percentage of its citizens enrolled in some form of higher education. And without exception, no country in the world has a greater percentage of its handicapped children enrolled in some form of specialized public education intended to meet their special needs.

Prior to the 1950s, most special education programs—be they for children with mental retardation or for children with visual, hearing, orthopedic, or other handicaps—were designed for children with relatively mild problems. The creation of a genuine parents' movement after World War II changed conceptions of the role of the public schools and the rights of children and their families. Without doubt, in mental retardation the parents' movement—generally anchored to the Association for Retarded Citizens— was responsible for the original development and the later deployment of programs for trainable mentally retarded children in the public schools. The coalition of parents, advocates, legislators, and citizen support led to landmark federal legislation and historic judicial decisions that have fostered an unprecedented inclusion of not only mildly but moderately and severely mentally retarded children in the public schools and related child development agencies.

Before the turn of the century, even mildly retarded children were prohibited from attending most public elementary, and quite certainly, most secondary schools. Between the decades that witnessed World War I and World War II, there was a modest development and expansion of programs for mildly retarded students in the public schools. Between World War II and the early 1970s, there was a nearly revolutionary explosion of programs for trainable mentally retarded children in the public schools as well as community programs for retarded adults of all levels of capability. During the latter part of the 1970s, and relatively unabating to this day, there has been another nearly revolutionary effort to insure the full participation of *any* retarded child (or, for that matter, any child) in the public schools. There has been a tremendous expansion of public educational programs so as to include all children—regardless of type or severity of handicap. This "zero reject" policy guaranteeing public school (or comparable educational opportunities) for all handicapped children was articulated in Public Law 94-142, but it gained much of its impetus from the parent movement. It derived its moral foundation from the working example of parent leadership, and its political strength from the mobilization *by* parents. Here was the articulation of society's fundamental respect for what parents seem to know naturally is good for their children.

It is possible that public education in the United States had its foundation in observations of the upper class that a need existed to create a system that would eventually prepare our ministers, doctors, and lawyers. And it can be claimed that universal public education was committed to the democratization of America, to the successful settlement of millions of unlettered immigrants, to the industrialization of America, and to the necessary social reforms required to maintain this as a decent society. It should be recognized that the development of special education programs for the most handicapped among us obtained from the efforts of consumers and their families *themselves*. Indeed, we should not forget that the American educational enterprise — with all of its imperfections — serves millions of people well, and part of this splendid achievement has been the special opportunities afforded handicapped individuals in our society. If there is credit to be given here, much of it must go to the demands of ordinary citizens, especially to the parents of handicapped children. At least during this period of the American experience, society proved that we need not be spectators of our condition but, rather, creators of a better future culture.

To appreciate the extent of progress made in the development of public school services for retarded children during the period from World War II to the present, we should remember that, prior to the War, the treatment of choice in the public schools was the special class or special school. Children with mild handicaps were often in regular classes, but that was more the case of a failure either to recognize handicaps or to do anything about them, rather than a conscious decision to provide special programming in regular classes for those children. Prior to World War II, few moderately handicapped children, and virtually no severely or profoundly handicapped children, found their way into the public schools — or if they did, their tenure was brief. Prior to World War II, there was homebound instruction for certain handicapped children, but this was often on a "catch as catch can" basis, and it was never available for children with chronic handicaps; that is, a child who had broken a leg, or one who had suffered from rheumatic fever, might be eligible for a homebound teacher, but never a quadriplegic child or a severely mentally retarded child. Of course, prior to World War II, there were many handicapped children in public and private residential institutions. But even at those facilities, schooling was not available to most; ironically, state schools for mentally retarded individuals usually provided schooling only for those children who actually did not belong at the state school, that is, very mildly retarded children. According to the philosophy of that day, those who genuinely belonged in the state school were placed there not for schooling but for housing.

Today, children with mild retardation are often found in regular class programs. They are now afforded the services of resource teachers, and their regular teachers are often able to receive specialized consultation and other help. Children with moderate and severe retardation are still typically found in special classes, but from time to time, these children also have been successfully placed in either part-time regular classes or other modified special education programs (Certo, Haring, & York, 1984). And, of course, such children are now in school while in years past many of them would have been excluded or exempted. Furthermore, there are now fewer segregated schools for mentally retarded children, even insofar as those with severe mental retardation are concerned. At the same time, there has been a concomitant and dramatic reduction in the institutional placement of mentally retarded children, and there have been substantial gains made in providing community alternatives for even the most severely retarded. While society has yet to be comfortable with the idea that there is more to life than merely trying to be like everyone else, it is more than ever before willing to support the rights of others who are different.

An indication of the progress that has been made in the development of public school options for mentally retarded children may be found by merely tracking the number of such children who have been enrolled in special class programs through the years. Prior to World War II, there may have been 50,000 to 75,000 retarded children in some form of special services in the public schools (Payne & Patton, 1981). Even that figure may be an exaggeration. Today, there are upwards of a million retarded children in special education programs. The general population increase doesn't account for this extraordinary gain. Again, we must look to social and legal milestones for explanations—the parents' movement, the civil rights movement, litigation, legislation, and an awakening Amrican consciousness concerning handicapped people. While it may be true that movements—like promises and legal mandates—are easier to articulate than implement, without them can there be reform, much less extraordinary gain?

The Revival of Conscience

Many believe that institutions for mentally retarded persons in the United States have failed so completely, have so lacked decency and hope, that they beg to be evacuated. Then why haven't they been evacuated? Why is it that, rather than evacuation, the insistent demand is for yet more evaluation? Those questions both illuminate the complexity of the deinstitutionalization problem and increase the doubt that there will be a general abandonment of the institutional model during our lifetimes—or our children's. While the exposés have been many, and while the reforms have been significant, little in the way of systematic deinstitutionalization has occurred. Wolfensberger (personal communication) has pointed out that there are essentially two types of deinstitutionalization: the genuine kind, which is normalizing; and the apparent kind, which mostly has to do with the shifting of funding for people from the state to the federal government, shifting the place of residence, and defining the new institution with terms and metaphors different from the old ones.

There are many reasons for our inability to take advantage of the now widely recognized hopelessness of the institution. For one thing, each state has a major investment in institutional facilities, and to abandon them might create fiscal and/or political embarrassment. Each state has an "army" of institutional workers, generally organized and represented in the state's legislature by people whose political careers are tied intimately to continued endorsement by the state's civil service workers. In each state, there is a network of companies and individuals who have for years enjoyed profitable business relationships with the state agencies responsible for institutions — businesses that broker foodstuffs, design and build facilities, and engage in one or more of the many enterprises that sustain the institutions; in virtually every state, there are institutions that serve as the only serious employer in the community, and hence, to evacuate the institution is to turn the community into a ghost town. So, the institutions endure and, to a large extent, prosper. It isn't enough that institutions fail the clients so completely, so obviously. Those who feed and are fed by the institutions *do not* fail as a result of the relationship. Indeed, their very survival depends on the continued life of the institutions. Insofar as the institution is concerned, for every ruined life there may be a successful career launched, or a dollar gained, or (in whatever respect) a life saved. The institution does not fail everyone.

I have stories to tell, some which may shock you. I have observations, polemics, and expository commentary. But I can't bring myself to relate most of those just yet. All I can do now is pull out what seems to me the *least* offensive, least painful of that mound of words. There are of course more dispassionate commentaries on the institutional reforms of the post-World War II period. Sigelman, Roeder, and Sigelman (1981) analyzed the extent to which the various states have deinstitutionalized retarded persons. They found great variation among the states, but what is hopeful is their observation, "No state has been entirely unaffected by the national movement toward deinstitutionalization of the mentally retarded which began to gather momentum in the 1960s" (Sigelman et al., 1981, p. 504). Zober (1978) reviewed the literature on the relationship between different characteristics within residential settings and adjustment to those settings made by various mentally retarded people living there. Note the following trends:

1. There has been a shift from a clinical model of mental retardation to a more humanistic model, leading to a change in the type of residential treatments viewed as most desirable.

2. Due to greater awareness of the influence the setting has on the development of the individual, there has been greater attention paid to the physical and social characteristics of the environment in which mentally retarded people live.

3. There has been much greater attention given to the deleterious effects of traditional large ward-like institutions. There doesn't seem to be very much doubt that, in contrast to small community settings, there is a greater possibility for social and other forms of deprivation in those large and impersonal institutional settings.

Possibly as important as any of the findings was the conclusion that, "The majority of mentally retarded persons at all levels of functioning have been found to adjust successfully in the community (pp. 78-79). Furthermore, "Significant increases in functioning have been found among those individuals who have moved from the large institutional environment to smaller, more homelike environments on the grounds of the institution as well as among those individuals who have been moved into various types of community residences" (p. 79). The prepotent conclusion flows naturally from the above: "There seems to be little doubt that manipulating the setting in which a mentally retarded individual resides to create a supportive 'normal,' 'homelike' environment may have a profound effect on functioning as well as life satisfaction" (p. 79).

While the institutionalization of persons with mental illness has slowed to a near halt, this is not the case for those whom we label "mentally retarded." There are approximately 149,000 people incarcerated in state institutions for mentally ill persons, approximately the same number as were in such facilities in 1900 (Braddock, 1981). By contrast, there are almost 10 times more people today in state institutions for retarded people than in 1900, approximately 126,000 (Scheerenberger, 1982). Of course, the actual numbers of mentally retarded people in designated state institutions have been declining since about 1965, but not nearly as dramatically as with the numbers of mentally ill persons. Some suggest that there has been less "dumping" in mental retardation, while others ascribe the difference to the greater effectiveness (or merely the more frequent use) of various drug treatment programs with mentally ill patients in contrast with their relative ineffectiveness (or less frequent use) with retarded persons. Be that as it may, the institutionalization of mentally retarded people continues at a fairly vigorous rate in the United States. It is ironic that the deinstitutionalization of mentally ill people has been ever so much more widespread than the deinstitutionalization of mentally retarded persons—especially when we consider that a major reason for the incarceration of mentally ill persons is that they can pose a danger to self and others, whereas a major justification for institutionalizing retarded persons is incompetence. Yet, the mentally retarded "client" is most apt to become a chronic "inmate."

There are, though, some silver linings in an otherwise cloudy and troubled sky. In Montgomery County, Ohio, a community acceptance study in which neighborhood opinions were solicited concerning homes for mentally retarded individuals disclosed that (a) the value of the homes was consistent with that of other properties in the neighborhood, (b) the homes were often better maintained than the surrounding properties, (c) general property values in neighborhoods with group homes enjoyed the same increase in market prices as those in other similar neighborhoods, (d) properties adjacent to the group homes did not experience declines in value, and (e) the establishment of group homes did not generate any greater turnover among properties than in similar neighborhoods (Mambort, Thomas, Few, Magin, & Torge, 1981).

In this survey, almost 90% of the respondents living near group homes believed that persons with mental retardation should have the same civil rights as others. Further, 77% of the respondents living near group homes believed that mentally retarded people should have the right to live in ordinary communities, 75% believed a group home is a better place for mentally retarded people than an institution, 46% believed the group home does not affect their own property values, and 64% believed that a group home can actually help a neighborhood to better understand and appreciate persons with disabilities.

More and more journals, books, case studies, and newspapers examine the devastating effects of institutionalization—journals such as *Human Ecology Forum,* a quarterly publication of the New York State College of Human Ecology; books such as *Humanizing Environments: A Primer* (Ostroff, no date), for architects and interior and industrial designers, with special emphasis on humanized environments for handicapped people; case studies such as *Heather's Story: Psychotherapy and the Practice of the Least Restricted Environments* (Blom, 1981), a beautiful and provocative account of how an adolescent girl with Down syndrome benefited from psychotherapy and eventually married another retarded person; and almost daily newspaper accounts of the positive effects of deinstitutionalization. Then, too, there has been the work of Vanier, mentioned earlier, the creator of L'Arche, an international effort to bring dignity and normal life opportunities to mentally retarded people. In a different vein, there has been the work of people such as Colleen Wieck (1980) on the cost of public and community residential care for mentally retarded people.

The Center on Human Policy of Syracuse University has taken hard looks at the various approaches, models, philosophies, and strategies—assessing the benefits and the tradeoffs. One of the more recent such examinations has been its evaluation of Title XIX of the Medicaid (Intermediate Care Facilities for the Mentally Retarded (ICF/MR) program (Atkinson, et al., 1981). The ostensible purpose of this program is to provide environments that are smaller, more home-like, and more humane. Millions of Medicaid dollars have gone into such facilities. Yet, the Center on Human Policy has expressed reservations concerning its impact on reforming services. Many of these new centers are 30- to 50- or even 100-bed facilities which, while not quite traditional institutional warehouses, nevertheless resemble certain aspects of the familiar institution. These centers have yet to demonstrate the proposition that "home-like" is a suitable substitute for "home." Some have concluded that not every new such program is an unqualified success.

To be sure, services expanded wildly during the period from World War II to the present. To be sure, institutions have been reformed—but only to a point. They are smaller, cleaner, better staffed, better funded, but they resist being anything but institutions. To be sure, the professionals have, if not mobilized for action, proliferated in numbers and (to a degree) in quality. Has the victory been won? There are doubts; the "numbers" testifying to victory seem too good to be true, maybe because they *are* too "good" to be true. There are even doubts that the most important battles have been fought. There is some feeling that the most important battles have yet to be defined, much less fought.

One such battle is the great stigma that is associated with having been a resident in a state school. Indeed, study after study—particularly studies of mildly or moderately retarded persons—indicate that the one thing ex-residents of state schools refuse to admit is the possibility that they were themselves actually mentally retarded (Edgerton, 1967). The stigma attached to being an ex-resident of the state school is apparently too painful and difficult to bear. The stigma not only tells about the past but it predicts the future. That is, the stigma carries with it the assumption that ex-residents of the state school may be able to change venue, exchanging the institutional bed for the YMCA bed. But they cannot change the immutable, the fact that they are mentally retarded. Hence, it seems that the only way for ex-residents of the state school for mentally retarded persons to reach the road to normalization is to deny ever having been in the institution in the first place. They must attempt to keep secret any fact associated with the history of their institutionalization. They must attempt to obliterate from their minds and their very lives the fact that they were once residents of the institution. That is not much of a way to start a new life, but for them it is the only way.

If you can understand the reasons behind this common reaction of the ex-resident of the state school, you will be better able to deal with not only questions concerning institutional reform but also the question connected with an even more fundamental issue: Is what's required reform or revolution?

Analogies to the problems faced by the mentally retarded person are everywhere. Relevant metaphors and stories can be found almost anywhere one turns. Stories have been passed on for generations by descendants of Chinese immigrants to this country between 1910 and 1940, when about 175,000 came to this "promised land." The experiences faced by such immigrants are not unlike those faced by the ex-resident of the state school: Both are perceived as outsiders, as different. And both suffer.

Once they arrrived on our golden western shores, the Chinese immigrants were locked up. They slept stacked, on steel bunks, six high. If they rebelled, they were punished as criminals. On the peeling walls of their jail "dormitories" are still visible poems written in Chinese, poems written to express their anger and anguish. One reads: "There are tens of thousands of poems composed on these walls; they are all cries of complaint and sadness. The day I am rid of this prison and attain success, I must remember that this chapter once existed" ("Untold Story," 1981, p. 84). And then there was Germany, and the more terrible analogue of the experience of the Jews. In *The Family Papers: A Return to Purgatory*, we (Blatt, Ozolins, & McNally, 1979) wrote:

> Years ago, but long after the horrors ceased, I forced myself to visit the Dachau Concentration Camp, now a memorial park bordered by attractive garden apartments and other common scenes. But within that still dreaded death camp, remnants of the holocaust linger. On hundreds of pictures, in dozens of languages, imbedded in every grain of dirt, written even on the shiny walls of the new facsimile barracks, there is a message: do not forget, remember what happened here, remember us, remember, I once lived. But the Jews were The People of the Book. They expressed their anguish and their pleas the ways all literate people express themselves, through their language. And because they knew that voices are eventually silenced, and theirs especially would be, they scrawled their message on the walls of the barracks: do not forget us.
>
> Today, in the United States, one can see scrawlings of the anguished. Today, in institutions across the land, one can find what remains of an American shame, but the words here are not in Yiddish or Polish or Russian. Because these inmates couldn't write, because many of them couldn't talk, because there was no one willing to listen, because there was no one wanting to understand, these institutional inmates used fingers instead of pens, and feces were their ink. But whether it was the fine hand of a former professor at the Univesity of Heidelberg or the ugly smear of a drooling mute, the message is constant: why are we forsaken?[1]

---

[1] From *The Family Papers: A Return to Purgatory* (p. 12) by B. Blatt, A. Ozolin, and J. McNally, 1979. New York: Longman. Copyright 1979 by Longman, Inc. Reprinted by permission.

Parallels can be drawn. What happened to Chinese immigrants on the Pacific coast of the United States, what happened to Jews in concentration camps, and what happened (what may still be happening) to institutional inmates are not unrelated. While services for mentally retarded persons "expanded" after World War II, institutional abuses were exacerbated. The more that was developed to relieve pain, the more that was developed to inflict pain. By no means, was either the extent or the type of suffering encountered by each group precisely the same. But there *are* parallels to be drawn. There is the paradox of not forgetting yet wanting to "pass." There is the paradox of the "healer" who assuages one pain, but who generates a new, yet even more terrible, pain. There is the paradox of the "new" life promised, through the new treatment, the new expert attention; while the person must pay a price every step of the way for the golden opportunity (which is too often "fool's gold") and the professional treatment (which may not have been needed to begin with).

My own attitude toward the institution evolved slowly and painfully. When *Christmas in Purgatory* (Blatt & Kaplan, 1966) was published in the mid-1960s, I still nurtured the hope that the institution could be reformed. By the time I was collecting material for *The Family Papers: A Return to Purgatory* (Blatt et al., 1979), I was convinced that institutions had to be dismantled, that meaningful reform was impossible. The following brief, previously unpublished excerpts from my diary, written in 1976 when I was collecting notes and essays for *The Family Papers,* will, I hope, give you an idea of what it's like to be a visitor to these places, once called asylums as a matter of course, now called asylums out of a sense of derision, disgust, and shame.

> Why did we visit these "homes" for the mentally retarded? What did we seek? What did we expect to find? About a decade ago, we barged into the workings of five state institutions for the mentally retarded. Quite literally, we forced, or bluffed, or wheedled our way into four of those places, plus one other which was more decent and whose superintendent and staff endorsed our intentions. From those recorded observations, *Christmas in Purgatory* (Blatt & Kaplan, 1966) was published. During the ensuing years, many laws and regulations were created to mitigate if not erase forever the mistreatment of institutional inmates. Many new programs were organized to provide more normalizing and humanizing institutional settings. New facilities were built. More people than ever before were trained for work with the disabled. Consumers and their advocates were welcomed to participate with policy and service delivery groups. Presidents of the United States, their cabinet members, and various other federal, state and local officials, as well as foundation heads and captains of industries, ordinary citizens and celebrity citizens—so many people were made aware of the plight of institutional inmates. Among the multitudes, a significant mass of those people pledged their personal and organizational commitments to a better if not final solution to the

"problem." "Deinstitutionalization" became a rallying cry for many. It became a priority of governmental agencies, as well as of voluntary and scientific societies. Polemics were shouted, or whispered, as the occasion commanded. Challenges were hurled. People made promises.

"Goodbye, you fuckin' doctors!" Those were the last patient words that we heard during the visit to this large and ugly state institution. We had been touring Building 8, a custodial dormitory for people the institution labels as severely mentally retarded. We had been in Building 8 ten years earlier and, with the possible exceptions that it's less crowded now and more inmates appear to be wearing clothes, nothing seemed to have changed. We saw the same headbangers, cryers, biters, shitkickers, vomiters, assaulters, screechers, rockers, and sleepers—all controlled by a few attendants who were sitting, standing, chatting, watching or drowsing. Once in a while, someone reached out and made contact.

Building 8 hadn't changed. Inmates still do not have clothes of their own. Each day arrives with a new chance at the clothes grabbag. Today might bring one a torn shirt and, who knows, even underwear. Tomorrow, one's luck may be better, a nice plaid flannel shirt in good condition, like a cowboy's. Or it might be worse—no underwear, or the wrong size shoes, or no shoelaces for the shoes, or a brown shoe and a white sneaker as a not so neat pair. Building 8 hadn't changed. There are still no activities for more than half of the inmates, no materials for recreation, no games, hardly any interaction of inmates with attendants. We've been here before, and it's no different, so we leave. A gust of clean fresh air pushes against us as the front door is unlocked. As we are about to escape from the terror inside, a scream shatters our pleasure in anticipating freedom.

"Goodbye, you fuckin' doctors."

We look up, and from a second floor window a man is standing, shirt off, angry face, waving a fist. We smile and wave and he waves back, and then a smile breaks out, and he waves again, this time with open palm. And when I leave the institution, I shout inside myself, "Goodbye, you fuckin' institution. I hope I never have to come back."

How could I have seen all this (and more) and walked away? How could I have left human beings there to die, knowing I would be leaving them to die? Still worse, how could I have left them, knowing that I would be leaving them to rot, until they were no longer recognizable as human beings?

Times have changed. Our conceptions and our constructions have passed through their primitive stages. But to rephrase Santayana, we not only repeat old embarrassments with unfortunate regularity, but we also fail to recognize their clever new disguises and to appreciate their threat to *our* welfare as well as the victims'. We're told that today's inmates' heads are not shaved for the purpose of illustrating microcephaly or hydrocephaly to clinic visitors. We're told that people have changed their attitudes, that we no longer think about mental retardation as a loathsome disease, that we no longer think about mentally retarded people as degenerates who might have been better off never to have lived. Yet, we also know that the State of California recently passed "death with dignity" legislation, and there are other states pressing for various laws to promote euthanasia and other forms of "killing the weak." We're told that the companies that manufacture institutional garb, furniture, and other paraphernalia are today more sensitive to such things as color, shape, form, appearance. But we ask, "Are they more sensitive to *our* sensibilities or to those for whom they have been created to serve?" This is a troubling question, but the answer is no less troubling. That's the problem. While everything has changed since the early 1900s, has anything truly changed? While we don't have inmates kept barefoot to prevent their escape from the institutions, for sure there are still naked (or clothed) clients somewhere today — alone in the world, alone with foster grandparents, alone in spite of the state and the bureaucracy, without anyone.

We heard from a famous scientist that religious expression is tolerated in the USSR. His trip to the Soviet Union confirmed for him that Christians, Jews, and other religious groups are officially permitted to express their religious beliefs in the few remaining houses of worship in that country. The secret police do not harass ordinary worshippers — people who "merely" go to church on a Sunday, or to synagogue on a Saturday. If those worshippers, however, attempt to get "serious" about their religions, they may find themselves in a great deal of trouble. It's one thing to attend church, but in the Soviet Union it's quite another to participate in a Bible study group after church, or worse still, in your home. Religious observance isn't prohibitied; but serious religious purpose is.

What does this have to do with the field of mental retardation today? The analogy is all too relevant to what seems to be occurring in our country in the name of alternatives to institutionalization. So-called alternatives are springing up everywhere — group homes, intermediate care facilities, foster homes, and apartment complexes. These alternatives are not only permitted, they are encouraged. Institutional alternatives, however, *must* abide by the regulations that sustain institutions — staff ratios, health codes, sprinkler systems, state surveillance, unionized employees, etc., etc., etc. So, while much of the old form of residential living has been altered because retarded people have moved from institutions to communities, virtually all of the *substance* of the old form — the institution — remains. This may be one reason why we have not made the progress that was originally envisioned to follow the creation of community settings. Anything goes, but nothing of substance goes. Of course, it's too early to determine "officially" whether the small community residence — albeit state controlled and supervised — is a better arrangement than the institution. Many observers feel that the current system is a significant reform of a bad system. Others have worried about the insistent reports of community abuses and inept community administrations. Notwithstanding, while we await better documentation concerning the influence of community programming for mentally retarded persons, there's no doubt that those programs have not only been created as a response to the cry for reform, but also that they reflect a genuine revival of conscience—however inept or misdirected the programs may be at the present time. This is all to the good. And such concern promises a *better* future society, even if it doesn't inform us how to create one good enough for the people today. Not taking the community alternative most seriously is even more foolish than eating one's seed corn; it's letting it rot.

The Mobilization of the Professions

In the second edition of his seminal work, *The Culture of the School and the Problem of Change,* Sarason (1982) asserted persuasively that if compulsory education requirements and the 1954 desegregation decision led to two genuine educational revolutions in America, then Public Law 94-142 must surely have precipitated the third. Sarason was right—even if his argument exaggerates. In our lifetimes, we have witnessed the metamorphosis of a relatively small and nondescript academic subculture (special education) into a monolithic entity equal in terms of power and influence, if not actual size, to the "main game" (education itself). Special education in general, and the field of mental retardation, specifically, have come of age. And probably, the most striking changes with the expansion of such services during the decades following World War II have been associated with the extraordinary increase in the sheer number of professionals as well as opportunities they enjoy today for specialized preparation.

The following may vivify the stunning increase of professional involvement in the overlapping fields of special education and mental retardation. In 1950, I became a member of the Council for Exceptional Children (CEC) and the American Association on Mental Deficiency (AAMD). CEC then had a few thousand members, and today it has more than 40,000 members. AAMD then had a few thousand members, and today it has 10,000 members. This mobilization of professionals to "conquer" mental retardation confronts if not contradicts Sarason's assertion that there will always be limited resources to accomplish the work before us (Sarason & Lorentz, 1979). Sarason has contended that there have been four great crises in America during the past 50 years: The Depression, World War II, the upheavals of the 1960s, and the recent realization that we don't control all of the resources that we feel are necessary. In essence, the quintessential question today is far different from the question of the Great Depression—

which was then related to how we could better harness our bountiful resources. And the question today is far different than the question we needed to answer during World War II—which was how we could quickly marshal our resources to defeat the enemy. And the question today is different still from the question we asked during the 1960s—which was not so much that we didn't have resources but that we didn't have the resources to simultaneously fight a war in Asia, explore outer space, and improve the quality of life here in America. The question today is: How do we live in a world of finite resources yet of gargantuan tastes and needs?

In view of the fact of finite resources, the aforementioned mobilization of professionals presents a puzzle. How did this mobilization of the professions occur? Why did it occur? What good is it doing? We again turn to Sarason to begin to unravel the puzzle. In one of his most illuminating papers explaining the development of community psychology in America, Sarason looked to the anarchist to explain his own worries. The anarchist—anxious that the state collects for itself unnatural powers, worried that the state neither has nor can develop the capability to serve the interests of the people—in a sense joins with the conservative in decrying the proliferation of the state's role in creating and delivering human services (Sarason, 1976). The worry is that, by its very nature, the stronger the state becomes, the more it breaks the will and spirit of the people, the more it enslaves the people. And the more powerful the state becomes, the more the people are robbed of a psychological sense of community. The more the state does for the people that they should be doing for themselves, the more the people are weakened physically, compromised morally, and bent spiritually. Big government robs people of the need or the opportunity to deal with their problems themselves, not because it is mendacious, not because it is without goodwill, not because it is irresponsible, but simply because large and powerful government is the way it is. When the state involves itself in the "running" of things, it usually creates a mess. For very different reasons, that is the essential philosophy of both the political (or philosophical) conservative and the philosophical (or political) anarchist. In a sense, their common interests, if not ideology, make it difficult to decide whether someone such as Thomas Szasz—the psychiatric myth slayer—is a conservative, an anarchist, both; or is he merely the Devil (a conclusion that may be endorsed by establishment psychiatrists)?

So we return to the question: How did this mobilization of the professions occur? What does it mean? The answer: government intrusion, unheard of resources made available for the first time, and extraordinarily attractive and powerful people (including the President of the United States) calling for an all-out effort. Special education and mental retardation became the glamour fields of the human services. The scullery maid became the princess, and the toad became the prince. Almost overnight, the special education teacher became a specialist, children in this specialist's class were depicted in the Sunday supplements, and the surplus World War II Quonset hut was turned into a modern schoolhouse. President Kennedy announced a War on Mental Illness and Mental Retardation. His successor, President Johnson, announced a War on Poverty, and pledged to continue the War on Mental Illness and Mental Retardation. The Kennedys and the Johnsons joined hands with great politicans and kings and queens from the entertainment industry — and, even once in a while with genuine kings and queens and princes — to wage battle against depression, ignorance, prejudice, illiteracy, human folly of all sorts, and unrealized human potential of any sort.

Part 4

THE POLITICS
OF MENTAL RETARDATION:
MONOPOLIES AND MONOLITHS

When You Walk with Moloch

When you walk with Moloch you pay,
More than you have,
You pay more than you know,
Less than he wants.

When you walk with Moloch you're with the devil,
Beelzebub!
Harpies,
And Yahoos.

Tread with care!
Step in slime, and you slip,
And you're trapped,
Engulfed.

Avoid state schools,
And state hospitals,
And state humanitarians,
And the state!

Each can make you wish for Moloch,
As each seeks to prove its goodness,
As each confirms the evil one,
And their gifts to his grand design,
And their murder of the kindest Brownie!

(Blatt, 1981, p. 106)

10.

The Industries

IN OUR PERSONAL lives, we are confronted with electric can openers or egg beaters that make people useless, exercycles and rowing machines that make us foolish, and elevators that make us flabby. We build buildings without windows, play games on our television sets, own cars to take us to the railroad, and build highways to encourage us to consume more gas and buy more cars for our journey to the Good Life. America seems to believe that it's better to spend money than to conserve it, better to find a complex solution to a problem, better to have "bells and whistles" on the game or the machine than to make it clean and functional. For generations, America's industries have profited greatly from our seemingly insatiable desire to spend, accumulate, consume, and discard. Even in sit-down restaurants, you will find in many places that the "china" is paper and the "silver" is plastic.

Likewise, consumerism infects the profession. At the annual convention of this society and that association, I get the feeling that I have been surrounded by the descendants of P.T. Barnum. Buy the "walking beam" and you may cure learning disabilities, buy the trampoline and you may cure reading failure, buy the new curriculum in music and you remediate arithmetic failure. Buy the reading series and you obviate the publisher's business failure. Like a pedant reviewing a concert with the complaint, "The Mozart symphony was fine, but the violinists' chairs were too far apart," we work on the chairs of life and ignore the music. To say that technology is misplaced is not an overstatement.

Yet there *are* professionals, technicians, and administrators who solve rather than create problems. Biklen and his colleagues at the Center on Human Policy at Syracuse University have written several guides concerned with the problem of mental retardation. For example, Biklen's (1977) *The Elementary School Administrator's Practical Guide to Mainstreaming* reached thousands of school principals and other administrators, hopefully to ease the way for the effective integration of handicapped children into ordinary school programs. There are other authors, too, who take seriously the idea that the biggest problem we have in the field of special education *isn't* money. For example, Don Caston, lecturer in-charge of the Handicapped Education and Aid Research Unit of the City of London Polytechnic has published a number of books and brochures that provide guidance to teachers and others in developing simple aids for handicapped persons. Their motto: It Isn't Clever to Spend Money. And they demonstrate that simple (and profound) declaration in numerous ways, especially by providing first-rate programs for disabled people. Thus, I don't want to leave you with a sense that all is lost or that nothing is done adequately. Quite the opposite; many things are accomplished in a splendid manner. Notwithstanding, I prefer to dwell on the great deal that needs to be corrected rather than on the impressive work that has been done in this field. Other books, other formats and forums, deal with those more pleasant (sometimes extraordinary) situations.

Why do the monopolies and monoliths thrive in our culture? For one thing, there are great fortunes to be made. For another, we don't take seriously enough Don Caston's dictum regarding the expenditure of money. Similarly, we don't take seriously the fact that it is not necessary, desirable, or effective to look for complex solutions to problems that may be amenable to more simple explanations. We should remember that common things occur commonly; or, as the old adage teaches us, when one hears hoof beats he should look for horses not zebras. This can be illustrated by the response I heard in 1982 from the University of Chicago psychologist, Bruno Bettelheim, to a young teacher who wanted advice about a child who banged his head when things weren't going his way. Bettelheim's off-the-cuff advice:

> Obviously, he needs to bang his head. The environment doesn't please him. Rather than try to convince him not to bang his head, or rather than to try to prevent him from banging his head, why don't you bring a pillow from home and place it between his head and the wall the next time he starts banging his head.

So many of the problems we encounter with retarded children require common sense, observational skills, and a teacher who deliberately and regularly thinks hard about the children in class or the clients at the clinic. It's much easier to *do something* about a problem, and it's much easier to *spend money* on the problem than it is to *think* hard and well about the problem.

In this chapter, you may note that my criticism is sharper than in other sections of this book—sections which, on their own, may not have been characterized as overly generous or positive. Although the field of mental retardation is hardly ever described as a monolithic industry, when you stop to ponder it, the idea cannot easily be dismissed. And while even monolithic industries may contribute to civilization, is there ever one that cannot stand criticism? A little criticism is better than no criticism, and leaders in our field may profit from a little criticism. The Nobel laureate, Isaac Bashevis Singer, tells the story about his grandfather who was asked the question, "Why is there a Devil? After all, if God is so omnipotent, so all-powerful, why did he permit the creation of the Devil?" He responded, "God not only created the Devil, he needs the Devil. God too needs critics." If God needs critics, don't we in the field of mental retardation *surely* need critics?

It may be that we in this field should consider the possibility that we have suffered with our own Vietnam. We have suffered with authorities who cut corners, academics who piously ignored the obvious, jurists who looked the other way, administrators who made excuses, and the people who pretended not to know that things simply were going sour. We in the field of mental retardation spend too much time measuring how well children drop marbles in holes, ignoring all the time the holes they live in, and the holes we professionals got ourselves into. We have spent our resources fighting for the clinical needs of retarded persons, when the quintessential issue has always been connected to civil rights. Our "enemies" exacerbate problems, and we minimize them—or vice versa; but we're never in agreement on either what the problem is or how serious it is. And unfortunately, most of us lie about what we see, what we think it means, and how we feel the problems might be solved. There are dilemmas, there are paradoxes, there are experts who argue with experts—to such an extent that the non-experts wind up being the experts. The courts intrude, often focusing not on compelling problems, but on those narrow issues which they are empowered to judge, issues that may not necessarily be most important, may not be important at all.

These are a few of the reasons why this is not a charitable chapter. These are also a few of the reasons why this may not be the most charitable book—that is, charitable to the professionals including myself. This chapter deals with the "business" side of the field, with that and other sides that are neither discussed in textbooks nor analyzed at professional meetings, with sides that some would rather leave unremembered—with sides that we must seek to understand better if we are going to understand our problems better, and ourselves better.

Treatment, Research, and Training Professionals

Mental retardation has always been an industry, and its professionals (like other professionals) have not been shy about living off it and (insofar as the leaders are concerned) controlling it. Consequently, it should come as no surprise that political and self-serving considerations have always been important to policy developments in the field. By analogy, an interesting example is the commentary offered by Cartwright, a prominent Southern physician who lived during the American slavery conflict, to "explain" the slave's character. Cartwright was puzzled why slaves tried to run away, but he finally figured out the cause: It was a mental illness characterized by the desire to flee, what the good doctor called "drapetomania" (Gould, 1981, p. 71). The black could no more control his insane need to flee than he could his love of a kind master. The cure: Slave owners should avoid either extreme cruelty or permissiveness; that is, their slaves should be treated like children if the disease were to be controlled. There were other "scientific" explanations of slave behavior, and "scientifically authenticated" treatments, just as today there are "scientific" explanations of the behavior of mentally retarded persons and "authenticated" treatments for their deficiencies.

Elsewhere, I developed the argument that education is a monolith, "no more capable of dealing with revisionism than any other monolith" (Blatt, 1977, p. 17). Education is a monolith as medicine is a monolith and other professions are monoliths. Hence, it should come as no surprise that a field such as mental retardation, powered by professionals, is monolithic. Let us look at those characteristics of the professionals who serve us, often with distinction, and it will be difficult to escape the conclusion that the ways our professionals are trained, the ways they are rewarded, the ways they protect themselves, the ways they perceive themselves, and the ways they are perceived by society among many ordinary citizens, as well as within the professions, the beliefs that:

1. There is a right way and a wrong way; there is established practice and quackery.

2. There are rules, regulations, customs, and values, from which there should be no significant deviation.

3. The public judges professionals by how closely the teacher, for example, behaves like others in his or her profession.

4. In unity there is strength; with a common agenda there is purposefulness; with common methods and procedures there is verification.

Not everything is bad about monopolies and monoliths, but it must be pointed out that *in private industry* there are laws prohibiting contrived orthodoxy. The opposite obtains in the professions. The greed of Rockefeller, Carnegie, and other oil and steel barons caused the creation of the Securities and Exchange Commission and the various anti-monopoly measures in the United States. The professions, on the other hand, not only continue to strengthen and refine their monopolies, but society praises them for their efforts. In the professions, monopolies are believed to be the antidotes to quackery and its permutations, despite some indications that they may also contribute to the disease. Teachers are required to complete certain courses before they can be endorsed to teach. Teacher groups are increasingly proclaiming that certification doesn't go far enough. Teachers now want to be licensed — in the same fashion that doctors, nurses, and psychologists are licensed. What may have begun as measures taken by the state to protect the public — licensure — are now viewed by teacher organizations as measures necessary to not only protect the public but to give enhanced status to the teachers. While teachers are waging battles to achieve licensure, doctors are waging battles to control the sizes of medical school classes. Each group is nurtured by its own distinctive unions — those of the teachers more resembling the union, that of the physicians more resembling the exclusive club. Should we trust the man who works with too obvious zeal to feather his own nest? Or, is it better to trust those who don't trust him?

The above comments may seem unfair and one-sided. No doubt, there is another side to the arguments concerning teachers' and doctors' unions, licensure for professionals, orthodox treatment practices, and conservatism in the professions. But of course, such professional perspectives are represented in most textbooks in those fields. I am assuming that you will examine that other side. The point here is not to present a balanced picture, laying out the good that professionals accomplish with each instance that I note a problem. Rather, I am making the point that treatment, research, and training professionals in the field are, for the most part, represented by large organizations that have powerful voices in federal and state legislatures. Indeed, those organizations employ substantial numbers of people to lobby on behalf of their members. And representatives of those teachers, doctors, nurses, social workers, psychologists, and administrators are not able to make their cases merely on the self-evident good works that their clients accomplish. There is an array of lobbyists, public relations specialists, and legislators who spend much of their professional lives convincing America that those professionals are necessary to foster the public good. And while of course that's all true, embedded in those claims is a degree of hyperbole cloaking self-interest. The professionals can take good care of themselves. The reader need not be unduly fearful for their future welfare. Better to pity the critic.

Most of society operates on the principle of "interchangeable parts." Certainly, industrial hardware is built and maintained on that principle. And oftentimes, human beings are viewed as interchangeable, especially those who are employed in "unskilled" and "semi-skilled" jobs. To a degree, even those in skilled and technical fields are trained and employed as if anyone with certain skills can take the place of anyone else with similar skills. The concept of "interchangeable parts" so permeates our society that it is rarely noticed, much less challenged. Some examples:

1. Rigid salary schedules for virtually all blue collar and technical workers. Furthermore, for most school teachers, social workers, nurses, and state and federal administrators, salaries are determined by the position one is slotted into and the years he or she has served in that position.
2. The ever more widespread utilization of objective competitive examinations for skilled and professional positions.
3. The popularity of competency-based instruction programs.
4. Unionization.
5. Stipulated procedures for arbitrating grievances.
6. Standard benefits programs.
7. Rigid retirement practices.

Of course, many of these practices — such as well-publicized stipulated grievance procedures, salary schedules based on seniority, and worker protection programs — were created because of employer abuses. It isn't an accident that unions have become remarkably powerful in the United States. Nor is it accidental that local, state, and federal salary schedules are for the most part determined by seniority. And of course, the civil service system is built on competitive examinations. These programs have accomplished good, and many would argue persuasively about the necessity for their creation and continuance. But at the same time, these practices reflect a society that employs individuals as if one person were interchangeable with another. In a fashion, the field of mental retardation not only employs its personnel as if one doctor (or teacher, or administrator) is interchangeable with another, but it also creates programs as if one developmental center in a state is not different from another, as if one regional center is not different from another, and as if one group home is not different from another.

The practice if not the theory of "interchangeable parts" is widely accepted in the field of mental retardation. This practice may be considered to be one of the primary problems in the field. Getting back to the fundamental principles, if all people are valuable, and if all people are different, wouldn't it appear that the main goal is to utilize humanity's many talents differentially?

Builders and Architects

When a Vice President of the United States was forced to resign on threat of criminal prosecution for accepting bribes, it may or may not have been noticed by the average citizen that *every* participant involved with him in alleged illegal "payoffs for favors" schemes was either a builder, an architect, or a land developer. It may not be noticed by most observers of bureaucracy that, year in and year out, the state is the largest customer of architects, builders, and land developers. The state appropriates money not only to provide services but to build facilities to house those services—with enthusiasm if not always in the public interest. It isn't necessarily true that state functionaries are crooked, but land acquisition and construction represent the biggest of big businesses. And where there is big business there is sometimes a compromise with, or even a disregard for, legality. Always, there is temptation.

In mental retardation, institutions (and now community facilities) have kept many an architect, builder, or land owner solvent. In several states, facility development is a billion-dollar industry. Of course, not all builders and architects are venal and avaricious. There are many who work very diligently to create healthful and beneficial environments. David Sokoloff is one of those architects who for years has been searching for better environments. His special interest is retarded persons, and together with colleagues in San Francisco, he created the Institute for the Human Environment. Gilroy and Sokoloff (1982) ask: Is there another way than that represented by the traditional institution? Is it possible to develop a true "community" that can substitute for high-cost professional services? Gilroy and Sokoloff proposed alternatives to the traditional professionally dominated support systems that the field of mental retardation has relied on for many generations. They laid out reasonable ways to enhance the physical, social, and economic lives of people with special needs, utilizing ordinary community facilities and services already in place for the general population. It all sounds too obvious to be true, but as Seymour Sarason has reminded us time and again in his writings, people simply don't take the obvious seriously enough.

A community based on the proposition that people with special needs can help themselves, as well as being helped by others, to be more self-reliant—that is an idea worth examining and working hard to achieve. The ideas of Gilroy and Sokoloff provide a ray of hope and an inspiring example of what *can* be done by the builder and the architect.

Merchants and Manufacturers, Organized Labor, and Bankers

What does the proletariat have to do with the bankers? Or with the merchant princes? Of course, most people have observed that the leaders of organized labor are as powerful and well known (if not quite as affluent) as chief executive officers representing the Fortune 500 companies. So in a sense, there is a relationship between labor and business. The relationship between the banker or the captain of industry and the mental retardation professional may not be as obvious. The leaders of a state employees' union are not, after all, as well known as the presidents of major industrial unions. But one fact connects all the "players"—all benefit from the mental retardation industry. The bankers raise the money to build or refurbish the institutions. The merchants and manufacturers fuel those institutions. And labor services them. These are not "cottage industries," but important and powerful in every sense. Consequently, there is great interest in the business and labor community whether there will be a deinstitutionalization effort or not in America. Why? It does not require mathematical wizardry to deduce that 6% (e.g., an architect's fee) of $20 million or $30 million (cost of constructing an institution) is a great deal of money. A construction program of this magnitude requires major contractors, suppliers, land developers, unions, and, especially, banks, which earn millions on the capital they raise to finance the enterprise. The question is: How can we terminate institutional building programs when, in many states, they are the sources for political support and patronage? In an analysis I did for a paper co-authored in 1977, the economics of mental retardation were likened to the game of Monopoly:

> Special education is big business. The Rand Corporation recently reported that government agencies expend $2.8 billion annually to serve mentally retarded youth (Kakalik, 1973). . . .
> Institutionalization is big business in New York, and in a fundamental sense, New York, our case example, reflects the national situation. The 1975 appropriation for the Willowbrook Developmental Center was approximately $62 million, more than a $20,000 expenditure per resident. In 1965, the per capita expenditure at Willowbrook, and at virtually every other state institution for the mentally retarded, was less than $4,000 a year.

Item. In 1965, New York State embarked upon a five-year $500 to $600 million mental hygiene construction program as part of a master plan for the mentally disabled (Legislative Commission on Expenditure Review, 1973). Forty major projects were approved, at a constsruction cost of $320.3 million. Furthermore, the program included an additional $188 million for modernization of existing facilities, plus $100 million to help construct community mental health facilities. By 1972, 23 of the original 40 major projects had been completed or were under construction; these exceeded cost estimates by 50% ($94 million), a discrepancy that inflation in construction costs cannot fully explain. When the revised total plan is implemented, 28 projects will have been completed at a cost of $343.5 million, $23 million over the original estimates. If there are no further delays, inflationary increases, union demands, or bright new ideas, the 7,500 beds that will be the basic product of New York's master plan will cost the state's taxpayers approximately $45,000 each for construction, and an additional one and one-half to two times that amount ($65,000 to $90,000) to meet fund obligations, to the banks, foundations, and other bondholders who underwrote the cost. . . .

Item. A study by the New York State Department of Mental Hygiene disclosed that residents in group homes for the mentally retarded required expenditures of $6,700 yearly, while instituionalized residents required $34,000. . . .

Item. A report issued by the New York State Assembly (Swift & Melby, 1976) revealed that family care for the mentally ill and retarded requires approximately $7 a day, while residential services cost from $50 to almost $90 a day. While family care and other community placement admittedly may require additional educational and treatment services, such services are frequently available through resources provided by insurance, city, county, or state programs.

There are fixed costs, some of gigantic proportions, which are not accounted for above: pension costs, government and other grants, various kinds of interest rates, and hidden costs that even the most penetrating search has yet to uncover. The question that crops up again and again is: Why does New York (and other states) continue to construct and support segregated facilities? Perhaps because there are currently 64,000 union employees in the New York State Department of Mental Hygiene, an increase of 10,000 in little more than three years. Perhaps because there are also contractors, builders, architects, real estate entrepreneurs, and many other people anxious to provide the best construction to any state for any purpose. Perhaps because there are merchants and manufacturers who would rather sell carloads of merchandise to institutions than run corner five-and-dime stores.[1]

Of course, capital (building) and operating costs are substantially higher in the mid-1980s than they were in 1977. Mental retardation is a bigger industry than ever, and the country has experienced an unprecedented infla-

---

[1] From "From Institution to Community: A Conversion Model" by B. Blatt, R. Bogdan, D. Biklen, and S. Taylor, 1977. In E. Sontag (Ed.), *Educational Programming for the Severely and Profoundly Handicapped* (pp. 42-44), Reston, VA: Council for Exceptional Children-MR Division. Reprinted with permission of Ed Sontag.

tion. For example, the New York State Office of Mental Retardation and Developmental Disabilities budget was approximately $1 billion in the early eighties, and it is getting bigger. In 1965, the care of a mentally retarded resident in New York State approximated $4,000 a year. In the early eighties it was $60,000, with at least one or two institutions spending $100,000. In a sense, costs are not only inexplicable but also incalculable. Precise figures hardly matter.

Parents especially are up against it. It isn't that all merchants who serve handicapped persons are out to gouge them, but they surely are out to survive, to make a living, and, if they can, to make substantial profit. As Calvin Coolidge once said, "Business is the business of America." Well, those who manufacture wheelchairs in this country not only have very good businesses, but businesses without a great deal of competition. Read what Hutchinson (1982) had to say in a recent issue of *The Exceptional Parent*:

> I have been in the process of buying my fourteen year-old cerebral palsied son a wheelchair since last March, which is eight months ago. This chair is a custom chair. I will not name the company. It is also motorized. He and I are frustrated at this point. . . . The cost of the chair is $3,450, which includes a $75 fee for measuring him. You can get a two-seated motorized golf cart for $1,900, a small farm tractor for $3,000 and a darned nice used car for $3,400. . . . We have for some time been concerned about the high cost of wheelchairs and the possibilities for competitive abuse in a market characterized by substantial sales to public institutions, significant underwriting by third parties and consumers who are at competitive disadvantages due to their absolute need for the product. In other words we are indeed a captive audience.
>
> In my case my insurance will pay most of the cost. That is not my problem. In March I was told I would have it in two months. By mid-July my son was asking every day. By August he was hoping he would have it for his birthday, August 7th, then in time to start school. It is now past Thanksgiving and he still does not have it. Maybe they will be kind and let him have it by Christmas. . . . I was told by an agent from the FTC that those that sell wheelchairs make 30 to 40% commissions on these chairs. That's a lot of money on a $3,000 chair.[2]

Pork Barrels and Politicians

It was during a year of leave from academe, as Massachusetts Director of Mental Retardation, when I may have lost my innocence about government and "men of affairs." For sure, what I experienced during that leave reified my disillusionment with a state's ability to offer direct services

---

[2]From "Wheelchairs" by E.F. Hutchinson, 1982, *The Exceptional Parent*, *12*(1), p. 7, 60. Copyright 1982 by Psy-Ed Corporation. Reprinted with permission from *The Exceptional Parent*.

to people. It was during this leave when sufficient data were collected to lead me to conclude that there is no hope for institutions, that there is no hope to truly reform them, that there is no hope that sustained good works can be accomplished in state schools for mentally retarded persons. It was also during this leave when I experienced firsthand the ways in which politicians and their hangers-on operate. First, the hangers-on.

I hadn't been in the job very long when I had an insistent visitor, an angry man who wanted to know why I was harrassing him. Not recognizing his name, face, or anything about him, I expressed puzzlement and the observation that he probably was mistaking me for some other bureaucrat in the building (and who could blame him for that?).

"No, you're the guy. I have been selling tile to the Commonwealth of Massachusetts for many years. I have not only built a wonderful business, but I have paid my dues to the party and to many philanthropies. I am a respected member of this community, and *you* are ruining my business. You are ruining my life."

Possibly, the recounting here is a bit melodramatic and not "exactly" how it occurred in my office in the State Department of Mental Hygiene in 1968. But, essentially, this rendition conveys what occurred. By my efforts to stop the building of large institutions, by my reactions to the various plans that were presented to a committee concerned with new facilities in the Commonwealth, this man's business was being affected. And he wasn't going to put up with it! I was informed that he was the closest personal friend of Governor so-and-so, State Senators X, Y, and Z, and distinguished and powerful politicians 1, 2, 3, and 4. Whether our industrialist actually knew all of those important personages, much less whether *they* counted him as close personal friends, isn't germane to the point here. While the *works* of government are fueled by the taxpayers, those who govern are personally sustained by private resources from industry, commerce, and even philanthropies and other nonprofit organizations such as universities. The people pay for constructing the state's facilities, but the vested interests— usually legal vested interests— support those who execute those works. There are two types of pork barrel: the one into which the Congress, the state legislature, or county assembly dips *for* their various constituents; and the one *from* the lobbyist, which is distributed *to* the executives and legislators of our federal, state, and local governments. Mental retardation, like every other important enterprise, engenders a lot of business. It isn't supposed to *be* a business, and it usually *isn't* a business. But it always engenders a lot of business. And where there's business, there are winners and losers, favors given and favors received, greed, and sometimes, illegal activity.

Quoting from the Romans, "The senators are good men, but the senate is a wild beast." As individuals, the senators are honest; but together, they may be devious at times; and how their work is eventually implemented requires constant vigilance by the people (Blatt, 1970b). Politicians as a group cannot always be trusted to carry out the will of the people. Consequently, deinstitutionalization and other reforms in mental retardation will not be achieved by merely letting the politicans follow the evidence to an inevitably proper conclusion. They *need* convincing, not only to teach them about mental retardation, but also to buck the tide of vested interests, which have other things in mind, and which are willing to pay to achieve *their ends,* rather than the common good.

Lawyers

Years ago, my heroes in the field were clinicians and scholars. But today, possibly the most visible if not always the most authentic leaders in mental retardation are the lawyers, judges, and legislators. Once, the most intriguing and discussed questions were, for example, whether placement of choice should be the special class or the regular class. Today, the most compelling discussions are whether or not children's rights are violated by placing them in special—restricted—environments. Once, Richard Hungerford debated the "functional" occupational education versus the "watered-down" regular curriculum. Today, Thomas Gilhool argues before the United States Supreme Court that an instititution should be closed down, that where a child resides (the community or the institution) and where that child goes to school (or *if* he or she goes) are more primary issues for society to consider than the type of special treatment made available or the content of schooling.

Once upon a time, the most serious and substantial issues in the field of mental retardation were clinical. Today, they are legal. Once upon a time, the prepotent objective was to *improve* clinical services and opportunities for the clients. Today, for many in the field the objective is to *free* the clients. Hence, as Herr (1979) argued, today we may think about mental retardation as a different field with "new clients." Herr contended that the lawyers, their affiliates, and consorts have been responsible for changing the rhetoric in the field from an emphasis on clinical concerns to legal ones, and from a discussion of what's going on in such places as Willowbrook, Forest Haven, Belchertown, and Partlow to a discussion on whether people are entitled to be in other places. Herr's provocative conclusion, however, is that while there are more legislative and legal avenues open to retarded persons today, there continues to be a serious shortage of trained advocates. He argued persuasively that a legal principle, or, for that matter, a legal decision cannot be retained as counsel for a client. Clients need lawyers, people to help them. He presented anecdotal evidence to support the contention that while things are much better today, insofar as protecting the legal rights of handicapped persons, great injustices are still perpetrated. He argued that there is a gap between advocacy needs and advocacy resources, and when retarded people seek legal or administrative relief without good counsel the actual doors to courthouses and bureaucracies remain shut. For the most part, good counsel isn't available to them. Hence, the call for still more lawyers and other legal advocates. Hence, a plea for these "new clients"—"new" in the sense that retarded persons more than ever before need legal, as well as (if not rather than) clinical services.

In spite of Herr's conviction and its popularity today, and in spite of his persuasiveness, while more lawyers would surely open more doors there remains the perennial question: Now that the doors would open, what's inside? How good is it? That is, what exactly is it that we are demanding for our clients? Are we doing them any great favors? And can (must) it be better? To be sure, something was terribly wrong for many years to bring us to the state we're in now, a state created in spite of the work of good clinicians. But without especially castigating the clinicians, why were they oblivious to issues of human and civil rights? Why were the abuses of segregated institutions and schools not regarded as part of the clinician's concern? Herr's concern is exactly right, as is the concern of the other lawyers and those who support modern legal advocacy. But something is also wrong with a society in which each person needs a lawyer to remain safe from harm. Who can dispute today the fact that thousands of people (especially handicapped and other disenfranchised groups) need and should have legal services? What troubles me, though, is that in our rush to provide such services and to guarantee human rights, clinical concerns seem to have become secondary—almost submerged in the wave of lawyers clamoring for open doors and advocates clamoring for open environments.

I will have more to say about this matter in the following section. But possibly because the lawyers *are* the "new heroes" for the "new clients," the urge to control the pendulum of excitement causes us now to be worried while we once simply said, "Amen." In the final analysis, it will be the responsibility of the larger society to find a place for handicapped persons; and in the final analysis it will be the clinicians who will be called upon to help ameliorate the learning disorder, to prevent further handicap, and to circumvent that which is believed to be unalterable.

We've learned in mid-twentieth century America that lawyers must be part of the team. But we must better understand that they can no more replace the family (the primary advocates), the general society (the primary normalizing environment), or the clinicians (the primary treatment specialists) than can the law replace the deed. Lawyers are good at seeing to it that society makes sincere attempts to give people that to which they are entitled. Lawyers, however, have no special preparation or experience to actually deliver on those legal guarantees. And lastly, we should not forget that the need for lawyers is a barometer not of how *just* the world is but how *bad* it is. In the ugliest totalitarian world possible, lawyers are prohibited. In a merely bad world, everyone needs a good lawyer to fight that bad world. There's something to be said about a world that needs but a few good lawyers to protect the citizens from occasional injustices. That is, we'll have a better world not when we have more lawyers but when we need fewer lawyers. Possibly, even the lawyers themselves look forward to that kind of world. In the meantime, we should be grateful to the Stanley Herrs and Tom Gilhools of society.

Advocacy

What the Golden Rule was to the ancients (and is to those who still hew to the Good Book), advocacy is to the moderns, especially those who seek to serve disabled persons. Almost, but not quite, the concept of advocacy *is* the Golden Rule. While once we were instructed to "Do Unto Others as You Would Do Unto Yourself," advocates today are guided by the proposition that they must work on behalf of another person as if they were working for themselves. In that manner, advocates *need* not be objective and *must* not be evenhanded. Advocates work on behalf of another person whether that other person "deserves" such efforts or not. Advocates must be less interested in serving society than in serving the particular individual for whom they advocate. Advocates must draw a line between their loyalty to the individual they serve and their general goodwill toward all people.

Like the Golden Rule, advocacy is a wonderful concept. But in a fashion, advocacy goes beyond the Golden Rule. While it's one thing to do for others as you would have others do for you, it's quite another thing to work for another as you would work for yourself. In the first instance, you are guided to treat other people as you *expect* to be treated by *them*. That's only decent and reasonable. If you're an advocate, you have agreed to treat another person as you would *treat yourself*—to "buy" into his or her viewpoints, to rationalize his or her behavior, to be as selfish concerning his or her needs as you are concerning your own. Advocacy goes beyond the Golden Rule, because you as advocate are asked not only to treat your client as you can reasonably expect your client to treat you, but to treat him or her as you treat yourself. It's a wonderful concept, but like anything that's wonderful, there may be negative side effects. I once discussed those side effects with colleagues, and then I was sufficiently stubborn and vain to put those ideas in writing. What followed caused controversy and hurt feelings. I knew then that what I had to say about advocacy, while not necessarily precise, was on the track of what needed to be said. Brief excerpts from that commentary are reproduced here:

> Dear Friend,
> We return to the most disturbing element of the entire advocacy movement—our intolerance. We know so little, but we act as if we know everything. When opponents raise sensible arguments, we shoot them down with slogans. When a perfectly decent family experesses anxiety about eight or ten unrelated mentally retarded people moving in next door, we call those citizens unfeeling, godless, and un-American. Ironically, we live by the golden rule, but more often we do to others no less than what others have done to the mentally retarded. We must stop that. We have neither all the answers nor all of the righteousness. We are no better and no more righteous than other people. Like the mentally retarded themselves, advocates are people, fragile people, people like those who work in institutions and even run them. If we have any special insights about where people should live and how they should be treated, it is only because we are now smart in ways in which we were once stupid. Our advocacy label is the license to work on behalf of certain others as we would work in our own behalf, but that is neither justification nor authority to infringe upon the rights of others. If we are not careful, there will be advocacy movements created to protect people who have been hurt by certain brands of our advocacy. If this happens, everything else we have done will have been for naught. We have preached that bad ends are not justified by good intentions. Now we must live by the belief that good ends are not justified by callous means. (Blatt, 1979)[3]
>
> Dear Friend,
> Once it took courage to join the "movement" against the institutionalizers, to be an advocate for the retarded, the other homeless, and the weak. Now it takes courage to decline the opportunity to join up. For the last decade advocates have become tough through dishing it out against almost overwhelming odds. But I hope we have not become so tough that we are not strong enough to take it, especially when the criticism is tinged with unfairness and is overstated in the same way that advocates overstate things to make points to hostile mobs.
> We need advocates because of the way our political-economic system works. It supposes that if everyone grabs as much as he can, everyone will have what he deserves. However, the poor, the weak, and the handicapped are at a great disadvantage in such a system. These persons have not been able to grab fair shares. Consequently, one solution to their plight is to assign advocates to take for the weak what they cannot take for themselves. The goal to institutionalize advocacy can only be a permanent state of siege between the weak and the strong, the poor and the rich. Those who grab the most for themselves or others come out the winners, but to wish a fair share for the weak is to repudiate the adversary model. As agents of social change we should seek to establish advocacy as a short-range expedient only as long as it is needed to counteract the destructiveness of a society

---

[3]From "Bandwagons Also Go to Funerals: Unmailed Letter 3" by B. Blatt, 1979, *Journal of Learning Disabilities, 12*(3) p. 11. Copyright 1979 by PRO-ED, Inc. Reprinted by permission.

gone wrong—a society where avarice and materialism predominate. As a long-range social goal we should seek to eliminate the need for advocacy or, at the very least, seek to minimize it. The systemic focus of social change should not be the establishment of advocacy networks as routine as fire departments or schools. Rather, the focus should be to reduce the raw frontier ethics of the survival of the strong. A truly civilized society is beyond the need for advocates. We should not have a system that serves the weak, like card players are served by the good or bad luck of who is drawn to advocate. Triage is not sharing.

When we fight for moral issues, we do so with the conviction that we are right. Our conviction is not the same as knowledge that we are, in fact, right. If we fail to understand that our conviction could be mistaken, we may become zealots who are at times stupid and dangerous. The dangerous consequences of being wrong are always present, even when we are aware of the frailness of our conviction. Therefore, we are potentially responsible for wrongs done in the name of justice. This responsibility cannot be dissolved by claiming certainty that we are right. Of course, we are tempted to fake certainty to be brave enough to act, but we should try as hard as we can to remember what we believe and are trying to impress upon others.[4]

As happened to so many other ideas, advocacy is now less of an unassailable idea and more of a good issue. It's also a problem. At least in part, the advocacy medicine is a new disease, possibly not as lethal as that which it was created to cure, but a disease nevertheless. Like most medicines, advocacy has its unintended negative side effects. "But even ordinary water can have side effects," so the rationalists advise the alarmists.

While it's been said that a functional test of advocacy is whether or not advocates work for their client as if they were working on their own behalf, it can also be said that, to the degree that anyone works on another's behalf, he or she is depriving that individual of working for himself or herself. This is a conundrum without escape, a circle with no detour. Parents are wonderful when they protect their young, but they are stifling when they give—when they insist upon giving—that same protection to their grown children. The consumer advocacy movement was built on the idea that families of the handicapped would work on behalf of the "cause" as no professionals could, as no ordinary citizens could—in spite of the humanitarianism of those other people. In large measure, that is so.

There *is* a problem, however. We are neither decrying the influence of the consumer movement nor suggesting its demise. Quite the opposite. But there *is* a special problem we must face. Advocacy—whether the consumer "brand" of the mother and father, or the citizen "brand" created by people such as Wolf Wolfensberger—must bridge the need for disabled people to be protected to the need each person has to be free, to take responsibility, to assume appropriate authority. It could be said that programs

---

[4]From "Bandwagons Also Go to Funerals: Unmailed Letter 4" by B. Blatt, 1979, *Journal of Learning Disabilities, 12*(6), pp. 7-8. Copyright 1979 by PRO-ED, Inc. Reprinted by permission.

for retarded individuals that are long on advocacy and short on responsibility are analogous to programs that have been created and are controlled by benevolent dictators. It's not enough to create something—even something good and decent—for people. Eventually, there must be the element of participation. Eventually, there must be something there that represents accomplishment by retarded persons themselves. In view of the development of such organizations as People First, The Association for Persons with Severe Handicaps (TASH), or The Center on Human Policy, it seems that we are learning to better value participation of handicapped persons—because we can learn from them, but moreover because they can help themselves in ways that other people cannot.

Another problem of advocates—exactly as it is a problem of the hospital administrator (who isn't a physician), or the athletic coach (who never excelled in the sport), or the film hero (who is intimidated by the real world)—is establishment of legitimacy. To advocate for another human being *as if* you were advocating for yourself is *not exactly* as if you were advocating for yourself. Everyone understands that it is perfectly understandable—albeit sometimes foolish, misinformed, or silly—to tell your doctor how he should dose you, or your tailor how he should clothe you. However, when someone presumes to tell the "expert" how to dose, tailor, feed, or measure *other* human beings, then that person is often accused of being meddlesome, a fraud, or a quack. The advocate who must inform the school that it is not properly serving a particular child may be on shaky ground because the advocate may not be "expert" in matters concerning instruction. And for sure, when the advocate informs the court that the hospital did not do right by his or her client, the court may wonder what expert knowledge the advocate has to make such strong and categorical assertions about medical practice. We ridicule the pretentiousness of someone who can't play the violin but believes he or she is qualified to be a concertmaster. To a degree, the advocate must overcome a similar if not identical reaction to his or her claim to speak on behalf of another person. It's a problem, and creates a tension that never quite finds resolution. But it has also been said that out of tension, out of strife, comes resolution. And so we have the paradox of the advocacy system, which is, on the one hand, a creator of tension and irresolution, and on the other hand, a force that can mitigate tension, resolve conflict, and even save lives.

The "Family": A Conspiracy Without Conspirators

For my commentaries on institutions, what they represent, and what they do to each of us—for commentaries of this sort, I have become known as a muckraker, a journalist. If truth be known, while I don't have any particular animosity toward journalists, I do have a distaste for muckrakers. And while I am not particularly proud of being of the Establishment, I am (in every way known to me) of the Establishment. So much for labels, at least for the time being.

I have tried to point out that people who work in the field of mental retardation are so numerous, so well organized, so influential on other people and other fields, that it is not possible for their concerns to be uninfluenced by political and economic realities, and vice versa. In this section, I seek to discuss the almost inevitable consequences of such prominence. As a field, mental retardation involves many full-time career professionals, technicians, and unskilled workers, and because there is an even greater array of professionals and nonprofessionals who come in and out of it according to various demands for their time and services, another reality is its "family" or "establishment" characterization. This is to say that the field of mental retardation is governed by more than federal, state, and local laws and practices. Furthermore, we are also "policed" by forces stronger than either the courts or accreditation agencies. Mental retardation is a field old enough, powerful enough, and sufficiently well identified to be more persuasive with its constituents than it is with the "outside world." In virtually every sense, the field of mental retardation is a "family." And while "families" bring comfort, stability, and strength to their members, when things go wrong they must accept their share of the responsibility. And so it has been with institutionalization in the United States.

In 1976-1977, we returned to the very institutions observed, photographed, and made public in *Christmas in Purgatory* (Blatt & Kaplan, 1966). In *The Family Papers: A Return to Purgatory* we reported on those and other visits to 14 residential settings for retarded persons located in seven states (Blatt, Ozolins, & McNally, 1979). In addition to the traditional institutions observed a decade later, the remainder of the programs seen represented ostensibly new models created in response to the "reform" intentions of the late sixties and seventies — small regional centers, community-based group homes, coordinated apartment complexes, and a community center that sponsored various kinds of independent living programs. For example, we spent two days at an intriguing farm community, relatively new itself but based on a much older religious philosophy. We spent some time in a group home supervised by the altruistic followers of a Canadian Christian visionary. And a day or two later, we visited a state school that the state had just designated as a "developmental center."

What follows are excerpts from the introduction to this study. It emphasizes the point that the field of mental retardation has been controlled by a "family," a confederation of individuals and organizations that has conspired to keep from the general public the "facts" about this field. It grapples with issues that are not publicly illuminated — the professional and personal motivations of the "family." What follows concerns itself with the various political and economic forces that drive and inform the field of mental retardation. You may conclude that—when we add up the influences and motivations of the treatment and training professionals, the builders and architects, the business people, labor, the politicans, the bankers, the lawyers, and the advocates—a persuasive case might be made for the existence of a generic category: "The Family."

> The Family knows things we haven't been telling the world about. Important things, more important than the Pentagon Papers, which were about senseless war and unnatural deaths. But the Family Papers are about senseless and unnatural lives, lives disfigured by a society which lays claim to the Declaration of Independence and the guarantee of justice for all people. War is terrible, but explainable. What we do in the names of mental health, human services and education is unexplainable because we do it to ourselves and not to the "enemy," and it's even more terrible because we do it to babies and don't quit our dirty work until dirt covers the evidence.
>
> And, who is this Family? It consists of all those who work, or say they work, with the problems of retarded people in institutionalized settings. It is the supervisors and superintendents and commissioners. It is the professional societies such as the American Association on Mental Deficiency and the Council for Exceptional Children. The Family includes government agencies such as the National Institute on Mental Health and the Office of Education, even groups like the Association for Retarded Citizens. From the attendants who show up for an impossible job every day, to prestigious professionals who often don't show up at all, the Family consists of everyone who should know better than to permit that hidden world to continue. And the academic community, which legitimates it all by issuing so-called credentials and generating so-called expertise, is also part of the Family. . . .
>
> Most institutions remain secretive and, almost instinctively, it seems, move to hide what goes on within their walls. The Family secrets continue to be well guarded from public sight. . . .
>
> But more impenetrable and sinister than overt secrecy is the misleading publicity with which the Family defends its dominions. The first thing one discovers in these places is that the official description of what goes on gives no clue to what one sees actually happening. The hypnotic language of humanitarian concern encapsulates the victims of institutionalization and seals their world off from examination or understanding or even hope. An elaborate camouflage of benign vocabulary—rehabilitation, treatment program, normalization, therapy, modularized privacy . . . —is thrown over the reality of idleness, segregation, neglect.
>
> If there is hope in what we have learned in our examination of institutionalization, it is not in any improvement of institutional life—imprisonment and segregation can be made more comfortable, but they can never be made into freedom or participation. The only hopeful sign is that while ten years ago and for generations before, those institutions were run by one happy Family, today they are run

by one unhappy Family. If it must become unhappier still before it changes its ways, then we are willing to contribute to the Family's unhappiness with our report.[5]

The question is often raised: With so many people in the "family" who knew about the serious mistreatment of inmates of state schools, why did it take so long to outrage the profession? Why are there yet people today in the "family" who profess disbelief about the past and who offer benign explanations concerning current practices in our institutions? There are many reasons to explain the silence of the past as well as misjudgments today—explanations ranging from vast delusions and "blaming the victim" syndrome to other forms of self-justification, misplaced loyalties to the system, and misunderstood allegiances to the professions. But as appealing as any of those explanations may be, there is the possibility that many people in the "family" simply didn't know (simply don't know) precisely how the institutional system works, what harm it generates, and what evil it radiates. How can that be? Isn't that always the excuse, whether mouthed by "good" Germans after the Holocaust or children and immature adults who "didn't mean it"? To be sure! That explanation very often becomes the unpardonable excuse. Notwithstanding, we have known people who have worked in institutions for many years, but never entered the back wards, never actually saw inmates in solitary confinement, never witnessed the beatings by staff or other inmates designated as "beaters." How could that be? Who are such people? The clerks in the administration building, the teachers in the institutional schoolhouse, the staff assigned to the dormitories—for the worker (more competent) "boys" and "girls"—the good boys and girls. What about parents and other relatives? We have known many parents of institutionalized children who for decades never visited their child's day room, and, for sure, never once saw an inmate of that unit in solitary confinement, or in a restraining camisole, or after a severe beating. There are many people in "the family"—some who actually work in the institutions, and many more who work on the outside (the professors, the doctors, the community social workers, the state commissioners, and those who staff the mental health clinics) who don't to this day appreciate what once went on in institituions, and, to a degree, what goes on today. Those people are very much like the visiting cousin who is given the nicest room in the house during a weekend stay, who always has fun on a visit because all the family members are on their best behavior during cousin Alice's vacation; in part at least, that's the definition of "vacation" (and "parent visit"). Of course, cousin Alice has a distorted vision of the home. When she arrives on Christmas, Thanksgiving, the Golden Anniversary, or the

---

[5]From *The Family Papers: A Return to Purgatory* (pp. 1-4) by B. Blatt, A. Ozolins, and J. McNally. Copyright 1979 by Longman Inc., New York. Reprinted by permission.

other special occasion, *everyone* is on holiday, everyone is on best behavior, everyone is there to make life happy for cousin Alice and themselves. People take pains not to expose their dirty linen to visitors. What the institutional teacher knows about the back ward is analogous to what cousin Alice knows about the family's dark secrets and embarrassments.

Life with the Decision Makers

As mentioned previously, in 1968, I spent a full year as Director of the Mental Retardation Program for the Commonwealth of Massachusetts Department of Mental Health at 15 Ashburton Place, Boston. The experiences I enjoyed (and those I didn't enjoy) are recounted in several of my previous books, especially *Exodus from Pandemonium: Human Abuse and a Reformation of Public Policy* (Blatt, 1979b). What follows describes my "life" there, excerpts originally published in the aforementioned book, but most recently reprinted in *In and Out of Mental Retardation: Essays on Educability, Disability, and Human Policy* (Blatt, 1981).

The DEFENSIVE MOAT: SOPHISTS' PARADISE
A man can get along, quite adequately and for many years, on the elegance of his language and the passion and conviction of his speech. One would suppose that this is the hallmark of the university professor, and so it may be. However, I have observed sophistry and pedantries much more frequently in 15 Ashburton Place and its tentacles than in the halls of ivy. Very few people at 15 Ashburton Place *must* make decisions, if they do not wish to make them. . . . Obviously, many choose to make decisions, but they elect to decide and are not required to decide. For some, departmental activities are one grand round of debating, discussion, more debating, and more discussion. The payoff for sophistry is rather good, considering the investment. Men have been promoted on the passion of their verbal convictions, rarely having been required to influence the life of one child, but having persuasively proclaimed their regard for the lives of all children. Further, the System is such that one learns quickly of the peril of making certain decisions and the impossibility of making others. Rather than torment oneself with the uselessness of trying to "buck the System" (and one hears this time and time again), many men make their peace with it. They give expression to their good intentions, good training, and anger in activities that appear vigorous and dynamic but are empty repetitions, which are heard by no one of any importance or influence, but reassure the speaker that he is doing his job and that he is on the side of the "good" people. (We should not discount the cathartic effect such activities provide the speaker.)

DECISION-MAKING and ACCOUNTABILITY
Few people are forced to make decisions because few people are accountable for

specific programs or activities. Obviously, those people who are accountable for specific activities must make decisions. How are these decisions made? A better question might be, "What causes an individual to make one decision rather than another?" For many months, my experiences at 15 Ashburton Place puzzled me because I was completely unable to "read" the System vis-a-vis decision-making. For example, several of what I considered to be very reasonable requests were denied by various business offices without explanation or apparent reason. Other requests were ignored. Still others were quickly and categorically honored to our complete satisfaction. There was no apparent logic to these responses. It seemed as if some mad table of random numbers was at work here, approving one thing, denying another, and ignoring the third. It must be admitted that, in each instance when I did require an explanation for a decision, there was some law or regulation or policy that seemed to lend credulity and wisdom to the decision. However, on other occasions, similar requests—in equal violation of the regulation or policy—would be granted. All one can do is speculate about the basis for decision-making at 15 Ashburton Place—as, obviously, one can't read the decision-maker's mind and there seems no logical pattern to his activities. My speculations have led me to three insecure and tentative conclusions: 1) It is thought much simpler and less perilous to make no decision, or to decide negatively, than to decide positively. 2) The System makes it more satisfying to decide negatively than to decide positively. 3) The process of working with laws, regulations, and policies encourages their utilization to prohibit activities and developments rather than to promulgate such activities and developments. . . . If a System is based on convictions and standards and precedents that make it easier, less perilous, and more satisfying to make negative decisions than to make positive decisions, to the degree that this assumption is true laws, regulations and policies will be interpreted in the light of their prohibitionary powers rather than in the light of their enabling powers. (pp. 314-317)

The industries in our field are political, defensive, organized, and less interested in the public good than they should be. Even those people on the highest level—the "decision-makers"—appear to worry more about how they are getting along than how the clients are getting along, more concerned with their careers than with their clients' lives. Of course there are many exceptions.

What is found among the professional and labor forces in mental retardation is found in *every* industry. Bishops want to be Cardinals and Cardinals want to be Popes. There is a Securities and Exchange Commission because business and industry can't govern their own affairs. Similarly, society demands autopsies, schools are required to appoint committees to deal with issues concerning handicapped persons, construction companies must satisfy building codes. Ralph Nader has become very powerful and very famous. It would be a mistake to conclude from the politics—from the cynicism, from the monopolistic and monolithic practices recounted in this chapter—that the mental retardation industries are particularly venal and particularly in need of reform. I believe that reform is necessary for the same reason that America once decided that the automobile is too dangerous an instrument for drivers themselves to set the speed limit. The purpose of this chapter was not to elaborate on the unique ways our field disregards its responsibilities and abuses its authority. Rather, I want to call attention to these problems because hardly ever are such problems brought to the attention of the student. And when on occasion they are brought to the attention of people in the field, it seems that hardly ever is the "problem" our doing but, rather, that there are "outsiders" who need to be watched, regulated, and punished for their wrong doings. Possibly that's no more than another example of the human condition. But we must expect more from *our* colleagues in *our* field. It was Pogo who remarked, "We have met the enemy and it is us." Well, we may have met the culprits, and they may also be . . .

11.

Social, Cultural, and Political Forces

WHAT DO THUROW'S "Zero-Sum" ideas have to do with mental retardation? What do the other social, cultural, and political ideas of the times? There are finite resources—even in the most affluent society. There are finite priorities and interests—even in the most altruistic and decent society. This chapter examines some of the forces that influence and inform our field—economic, legislative, judicial, political, and civic.

The Zero-Sum Society

There is the apocryphal story about the general and his troops during a religious crusade. From town to town and village to village the army moved, leaving behind smoldering ruins and murdered people. Eventually, the destruction and killing got to his men, and they asked how they might better discriminate between who should die and who should live, which homes must be spared and which must be burned. "Kill them all. God will determine who were Catholics," commanded the leader. And so today; there appears to be little that is reasonable and decent about the social, cultural, and political climate in America. In spite of the temptation, the burden of guilt cannot be placed on one or the other political party or one or the other social movement. It appears that, especially today, while everyone is in a sense the victim, everyone is in a sense the culprit. The Flower Children of the sixties are today's bankers. Abbie Hoffman writes books, and Jerry Rubin sells stocks. And while it is true that Reaganomics changed the pace and tone of government from one apparently more concerned with the "common good" than the "individual good" (as if these were mutually exclusive values and ideals), it was both Republican *and* Democratic voters who put Mr. Reagan in office. And furthermore, there are many Democratic state administrations that have eagerly followed the Washington lead of cutting taxes, cutting services, and shrinking the safety net. It was not only the Director of the Office of Management and Budget who said that government is not created to provide services for the people. His voice was backed by the throngs—Democrats and Republicans, middle-class blacks as well as whites, men and women, *the people* (if not "the masses"). A government would not attempt to justify the use of catsup as a vegetable in children's school lunches (which ours tried soon after Reagan's election) if it didn't believe that this was something the people could and would tolerate.

There are some among us who would claim that we are a society that seems bent on despoiling our land, polluting our atmosphere, fouling our nests, and turning away from those who need us. Maybe we should remember Thoreau's remark that, if we took as much time and care in creating our environments as birds take, we too would sing like the birds. There are some who feel that, had we remembered why we in this country fought our Revolution 200 years ago, today we would take as our first priority the needs of those who are defenseless, handicapped, sick, and aged. We seem to have forgotten that *every* revolution ever fought anywhere was to bring greater freedom and opportunities to the disenfranchised, to the powerless, to the have-nots. And while governments created from altriuistic ideals and the purest of motives have gone wrong, there's one thing "everyone" knows; and that has to do with the reasons why people rise up against their masters and why radical new governments are formed—which is always to free the people and bring more decent opportunities to life. It is not news that things go wrong, both during a Revolution and through the years of its aftermath. We must grope to comprehend better what has gone wrong *here,* in this land of plenty, this once-haven for immigrants from every part of the globe, this once-land of opportunity. And we must remember that "anybody's" right to be wrong is what we pay to give us the right to complain.

In *The Zero-Sum Society,* Lester C. Thurow (1980) suggested that extreme measures are required to address the vast problems facing the country— declining prominence in the world, our declining productivity, our inflation and poverty, our loss of resolve and confidence, and our tarnished halo. Our nation once generated great affluence; it is now much more ordinary in that respect, though hardly one of the "have-not" nations. The Middle East oil countries, but also Switzerland, Denmark, West Germany, and Sweden, outstrip our standard of living. Then there's Japan, whose economic growth has been stunning and rapid, and is expected to surpass our economic status before too long. What has happened to America, to this vast energy-rich, materials-rich, land-rich paradise that our settlers inherited? That is Thurow's question. And he offered an answer. He also offered a solution for the renascence.

According to Thurow, the "Zero-Sum game" is at the core of our economic problems. These problems are solvable, but there will be a price to pay. A liberal economist, Thurow defined the Zero-Sum Society as a mixture of gains and losses; for every loser there is a winner, and the only way we can have winners is to be willing to live with (or tolerate) losers. The problem has been that we, in this country, have simply not been able to accept an economy that has a significant Zero-Sum element. We will never have a situation in which the losses exactly equal the winnings, and we do not want a situation in which the losses far outnumber the winnings. Unfortunately, it is not possible to have a situation in which the winnings substantially exceed the losses.[1]

Is there a way to ameliorate the problem? The heart of the matter concerns how we might narrow the gap between the "have-nots" and the affluent. It is Thurow's conclusion that, to make any significant progress toward that objective, the more affluent must in some fashion be willing to take less for themselves. Will the more affluent—those who have the power, own the companies, have the heaviest taxes, run the universities, and mold opinions—agree, however reluctantly, to take less of the country's riches and benefits for themselves? This is not a rhetorical question. Indeed, it is an open, yet untested question. If there is any evidence or a clue to the answer, it suggests that people will not willingly, and for certain will not easily, give up anything to which they have felt entitled; they will not want to do without what they have learned to accept as rightfully theirs. This leads to other points of view, less generous, more conservative, throwbacks to our early history of rugged individualism and unrestricted opportunism.

Irving Kristol (in Goodman, December 6, 1981) and many other so-called neo-conservatives offer a strong case in support of tax and budget

---

[1]Of course, there are people who envision a future society in which gains can be achieved for some without others losing. Of course, that would be my preference; and we should not take the zero-sum structure as inevitable. Yet, we should also remember that the glory of the British Empire was achieved while many of its colonists (and also citizens of England itself) were suffering; and today's attacks on America's schools are, at least in part, related to their egalitarian emphasis. The grand human experiment remains unfulfilled—a society that offers an excellent quality of life *for all of the people.*

cuts, government deregulation, and government withdrawal from social programs as the solution to both oppression of the people by "big brother" and most of today's economic and social ills. Their point is that a "free market" frees the people. The belief is that a reduction in taxes stimulates private investments, which in turn results in increased government revenue; and across-the-board budget cuts and government deregulation free cities and states to make wiser decisions for the people, decisions that the federal government usually gums up or doesn't get around to. The neo-conservative claim that their philosophy is intended not only to benefit middle and upper class America but the poor themselves. Their claim is that America's social programs have failed the nation as well as the intended beneficiaries.

Of course, there are other economic as well as political philosophies. Notwithstanding the much-bandied labels of economics as the dismal science and politics as the corrupt one, it is useful to remember that virtually all political philosophies (at least those articulated in America) claim to serve people in need. Lester Thurow, however, was one of the few to articulate (the unthinkable thought) that to *truly* serve those in need there will have to be a redistribution of the nation's resources: For every loser, there must be a winner. The question to be asked is: Isn't it time that the "losers" in our society were given an opportunity for at least a modest win now and again? But that question leads to another one: Will we need a reform or a revolution to set America's house in order? That is not a rhetorical question. And, that should not be a question asked only by cranks, zealots, and the other eccentrics always on society's fringes. Thoughtful people, even some on society's fringes, also ask troubling questions.

Legislation

If the nineteenth century was the era of philanthropy on behalf of the disenfranchised, and if the twentieth century has been the era of true democratization, the 1960s was a period when the disenfranchised were remembered — not as charity cases, not as problems, but as *citizens* with rights and with capabilities for contributing to our society. Never before has there been a time when so much legislation was passed on behalf of persons who were old, weak, handicapped, and needy. There are some who sadly predict that *never again* will we experience a time of such genuine concern and action on behalf of all those who have been disenfranchised almost since the beginning of recorded history. But the good news is that we should never say "never" and expect to be eventually right.

Recently, a national examination of cities in the United States revealed that Syracuse—my community—is ranked as one of the most desirable in which to live. How could that be, especially considering the area's severe winters? It may not be entirely facetious to suggest the hypothesis that the severe winters are exactly the cause of the favorable ranking. The Syracuse area has little pollution, excellent water supply, few traffic problems, a low crime rate compared to larger cities, and excellent schools and universities. But what do excellent water and a low crime rate have to do with our harsh winters? Well, look at it this way: With more moderate winters, we would probably have many more residents. That situation would surely change the traffic situation; it would be harder to control air and water pollution; and the schools might be more crowded. And frankly, between the months of December and March, it's probably too cold to roam the streets to commit mischief. Perhaps the low crime rate is related to the bad weather! It is not entirely facetious to conclude that Syracuse is one of the most desirable areas in which to live because hardly anybody wants to live there.

It is not facetious to conclude that Public Law 94-142 was enacted because we want to do more for handicapped children, because heretofore we've done so *little* for handicapped children. Like the "popularity" of the City of Syracuse, P.L. 94-142 is so "good" because we're so "bad." Public Law 94-142 is at once an expression of the generosity of the American people as well as an admission that for generations we have failed handicapped persons. Otherwise, why the need for a federal law to insure the inclusion of handicapped children in our public schools? No such special law is needed to insist that local communities take care of the educational needs of its nonhandicapped children. A true gauge of the progress of our educational programs on behalf of handicapped children will be the time that is required for P.L. 94-142 to be rescinded—not because we won't any longer believe in its provisions, but because we won't need to be reminded that handicapped children are *entitled* to such guarantees.

What are the key provisions of this law, of which the "protection" clauses went into effect in 1975?

1. Under it, states receive funds equal to the number of handicapped children between 3 and 21 receiving special education services multiplied by a specified percentage of the average per-pupil expenditure in public schools in the United States.

2. To discourage states from including nonhandicapped children in the program, the law provides limitations on the numbers who may be counted (to a maximum of 12% of total school-age population between the ages of 5 and 17).

3. To qualify for participation, the state is required to establish policies

for all handicapped children between the ages of 3 and 21. Such policies do not apply to children 3 to 5 years and 18 to 21 years where mandatory services are inconsistent with state law or court order.

4. The law requires that an individualized educational program must be developed for each handicapped child. First priority must be given to unserved children. Severely handicapped individuals who are not receiving adequate services will be given second priority.

5. To qualify, a state submits a plan that guarantees that federal funds will be used in a manner consistent with the law's requirement; includes a program for personnel development; provides free services for children placed by local educational agencies in private schools; guarantees that federal funds will supplement and increase rather than supplant state and local funds; prescribes a program evaluation system; provides for an advisory panel on unmet needs; and provides specific procedures for record keeping and accountability. Each participating local educational agency must submit a plan similar to the aforementioned.

6. Due process safeguards have been incorporated into the requirement for state and local participation. Federal and state monitoring procedures are included. All participants must include affirmative measures to employ qualified handicapped individuals (which may raise the issue of "deviant" staff serving "deviant" clients). Lastly, the legislation requires the Commissioner of Education to conduct whatever studies are necessary to adequately report to the Congress on progress achieved as a result of this legislation. (Blatt, 1978)

The due process provision is one of the important facets of Public Law 94-142. This is not a new guarantee, but a rearticulation of fundamental principles advanced in the Constitution. In its due process clause, the United States Constitution insists on *fair* treatment for all people. No one under the protection of this nation shall lose his life, liberty, or property *without due process of the law*. The term "due process" has been widely misunderstood. What the constitution stresses here is not the guarantee that all people should always be treated justly (although this is clearly the hope if not the expectation), but rather that all people should always be treated according to the rules.

Budoff and Orenstein (1983) recounted the experiences of parents who engaged in the due process system in Massachusetts, created to consider appeals of school decisions concerning special needs children. In Massachusetts, a child suspected of having special needs is referred for evaluation. The referral can come from the principal, a teacher, the parents, the social worker, the family doctor, or the child. A multidisciplinary team engages in an evaluation and develops an individual educational plan for the child. The appeals process is put in motion when the parents reject the educational plan. Hearings are held, witnesses in support and in opposition to the plan give testimony, and within 30 days of the testimony a decision is rendered. There are rules for the hearing process, for who conducts it, for how it's scheduled, and how promptly it must proceed. There are also rules governing further appeal efforts. As I read Budoff and Orenstein's account of parents' experiences with the due process system, I concluded that the law can mean both the realization of a dream and the endurance of a nightmare, for it seems to inflict new burdens as it removes old ones. Further, their account led me to question whether an adversarial system is the only (or the best) way to insure fair treatment for children and their families. Does every child with special needs require elaborate legal safeguards in order to receive a decent education? If a handicapped child in Massachusetts (for example) needs the federal "club" of Public Law 94-142, the state "club" of Chapter 766, advocates, lawyers, and hearing officers, in order to get what other children get simply by showing up at school each day, what does this say about the decency of this society? What does it mean that due process in special education is both hailed as a remarkable reform and decried as a nerve-wracking, time-wasting, degrading experience — by school officials and parents alike? While the special education appeals hearing may be necessary (and a genuine reform of a more corrupt earlier system), it's a necessary evil. Possibly, one of the "necessary evils" of due process has to do with who takes advantage of the opportunity. The Budoff and Orenstein data suggest that few poor people know about or pursue due process, though it's doubtful that they have any less need for it.

Public Law 94-142 engendered considerable debate before it was passed, and since its passage, has been frequently attacked by the White House, by a growing group of professionals who feel that mainstreaming has gone too far, by school administrators who worry about budgets, and by certain consumer groups. The law was originally passed because of strong political pressure on the Congress to develop a national protective policy on behalf of handicapped persons that would insure the education of *all children* in our schools. Recently, there has been a growing political force seeking to repeal that legislation. Public Law 94-142 did not merely happen. There were major political, legislative, and societal events that led to the establishment of this national federal policy.[2]

As early as 1827, Congress passed Public Law 19-8, designed to provide land for the establishment of a residential facility for deaf persons in Kentucky. During the next several decades, Congress passed legislation to assist in the development of institutions in Washington, DC to care for mentally ill (1855) and deaf (1857) persons, and in Kentucky for the development of materials for blind persons (1879). Eventually, the original District

---

[2] I am grateful to Nazzaro (1977) for guidance in the development of this section.

of Columbia Institution for the Deaf was transformed into a major college, Gallaudet, in 1894. In 1896, Congress created what has now become the United States Department of Education, the federal agency which from the beginning has assumed strong leadership to promote programs on behalf of handicapped persons. But it was not until 1917 that the then United States Office of Education began publication of a regular bulletin on exceptional children; and a year later Public Law 65-178 was promulgated for the purpose of providing rehabilitation for veterans of World War I.

Over the years, extensions, elaborations, and new emphases have been introduced into the laws passed on behalf of not only veterans but of all handicapped people. In 1927, Public Law 69-655 amended the Interstate Commerce Act, thus permitting a blind person and a guide to travel for one fare, and a few years later (1931) the United States Office of Education established a section on Exceptional Children and Youth. In 1934, the Commissioner of Education brought together representatives from 15 major groups concerned with the education of exceptional children in order to consider greater coordination of their efforts. Through the years of the Depression and until World War II, various federal laws were passed: to provide talking books for blind persons, to allow seeing-eye dogs to accompany blind persons during interstate travel, to provide special postage rates on materials for blind persons, and to encourage sheltered workshops for them.

After the War, those important efforts on behalf of visually impaired persons were extended to all handicapped individuals. Public Law 80-617, the Civil Service Act, was amended in 1948 to prohibit discrimination in hiring physically handicapped persons. Public Law 80-402, created to encourage international exchange of students, teachers, and leaders in fields of specialized knowledge, including the broad field of special education, was also passed in 1948. In 1949, Public Law 81-162 authorized an appropriation for the work of the President's Committee on "National Employ the Physically Handicapped Week."

The Cooperative Research Act was passed in 1954, earmarking two-thirds of a million dollars for educational research with mentally retarded children. A few years later, in 1958, Public Law 85-926 was passed, providing grants to institutions of higher learning and to state education agencies to encourage training of teachers of mentally retarded students. That original landmark legislation was amended to provide federal support for preparing teachers and leadership personnel in all areas of special education. Further amended legislation of 1963 provided for federal resources to construct mental retardation and community mental health facilities to serve handicapped persons, to train those who work with handicapped persons, and to study the problems related to the needs of handicapped individuals.

During the sixties and seventies (and indeed until this day), there have been many important legislative acts implemented to serve handicapped persons, train those who would work with handicapped persons, and study the causes and consequences of various handicapping conditions. Perhaps none has been as significant as Public Law 94-142. To a great extent, the Anti-Poverty Act, the National Defense Education Act, the Civil Rights Act, the Elementary and Secondary Education Act, various special education acts, various amendments to the Vocational Rehabilitation Act, and various early education acts all paved the way to the development of the Education of All Handicapped Children Act, Public Law 94-142. As federal facilitating legislation was passed act by act, and as the states responded with their own implementing legislation, what had once been a small federal effort became a major national priority on behalf of the education of handicapped individuals.

And tomorrow? It's difficult—painful—to predict. Ronald Reagan's "New Federalism" has sought to decrease direct federal involvement in programs for handicapped persons (indeed, in *many* educational and social welfare programs). There are indications that Public Law 94-142 is destined for such massive revision that it will be unrecognizable, at best, or perhaps even terminated completely. As with everything, time will offer the most precise understanding.

Litigation

During the late 1960s and 1970s, advocates and other citizen groups learned that courts can address problems ignored or misunderstood by various bureaucracies charged with running the schools and the other health, education, and welfare agencies. Parents went to court to seek relief for one injustice or another perpetrated against their children. Groups of parents went to court to claim that they represented not only themselves but large classes of individuals who suffered from similar injustices. It can be said that the major reforms in mental retardation were, if not begun, at least strengthened as a result of class action litigation.

During the seventies, litigation in Pennsylvania, New York, Massachusetts, Tennessee, Nebraska, Washington, DC, Alabama, and elsewhere changed the entire country's conception of the nature of a segregated environment (based on the "least restricted environment" principle); who is entitled to publicly sponsored schooling (based on the philosophy of "zero reject"); personalized education (based on the implementation of Individual Education Programs); "peonage" (based on disclosures that resident workers in state schools were not compensated); and what it means to live normally (based on concepts of normalization and mainstreaming). All these ideas were examined and reinforced by the courts. Of course, litigation is never without its unintended consequences. While the courts order children to be integrated, or that individual education programs be developed, or that X treatment be given, or Y therapy be made available, they are too often silent about important basics — such as reading and arithmetic skills for mildly retarded children. While a court orders Willowbrook Developmental Center to reduce its population from more than 6,000 residents to 250 residents, it is unable to convince the State of New York to implement the decision or to understand why it was made. What is right about litigation and subsequent court action is exactly what is wrong with it. It is an intrusion by outsiders, on the one hand. On the other hand, it is a necessary intrusion when those in authority and with responsibility either do not assume the authority or fail to meet their responsibilities. Litigation may address the problem at issue, but in doing so it may engender unintended — negative — side effects. The court, for example, orders the initiation of X program; the equally valid Y program is terminated to meet the costs of the new mandate. The court, for example, orders an end to "peonage" in the state school; adults for whom work had been meaningful and necessary then must stop working and submit to torturous idleness and boredom. Among the earliest and most important litigation connected with the education of children, and thus connected with special education, was *Brown v. Board of Education* in 1954. This case affirmed the rights of all children to participate in unsegregated schooling. The Supreme Court ruled that segregation by race is unconstitutional, a decision that led to later lower court rulings on the equal protection of all children from segregated schooling.

One of the earliest comprehensive cases specifically concerning retarded individuals was the *Pennsylvania Association for Retarded Children v. Commonwealth of Pennsylvania* in 1972. Brought by a number of parents representing their mentally retarded children, this class action suit fought the exclusion of retarded children from free public programs. The decision of the United States District Court in Pennsylvania affirmed the right of these children to appropriate education from preschool through all their developing years. Furthermore, the Court ruled that this right must be articulated in the least restrictive setting — so that education and/or habilitation can be offered in an environment that separates these students from other students only to the degree necessary to insure appropriate programs.

In 1972, the United States District Court in Washington, DC heard *Mills v. Board of Education of the District of Columbia,* a class action suit brought to insure the appropriate participation of all exceptional children in the local public schools of the District. In 1973, in *San Antonio Independent School District v. Rodriguez,* the United States Supreme Court confirmed again that education is a fundamental right of *all* children.

In *Hobson v. Hansen,* the District of Columbia District Court in 1967 considered the argument by plaintiffs that schools should not use IQs to place children in ability tracks. In general, the Court examined the impact of various school classification (labeling) practices on opportunities afforded impoverished children. In 1972, *Larry P. v. Riles* in the California District Court also examined the effects of labeling, and furthermore, carefully weighed the extent of misplacing black children in classes for retarded students. In another litigation arena, the courts examined legal aspects of institutional placements. An important case, *Wyatt v. Stickney* (1971), began in the early 1970s the long court test of the rights of institution residents to treatment.

The several so-called Willowbrook cases, beginning in the early 1970s and continuing to this day, have been concerned with deleterious effects of large segregated institutions on the lives of mentally retarded residents. Of course, there have been many many other cases in state and federal courts that have addressed issues concerned with equal protection, due process, freedom from cruel and unusual punishments, and with other constitutional guarantees that may have been systematically denied retarded people in our society.

America is a litigious society; and while some decry this, others applaud the emerging argumentative character of the American consumer, the voter, the individual with a special interest, the individual in search of an interest. In no more profound manner has the field of mental retardation been split than as a result of litigation. Some see litigation as the "salvation" of the abused and disenfranchised, while others see it as the work of the devil, of adventurers and assorted other "Johnny-come-latelys" intent on "making their mark" rather than "paying their dues." And so we have situations where friend testifies against friend, colleague against colleague, one professional or scientific organization against the other. We have the situation where an organization — such as the American Association on Mental Deficiency — enters into litigation as amicus curiae (friend of the court), but essentially provides testimony on behalf of a plaintiff who is suing a distinguished member of that very organization.

As mentioned, litigation on behalf of mentally retarded persons came of age with *Pennsylvania Association for Retarded Citizens v. the Commonwealth of Pennsylvania* (1972) and *Wyatt v. Stickney* (1971). Those landmark cases and the multitudes that followed established several important principles that have since guided the courts, state departments of education and mental retardation, the federal government, and people everywhere:

1. Mentally retarded people shall be placed in the least restrictive environment which provides appropriate habilitation and other developmental opportunities.

2. No child shall be excluded, exempted, or suspended from publicly supported schooling.

3. Handicapped persons are entitled to the same protections under the United States Constitution and our federal and state laws as any other people.

What has all this litigation meant to handicapped people, to society? While it can be estimated that 80% to 90% of the litigation in this area during the past 20 years was decided on behalf of the plaintiffs (the handicapped individuals and their families), there has not been a *commensurate* improvement in opportunities and programs for them. For sure, today there are more thoughtful programs, and the laws are better heeded by officialdom. But there is much yet to be accomplished insofar as the day-to-day lives of handicapped people are concerned. Added to the burden of what needs to be implemented are problems connected with the erosion of guarantees heretofore stipulated. For example, we have hardly begun to put into practice what legislatures and courts have authorized, and yet the opponents of school integration, zero-reject, deinstitutionalization, and equal rights for handicapped individuals have succeeded in modifying a number of the laws, overturning a number of past court decisions, and reducing federal, state, and county allocations for programs and other services for handicapped persons. The period of the thirties through World War II may be characterized as a time of consciousness raising; the period of the fifties and sixties may be characterized as a time when conscience acted (legislation was promulgated); the period of the seventies may be characterized as a time of litigation and program building. It is not inconceivable that historians will later characterize the eighties as the time when society broke faith with its earlier promises, as a time of reaction, a time of return to the dark days before the people were enlightened.

Of course, some of the disenchantment has been brought on by the field itself. A program is developed—a small, carefully nurtured group home. It's so successful that a second group home is developed and placed in the same neighborhood. That too succeeds. More homes are created, eventually so affecting the neighborhood that there is no longer a normalized environment for mentally retarded people but there is an abnormal environment for the citizens who lived there originally. In mental retardation, nothing fails like success.

Much of the confusion, much of the demoralization, and much of the litigation in the field grew out of inept policies. Litigation itself, for example, was a good idea, but has been so overused (and sometimes for the most trivial purposes) that it is now often as oppressive as the inequities it seeks to address. And so we find that the field of mental retardation suffers from too much and too confusing legislation, litigation, politics, and bureaucracy. Because too few people are willing to assume responsibility for their actions, we have a greatly regularized mental retardation system in the various states. Because too many of us have lost our faith in the laws, we litigate, possibly beyond reason. And because our laws are sometimes too severe, complex, or incomprehensible, we break them. There is a pessimism in the field — one which does not admit that the human being is changeable (educable), a pessimism which causes us to be annoyed with each other, to distrust each other's motives, and to seek relief in the courts for our anger and despair.

In a recent unpublished paper, Biklen found fault with the courts for their less than aggressive protection of the rights of disabled people. In June, 1982, the United States Supreme Court decided that a deaf child, Amy Rowley, was not entitled to have the assistance of a sign language interpreter for all of her academic classes (Board of Education v. Rowley, 1982). Biklen makes the interesting observation that, at first, it appeared as if Rowley would win her case. Indeed, the District Court, and then the Appeals Court, affirmed this child's right to sign language assistance. But eventually, the majority opinion of the Supreme Court confirmed that, while the school must provide Amy with a program that has some educational benefit, it need not provide her with greater opportunity than that afforded her nondisabled classmates. As long as Amy is able to achieve passing grades *without all possible special help,* the school need not provide all possible help for her. As Biklen pointed out, the Supreme Court ruling has important implications for the field of special education. Because of it, the schools now have greater latitude to decide what is or is not fair for each child. The schools need no longer be concerned with optimal programs. Rather, the schools must meet a far lesser standard. That is, a deaf child may be given a hearing aid or tutorial assistance instead of an interpreter if the school decides that those services are as beneficial (in helping the child achieve passing grades) as an interpreter, and that even without an interpreter the child will still pass his or her subjects.

I summarized this case briefly in order to illustrate how the balance of sentiment has shifted during the past few years — ever so slightly, but noticeably. More and more, the courts are (again) deciding on behalf of defendants rather than plaintiffs. More and more, the legislatures of our country are reluctant to either pass progressive legislation or to fully implement current legislation that would cost the taxpayers money — money which the legislators say the states do not have, and money which the taxpayers say they do not want to give for such purposes as providing the fullest educational opportunities for handicapped individuals. Here again, we have a situation for which nothing succeeds like failure and nothing fails like success. As discussed, until recent years, almost every case brought before the courts on behalf of handicapped plaintiffs was won by the plaintiffs. The more such cases were won, the more popular litigation became.

It would seem that everything breaks, including good ideas that are extended too far, even good intentions that have forgotten their original purpose. Litigation was once a great means to redress injustice. Today, it may be as often as not just another aggravation between what we want to accomplish and that myriad of ever-present roadblocks and discouragements. In the field of mental retardation, there is no question that litigation works. But now there is a new question: "How much good does it do?"

Politics

The last chapter examined the politics of mental retardation in terms of the people in control; this discusses mental retardation in terms of various social, cultural, and political forces that have created and now sustain the industry. How many of us understand how the idea of a law is created, how it is moved from idea to legislation, how it is worked over by politicians along the way, how it is executed by government executives and bureaucrats, and how it is received and fine-tuned by the public—the final and most important judge in a democracy? Boyer and Hechinger (1981) have claimed that the declining confidence in our country, its government, and its institutions, is related to our stupidity about the ways we create, pass, and promulgate our laws and other governmental business. Nearly half our eligible voters fail to turn out for presidential elections; and half our citizens do not believe that political institutions can solve such problems as energy shortages, inflation, and crime; and half do not believe that the electoral process determines how the country is run. The most serious question is not what we can do about all of that, but, Why don't the people vote?

There is little confidence in our elected executives, little confidence in Congress, little confidence in our doctors, and little confidence in our professors. Apparently, we have the *most* confidence in the conclusion that our leaders and institutions are not to be trusted. In some ironic manner, what we didn't know about institutions for retarded persons permitted us to keep supporting them; but what we didn't know about our better institutions—our Constitution, our courts, our Congress—permitted us not only to ignore them but to disdain them. What we all need is a basic course on the idea of America, how it works, why it doesn't work better, and how we can make it work better. Of course, it will be infinitely easier to teach such a course to young children over a period of time than to unwilling adults.

Throughout this book, I have emphasized the role of political forces—both inside and outside the field. A crucial, if neglected, aspect of political power is intimately related to the question, Why don't people vote? One question begets another: What is the meaning of citizenship?

Citizenship

Citizenship and civic action are ennobling ideas. But they are also vexing and puzzling, vexing because they sound almost pretentious (yet necessary), and puzzling because, while everyone knows what these ideas mean and how they can be used, hardly anyone knows how to foster them. Scarcely 50% of the nation's eligible voters actually vote. Yet, educators and others in positions of leadership are lost for ways to teach concepts of citizenship. We are lost for ways to interest people in citizen action. We are not even certain if we ourselves are seriously interested in being part of a mobilization effort for citizen reform—whether it be reform of the schools, reform of the mental health system, or reform of our ways of living with one another.

What does it mean to be an active, responsible, citizen? And again, how can active citizenship be fostered? An initial notion may be to persuade people to go to the polls. But perhaps we should reconsider that impulse; perhaps we should first try to find out *why* people don't go to the polls. Perhaps we should first find out *why* people aren't as interested as they should be in the schools. Perhaps we should first find out *why* even decent people abide indecent state institutions.

Once upon a time (really not too many years ago), parents of retarded children mobilized to establish extraordinary political and social power on behalf of handicapped persons. Through their efforts, preschool classes grew in virtually every city and town in America—where once there were none. Through their efforts, sheltered workshops and job training programs grew—where once there were hardly any. Through their efforts, laws were changed or new ones were promulgated to guarantee the right of every child to go to school. Perhaps, so much seemed to have been accomplished that those citizens saw less and less reason to remain mobilized as an army for this good cause. The problem today, however, is not to publicize word that the work of citizens is completed. Rather, the task today is to counter the deep, pervasive—but mistaken—impression that this work is completed. Here lies both the danger and the challenge.

In this chapter I have attempted to examine briefly legislation, litigation, politics, and civic responsibility. I seek only to whet the reader's appetite for further exploration of these issues.

12.

Aspirations and Values

IN THIS CHAPTER, I continue to explore the dilemmas and paradoxes in the field of mental retardation. Because they are rarely discussed does not necessarily mean that they are unimportant. I assert that a first responsibility of the community is to ensure that *everyone* has useful work to do—even if a *modern* farm must have the cows milked by hand, just to make jobs. Yes, that *would* offend some persons' sense of rationality, especially since American society has not, for the most part, been willing to "make work" for healthy unemployed persons. I discuss technology, how it helps, and how it can interfere not only with purposeful work but also with human interactions. I share some of my worries about a relatively recent trend in our society—the bureaucratization of values—using Ralph Nader as a case example; he has both performed a remarkable public service and also fostered the new "disease" of over-regulation. And lastly, I return to the "life and death" issues—killing babies, euthanasia, the value of a human life. All of these issues are related to the question of values in the field of mental retardation. It is critical that such values be carefully considered in order to understand their fundamental contribution to the shaping of the field.

Moral Goals and Technical Means

Moral goals obtain from moral convictions, not empirical evidence.

Of course, we must utilize *technical means,* all the hardware and software and professional expertise available to *achieve* those moral goals. We know a great deal today about immunizing all children against measles, diphtheria, and other child killers. We know more about the ravages of malnutrition. We know and do more about those problems than ever before. Well baby clinics, food supplement programs, health education efforts, and welfare plans have been established. That's all to the good. However, the *goals themselves* should be natural consequences of what we believe, what we aspire to become, and (conversely) what we disavow. We must always be focused on the goals. There has been confusion in the field, and the confusion has led to unfortunate consequences. For example, experts have been called by the courts to testify concerning whether retarded people have greater opportunities for development in the institution or in the community, or, for that matter, whether it makes any significant difference where they are placed. But the primary question should be whether this society will allow people who have not been judged as dangerous to themselves or others and who have not broken the law to be institutionalized "for their own good" or "for the good of society." That's the prepotent question! Of course, it's true that some people have greater opportunities to develop, or to avoid physical or mental problems, in one type of environment rather than in another. But this is not only true of mentally retarded people. It's true of everyone. What professor will deny that he or she would probably write more books if forced by the dean or department chairperson to spend 20 hours a week in the library or laboratory? Then why don't we require professors to spend more time in the library? To avoid a horrible mess, and to avoid a totalitarian state, people are permitted to do more or less anything that pleases them—just as long as they don't break "too many" laws, or endanger themselves, other people, or society. Such indulgence appears to work well in a democracy. There are people who are relatively happy, relatively free, relatively responsible for how they conduct their lives.

The question remains vis-à-vis retarded persons: Why do we require scientific "proof" that they are entitled to freedom? I assert that scientific evidence is irrelevant to freedom. I assert that all persons, if they are not a danger to themselves or to society, are entitled to freedom. This is a fundamental part of my values, my beliefs. This belief cannot be tested empirically, yet it provides a basis for action. It provides a basis for the formulation of goals, it can be realized in the form of social policy. Camphill Village, an intentional community in rural New York, comes immediately to mind because it embodies the notion of freedom (Blatt et al., 1979). Retarded residents live there by choice—and would probably remain there even if they were miraculously cured. Camphill Village is a model community for a group of about 150 people, about half diagnosed as mentally retarded. Camphill has a lovely modern barn as well as modern homes, work places, and machinery. Consequently, the first-time visitor might be surprised to find that the farm workers, all of whom would be diagnosed as mentally retarded according to conventional criteria, milk cows by hand. Further, a worker is assigned to hold each cow's tail during the milking. What's so modern about all of this? Nothing, but everything. After the cows are milked by hand and the milk is collected in pails, subsequent handling is with the most up-to-date equipment—electronically pumped to an upper level of the barn for pasteurization and refrigeration. Then why the hand milking? Everyone at Camphill Village has a job, a *real job,* and everything is precisely figured out so that people aren't standing around with their hands in their pockets or playing meaningless games. Thus, they hand milk the cows, because it's much better for people to be *needed* to milk cows than to have a machine do the milking while they (who could accomplish that work) have nothing to do. This is an example of *utilizing* technology to implement moral goals, to the best advantage for human beings. A major moral goal is for everyone to work—to be useful to society—and that goal takes precedence over getting the most return on each cow; better we should insist on the most return on each person. I worry about a society that seems to have run amok with its technology. I worry about office building windows that do not open, especially in those communities with few humid days during the summer. I am puzzled when I cannot find an ordinary staircase in many college and office buildings. If, in those buildings, architects had designed staircases that were easy to find and as inviting as staircases of old, the occupants might have been able to do with one less elevator and a lot less energy consumption.

What does all of this have to do with mental retardation? A great deal. Technology is too often perceived not as a means to achieve moral goals, but as a statement in and of itself. If people can be made useless by technology—made useless while cans of peas whirl around innumerable electric openers—then worrying about robots is not as paranoid an activity as some people make it out to be. If the goals are indistinguishable from the technology, then we are being driven not to a better world but merely to a less sweaty world. There is a difference between the goals we stand for and what we merely stand, what we are willing to put up with. There should be a difference between unnecessary and necessary technology, between something useful and a merely interesting gadget, gimmick, or new invention. Possibly, much of the technology that has been reputed to aid us in our work in mental retardation has simply been another way of making the clients or the caretakers less useful to each other or to society. Goals in this field must be primarily judged on moral grounds. Technology must be judged on how well it serves to progress toward moral goals. All other considerations are secondary at best, and sometimes either unrelated or inimical to our goals.

Naderism and the Bureaucratization of Values

With every technical advance or new program on behalf of society, there is the possibility of unintended negative consequences. Witness the great national highway program (and clogged roads), and the great communication networks (and new worries about the effects of television on social discourse). Witness the proliferation of federal, state, and local laws and regulations. Who today does not worry about loss of freedom, about red tape, about the burgeoning civil service? Enter Ralph Nader.

Nader may well be more derogated by American big business than even Karl Marx or Franklin Delano Roosevelt — and Nader is alive, still capable of yet more "mischief." Ralph Nader is neither one-dimensional nor uncomplicated. Even to sympathizers his work and influence present characteristics of a mixed blessing. Of course, he provided a great service to Western Civilization if for no other reason than by reminding us that, if Charles Darwin was right about the "survival of the fittest," by definition there are times when even the most altruistic survivors must behave selfishly. If "advocacy" is when you work on another person's behalf as if you were working on your own behalf, then "survival" requires you to work (at least from time to time) on your own behalf as if you come first. This is not to say that people cannot rise above their selfish motives and behavior. Our history is replete with great acts of heroism, of sacrifice, and even of martyrdom. But if people were not characteristically selfish, or at least self-interested, then there would not be a need for such words as "sacrifice" and "martyrdom."

What Ralph Nader did was to call attention to the selfish interests of our various industries and government agencies. He reified a well-known lesson, one that forms the basis for most of our laws and practices. For example, we do not ask the trucking industry to set the toll rate on the turnpike, and we do not ask the telephone company to set its own rates. We do not permit the university student to determine when he or she deserves a degree. And we do not permit the university to determine whether or not it deserves accreditation. Nader called attention to certain aspects of our business and government communities that were not sufficiently regulated. Notwithstanding, the "disease" Nader sought to cure — unregulated industry and government — if too vigorously "treated" spreads another disease, one threatening to reach epidemic proportions — bureaucratization.

We observe bureaucratization everywhere — in the paperwork doctors must now attend to, for example, in order for society to control their self-interest. We see bureaucratization in the field of mental retardation and wonder whether the plethora of paper and standards cure or exacerbate the problems they were meant to solve. Once, institutions were unregulated.

This lack of regulation was thought to be the source of unconscionable, inhumane conditions. We created accreditation commissions. But what do they do? They seem to be preoccupied with matters such as square footage allotted for each bed or with the fire-resistant qualities of materials used in the dormitories. These are not unimportant concerns, but they are surely secondary to the primary question, about which the commissions and other official bodies remain relatively silent: "Should we have the institution?" Or, "What is going on here that can't go on in the community?" The rationale for institutions and programs used to be connected to what was done and to whom; today it is connected to what the place looks like, how many people are served, and how many people are available to care for them. It seems that we have given up on the idea that we can examine and evaluate the *substance* of an environment and program. It's as if, because we don't know anything about whiskey but we know a great deal about glass, we should evaluate Johnnie Walker Scotch on the quality, the appearance, and the durability of the bottle.

We should not be misled. The great deal we have achieved with our various commissions and accrediting agencies insofar as the maintenance of standards has little to do with fundamental questions, such as: Is this good for people? Are there better ways? Are we on the right track? That is, we now have the "machinery" to learn more and more about the particulars of the "nuts and bolts" of institutions and their programs, but we persist in learning little about what they do for people and (even more importantly) whether they're necessary. Much of this perceived problem can be laid to movements of the past 20 years to bureaucratize values. Mental retardation suffers not from what we don't know about the institutions but from what we don't know about the world. In this regard, Ralph Nader is of limited help.

> Nader seems to want to overcome . . . evil by a bureaucratized society, one to be controlled by the people to be sure but, nevertheless, people who would weigh everything, test everything, define everything and be suspicious about anything. Possibly, at this time what is needed more than . . . Nader is a good poet who would give us some hints on how to live better with each other . . . .
>
> Maybe we needed Nader when he came along. But I'll take Robert Frost. (Blatt, 1981, p. 345)

Of course, there are times when the bureaucratization of values might be necessary, times when the bureaucratization of values might insure life. During recent years, courts in the United States and the United Kingdom have ruled that parents in consort with physicians may elect to deprive their children of life-sustaining procedures. Until eventually overturned by

California's highest court, the natural parents of a child with Down syndrome were permitted to withhold the necessary surgical repair of his heart. In Baltimore, the natural parents of a newborn with Down syndrome were not challenged by a university medical center when they elected not to permit surgery that could have prevented their child's death two weeks later. And in England, a court exonerated a physician who deliberately injected a lethal dose of a drug in a newborn with Down syndrome. The latter two are instances of what might be called the "bureaucratization of death," the former the "bureaucratization of life."

The Department of Justice is prepared to intervene actively in such cases ("Justice," 1982). At least until a newer or stronger bureaucratic edict changes policy, the Department of Justice will vigorously argue in court that parents do not have the right to refuse to permit necessary medical treatment that might prevent the death of a sick child. Furthermore, the Department of Health and Human Services let it be known that federal aid will be denied to any hospital that refuses to provide necessary care for retarded and other handicapped infants. So here we have an instance where a federal bureaucracy — the Department of Health and Human Services — informs the medical community that it is suspected of making bad decisions concerning the protection of human life, and consequently, the bureaucracy will deny funds to hospitals that continue to kill babies. And furthermore, the second arm of government, the judiciary, announces that, when it learns about parents who refuse necessary treatment for their child, it will through the court attempt to save the life of a child whose very parents want to see it killed. In this brief commentary, we have *both* the reasons why bureaucratizing values causes great harm *and* why it's often necessary. Here we have instances where at times the disease (bureaucratization) is the cure, and at other times the cure is the disease. Why is it that, in this field, what we do best sometimes causes the most mischief (bureaucratize and litigate)? And why is it that we have the most difficulty in accomplishing that which may help people (e.g., create a normal environment for the disabled or manage a mainstreamed special education program)? Why is it that our institutions do best what other agencies do well (e.g., run laundries), and they do poorly what only they can do (provide living environments for their clients)?

With all of the problems attendant with the bureaucratization of values, I do not want to suggest that people such as Ralph Nader are or were unnecessary. I only want to point out that the bureaucratization of values entails some unintended and undesirable consequences. As I have stressed, though, such bureaucratization is in some instances necessary to insure the preservation of life. Thus the dilemma, a dilemma that certainly does not leave the field of mental retardation untouched.

We Need Not Be Strangers

Aspirations and values cannot be adequately understood apart from that which we work to forget—our mortality. Later in this book, I write about the "Amnesia of Mental Retardation." There are certain matters that humans choose (or are compelled) to forget or ignore. This is by way of saying that we are burdened with long-standing taboos. All of us must die some day, and all of us must face pain, unhappiness, disillusionment, despair. But only the young or the foolish can live without being preoccupied at times with that which is taboo at other times; it is even possible that those may be among the most meaningful periods of our lives.

We need not always be strangers to that which is now the unthinkable, and, for sure, the non-discussable. Like death itself, mental retardation is much easier to face when it does not visit us as a stranger. That which should be most familiar to us is often a stranger. Death, mental retardation, love, friendship, nature (especially the animal world) are such strangers to human beings, are so frightening. The man with cerebral palsy walks haltingly on the busy city sidewalk, and as he passes, people turn their heads away and make a psychological if not physical path for him. It's almost as if he's the most feared gunslinger in town, because no one—simply no one—wants to get in his way, wants to look toward his eyes and meet them.

Why? Human beings avoid that which is different; for that which is different is oftentimes perceived as unpleasant, and if not entirely unpleasant then anxiety-provoking. People avoid death and mental retardation, in part, for the same reasons they avoid unfamiliar faces at the cocktail party. They too are strangers. As long as mental retardation is a stranger to society, as long as mental retardation is a stranger to the family, it will be unresolved as well as misunderstood in the home. There is no way we could (or should) want mental retardation in the home, but there is no good reason why we cannot accommodate it, and thus make life less arduous for the person so afflicted as well as the rest of the family.

The reality of mental retardation is plain enough—it is not sought, appreciated, wanted, or easily tolerated. We are able to comprehend all but the last, because while there is always the question of whether it can or cannot be treated, it *must* be tolerated. As far as we know, mental retardation is chronic, it is either tolerated or made much more serious than it needs to be. It is either tolerated or it will make us more unhappy than we need to be. Mental retardation need not be looked upon as a blessing in disguise, but neither need it be looked upon as a completely unmitigated disaster. There are things a family (or a community) can learn from one of its members who has mental retardation. There are things a family can learn from each other in dealing with, in sharing with, in loving one of its members who has mental retardation. There are things a family can learn about death that makes it easier for the dying person as well as the rest of the family. There are things a family can learn about mental retardation that not only make living easier but also make their common experiences more worthwhile. No one should seek death nor should one seek mental retardation. But as death is unavoidable to everyone, mental retardation will happen for sure in some families. And furthermore, the fact of mental retardation will remain with such families forever, even if the individuals themselves are actually "cured." No one escapes remembrance of mental retardation in his family, as no one ever forgets a departed mother or father. But to put it still another way, no one ever forgets mental retardation in a family as no one ever forgets a first love, a first triumph, the first momentous encounter with life. Mental retardation is a genuinely momentous encounter with life. Whether it happens to you or to a loved one, it is an unforgettable experience. The paradox is that most of us act as if we not only can easily forget it, but also as if it is already forgotten. In that sense, mental retardation is simply another version of the death experience — or the love experience.

Why Opportunity Eludes Us

Some settings do not afford the "opportunity" to achieve moral goals. In complex organizations, the situation is often messy. It's to be expected. A case can even be made that in the university the mess is not a compelling problem (Blatt & Ozolins, 1981). A great university isn't created by cleaning up the mess, but rather, by uncovering and developing good professors to work with potentially good students. "Opportunity" is what makes settings exemplary. The potential for genuine greatness is enhanced when there is *freedom* for people to develop, when there is *freedom* for the "unexpected" to occur. Again, this argument makes the case for an open as opposed to a closed environment, for democracy as opposed to totalitarian rule. The mission of *any* complex human setting should aim at steering itself toward the maximization of the "unexpected," and to do this requires the organization to deal with individuals, not with people who are conceptualized as "replaceable parts." Of course, there are risks involved with such a strategy. People are appointed and people are supported on "speculation," which always entails risk. But whenever there is speculation, there is the opportunity for something fresh, soemthing exciting, something healthy to develop and flourish. Essentially, that is the case for abiding with the little (and even some of the large) messes in the university. The mess isn't always a symptom of disease, but rather, of cure.

The situation in the segregated environment is different. Opportunity eludes us in the segregated environment because the messes there *dominate* the culture of the place. Where there is segregation, where there is repressiveness, the mess becomes the figure and whatever is good is the ground, soon to wither away, now to be ignored.

Before me, I have a report sent anonymously. What follows is the unsigned covering memorandum to the report:

> Dear Mr. Blatt:
>
> I am a worker here in the Department of Mental Retardation and Developmental Disabilities. I am writing to you to give you a copy of a report I got hold of in my office. I am in grad school now and have heard that you are very serious about helping the retarded. I cannot give you my name because I am afraid I might get fired if anyone found out I sent this report to you. The report is about a hospital for the profoundly retarded. I have heard that very little is being done to help those kids. This report talks about that problem and about the way the staff continue to do nothing.

What does the report say? A consultant was brought in from another state to look at a comprehensive instructional program at a converted hospital. It had been created to handle overflow discharges from a large institution, one that had been ordered by the federal court to reduce its census by several thousand. At the newly created institution, the per capita expenditure for each resident approached $100,000 a year, and, quite possibly, now even exceeds that amount. The institution, the report said, had poor morale, and the in-service training program for professionals had been judged by participants themselves as inadequate and unhelpful. Management was not effective or supportive, staff did not implement new procedures, and there were mismatches between the competencies of the workers and the jobs that they were expected to perform. There were widespread feelings of confusion among professional and technical staff, and there was resistance to try anything new or different; there was reluctance even to attempt to meet the mandates of the court itself, or the various federal and state laws that require certain procedures and programs. In a word, the situation was a bad "mess." But different from the "mess" in the unviersity — a creative mess, in a sense — there was little here that was not messy, and there was little here that portended future program and morale building.

Why? We return to primary questions: What are the goals? What are the means to achieve the goals? In this case, the goals revolved around providing a "better" institution. The strategy for achieving the goals appears to be embedded in setting down the values which people *should* embrace but were little more than *told* to embrace. Here we have a prime example of what we termed earlier the "bureaucratization of values."

Paradoxes

Our neat plans work precisely only on paper. In human affairs—especially when dealing with complex and serious matters, there are always paradoxes. Even our beautiful Constitution needed amendments. And if there were not paradoxes, we would not need a Supreme Court. Even if our goals are moral and our values are clarified, we will still face unresolvable paradoxes. Consider the following.

A Communicable Disease

Imagine the following situation; it shouldn't be impossible, for there are those in a small central New York community who need not imagine it because it is embedded in the reality of their lives. A young boy was a resident of the nearby state institution. It was decided to return him to the community, to a more normalized life experience. As are millions of other children in America, a day or two after Labor Day he was brought to the local public school by the group home supervisor. Everything was in order, with the exception of an unsolvable complication. The child had an incurable and highly transmittable type of herpes. The contagion is transmitted by mouth, through his almost constant open sores, and from his urine. He was enrolled in the class for severely and multiply handicapped young children—children who cannot fend too well for themselves, children who touch things and other people, children who like to hug and kiss. Advocates for the child insisted that he remain enrolled in the class. But the teacher threatened to resign if she was forced to change the diapers of this child who might have infected her and others with an incurable disease. The parents of the other children in the class threatened to sue the school department, the state, and whoever else they found responsible for the situation—claiming that their children also had rights. What would you do?

I have indicated time and again my conviction that every individual deserves to live in an ordinary community in as unrestrictive an environment as possible—if the individual is not a danger to self or others. Clearly, this particular child was perceived to be a danger to others, despite his innocence. Would you exclude him from instruction in the school and offer him a homebound teacher? That might provide the child with appropriate learning opportunities, but it would not do very much for his social and psychological needs. Would you insist on his right to attend the public school, this despite the possibility that others may be harmed by the decision? This is but one of many paradoxes that face those who would devote themselves to this work.

Sexuality

The following story was told to me by a distinguished colleague who specializes in sexuality and human development. A large old institution, which was being "battered" by parent advocates on the one hand, and the courts on the other, asked my friend to come to the institution to advise it on yet one more serious problem—widespread homosexuality. He called me for advice on the matter, since he had not had much experience with institutionalized retarded people. I offered one suggestion or another, but ended my commentary with the somewhat sarcastic remark that the only thing that institutions ever cure is heterosexuality. I implied that he would not be able to solve this problem. I asked him to call me when he returned to our campus from his visit to the institution so that I could hear about his experiences.

About a week or two later, I received that call. Yes, he had been to the institution, and yes, he had advised them—to integrate the institution's adult dormitories. My friend made a strong case for bringing men and women together, thus creating a more natural atmosphere. The recommendation sounded reasonable to me, but I asked my friend to call me if there was any further communication from the institution.

About a year later, my friend did call with the information that the institution had asked him to return for a second visit. There was a new problem. After the men's and women's dormitories were integrated, there was successful intermingling of the sexes, too successful; before long, several women became pregnant. This turn of events deeply disturbed the institution's administrators, and deeply grieved relatives of the pregnant women. "Now, what was the institution to do?" was the new question posed to the famous consultant. He told them quite frankly that he did not have a solution to this problem that would not exacerbate the old problem. The solution to one dilemma begets another, and that another. But as he later found out, one creative administrator at the institution *had* a solution. That person placed observers in the co-educational dormitory, their only task being to find out where the sexual activity was taking place. Soon enough, it was determined that the sexual activity was taking place on the grounds of the large old campus, particularly in an area where there were several old large trees. The solution would be simple. Cut down all of the trees. Clear the field, so there would be no good place to hide. The order was given to cut down the trees. But at the last moment, an attendant working at the institution—who was also a member of a local environmental group—secured a court order to prevent the destruction.

Normal sexual expression in an abnormal environment such as an institution appears to be one of those unsolvable problems. That is, the institution *must* have sexual problems. As it gropes to solve the problem of homosexuality among the residents, it increases the problem of undesired pregnancies. As it seeks to provide residents not only with a sense of freedom, but with actual freedom, it creates new dilemmas—such as thrusting a severely retarded person into a position where *he* or *she* is asked to consent (or not) to sex with another human being. Can a severely retarded person give informed consent? Is it not a non sequitur to think in terms of a severely retarded person being truly informed about anything? And if such an individual can be, then what does the term "severely mentally retarded" actually mean? What does it mean when an attendant at the institution reacts with the following comment when observing two clients fornicating, "Stop, put your clothes on. It's time for snacks"? And they obey. And that's it!

I am not calling for a return to the repressive institutional environment of years ago. That environment too caused many problems related to the sexual needs of the residents there; and it provided even fewer solutions than we have today. It appears to me that sexuality, like the very definition of mental retardation itself, offers opportunities to explore virtually every facet of the problem of mental retardation. And furthermore, because sexuality presents dilemmas not only to those of us who must work with retarded persons, but to all society, it also presents us with opportunities to reflect on society's general condition from the special vantage of seeing this issue in terms of a particular problem in which we have deep interest and experience. Consequently, while there are ironies and paradoxes embedded in the examination of sexuality of mentally retarded people, there are also opportunities to learn. For example, there is the paradox that, when people are given complete sexual freedom, one inescapable conclusion is that they are no longer thought of as people. To put this another way, we can view society's complete tolerance of any and all sexual behavior of a certain group of human beings much the same way society tolerates any and all sexual behavior of animals. A man isn't concerned when he sees a dog mounting another dog in the street. He doesn't dwell on the possibility that both dogs are male, or female. And he's not embarrassed for either the dogs, or himself, because the behavior is practiced in public. But a man is embarrassed—and sometimes distraught enough to call the police—when he encounters human beings publicly engaging in sexual misconduct (it's always *misconduct!*). Then what are we to make of the complete toleration of homosexual, heterosexual, or any sexual behavior of institutional residents? Is it human freedom that is being offered them? Or are they tolerated exactly as animals are tolerated? As we work toward examining such questions, we also work toward coming closer to a better understanding of these people as human beings, and of the concepts of "competency," "independence," and "responsibility." I am not calling for repression, but I am also not advocating for license. I want it to be remembered that only animals are permitted complete sexual freedom in our society. Human beings deserve better. Ironically, this is an instance in which human beings deserve the benefits of certain restraints. At least part of the definition of being a human being includes the restraints and responsibilities imposed on the person.

Wolfensberger (1982) in an unpublished paper, developed a position on a Christian approach to the sexuality of retarded people. Recounting past attitudes towards sexuality of retarded persons, he reminds us that these people were either treated as eternal children — or incapable of having sexual drives — or, if their sexuality was acknowledged, it was repressed. Today, the situation appears to be far different. Their sexuality is recognized with a vengeance. Many retarded people today (even more than people not retarded in this liberal society) are often encouraged to pursue sexual pleasures, to feel free to do anything that makes them feel good, to gratify their sexual and other urges, and not to suffer guilt (since suffering itself is considered evil, more evil than any sexual act could be). Of course, not all retarded people are encouraged to lead sexually permissive lives, as there are many ordinary people still today who practice the virtues learned in the churches and from traditional parents. But it's surely true that mentally retarded people today are more than ever before encouraged to express their sexuality. And there are some who are possibly urged, if not forced, to express sexual behavior which, just a mere decade or so ago, would have been considered reprehensible, if not illegal. Wolfensberger isn't the only one who worries about certain practices today with retarded people — practices which, even in the most favorable light, causes great anxiety among families, such as: giving retarded people money to "buy" sex, teaching retarded people how to masturbate, taking retarded people to pornographic movies, and hiring prostitutes or other "surrogates" to initiate the retarded persons into sexual activity.

As a teacher of retarded children, I once avoided confronting my pupils with their sexuality. As someone now removed from regular direct contact with retarded children, I seem to seize upon opportunities to dwell upon these matters. It might have been better had I dealt with such issues when there were live people under my charge who needed my guidance. On the other hand, the problems are such that they are often botched by even well-meaning and informed teachers — and much more so when the teacher is uncomfortable. "Better late than never," so the saying goes. Besides, as the tardy worm may have commented on missing the hungry bird, "Not only is it never too late, but there are occasions when one can only be saved if late." While probably not as desirable as otherwise for some people, that's the way it may be for others with regard to their sexuality.

For some people — for some mentally retarded children — not dealing with these issues early on leads to ugly, irreversible consequences, possibly even life-threatening consequences. During a recent trip to a southeastern state, I met with a group of parents whose children were in the educable and trainable classes in a local county school system. All of the children were segregated in special classes, with the more seriously retarded students in special schools. I learned that 60% of the moderately retarded girls received hysterectomies between the ages of 10 and 13, for reasons reputed to be connected to "menstrual hygiene." Of those not surgically treated, a large proportion of teenage and adult retarded women in that community received monthly injections of depo provera, which is considered to be a dangerous drug associated with lethal side effects. I also learned that mildly retarded girls and women were either sterilized surgically or were on some other birth control regime. This practice was—and is—so common that parents who resist school and medical advice of this kind have been viewed as uncooperative or unstable. Possibly, segregated schools and widespread sterilizations are to be expected from a system that introduces its segregated school curriculum with the following paragraph:

> The students are very happy at _____ School, therefore the parents are happy. The students don't realize that they are different from anyone else. They have the same things that anyone else their age has. They would know they were different if they were placed in a class in a regular school. They are accepted here and provided the same activities as a "normal" child.

I wish I were not so cynical about so much of this business. I wish that every American not only knew of the Constitution and the Bill of Rights, but also believed in the idea of America, why it was created, what it was meant to be. Reform and change are nurtured during periods of discontent. Unhappily, this is a time in our field—if not in the larger society itself—when there is widespread discontent, but also widespread complacency, even reactionism. We live in a puzzling and dangerous period of the American experience. We seem to have neither the persuasive people who could tell us truthfully what we are, nor those who could tell us prophetically what we might become. We seem to have neither adequate reality in our grasp nor vision in our mind.

Withholding Treatment

We pause here to resurrect a recurring scene in this book—one exemplifying the ambiguities and dilemmas embedded in the moral choices some confront regularly—the ethics of withholding medical and other treatments from disabled people. On one level, there's the dilemma in providing "expensive" services to severely handicapped children in the schools while others are denied more ordinary services. Is it morally defensible to give the severely handicapped child an opportunity to go to school — a decision that may involve a low teacher/pupil ratio, special equipment, and special facilities — when other children are not afforded opportunities for advanced mathematics, or classic languages, or driver education? On another level, there is the newborn with several serious physical anomalies whose parents are asked to choose between his or her life and death. And so we have the question: Can a moral community permit (or insist upon) tragic choices? Should parents have the right to order their severely defective babies to be killed? Do we permit parents the choice of killing their nonhandicapped children? If a parent can be offered a choice to terminate the life of a defective baby, why can't another parent be offered the choice to terminate the life of a son or daughter who is a murderer? Do parents own their children? Can one human being own another human being? Abraham Lincoln had something to say about this matter.

This is not a question that permits finite understanding. On the face of it, it can be argued that a community can't be moral if it makes tragic choices — if it allows the parents to decide on the life or death of their child. On the other hand, however, there is the argument that it is exactly that quality in a community which makes it moral. That is, the community that will not make a moral choice is immoral. Let's examine the case of the parents who are confronted with the life or death of their child. If they are not given a choice because there is a law that makes choice unnecessary, a law that regularizes euthanasia — then we have regularized immorality. Then the choice is neither moral nor anguishing, but rather, purely economic. Most choices made by government are not tragic; most choices made by government are in the best interests of the larger society, and usually, are driven by economic, political, or practical considerations. A law does not permit moral choice. Therefore, in this regard, the law is a two-edged sword. While we can claim that a community that permits babies to be killed upon parental consent is not a generous community, at least it permits the element of choice. If the society itself elects to regularzie euthanasia, though, then choice is abdicated, then what once required oftentimes an agonizing moral decision now is left to administrative implementation of economic necessity, then the rare exception can become the regular practice.

We must remember that Hitler and his Nazi confederates once developed a euthanasia program on a "quality of life" issue. Hitler decided that life devoid of value is meaningless, and consequently, killed the Jews, the Gypsies, the Slavs, and others who failed to meet the Nazi ideal for human existence (Wertham, 1966). Duff (1981), a medical professor who has advocated euthanasia with "severely defective children," calls for proactive family involvement in life or death decisions involving such children. For those parents who are clearly incompetent or irresponsible, he has recommended hospital resolution of such problems. In this manner, he has concluded that the medical profession will go a long way toward coping with what he terms "medical Vietnam." Elsewhere, I have commented negatively on the right of families to deny life and on the regularization of euthanasia — either by hospital or court initiative. The point of the above argument extends the discussion: If there are any choices to be made — that is, if we continue to foster an imperfect moral community — then the choice must be made in such a manner as to require anguish and soul searching. That is, if the choice must be made, then it must be a "tragic choice" and not a legal one.

Paradoxes are Inevitable

Work in the field of mental retardation will confront you with an almost endless array of irreconcilable paradoxes, some of which are crucially important to you, to your clients, to society. In America, most people believe that every problem can be overcome, every puzzle can be solved. Yet, in reality, there are problems that are unsolvable. People still die from the ravages of cancer. People still die from the destructive consequences of a damaged heart, or a broken heart. While we have accomplished a trip to the moon, travel to even the nearest of our planets seems beyond our reach. There *are* problems that defy solution. It seems that society would be better off all around if it could recognize the existence of such problems. I will have succeeded in this book if I leave you with the realization that some problems do defy neat solutions; yet we must not on this account accept the problems themselves.

Part 5

SOCIAL CHANGE
AND THE PROFESSIONS

VICTIMS and VICTIMIZERS

In the back ward, who is the
victim, and who is the victimizer?
  Each is; all are.

Who is dehumanized, who are the
cruel, and what is cruelty?
Each is; all are; everything!

In any institution, if there is a
back ward, can there be anything but
back wards?
  In that institution, as the back
ward continues to exist, are all people
chronic victims and pervasive victimizers?
  In that institituion, is not the
  term "back ward" a synonym for
  "institituion"?

He who victimizes others is the victim
of his inevitable dehumanization,
  As he who is dehumanized must contribute
to the dehumanization of others.
  All men — willing or unwilling, knowing
  or unknowing — are victimized during the
  trials of living as their debasements and
  agonies victimize other men.
  Our way of living tests each man's
humanity, assaults it, and sometimes is its conquereor
  As each man contributes
  to our way of living, to his
  own dehumanization, to the dehumanization
  of all others,
  As each man is his own victim and victimizer.
    (Blatt, 1981, pp. 107-108)

13.

Ideals, Practices, and Declarations

WHAT ARE THE ideals of mental retardation practitioners? What are the practices of mental retardation idealists? And what are the goals? I turn now to those questions in terms of testing, diagnosis, placement, and treatment. It is necessary to think about these questions in terms of professionals who (believe they) know more than enough and consumers who (believe they) do not know enough. The professionals—even the professional advocates—may "know" and do so much for the consumers that the consumers do not (or cannot) do enough for themselves—which is, of course, the ultimate goal.

Inevitably, we must return to the Golden Rule, but we must strive for an extended, or different, if not deeper, understanding than what we learned in our schools and places of worship. Yes, do not do unto others as you would have others not do unto you. But also, try to do for others as *they* want done for themselves. Especially for those whom society perceives to be "different"—those who are disabled, disenfranchised, old—let us try to see them as *they* see themselves, and let us try to help them as they want to be helped—not only as we think we would want to be helped if we found ourselves in their circumstances.

It seems inevitable that some readers will disagree with my commentary here. People do indeed differ on ideals and goals—even people of goodwill.

The Golden and Other Rules

There is a story of many variations, many colorations, told for many purposes, told in many tongues and contexts. As part of its cultural baggage, every group knows and passes on such a story from generation to generation. It goes something like this:

> In a small ghetto village, a newly arrived couple visit the local Rabbi, obviously worried.
> "Rabbi, we were forced to move to this town because my husband's work must take us here. But we didn't want to move. We lived in a wonderful community. The people were all friendly, honest, compassionate, caring. Everyone helped one another. Everyone was a good neighbor. Everyone could be relied upon, could be trusted. It was the perfect community."
> "You will find this to be such a community," the Rabbi responded.
> By chance, a second couple came to see that Rabbi a few days later, also newly arrived, and also from the very community where the first couple had enjoyed such an ideal life together. But the second couple appeared glad to have escaped that town.
> "Rabbi, we are so pleased to be here. I hope we find life better here than where we had lived. There, the people were mean, nasty, dishonest, cruel. They weren't friendly. They didn't care about neighbors. It was a terrible place."
> "I am sorry to tell you that you will probably find this town to be very much like the town you came from," lamented the Rabbi.

It is not necessary to spend much time here drawing the obvious lesson from the story. It is necessary, however, to spend a great deal of time trying to fit that lesson into the practice of your life. Opportunities to improve the world, for all people, are everywhere. Even in our practical world, we can improve virtually every aspect of the ways we treat each other, the ways we help each other, the ways we provide for others as well as for ourselves during times of need. But as the preceding simple story teaches us, our behavior is reciprocated in kind. The human being is a mirror. When people see good in us and in our works, they behave accordingly. When people see suspicion, mistrust, and calculation, they also behave accordingly. Rule One is the Golden Rule. Rabbi Hillel once remarked in another context that everything else about ways to change the world, or ways to improve society, or ways to leave the world a better place are variations or commentaries on the Golden Rule. There are other Rules and the teachings of other religions, but none to my knowledge contradict this precept.

Such technical matters as testing and diagnosis, placement practices, treatment protocols, and administrative configurations may seem far removed from the Golden Rule, but they are not. To what purpose do professionals engage in these practices? How do they go about achieving their goals? In mental retardation, more important than theories about universal aims, learning, educability of intelligence, and prevention is the idea of doing for others as you would have others do for you (or as you would have done for yourself). Not straying too far from that idea will help the worker in mental retardation more adequately fulfill a decent mission. The Golden Rule is not tin or lead because God sees everything. Trust God more than mortals. But trust people too. Even this world can be good. And it can be better.

There are ideals and there are realities—practices. An ideal never put to the test is the virtuous person never given the opportunity to sin. In that sense, the ideal is neither good nor bad, neither important nor trivial; the idea unexpressed is nothing more than another idea.

In the field of mental retardation, many leaders seem to support liberal—indeed, radical—ideas. Notwithstanding, in the field of mental retardation, many leaders seem to engage in reactionary—regressive—practices. Some might conclude that therein lies the most prevalent, and, quite possibly, the most serious deception in the field. Quite simply, many leaders in mental retardation do not practice what they preach, or, conversely, do not preach what they practice. Many other groups in society can justifiably be accused of similar hypocrisy.

Testing and Diagnosis

A test leads to a judgment, a diagnosis. The diagnosis should lead to a prognosis, a prediction, which naturally leads to a placement (or refusal to make a placement, or a termination). But underlying all testing, all diagnoses, and all placements, is an orientation, or for want of something more precise, there is a philosophy, a prejudice, a principle, a reason.

How do diagnosticians find and shape their reasons, their principles? From their studies, from their professional experiences, but also from the ethos of their very cultures. While the professional influences the public, the professional is not immune to the blandishments and the interests of that same public—even on issues connected with the professional's area of competence. So, when a survey of the 25th reunion classes of Harvard, Yale, and Princeton revealed that many alumni of those distinguished universities believe that blacks are intellectually inferior to whites, it is not unreasonable to suggest that such influential (if not always informed) viewpoints bear discernible relationships to the viewpoints of other well-educated citizens—psychologists, teachers, physicians, and other professionals ("Poll," 1982). In that survey, no more than 37% of Princeton graduates, 46% of Yale graduates, and 54% of the Harvard graduates would agree that blacks and whites were intellectual equals. The rest either disagreed, weren't sure, or didn't respond to that particular question. After examining the report, one still-loyal son of Harvard remarked, "It shouldn't be that way."

If diagnosticians would but admit how difficult it is to make judgments concerning mental retardation and/or mental illness, everyone would be better off—patients, of course, but even the diagnosticians themselves. A study by Rosenhan (1973) and his colleagues, which described what occurred when they presented themselves for admission to psychiatric hospitals, offers insight into the diagnostic process. All complained of the same faked symptom; they heard voices. Eleven of the twelve mentally healthy "actors" were admitted with diagnoses of schizophrenia. Discharged one to seven weeks later, each of those 11 was labeled "schizophrenia in remission." The 12th "actor" was admitted and later discharged with a diagnosis of "manic-depressive psychosis." Nobody on the staffs of the hospitals even questioned the original diagnoses, even though the pseudopatients acted (or thought they acted) quite normally and cooperated fully. Rosenhan, a Stanford University psychologist, and his colleagues found that the other residents— presumably genuinely ill patients—may have been more perceptive. One of the "actors" was told by one of the inmates, "You're not crazy, you're checking up on the hospital."

Of the 12 hospitals that admitted these patients, three were top-ranked, AMA-approved hospitals with extensive residency programs to train psychiatrists and other mental health workers. Insofar as the "treatment" given these pseudopatients, here too the news is depressing and damning. These presumably sick people tried but were unable to establish communication with staff members. They were ignored for the most part. For example, when the pseudopatients questioned medical staff members (or asked for help), responses bordered on the bizarre, being neither relevant to the questions nor mindful that patients are entitled to some semblance of concern, if not immediate service. The pseudopatients reported that they were deprived of all sense of privacy, that their physical examinations were conducted in the open, that they couldn't even attend to their toileting needs unobserved.

It is possible that staff in other medical fields would have been brought up on charges of neglect, incompetence, and carelessness had they treated their surgical, medical, orthopedic, or other patients in so inept a manner.

Placement and Treatment

Practitioners in mental retardation experience the same problems as other professionals—politicans, businesspeople, ministers—in expressing their ideals in the practical world. It's within such confrontations that dilemmas are created, sustained, but often unresolved. The nature of our parents' rearing practices, the nature of our education — ironically even our moral education — the nature of the society we live in and, just as importantly, the nature of the society we want to create, forces upon people a test between their religion (or humanist philosophy) and the so-called real world. From early childhood on, who hasn't repeatedly learned a variation of the lesson that it's the good sailor who loves the wind but respects its dangers? Is there a mental retardation professional who hasn't learned to articulate support for the normalization principle while, nevertheless, he or she is acutely aware of the pitfalls embedded in the principle itself and those associated with its implementation? Of all the decisions that practitioners in mental retardation make, this dilemma between ideal and practice is no more extensive or apparent than in the placement-treatment-implementation scene.

The previous section briefly examined "testing and diagnosis" in terms of moral dilemmas. If a child is diagnosed as "severely" mentally retarded, a local school department I know of receives a triple reimbursement to support that child's educational program; if the child is diagnosed as "moderately" mentally retarded, the school department receives a double reimbursement; and if the child is merely "mildly" mentally retarded, there is but a single special reimbursement. Of course, if the child is not diagnosed as mentally retarded, there is no special reimbursement. The disposition may then be, at least on occasion, to diagnose so as to make the agency eligible for special reimbursement and, secondly, to exaggerate the severity of the handicap so as to increase the level of reimbursement.

Once maximum reimbursement is secured for the client, the placement and treatment of the individual is dealt with on different terms. While more financial aid is received to the degree that the client can be designated more severely handicapped, less money needs to be expended by the agency to the degree that the client can be designated more in need of generic group services rather than specialized individual services. Consequently, the practitioner may sometimes experience a conflict between training (which discourages unnecessary labels) and the budget regulations (which encourage unnecessary labels); the obverse conflict arises when the practitioner seeks to place the client in the least costly program, when the client actually needs a specialized, relatively expensive treatment.

While practitioners encounter difficulty reconciling the drive to meet a budget with the desire to help a client, they encounter other moral as well as practical dilemmas. An interesting problem was raised by Cassileth (1982) with respect to an increasingly popular approach to "treating" cancer. There have *always* been unorthodox cancer therapies, laetrile being merely one of the latest and prominent. As Cassileth explained, for generations people have been exhorted to try Doctor Bye's Combination Oil Cure, Dr.

Chamlee's Treatment for curing the blood of cancer viruses, Dr. Leach's Cancerol, and many others. Of course, such prescriptions are now dealt with by conventional medical laws and regulations that have been designed to avoid or ferret out quacks, charlatans, and bogus doctors and their therapies. However, the new "therapies" represent a *natural* approach to malignancy. They rely upon "cure through purification and the body's capacity to heal itself" (Cassileth, 1982, p. 1482). They are very much like the old homeopathetic and naturopathetic philosophies and other religious and medical approaches to purifying the body and the mind. How can society prohibit individuals from selling natural foods, carrot juices, sunshine, anxiety reduction, spiritual and physical homeostasis, religion, "getting it all together," or the avoidance of unnatural, toxic or otherwise harmful treatments and foods? Of course, those who sell these natural "therapies" to patients also advise them not to embark upon unnatural (possibly more effective) treatments — advice that may eventually kill them.

What does all of this have to do with placement and treatment issues in mental retardation? A great deal. If you think about it, the analogy of natural treatments to mainstreaming is striking. If you think about it, the analogy of the cancer ward to institutionalization is striking. And while I am biased toward mainstreaming and deinstitutionalization, I am not biased toward everything that is merely natural, everything that merely mainstreams or deinstitutionalizes. While institutionalization programs in America during this century could have been viewed exactly the same way many Americans viewed Vietnam, certain bogus mainstreaming and deinstitutionalization programs can be viewed as little more than dumping people into inappropriate settings and forgetting they ever existed. I have said before that anything good in society is mainstreamed; anything therapeutic must in some way be connected with normal life. But this is not to say that a person with acute needs can recover from his or her illness or malaise by being neglected or eating natural foods. When people are sick, they may need a hospital. When people are poisoned, they need an antidote. Children who can't read need remediation. Children who have seizures may need some sort of drug treatment. Children who are blind may need to be taught by a specialist to read by the Braille or other special method. Deaf children may need special amplification or training in lip reading or sign language training. People with special needs also need special consideration — special treatments. In and of itself, a natural approach to a problem is not necessarily effective. It is only useful when a natural approach is required. When special measures are needed, they must be employed. In no way is this argument antagonistic to the concepts of mainstreaming and normalization. Indeed, it's "normal" for sick people to see doctors and for needy people to seek help. It's abnormal — as well as cruel and indecent — to ignore the special needs of people with special problems. And such indecency is not mitigated by using such terms as "mainstreaming" and "normalization." Trendiness is chic, fun, "in." Mainstreaming is chic, trendy, "right on," as they used to say. But it's not right for everyone all the time. That's why specialists and special methods will never go out of fashion. At least, I hope they won't.

When considering the issues of diagnosis and treatments, it is important to recognize that there is a difference between a prediction and a policy, an expectation and an insistence. It's one thing to predict (or to expect) that, in any group of severely retarded children, there will be X number who will not learn, who will never be of clean bodily habits, who will not be able to understand others, or be understood, and who will be of danger to themselves or others. Similarly, in any university, there will always be professors who will not publish important scholarly works, who will not teach well, and who will not serve the academic community as scholars. That's a prediction, not a desired outcome. It is an expectation based on prior experiences of how the world seems to operate. But if policy stated that professors would not publish or teach well or serve the academic community, then the university would be in greater trouble. In the same way, if policy states that some children are not educable, that's a different problem than when we recognize that there are children who aren't learning. Consequently, when I remark upon the clinical virtues, if not the established truth, of the educability hypothesis, it isn't because I insist that all children will learn. Rather, I insist that all children can learn, must have the opportunity to learn. When we as a profession better understand the difference between a prediction and a policy, we may be able to create better policies. Then, we may be able to live better with ourselves and other people.

I conclude this section with a *fable*; like many fables, this one is based in part on that which we have seen and felt. Like other fables, this one is not completely untrue. Once upon a time there was a superintendent of schools who figured out how to save his school system if only the state education department would designate the truants in his district as handicapped.

"After all," he demanded to know, "isn't the truancy problem the most significant factor in low student achievement in our district? Of course! Then it's clear! Truants must be identified as having handicapping conditions."

And to his confidants, this advocate on behalf of truants and others downtrodden, confided, "If we could only get the state education department to permit us to designate truants as handicapped, then we can claim reimbursement for their non-attendance in our schools. It's a wonderful way to help ease desperate budget problems. As you know, today when the truant doesn't come to school, we lose dollars. If that same child were labeled 'truant-handicapped,' we would *get* dollars instead of lose dollars.

For those who are truant on occasion — when the weather is warm and the kids want to get an early start at the fishing hole — they would be categorized as 'mildly truant,' and the school district would receive a special reimbursement from the state for their non-education. And if the child were more frequently truant, then he or she would be labeled 'moderately truant' and we would receive a double special reimbursement. But if the child were habitually truant, we would receive a triple special reimbursement. The less the truant came to school, the more we would be reimbursed for avoiding his or her educational problems."

"Chief, that's a splendid idea," the staff chorused.

"But I'm not finished. If we can convince the state education department that truants should be labeled 'handicapped,' then we also solve the single most embarrassing problem we have."

"What's that, Chief?"

"Our district-wide reading and arithmetic achievement scores! Each year, the state requires us to publish our achievement scores, and each year they go down, down, and down. And some year, they'll fall off the newspaper. And we will fall."

"But, chief, what do our handicapped truants have to do with the district-wide achievement tests?"

"Nothing! And that's the point. Nothing, which is everything! Don't you remember? We do not have to include children who have gone through committees for the handicapped students in compilations of those data. And who are our poorest students, our most intractable learners, our most underachieving pupils? The truants. Those are the ones who are driving our achievement scores down. If we label them 'handicapped,' then we can remove their scores from the achievement averages and — eureka! — our scores will go up dramatically."

"Chief, you're a genius," the guys gushed.

"I'm not finished. If we get away with this, there is yet another bonus, a big one, maybe the biggest one politically speaking. If truants can be designated as handicapped, then we can with one broad brilliant stroke solve the racial imbalance that has been plaguing our schools."

"How?" the staff whined.

"It's so simple, so beautiful. Why haven't any of you ever thought of this before? Why I always have to do the thinking for us constantly irks me; but never you mind. Listen hard, this is stunning. We assign our handicapped truants to schools on the basis of their race. White truants will be placed in black schools, and black truants in white schools. Because none of them attend school frequently, and because some of them never attend school, I don't expect we will have serious objections from parents or, for that matter, from the children themselves in placing them wherever we want. And the schools themselves will be delighted. Since they won't be seeing very much of the children anyway, those placements will both balance the racial composition in our schools while there will be no disruptions of programs or feelings."

With bold insight, one school district was able to reap large reimbursements for the non-attendance of children to its classrooms. At the same time, the district enhanced its academic standing in the state without adding one remedial teacher to its rolls, or spending one extra minute either teaching its children to read or its teachers to teach. And best of all, without busing children, without inflicting children on schools that didn't want them or — conversely — inflicting schools on children who did not want them, for the first time the district was approved as racially balanced. For the first time, the liberals, the Civil Liberties Union, the black caucus, the Hispanics, the women, and the other alleged trouble-makers were given racially balanced schools.

Picture this headline in the local paper:

SCHOOLS BALANCED, SCORES UP, DEFICITS DOWN,
ALL IS WELL WITH THE WORLD

More on Goals and Freedom

Maxwell Evarts Perkins, the great Scribners' editor who "discovered" Fitzgerald, nurtured Hemingway, and helped to "create" Wolfe, and who through his distinguished career kept "finding" such greats as Erskine Caldwell, Allen Paton, James Jones, and many other gifted writers, used to remark that his Evarts' genes caused him always to look for the difficult way to do things. "Living against the grain," he would say (Berg, 1978, p. 5). Less willingly than Perkins but just as surely, retarded people "live against the grain." Their lives are hard — mainly because of their limitations, which make easy jobs difficult, which make the mundane exotic.

But mentally retarded people also "live against the grain" because *we* insure that they do, inevitably if not deliberately. For mentally retarded people, the world is often strange and inhospitable. For some mentally retarded people, living in ordinary society is living better than what they feel they have a right to expect. For some mentally retarded people, having a sense of dignity, having a few possessions, finding a little happiness is not the fulfillment of expectation but the acquisition of rare gifts. If our goals for retarded persons are to have meaning, if they are to be worthy of the suffering that must be relieved and the needs that must be met, as Max Perkins might have remarked, they must "go against the grain."

Gerald and Sarah Murphy, once heirs to the Mark Cross fortune, were expatriates who spent much of their lives in southern France, amid the splendor of captivating scenery as well as enchanting poets, artists, and other intellectuals who gathered around them as bees gather to honey. There was a saying concerning the Murphys, which was also the title (as well as the substance) of a book and articles written about them, "Living Well Is the Best Revenge." And so too for those termed mentally retarded. "Living well" may indeed be their "best revenge" for the suffering inflicted on them, for the unnecessary pain and drudgery that so many of them encounter.

What are the goals to insure the good life? For retarded persons, these are not self-evident. That is, they may not follow directly from the goals for other people. For example, after the folderol is reduced to plain English, when we look at education the major goal is to provide the child with both a sense of competency and academic skills. For most children in the schools, academic competency is the prepotent goal — the area of emphasis, the area that deservedly requires the lion's share of the school's money, the area that deservedly requires the lion's share of the time and energy invested in the academic enterprise. From that primary goal — academic competency — come the other important (*but not as primary*) goals: vocational competency, social competency, and physical competency. While these four goals remain similar for retarded children, their order of importance is reversed. For the retarded child, physical and social competency become paramount, vocational competency is very important, and academic competency is least important.

Why? Is there justification to focus a curriculum extending through 12 to 15 years primarily on a goal which, at best, results in success only if judged against childish standards? That is, by definition an educable mentally retarded child will not at maturity read with understanding at a level beyond fourth or fifth grade. To focus an entire curriculum on the attainment of a few grades of reading after many years of arduous work simply doesn't make great sense, either in terms of cost to society or as effort expended by the pupil. On the other hand, there are many retarded people who have physical and social capabilities such that they can develop *those* characteristics to a degree that would not only insure a longer and healthier life but also the attainment of certain vocational and social aspirations. It's now well known that many moderately and some severely retarded individuals can enter the job market and at least partially earn their way; indeed, there are many retarded people who are capable of making substantial contributions to society.

What is the general goal most people have insofar as their outlook on life is concerned? To live good, decent, appreciated ordinary lives. Mentally retarded people have the same goal despite the fact that they are "exceptional" people. Notwithstanding, they don't want to be exceptional; they want to lead good and decent ordinary lives. It's probable that there are many so-called "ordinary people" who want to lead exceptional lives, but most mentally retarded people will settle for a satisfying ordinary life. Under what circumstances can they accomplish this? Incarcerated? Under the yoke? Under close scrutiny? In an institution? Of course not. People must be free. The goal of freedom should never be far from the programs, the activities, the benefits, the resources and policies that are promoted and promulgated on behalf of mentally retarded persons. Overarching all goals, all considerations, all legislation, all litigation, EVERYTHING, is the goal of freedom for retarded people. To understand that is to understand almost all that is of primary importance insofar as what we need to know about mental retardation. Not to understand that is to understand little of anything that's important.

Declarations to Live By

What follows are two declarations: one brief excerpt developed by a group from Syracuse University's Center on Human Policy and another excerpt from the United Nations. Of the first declaration, I should modestly mention that it has received widespread dissemination, and has been embraced and supported by thousands of consumers, families, professionals, and other citizens. Of course, the United Nations declaration has received worldwide notice. These statements are reprinted because, while they are known to many, their relative significance in a world of more than five billion people is dishearteningly meager. Even among those who have read these words and support them, there are few who actually live by their guidelines for insuring better lives for all of us. They both represent affirmations of the rights of disabled persons to services and ultimately to respect and personal dignity. They are offered here as guides to public policy and societal practices.

A Declaration on Human Rights and Responsibilities

I Freely Sign This Declaration Affirming

- *that, as human beings, all people are inherently valuable,*
- *that all people have essential rights and privileges,*
- *that, included in these rights, all people must have access to a broad spectrum of services and opportunities to insure their physically, spiritually, socially, and psychologically optimum development,*
- *that such development is enhanced in integrated open community settings,*

- *that among those who have been most frequently detained in segregated settings, and who have most often been denied their basic rights, are devalued people with special needs — the so-called handicapped (e.g., physically disabled, mentally retarded, emotionally disturbed), the elderly, and the disadvantaged.*

United Nations Declaration on the Rights of Disabled Persons

General Assembly Resolution 3447 (XXX)
Adopted December 9, 1975

- Disabled persons have the inherent right to respect for their human dignity. Disabled persons, whatever the origins, nature and seriousness of their handicaps and disabilities, have the same fundamental rights as their fellow-citizens of the same age, which implies first and foremost the right to enjoy a decent life, as normal and full as possible.

- Disabled persons have the same civil and political rights as other human beings; article 7 of the Declaration of the Rights of Mentally Retarded Persons applies to any possible limitation or suppression of those rights for mentally disabled persons.

- Disabled persons are entitled to the measures designed to enable them to become as self-reliant as possible.

- Disabled pesons have the right to medical, psychological and functional treatment, including prosthetic and orthetic appliances, to medical and social rehabilitation, education, vocational education, training and rehabilitation, aid, counseling, placement services and other services which will enable them to develop their capabilities and skills to the maximum and will hasten the process of their social integration or reintegration.

- Disabled persons have the right to economic and social security and to a decent living. They have the right, according to their capabilities, to secure and retain employment or to engage in a useful, productive and remunerative occupation and to join trade unions.

- Disabled persons are entitled to have their special needs taken into consideration at all stages of economic and social planning.

- Disabled persons have the right to live with their families or with foster parents and to participate in all social, creative or recreational activities. No disabled person shall be subjected, as far as his or her residence is concerned, to differential treatment other than that required by his or her condition or by the improvement which he or she may derive therefrom. If the stay of a disabled person in a specialized establishment is indispensable, the environment and living conditions therein shall be as close as possible to those of the normal life of a person of his or her age.

- Disabled persons shall be protected against all exploitation, all regulations and all treatment of a discriminatory, abusive or degrading nature.
- Disabled persons shall be able to avail themselves of qualified legal aid when such aid proves indispensable for the protection of their persons and property. If judicial proceedings are instituted against them, the legal procedure applied shall take their physical and mental condition fully into account.
- Organizations of disabled persons may be usefully consulted in all matters regarding the rights of disabled persons. . . .
- Disabled persons, their families and communities shall be fully informed, by all appropriate means, of the rights contained in this Declaration.

14.

Practitioners and Scholars

CHAPTER 10 discussed the industries in mental retardation—the treatment, research, and training professionals, the builders and architects, the merchants and manufacturers, politicians, bankers, lawyers, the Establishment shakers and movers, the advocates, the people who live for and by retarded individuals and their families. In this chapter, I discuss some of those same people—but here in terms of the practice of their professions, the living of their lives, rather than the politics of their professions. Of course, one discussion not only overlaps with the other, but one discussion is inexorably grounded and embedded in the other. You will see this as we examine the work of teachers, professors, diagnosticians, and therapists. Some are essentially practitioners, others scholars, still others both.

Why do people come into these fields? Why does the teacher decide not only to teach but to teach retarded children? Or why does the psychologist specialize in work with these clients and their families? There are those who come into the field of special education because this has always been the plan, and there are those who come into the field of special education because this is the only plan now available. And so too with doctors and other practitioners.

How does one go after a goal? Better, once the goal is established, how is it pursued? And what about the means? There are those in this field who are courageous, some might even say reckless, about the goal they pursue (be it deinstitutionalization *or* institutionalization, for example); but those same people may be quite conventional in their means to achieve the goal. Conversely, there are those who have the most innocuous goals, who are viewed as conservatives in all respects, *until* they are seen in action. Who is the conservative, and who is the radical are questions that do not lend themselves to obvious answers.

Let's examine briefly a few of the people who pursue goals on behalf of mentally retarded individuals and their families. Let's look at the work of these practitioners and scholars. From much of the published expressions of their goals and activities, it may be concluded that their means vary more than their goals. Another way of saying this is that means more than goals may better reflect attitudes.

Teachers and Professors

What makes a good teacher? Or do method and curriculum rather than teaching distinguish one class or child from another? And whatever the significant factors are that contribute to learning, what are the goals — for children, for those with special needs? These are some of the questions considered here.

Classroom Variation

As I wrote in a paper on theories and methods in special education a number of years ago, we have witnessed a profusion of methods, curricula, and special administrative designs. There has frequently been insistence that each be taken seriously as a "solution" to compelling pedagogical and/or psychological problems. But as I commented then:

> It is suggested that each great methodological contribution begins with an individual who is interacting with a child, or a group of children, in such a way as to promote extraordinary change. This change is observed by either that individual or others and causes astonishment and excitement. Why are the children doing so well? Why are they learning to read so quickly? Why is mathematics no longer a horrendous puzzlement? Or, why is this sick person getting better? Closer attention is given to the interaction between the teacher (or therapist, or experimenter, or psychologist) and the child. A careful description of the interaction is reported. From this inductive approach, a recording of the educational or therapeutic presentation is prepared; a method is obtained. The teacher is teaching in a certain way, using a certain style, and promoting certain desired responses. Various people develop collaborations around the method. They study it in its original natural setting. They experiment with it. They refine and modify it. They become infatuated with the notion that the gains they observe are dependent on the order, style, and materials of presentation. They learn a lot about this method, the

responses it ordinarily generates, its frailties, the problems it creates and how to overcome these, and its most efficient utilization. They train others to use the method. They write books about it and develop elaborate ways to present it, test it, and relate it to a host of other methods, treatments, and conditions. Hence, we have literally thousands of studies completed on how infinite varieties of individuals behave in psychoanalytic settings, what their behaviors mean under innumerable circumstances, what responses are pathological, and what responses are healthy.

There are several things that strike me about individuals who were reponsible for the development of spectacular methods. From scientific history, and my own observations of some current workers, each appeared to be a gifted teacher and interactor. Each appeared to have a dynamic quality that attracted the attention of other individuals. Each appeared to have a magnetic, almost charismatic, personality that brought droves of disciples into the fold. Each was a great teacher. An analysis of the research relating to special methodologies produces other interesting conditions to speculate about. From the sensationalistic method of Itard and Seguin to the present work of Doman and Delacato, Omar Moore, the new math, and the special reading programs, verification studies of special methodologies categorically find less spectacular, less promising, less comforting results. Omar Moore has demonstrated more with an automated or non-automated typewriter than have those who replicated his work. The most spectacular changes observed in children utilizing the Doman-Delacato methodology can be observed at their Institute for the Development of Human Potential.

There is no doubt that some methods work well. Further, there is no doubt that some methods work better for some people than other methods. Still further, there is no doubt that some methods are more logically conceived, implemented, and utilized than others. There is a great deal of doubt that any method is very far removed from those who employ it, understand it, have faith in it, and experiment with it. (Blatt, 1967)[1]

It is interesting to note that colleagues who read this work in manuscript insisted that I must not even mention this methodologist or that one because it might appear that I endorsed unproven or lightly regarded work. This is exactly the point. Those controversial methodologists were unable to generalize their models, which is not to say that they were unable to produce the claimed effects themselves.

The more work that has been done on comparing children in special and regular classes (or children taught by method A in contrast to method B, children in open as contrasted with closed classrooms, children who receive a great deal of intervention X in contrast with children who receive a great deal of intervention Z) the more I am convinced that "answers" to

---

[1]From "A Hypothesis of Theories and Methods in Special Education" by B. Blatt, 1967. In J. Helmuth (Ed.), *The Disadvantaged Child, Vol. I* (pp. 70-71), Seattle, WA: Special Child Publications. Reprinted by permission.

the vexing questions concerning "best method," "best pedagogy," "best curriculum" lead to dead ends.

> What have we learned from these efficacy and methodology studies? Or how may we interpret their relatively uniform findings? We have concluded that the accumulation of evidence leads to a clear rejection of even the legitimacy of the form and content of these two questions asked rhetorically. The special versus regular class dichotomy is not a defensible independent variable. Although there may be powerful exceptions to this hypothesis, the regularity of data findings suggest strongly that children's experiences are not systematically different in a consistent way if they are in one or the other class. A child can have individual attention, warmth, support, friends and an exciting program in either class. Furthermore, his home can vary independently of the kind of class he is in. For many children, the home contributes so potently to variance that it may well drown out any differences connected with educational programming. (Blatt, 1981, p. 73)

It's quite possible that, in the assignment of variables for research on teaching, the field of education would have been much further along in understanding the complex teaching-learning interaction of children and teachers had we "controlled" for method, curriculum, and administrative organization, and had we rather experimented with such variables as teacher variation, child variation, and teacher-child interactions. Of course, virtually all educational research assumes *exactly the opposite* methodological position. Most such studies are designed so that ages, backgrounds, and educational experiences of teachers (and children) are "neutralized" through some sort of randomized procedures. This is accomplished in order to achieve comparability among groups on variables that are important, but that do not constitute the major differences among those groups. Once there is assurance that Group A is similar to Group B insofar as teacher and child characteristics, an intervention is imposed—be it a new curriculum, a promising method, or an experimental organization. Almost invariably, the results of such studies indicate that there are no differences between groups who receive Method or Curriculum A in contrast with Method or Curriculum B. It is possible that what we now consider to be greater sources of independent variation (methods, curricula, and administrative organization) are less fruitful variables than, for example, teachers, children, and their interactions. It may well be that in those teacher-child interactions we might find clues to better teaching and learning.

Teachers

The teacher is someone who must be taken seriously if the pupil is to get anything out of the experience. What we want from teachers of retarded persons may be qualities consistent with the following:

a. Someone who takes care and interest in unraveling problems; someone who enjoys learning.

b. Someone who believes those problems are compelling and important.

c. Someone who has become convinced he or she has a special capability to share his or her interests with other people.

d. Someone who wants to sustain a relationship that involves a mentorship burden, and who is not uncomfortable with such a responsibility.

Of course, all of the above traits are not easy to obtain. But those are exactly the traits that seem necessary if teachers are to succeed.

The teacher must be objective, which is not to suggest indifference. Each of us must fulfill certain responsibilities. Objectivity may sometimes seem like indifference; the crucial difference for the teacher is the desire to be responsible. That's the mark of the professional, in contrast to the individual who is there for the ride, or the fun. Professionals cannot simply do things for pleasure; and while there are times when they surely do something that affords great pleasure, when that occurs it is a coincidence, because professionals must do many things out of a sense of responsibility, in fulfillment of the code or contract they agreed to in accepting their professional role.

Normative vs. Clinical Teaching

Normative teaching is based on presumed a priori understandings of what pupils are like, what they need, and how they should be taught; in contrast, clinical teaching requires the teacher/clinician to hold back on judgments concerning children's characteristics and how they might best be taught until better and direct understanding of children is obtained through careful observation and experimentation. One way to conceptualize the difference between normative and clinical teaching is that the former involves a deductive approach whereas the latter involves an inductive approach. The deductive teacher seeks to find a carefully contrived category in which to place the child. Achieving that, the teacher proceeds in a prescriptive manner, "knowing" what the child needs and how to provide a proper program. The inductive teacher does not rely as much on prior diagnoses and standard programs and methodologies to achieve an appropriate learning environment for the child. The inductive teacher will spend more time observing the child, exposing him or her to various methodologies and content, and working toward the achievement of a program for the child that is based on his or her unique needs and interests. The various psychoeducational models can be characterized as being more inductive than deductive, more clinical than normative, more experimental than formal, and more creative than technical. Suffice it to say that there are few mental retardation programs that can be legitimately characterized as psycho-educational. Indeed, few programs do not have a beginning context grounded strongly in official diagnoses and well-tested standard approaches to teaching children with similar problems.

Possibly, what may best characterize the various psycho-educational models is that they reflect the idea that the various curricula, methods, administrative organizations, and equipment provide interesting "historical" perspectives to help a clinician establish a program for a particular child. It may be claimed that the psycho-educational approach is less concerned with medical, educational, psychometric, social, behavioral, or other classification schemes, and more concerned with what a child looks like here, in this particular learning environment, and what that child may need here in this unique setting. Of course, there must always be compromises made between the desire to create a truly unique program for a child and the practical problems a teacher has in providing a total class with optimal opportunities to learn.

Educational Goals

In 1963, I directed a study of the education of Rhode Island's handicapped children (Blatt, 1963). I also assumed personal responsibility for examining the state's programs for retarded children. In that section of the report, I worked out what I then viewed as minimum essentials and major goals relative to educational programs for such children. Now, 20 years later, I reexamined that statement, and (except for some words and tones that I would today modify) those convictions remain.

While I truly believe that teachers and other clinicians must behave as if capability is educable, I also know that we have yet to demonstrate sufficiently the educability hypothesis. Consequently, it would be imprudent to discard the conventional special class option for some children or the "occupational education" option for others. It would be imprudent to deny a growing emphasis on functional education as the handicapped child gets older—and as prospects become dimmer that eventually the child can be best served in a standard regular program. In my view, to this day Hungerford's Occupational Education Curriculum remains a thoughtful approach to providing for the educational needs of many mildly retarded children. In my view, the dictum that we should not unnecessarily "experiment" with human lives is as true in education as in medicine. All things considered, the following seem to me to be the most reasonable minimum essentials and major goals; each is discussed in detail in my 1963 report:

1. Minimum Essentials:
    a. Early helpful diagnosis and prognosis for all children with learning problems.
    b. Early educational intervention for all children with learning problems or who reside in certain cultural areas that are characterized by high incidences of school failure.
    c. The special class program, among the last (not first) resorts, should be available both to those children who are unable to profit sufficiently from pre-school programs and to those children who are not diagnosed as mentally retarded during the early years.
    d. Open doors. Each child should be given every benefit of the doubt and as the doors are open for children to enter special classes at many points during their school careers so, too, the doors should always be open for them to return to the regular grades.
    e. Extended opportunities beyond formal education. Opportunity to learn should be available to all, even beyond the normal years of public sponsored education.
    f. The special education program should prepare the child for a productive and satisfying life as an independent (or in the case of some trainable children, as a dependent) citizen. Especially, in secondary programs for educable children, attention should be given to: analyses of possible vocations, analyses of strengths and weaknesses of individual children, and preparation in both the manual and non-manual areas associated with particular vocational choices.
    g. Social Development. An educational program which encourages students to: offer suggestions, engage in varieties of responsibilities as part of the teacher's intent to provide another learning opportunity, help each other and share during activities, and make evaluative statements regarding their own work, is providing an environment where children may develop the social as well as intellectual skills needed for economic and social independence.
2. Major goals. Related to the previously discussed minimum essentials, are the following goals which we consider to be major, and reasonable, insofar as special programs for mentally retarded children are concerned:
    a. Those children who have been differentially evaluated, realistically and conscientiously educated, who have been afforded all known programs and therapies to circumvent, ameliorate or prevent the learning difficulty, can be expected to achieve a level of scholastic, social, and vocational proficiency commensurate with their abilities.
    b. Those children who have received an adequate special education program (i.e., have been taught and practiced those essentials needed for a pro-

ductive and satisfying life), have been afforded the benefit of specialized placement, and have had available to them those normal habilitation and rehabilitation services, can be expected to secure, hold, contribute, and "grow" within an occupation or sheltered employment.

  c. Those children (educable) who have received the benefit of our best and most enlightened professional services can be expected to become relatively indistinguishable (normal) as contrasted with other citizens within their community. (Blatt, 1963, pp. 58-61)[2]

As noted, I believe that these minimum essentials and major goals are still applicable to special education. It is important, however, to place these guidelines within an overarching context that recognizes the crucial role of the individual educator. In this regard, it is useful to turn again to Jean-Marc-Gaspard Itard, who in 1801 wrote:

> Cast upon this globe without physical strength or innate ideas, incapable in himself of obeying the fundamental laws of this nature which call him to the supreme place in the universe, it is only in the heart of society that man can attain the preeminent position which is his natural destiny. Without the aid of civilization he would be one of the feeblest and least intelligent of animals—(Itard, 1962, p. xxi)

Education, of course, is one of the primary means by which civilization is transmitted from one generation to the next. Thus, while educators use tried and true methods, and while the everyday activities of the schoolroom may seem mundane, they *can* have a vision. They can dream and plan for a future society in which the people will know how to prevent mental retardation, how to ameliorate it, how to reverse it. Without education, the human being is one of the least intelligent of animals. With it, we may find yet better ways to reinvent society. There can be a finer world for people, and much of such promise must come from the education we provide for our children. Education and educability remain the ultimate goals for everyone.

Ideas Worth Remembering

Kay Long's (1977) *Johnny's Such a Bright Boy, What a Shame He's Retarded* is not only a novel but also an exposition on current problems in special education. Long was not concerned just with the professional literature or what occurs in the schools; rather, she explored the relation between these spheres in the practical context of a society that is ever changing. Her pro-

---

[2]From *The Education of Handicapped Children in Rhode Island* (pp. 58-61) by B. Blatt, 1963, Providence: Legislative Commission to Study the Education of Handicapped Youth. Reprinted by permission.

tagonist is Maggie Callahan, a teacher imbued with mainstreaming philosophy, who is attempting to create an integrated program for her pupils. She encounters great prejudice and resistance to the idea of a "least restrictive" alternative for her students. There is a lesson to be learned from this novel: Implementing a truly educational mainstreaming program is difficult. Those who oppose mainstreaming cannot be merely dismissed as "bad guys." The problems the schools face in mainstreaming handicapped children are real and serious. Further, the problems are a complex subset of much larger problems faced by an entire community. In the final analysis, while P.L. 94-142 is very important to handicapped children, it is also very important, although less obviously so, for a community to look after its economic, political, and cultural affairs. That reality makes life difficult for idealists in special education, or, for want of a better descriptor, for "mainstreaming purists." Such understanding leads inescapably to the realization that even the mandates of federal law must be modified or delayed to fit the fabric of a community. It means that the letter of the law must be tailored to an individual in such a way that he or she is enabled to contribute to its spirit. It requires of all of us great patience, careful judgment, and a sense of responsibility. At the end of Long's novel, Callahan resigns from her job, ostensibly a failure. But she is a failure, though, only in the sense that she did not succeed in her attempt to be a "social engineer" of change. In spite of the missteps and errors she made along the way, she touched many people, and consequently, made important contributions toward the goals that eluded her professional efforts. The novel leaves us with the most important understandings—that the problems we have in education are not the result of viciousness, that people are *concerned* with the welfare of their children and their communities, and that in the end good people will prevail.

Sweeping federal mandates or crusading individuals *will not* revolutionize the schools or the communities. While we may be impatient for immediate fundamental changes in our schools, it is possible that we should be satisfied with the real gains that have been made through thoughtful and carefully crafted planning and implementation efforts. Again, Long's (1977) book brings home the realization that *people are people*. And although we must be committed to undoing the indecency of segregation and abuse in special education, our zeal must be tempered by the recognition that we, like all good people, are fragile human beings who act wisely as well as foolishly and who will always have incomplete data and insufficient resolve.

Professors

Although professors write most of the books on retardation, there is rarely mention of professors in those books. This is not unique to the field of mental retardation, but is characteristic of textbooks in general. It is unfortunate, not because professors are such a "special lot," but because students can, I think, learn something from studying the professoriate.

Some observers believe that professors are typically so far removed from daily participation with children in the schools that they should not be writing books and papers for clinicians. Immodest as some professors may be, most would agree that this is a serious question that deserves examination. Without doubt, clinicians face problems that require fresh and continuous participation in the clinical setting. On the other hand, professors of moral philosophy are judged on their scholarship, and not on the manner in which they conduct their personal life. Theologians shouldn't be evaluated on the amount of their participation in religious activities, or even the quality of their personal religious experiences (wherever they occur). So, what can the "real world" learn from the university, if anything? Specifically, what can workers in the field of mental retardation—teachers, psychologists, residential administrators, commissioners of mental retardation, advocates, and others—learn from professors and the place where they work, which to a great extent is where professors' minds and souls live, the university? For one thing, the university fosters the generation of new ideas and methods. Moreover, the university to a great extent is a microcosm that reflects the values of the larger society. How will future historians characterize our society? Our descendants will make the final judgments, just as people made compelling judgments about the Old and New Testaments, the Renaissance, the works of Leonardo and Michelangelo only centuries afterward. And, just as there was once an ancient society that is now remembered for its great civilization (Athens) and just as there was once an ancient people who is now remembered for a great book (the Hebrews), so it is possible that our society will be remembered as the one that brought to consciousness the right of everyone to be free, to pursue decent lives, to eat regularly, and to be governed by laws that protect everyone equally. It isn't that this society has stamped out hunger, or injustice, or cruelty, or want. It isn't that this society has reduced the number of hungry people in the world, or reduced the number of disfranchised— those without countries to watch over them or neighbors to care about them. Rather, this society, as none ever before, has articulated the rights of people and what all of us must do to guarantee those rights. So while it's true that children continue to starve in Africa, it is equally true that there are people in the United Nations who worry about and try to alleviate such problems. And while it's true that mentally retarded people unnecessarily languish in institutions, it's equally true that there have been stunning court victories, new legislation, and insistent advocates who speak out against such injustices, and, at least in part, do something about them.

Of course, the university cannot claim responsibility for every social advance of this century. Yet it can be argued, I think, that the university plays an important role in social change. The university affords the possibility for truly different and valuable ideas to be articulated, to take root, to gain currency. As imperfect as the university may be, it does provide an atmosphere that encourages the development of fresh perspectives on some of society's most complex problems. In several respects, the university represents a microcosm of society, and thus society can learn important things from observing the university and its professors. The following observations, I hope, will give you some insight into how the university and its professors function:

1. *The Concepts of Professor and Teacher.* The authority of the professor and the authority of the public school teacher are quite different. The hierarchy in the public schools is such that the superintendent makes most important decisions that are not made by the school board. The principal makes certain fairly important decisions, the teacher makes a few decisions, and children and parents make even fewer decisions. Decisions in the public schools, thus, are made on the basis of certain carefully developed hierarchical lines of authority and responsibility. Superintendents (or principals) appoint teachers, retain them, and eventually tenure them. On the other hand, in the university, the teachers—the professors—have certain inviolate responsibilities and authority, which cannot be abrogated by the president of the university or even its board of trustees. In the university, professors are primarily responsible for appointing and promoting other professors. Indeed, the professors select their deans and influence the selection of their president. Similarly, professors control curricula in the university. The courses they propose and endorse and the curricula they create find their way into university catalogs. The dean can suggest, prod, plead for certain curricular developments or actions, but essentially professors make the final decisions about curriculum, staff, and students.

2. *The Concept of the Brimming Cup.* In the university, "bigger," "newer," or "shinier" are not necessarily perceived as better; "economy of scale" does not apply. The largest university is not necessarily the greatest. A large state university may have many more new buildings than either Harvard or Yale—but it is not judged as better.

3. *The Idea That Honesty Can Change Behavior.* At its best, the university is honest with its professors. Honesty encourages the exchange of information that hopefully leads to progress and improvement. There is more self-criticism and mutual criticism in the university than in the larger society. When it's working well, the university operates as

if people who are told the truth will not become insane, and indeed, they may even be more thoughtful having been told the truth. In the university, not everyone is promoted, not everyone is tenured. In the university, everyone does not receive identical salary raises.

4. *The Idea That Education is Serious Stuff.* Socrates was sentenced to drink hemlock because the elders of Athens did not like his curriculum. Of course, the university does not force professors to drink hemlock. But education is, I think, taken much more seriously in the university than it is in the community. In the university, professors are expected not only to teach but to learn. They are expected to be learners *forever,* and they are banished from the university (i.e., are not tenured) if they fail to demonstrate that they do learn (i.e., do not publish). This is not the case in the public schools where all the teacher's time and energy are devoted to teaching children. Possibly, that is why universities remain exciting places for most professors, while the public schools have become dry, dead places for many teachers. Possibly, that is why there appears to be much less talk about "burnout" in the university than in the public schools. What's taken seriously by adults in the university is viewed on the outside as children's games — reading, writing, arguing. The university preserves the idea that education is serious stuff.

5. *The Idea That Resources Are Never Sufficient.* A popular fallacy is that resources are sufficient to meet needs. In fact, there has always been a discrepancy between what is needed (i.e., what is wanted) and what is available (what we can afford). The misconception that this gap can be bridged infects both the university as well as the larger community, although the university seems to endure the fallacy more gracefully, if not more honestly, than the larger community. But then there is the Brimming Cup: The secret to sufficient resources is to need less. Whatever the resources, those who want more will never have enough.

6. *The Idea That There is Virtue in Heterogeneity.* Professors are hired individually, and the major criterion for such appointments is usually the ability of candidates to demonstrate that they are individualistic, sufficiently egocentric to know where they are going, and confident that the journey is important. That is probably why it is often difficult to cooperate with professors without struggle, especially on assignments that are perceived to be mundane, such as serving on committees or attending meetings. In public schools and residential facilities, people are often hired on the basis of how much they look and think like those already on the job. Possibly, both the university and the outside agencies would be better off if professors were a little less individualistic and public school administrators and teachers were a little more individualistic.

7. *The Idea That There is Virtue in Not Striving to be Taken Too Seriously.* The university used to be known as an environment intent on comprehending rather than mastering the world. That we have become more practically minded and pragmatic may be all to the good, but the university nevertheless remains essentially a place that isn't taken too seriously by the larger society. That is one of its worries, but it also may be its saving grace. Professors can speak from conviction unhampered by the concern that their every word is going to be recorded, weighed, and judged, and that what they say will be instrumental in shaping public action as well as opinion. Quite the opposite. What school superintendents say, on the other hand, will influence school boards, principals, and eventually, teachers, parents, and children. Professors can speak as honestly as they wish (or can), while public school administrators and state commissioners of mental retardation must be guarded in speech as well as action. That is why the American university is not closed down when a new government takes charge. Who cares what university professors think and say? Everyone cares what the state commissioner thinks and says. Of course, the university eventually shapes most opinion and much action. After all, future presidents, judges, legislators, opinion molders, merchants, bankers, and kings have their formal education in the university. Virtually all the world's leaders have stopped at the university—some for significant periods of time—to learn, to be persuaded, to shape their ideas and ideals, and to be "placed" in the larger society.

8. *The Worry That, While Professionalism Serves Society, It Is Also One of Society's Diseases.* It is ironic that specialists are needed to prevent or cure the illness, to ameliorate the problem, to solve the puzzle, but specialists also separate people. In the university (when it works as it's supposed to work), scholarship is "king"; titles, degrees, and honors do not rule; scholarship does. Of course, it doesn't always work that way, but the importance of scholarship has more currency in the university than out of it.

9. *The Belief That Everyone Deserves to be Involved in Education.* In the public schools, the teachers and school administrators act as if they know best about education. Indeed, a few think they know everything about education. In the university, that startling idea may attract some support, but many know better. Professors learn from their students, and the good ones are not only grateful but they even credit their students in appropriate ways. On any day on any major campus, many outsiders come in to lecture, demonstrate, harangue, or perform. Those visitors do not always have doctorates and they are not necessarily professors from some other university. In the university, there is often the search

for people from outside the ranks who can teach us about things we ourselves are unable to master without help. Mental health administrators, commissioners, and public school personnel do not seem to reach out in that way.

10. *The Conviction That We Must Try Harder to Tell the Truth.* Everyone lies, and the university is not immune to telling or believing lies. But it seems that the university tries harder to nail down the lie, to expose and discredit it. We have liars amongst us, but we don't suffer liars gracefully.

11. *The Insistence That We Must Try Harder to Learn From History.* As I said before, nobody learns easily or well from history, and the university is not entirely an exception to that adage. Nonetheless, the university seems to take history more seriously than does the outside world. This may be so because universities have history departments and large libraries, or because there are more people in the university who either have better memories or store their data for easier retrieval. Whatever the reasons, people in the university are a bit more apt to learn something from history than those on the outside.

Of course, while the world can learn important things from the university, those within the university have much to learn about the world—in particular, the art of communication. In the field of mental retardation, we have not taken seriously enough the need to communicate our concerns and interests to the larger society. As a group, we are not as literate as we should be, as we are expected to be, or as we think we are. We are especially inept during those few opportunities we do have to communicate via radio and television to large segments of the general population. And of course, it's essentially through those mass media channels that we can hope to spread word concerning our accomplishments, needs, worries, and interests. The general public does not read the *American Journal on Mental Deficiency,* and for the most part, we do not write for the *New York Times.* Consequently, if we ever hope to reach beyond our immediate professional family, we must take more seriously, and become more competent with radio and television. Professionals listen to and see radio and television; but we don't know how to use them. Why is there such ignorance of these potentially powerful instruments for communicating our ideas and values?

We express our research and clinical finds in scholarly journals and books. We tend to think of our work and our goals as scholarly rather than popular. Thus the idea of "performing" on television (even public television) or being interviewed on the radio (even when it's the noncommercial college station) smacks of the marketplace. The university is known for its scholars, who write books few people read, its presses, which publish books few people buy, and its laboratories, which produce data few people understand. The university does not pander to popular opinion, but to things more permanent—knowledge and wisdom. But the university, its professors, and the students they train should not remain aloof from either public opinion or public education. Scholars have a responsibility to communicate to the larger society, especially when their work is connected to the welfare of the society. That is, we in the field of mental retardation must make strenuous efforts to reach out to the parents, the clients themselves, and the citizens who are unfailingly asked to support the programs we espouse. We must remember that the goal of even the most pristine scientist is inevitably connected to making the world better than it is now.

There are people in America waiting to hear, waiting to see what professors are up to. And we have important things to communicate to those people, if we would take more seriously the power of the popular media, and if we would take more seriously the importance of our work. At the root of this problem is the fact that the scholarly professions have not considered radio and television as media that can stand alongside books, articles, and public addresses to express worthwhile concerns. Especially in the field of mental retardation—which is linked so inextricably to real problems and real suffering—we should strive to communicate more effectively to the larger society. Especially in this field, which touches people in every walk of life and in every circumstance, we should not confine our communications to narrow professional or other parochial constituencies.

Clinicians

Medical Practitioners

Mentally retarded people probably appreciate better than most of us the virtue in attempting to *understand* others even when you know for certain that *you* are not being understood. Among professionals, doctors and nurses are perhaps more *understanding* but less sensitive to the needs of such individuals. A great deal has been written concerning the inability or unwillingness of health professionals to come to grips with chronicity. That is, doctors, nurses, and other health professionals seem to be most comfortable in treating people who are expected to get better. It is almost as if incurability and inevitable death are insults to medical practitioners. It may sound terribly romantic, but death may be the "enemy" not only of the doctor, but it may also be a reflection of his or her own imperfections and mortality. As with the rest of us, doctors and nurses may have poor memories when it comes to confronting mortal certainty.

On the other hand, the much admired and respected medical tradition is not based merely on hyperbole and the public relations efforts of the American Medical Association. Indeed, teachers, psychologists, social workers, and others could do much worse than to consider seriously the essential ethos of medical practitioners. Specifically, they are trained that the patient or client comes first. It is not that the patient or client always gets first priority, but that is the rule, and it seems to be breached less often in the medical and allied fields than in other professions. When someone sees the doctor about an illness, the primary tasks of that doctor are to relieve the suffering and ameliorate or remedy the condition. When the patient sees the dentist because of an infected tooth, the patient expects the dentist to clear up the problem, which the dentist usually does. When a patient sees the doctor because of a rash, the flu, or cancer, the patient expects the doctor to exert every effort to cure, or, if that is not possible, to relieve the pain and ameliorate the condition as much as possible.

This is not always the case when the school psychologist sees a child in difficulty. Here, all too often the objective of the psychologist seems to be to nail down and label the problem, not necessarily to treat it. Likewise, all too often the work of the teacher seems to be devoted to separating those who can from those who can't learn — rather than trying with every idea or trick *to make it come true* that the child will learn. In a sense, thus, there remains much to be learned from the health professions. And much that they accomplish deserves our attention, and, if not veneration, our respect.

As I have indicated previously, the post-World War II era witnessed several successful prevention breakthroughs in mental retardation. PKU, Tay-Sachs disease, and RH incompatibility are now much better understood, and, to some extent, under preventative control. Today, we know a great deal more about the effects of rubella on the fetus, and consequently, effective programs have been instituted to prevent this disease. We also know more about the effects of alcohol and drugs on the growing fetus. Expectant mothers are more seriously and sensibly advised concerning their personal care and habits during pregnancy.

But after all is said and done, there is *no* "magic bullet." Of course, today we know ways to prevent much of mental retardation, and to even ameliorate certain culturally determined forms. Furthermore, there are prospects for cure in future generations. Even after all amelioration and cure, however, society will still be left with severely disabled people. Mental retardation remains in large measure unpreventable, irremediable, and without significant prospects for amelioration insofar as many of the most severely afflicted children are concerned. This is not to say that new preventive measures, and even new cures, are impossible to envision in later years. Notwithstanding, as I have also stressed throughout this book, the only genuine "magic bullet" that can be offered today (or in the foreseeable future) lies in the way we conceptualize what human beings are, what they are entitled to as human beings, and what responsibilities society has toward human beings.

Although medical practitioners no longer need to play the central and dominant roles they once enjoyed in this field, there is much profit in actively enlisting their involvement. And while the "magic cure" cannot be expected to come from the medical profession any more than from others, several critically important medical discoveries have been made during the past 30 or 40 years that have prevented mental retardation in thousands of people, that have prevented untold suffering, expense, and burdens to family and society. That the health professions have been unable to prevent or cure mental retardation for the throngs—the millions—is no more a criticism of that group than it is of society in general, except of course that the medical profession may have promised more than the others.

The quality of medical care, of course, does not inhere entirely in technological advances. A recent trip to Indonesia convinced me of this fundamental fact. The following brief excerpt from my diary of that trip addresses the limitations and positive aspects of medicine by focusing on how a relatively poor country seemed to offer better care for its handicapped citizens than the most affluent civilization on earth. Possibly, when we understand how a small rural Indonesian institution could offer such excellent medical care, then we will be persuaded that the "magic bullet" is nothing other than a variation of the Golden Rule:

> We were met at the door of the institution by the nurse in charge. She was an old woman, recently retired from a position in a general hospital. She was assisted by eight or ten young women who are also called nurses, but who probably don't have any formal nursing training. There was also an old man who serves as some sort of caretaker for the facility.
>
> The main floor consisted of a couple of small dormitories, a staff dining room, some sort of a reception room, and possibly another small room or two. The cribs were lined up side by side. We went from crib to crib. One blind child was trying to get about by himself. He was the only child who seemed to have the freedom of the dormitory. We asked if he was being taught anything. No, there was no itinerant teacher of the blind to come to teach him—no Anne Sullivan for this child. We moved on.
>
> In the next crib was a child with hydrocephalus. His enormous head tells that there may be little hope here. Through Julie, our interpreter, we asked the head nurse if a shunt operation had been attempted. We learned that not only

was it not attempted, but such an operation was unknown. We moved on to a child with beautiful eyes who was lying in his crib, staring. He seemed to want to say something to us, but we don't understand Indonesian. We moved on to the next crib, and the next, and then to the next room. We asked about the rest of the institution, but they told us that was it. There was a second floor, which served as a dormitory for the nurses. We chatted for a few more minutes and thanked each other for the visit. We were grateful and they seemed very grateful.

In some respects, this institution was exactly like Willowbrook, Belchertown, Fernald, and the others. There was nothing here for the residents to do. It's a typical institution. But this institution smells sweetly—it's clean—unlike our institutions.

We were in an institution whose entire operating budget is 10,000 American dollars per year, less than $700.00 per resident. And we returned to a land where yearly institutional budgets for 3,000 residents often run higher than $75 million—$30,000 per resident—and sometimes higher than $90,000 per resident.

Of course, we know that the average Indonesian doesn't earn $700.00 in a year, and even if he did, one cannot compare Indonesia to the United States in this regard. And we know that in America, children with hydrocephalus are afforded shunt operations to sometimes prevent the devastating effects of this malady.

How could it be that in Indonesia, which hasn't yet discovered shunt operations, a country that spends only $700.00 per year, per child in an institution, a country whose city streets stink, could have created an institution whose dormitories smell sweet? How could it be that a country whose dollar was devalued a third during the few days we were there, whose average citizen doesn't read, whose institutional superintendent doesn't have a college degree, who doesn't know about Braille, who doesn't know about peripatology, who doesn't know about all the things which make life beautiful in the United States, can run a cleaner and more decent institution than we in New York State run?[3]

There are no "magic bullets," but medicine and education are important substitutes. There may not be many miracles to count on, but there is significant good that well-trained dedicated people can accomplish. Of course, medical practitioners are not without problems. In a perceptive paper, McCue (1982) discussed the effects of stress on physicians. Medical students, residents in training, and even experienced practitioners often encounter persistent and debilitating stress connected with their responsibilities as physicians. Doctors deal with people who are, for the most part, suffering (or fearful that they will soon suffer), and who have other fears connected with how they will feel, function, and look if an illness is not controlled. Doctors also work with patients who become sick from the treatment itself. That is, it's sometimes necessary to inflict illness to cure illness;

---

[3]From "Rediscovering the Nineteenth Century" by B. Blatt, 1980, *The Exceptional Parent, 10*(3), pp. 52-53. Copyright 1980 by Psy-Ed Corporation. Reprinted with permission from *The Exceptional Parent*.

and cancer patients aren't the only ones who have such worries. What patients often confront, if but fleetingly, is mortality.

Added to the doctor's tension and burden is that patients perceive in the physician such enormous power to provide relief from pain (with drugs) or to inflict pain (with other drugs). Further, doctors face uncertainty about whether to treat this way or that way, a stress that is exacerbated by a patient who not only *believes* that certainty can exist if the doctor knew enough, but who *demands* that certainty exist in his or her case. All the while, doctors know that many of their decisions, conclusions, and specific treatments are approximations of what they think is best and (more often than they might admit even to themselves) that these approximations are not perfectly precise or beneficial. A new dimension is added to the problem when there is an insistence on "truth": For everyone there is eventual death, but immortality is demanded; or, because the physician needs to "know," he or she probes into the most personal, sensitive, and secret, lives of his or her patients. The doctor must know about what the patient drinks and how often, what the patient's sexual habits are, what the patient's insides look like—probing that angers people. And with each probe there is a threat to the patient's self-worth. Why do doctors put up with it? It has been suggested that only out of crisis can there be true maturity, only out of a tested reality can dreams have temporal meaning. For some doctors, life could not be more satisfying. For others . . . .

Is it any wonder that physicians, even excellent ones, often have stressful times that can interfere with their medical practice as well as their family and personal lives? For the physician responsible for a patient who is mentally retarded, those stresses can be exacerbated. Whereas cancer, heart disease, mental illness, epilepsy, and leprosy can be cured, mental retardation presents a more chronic picture.

Among medical practitioners—internists, orthopedists, pediatricians— few elect to devote themselves to the medical treatment of retarded people. Even psychiatrists are "warned" during their training that mental retardation is a dead end, a field inhabited by chronic patients who are doomed to live uninspired lives which, for all concerned, might better not have been lived. I may be painting the scene too negatively. There may be more doctors than I think who find fulfillment in treating retarded people. By and large, though, doctors want to treat healthy people, and if they can't always treat healthy people, they want to treat people who will get better. Indeed, for most doctors, cure or maintenance of good health seems to be the main goal insofar as what they expect in the way of emotional and psychological payment for their years of sacrifice and training. Quite simply, most doctors seem reluctant to treat retarded people and seem to derive little joy from whatever healing they accomplish with those patients.

Psychologists, Psychiatrists, and Related Professionals

Like psychiatrists, psychologists have not been encouraged by their professors or organizations to devote their careers to the study and treatment of retarded persons. And what has been described as a "dead end" for psychiatrists has sometimes been written off as a "no beginning" for psychologists. To be sure, this field has enjoyed the contributions of a handful of the most distinguished psychologists and psychiatrists America has produced. Nevertheless, while their quality is impressive, their numbers are small.

In the third edition of *Psychological Problems in Mental Deficiency*, Seymour Sarason (1959) discussed the future of mental retardation in the way of improved professional training. He envisioned a world more depressing than encouraging, more to avoid than to work toward. "There is little reason for believing that professional interest in the psychological aspects of mental deficiency is likely to change in any noticeable way in the near future" (p. 370). His prognostication was extrapolated to all areas of professional interest.

Now, more than 20 years later, we must judge whether Sarason's pessimism was a prophesy or an unnecessary worry. More recently, Sarason (1982) has addressed new concerns, particularly insofar as the field of psychology is concerned. His pessimism remains, although the reasons behind it seemed to have changed. From his considerable experience with professionals and other workers in the field, he concluded in 1959 that there was a general attitude that working with the retarded individual is dull and unrewarding. He concluded that people in psychology and psychiatry were in common agreement that there was little in the field that promised the research worker opportunities for engaging in fascinating or important problems. He found that most educators, psychologists, psychiatrists, and other professionals shared the belief that mental retardation does not require of the professional very much specialized knowledge or preparation. And he observed that many professionals felt perfectly comfortable making recommendations to families concerning their retarded child — without having had training or experiences in working in this field, or even very much knowledge about it.

In his more recent book, Sarason (1982) called for a meticulous evaluation of the adequacy of various professional training programs that could or should be connected with the field of mental retardation. He claimed that such evaluations have not yet been attempted, and they are very much needed. He ended his pessimistic discourse with the implied conclusion that, without substantially greater interest by the various professional groups in the problem of mental retardation, without the assignment of greater resources and talents to the preparation of professionals, little will change; retarded persons and their families will continue to receive inadequate services.

In the years since his original discourse, we have made progress. But with the exception of the field of special education—and to a much smaller degree pediatrics, social work, and psychology—little notice has been given to Sarason's worry, and consequently, little attention has been given to the training of people for this work. Individuals can complete graduate training programs in the various psychological areas without ever needing to confront the problem of mental retardation; even students preparing for positions as regular class teachers receive at best a smattering of course work, modules and related experiences connected with handicaps in general. While perspectives of these various professionals have been widened in recent years, and while there is greater range among their concerns and responsibilities, mental retardation essentially remains today the work of specialists and affected families. We have yet to heed much of Sarason's early admonitions and advice.

The first "professional" practitioners in the field were the priests, and their responses to mental retardation during the Middle Ages through the period prior to the so-called Enlightenment were marked by whatever it was those in the Christian community did for weak, homeless, and unwanted people. That is, the first "professionals" were those who offered the "village idiot" shelter, sustenance, and salvation. The first scientists in the field were the doctors—Pinel, Itard, Seguin. There were a few before those "greats," many during their lifetimes, and a relative throng after. The early twentieth century through World War II was marked by a surge of participation by educators, teacher educators, school administrators, and pedagogues of various stripes, persuasions, interests, and motivations. As the educators became more involved, except for institutional superintendents (and their counterpart commissioners in the state mental hygiene offices), the involvement and influence of medical practitioners became more constrained, and eventually, almost nonexistent outside of that narrow band of institutional psychiatrists who continued to manage institutions and other state-sponsored programs until recent times. With the exception of a few pioneering psychologists who contributed mightily to scientific understanding as well as to humane practices in the field (e.g., Alfred Binet, J. E. Wallace Wallin, Edgar Doll, and Alfred A. Strauss), the list of names of modern psychologists who come readily to mind as primary (or even "serious") workers in this field remains lamentably select: Seymour Sarason, Edward Zigler, C. Edward Myers, William Sloan, Wolf Wolfensberger, a few others, and of course a larger number of younger professionals.

Arrogance

As a group, clinicians sometimes have been accused of being arrogant. Among them, there is probably no group more vilified for "arrogance" than physicians. But a case can be made for arrogance on the part of physicians, and Ingelfinger (1980) makes it brilliantly. By extrapolation, I suggest that the argument applies to all clinicians. Clinicians have been known to be authoritarian, paternalistic, and dominating. Sarason has spoken of "professional preciousness." Others have written about the callousness, the "distance," the coldness of the clinician. The more charitable who write with disfavor about that side of the clinician sometimes use the term "overly objective." And Ingelfinger (1980, p. 1507) himself has admitted that "physicians are indeed arrogant in their behavior to their patients." While all his arguments about why this is so are interesting, possibly the most persuasive comes from his personal experience:

> Although I have subscribed for some time to the principle that the physician must be authoritarian and paternalistic to some degree, my experience as a patient has substantiated that belief in the strongest way possible. If you will forgive me for being both anecdotal and personal, let me tell you how the lack of authoritarian decision brought agony to me and my family. About a year and a half ago it was discovered that I had an adenocarcinoma, a glandular cancer, sitting astride the gastroesophageal junction. Ironically, this has been an area of the gut to which I had paid much attention in my professional career as a clinical investigator and consultant; therefore, I can hardly imagine a more informed patient. The need for surgery was indisputable if I hoped to continue to be able to swallow. But after a successful operation my real dilemmas began. The surgeon had found no visible evidence that the cancer had spread. But this proved nothing, because cancers can spread to form tiny nests of cancer elsewhere — micrometastases. The current medical practice is to assume that a patient who has had an operation for any of a variety of cancers (including the type I had) should also be given prophylactic treatment in an effort to eradicate the micrometastases before they enlarge. For this purpose both chemotherapy and radiotherapy are being used extensively. So one question was: Should I have chemotherapy, with all its side effects? And if chemotherapy, what kind? Even more debatable was the question of whether I should have radiotherapy. There is no generally acceptable evidence that residual nests of adenocarcinoma cells will respond. In addition, radiation would involve for me a number of complications, such as fibrosis of the lungs, and the possibility of a host of less frequent but nevertheless serious side effects. At that point I received from physician friends throughout the country a barrage of well-intentioned but contradictory advice. The question of prophylactic radiotherapy was particularly moot. As a result, not only I but my wife, my son and daughter-in-law (both doctors), and other family members became increasingly confused and emotionally distraught. Finally, when the pangs of indecision had become nearly intolerable, one wise physician friend said, "What you need is a doctor."

He was telling me to forget the information I already had and the information I was receiving from many quarters, and to seek instead a person who would dominate, who would tell me what to do, who would in a paternalistic manner assume responsibility for my care. When that excellent advice was followed, my family and I sensed immediate and immense relief. The incapacity of enervating worry was dispelled, and I could return to my usual anxieties, such as deciding on the fate of manuscripts or giving lectures like this.

If arrogance in the sense of paternalism and dominance is an ingredient of beneficial medical care, these qualities have to be used appropriately. To the extent that paternalism and dominance are infected by some of the other meanings of arrogance, a physician's conduct with patients is correspondingly worsened. Thus, if his paternalism is accentuated by insolence, vanity, arbitrariness, or a lack of empathy, the care he attempts to provide his patients is nullified. In other words, a physician can be beneficially arrogant, or he can be destructively arrogant.[4]

Ingelfinger's last remark makes the point: arrogance can be beneficial, but it must be of a type that aims toward *benefiting* the patient. There is no place for insolence, vanity, meanness, or condescension. The safeguard to unwarranted or destructive arrogance is, of course, magnanimity. The best of our clinicians are magnanimous. That is at least as important to remember as the certainty we expect of our physicians, psychologists, and other clinicians.

Finally, it is important to note that, notwithstanding their considerable accomplishments, our clinicians must work yet harder and better to repair the mistakes of our predecessors and to prevent more of their own. Then, they can leave to others the vindication of the particulars as well as the purpose of their involvements. The cornerstones of the clinical ethos are magnanimity, competence, and conscience. The "disease" of clinicians is to believe the myths about themselves, their magic, and their superiority. Again, the antidote is to remember that people are people, that all people are equally valuable, that every life has meaning or no life has meaning, that if the spirit lives for one human being it lives for each human being, that good beliefs must stay with a human being forever, hanging on and growing deeper and better as the person grows older and wiser.

---

[4]From "Arrogance" by F.J. Ingelfinger, 1980, *New England Journal of Medicine, 303*(26), 1509-1510. Reprinted by permission.

Part 6

BEYOND THE
SCIENCE FANTASY:
PERSPECTIVES ON
WHERE WE HAVE BEEN,
WHAT WE HAVE BECOME,
WHY IT IS IMPORTANT

Antonyms and Dissonyms in the Pariah Industry

When should one's behavior reflect logic,
    When history?

When is the goal the "cool out,"
    And when are the means the goal?

When is the conciliation to set goals,
    When to continue the defense?

When is the credential needed,
    When the competency?

When is one's discipline,
    What is one's being?

What is the beast in a human,
    What is the burden?

What is the scratch,
    What is the itch?

Define impartiality;
    Contrast honesty.

Facts,
    Insights.

Burton Blatt

15.

Banishment: The Creation of Monsters

THERE IS SOMETHING about our past in mental retardation—our institutions and schools, our segregation policies and practices of all types—which appears to promote intentional amnesia, a theme discussed later in this book. Consequently, we must work hard to remember certain things, and we must encourage others to remember. What?

We must nail down *The Lie That Has Failed*—and will continue to fail, the lie that there are human lives without value. It is from the dissemination and acceptance of this one lie that justifications are created—often clothed in research and scholarly pronouncements—to kill newborns, to incarcerate others, and to deny to still greater numbers of people rights the rest of us enjoy (and take for granted) and the protections to which all people are entitled.

This chapter deals with the effects of banishment on the human spirit, on development, even on those not banished. It includes the history of "solutions" for dealing with people who are "different"—mentally retarded persons, philosophers, "monsters," or even distinguished university professors who have grown old and must leave the campus. You will see that now, as in the time of Socrates, banishment is punishment in some ways as brutal and serious as execution. It robs the person of human affiliation, of a purpose in a community of dignity, of a reason for behaving as a human being, of a reason for living. Banishment is very serious stuff—and should not be the concern only of those in mental retardation. Everyone must be concerned. Nail down the lie that causes such despair, such destruction, death itself.

Banishment

In ancient Athens, the highest punishment was banishment, *not* execution. In modern Western civilization, the highest punishment—capital punishment—is execution, not banishment. While it would be difficult for us to think of anything but execution as the most severe punishment, there is reason to suspect that the ancient Athenians would have found it equally difficult to think of anything other than banishment as the most severe punishment. That is why we in this culture experienced such difficulty in comprehending what compelled ostensibly sane and educated Japanese pilots to volunteer for Kamikaze missions during World War II, or why young men seemed eager to sacrifice their lives to kill Americans in Lebanon. That's why most of us find suicide incomprehensible.

Society's "monsters" aren't born. They are created when two conditions are at work: Such individuals believe that society perceives them as monsters, and they accept society's judgment. Unfortunately, ordinary people find it virtually impossible to understand how and why a human being can become a monster. Unfortunately, otherwise sensitive people are insensitive to the effects of self-perceived ugliness and actual or self-perceived banishment. Mentally retarded people are prone to the conditions that can lead to the creation of "monsters." For retarded people, the danger in becoming the "monster" is much more serious and infinitely more real than any threat they present to the general welfare of society. The burden of, and the price which must be paid for, the affliction, imposes a greater penalty on the retarded individual than on any other person or the collective society.

In John Irving's (1981) novel, *The Hotel New Hampshire*, one of the memorable characters is Susie, who lives in the skin and acts the role of a bear. Pale, pockmarked, with straggly hair and unattractive body, Susie adopts the costume of the animal rather than try to live the life of the human.

"What you see," Susie said, "are the ravishment of acne—my teenage misery. I am the original not-bad-if-you-put-a-bag-over-her-head girl" (p. 219).

Susie could not face life as a physically ugly person, day in and day out. And so, this otherwise bright, interesting, sensitive, caring person took the disguise of a monster before society made the judgment for her. What a price to pay for pock marks and straggly hair! And what a price some retarded people pay for their inability to read better than at a fourth-grade level with interest and profit. This chapter explores how monsters are created.

In a profound sense—in principle if not with all of the familiar particulars—many people are banished in contemporary America. Old people are banished to convalescent homes, and worse. Retarded people are banished to institutions. People have to retire who do not want to and should not have to retire. This editorial in a popular magazine neatly sets out part of the problem:

> The prevailing vision of the good life in America has for some time included early retirement. Numerous voices speak in its behalf, from insurance companies to unions to government agencies. Quit while you're ahead, still healthy and young enough to enjoy a generous spread of the sunset years. Not only should you enjoy the fruit of your labors in this most bountiful of countries, say the many voices, but you should also give the young folk their chance to move up by exiting gracefully. There are, you are told, numerous benefits—tax, medical, recreational, psychological. It is not only foolish to overlook the opportunity; it is downright un-American. So why not do it? Why not? Because it will probably be the worst decision you have ever made. Here's why.
>
> To begin, it is an immediate, and usually irrevocable, step into second-class citizenship. Once retired, you are one with blacks, Hispanics, the handicapped, homosexuals, jailbirds, the insane, the retarded, children and women: America's Third World hordes. America doesn't like old people, and retired people are old people, whether they are 45, 55 or 65. Old people clutter up the landscape. Their families don't want them. Their communities don't want them. They are a nightmare vision of everyone's future. They are of interest mainly to doctors and hospitals, real-estate brokers and travel agents—but not as people, rather as bodies from whom some final payments can still be exacted.[1]

Professors are surely among those who are sometimes banished before their time, before they have completed their work, before they have made their final contributions to students, to their scholarship, to society (Blatt, 1982). In our society, it isn't always weak and handicapped individuals who are banished. All of us are vulnerable and can suffer the most serious indignities, the most destructive decrees—exclusion from our psychological or social home, from our physical home, from our work and friends, exclusion from life as we knew it. When we speak of banishment in the 1980s, we speak on behalf of handicapped and weak persons; but we also speak on our own behalf. That's why, at once, this chapter may be the most serious and most personal chapter in this book. That's why there is the claim that this issue

---

[1] From The first step to the cemetery by Kenneth Bernard, Feb. 22, 1982, *Newsweek*, p. 15. Reprinted by permission.

concerns life and death — yours and mine. As we banish retarded persons to institutions, we increase the expectation that we too may be banished some day.

In an early twentieth-century book on medieval English hospitals, Clay (1909) described a set of rules for dealing with the leper:

> When leaving the Church after Mass the priest ought to stand at the door to sprinkle him with holy water. And he ought to commend him to the care of the people. Before Mass the sick man ought to make his confession in the Church, and never again; and in leading him forth the priest again begins the *Responsorium* Libera me, Domine, with the other versicles. Then when he has come into the open fields he does as is aforesaid; and he ends by imposing prohibitions upon him in the following manner: —
>
> "I forbid you ever to enter Churches, or to go into a market, or a mill, or a bakehouse, or into any assemblies of people.
>
> Also I forbid you ever to wash your hands or even any of your belongings in spring or stream of water of any kind; and if you are thirsty you must drink water from your cup or some other vessel.
>
> Also I forbid you ever henceforth to go out without your leper's dress, that you may be recognized by others; and you must not go outside your house unshod.
>
> Also I forbid you, wherever you may be, to touch anything which you wish to buy, otherwise than with a rod or staff to show what you want.
>
> Also I forbid you ever henceforth to enter taverns or other houses if you wish to buy wine; and take care even that what they give you they put into your cup.
>
> Also I forbid you to have intercourse with any woman except your own wife.
>
> Also I command you when you are on a journey not to return an answer to any one who questions you, till you have gone off the road to leeward, so that he may take no harm from you; and that you never go through a narrow lane lest you should meet some one.
>
> Also I charge you if need require you to pass over some toll-way (*pedagium*) through (?) rough ground (*super apra*), or elsewhere, that you touch no posts or things (*instrumenta*) whereby you cross, till you have first put on your gloves.
>
> Also I forbid you to touch infants or young folk, whosoever they may be, or to give to them or to others any of your possessions.
>
> Also I forbid you henceforth to eat or drink in any company except that of lepers. And know that when you die you will be buried in your own house, unless it be, by favour obtained beforehand, in the Church."[2]

The above commentary reflects harsh and indecent treatment of the leper.[3] Of course, our asylums are much cleaner today, language more

---

[2]From *The Medieval Hospitals of England* (pp. 275-276) by R.M. Clay, 1909, London: Methuen. Reprinted by permission.

[3]Wolfensberger (personal communication) has argued that this characterization of the treatment of lepers is an historical myth and that ancient treatments, customs, and rites deserve interpretation in a larger context. For example, in earlier centuries many churches were architecturally adapted so lepers could participate without contaminating others. Even so, however, the characterization

euphemistic, and resources allocated for such treatments more plentiful. But in the most fundamental ways, how exactly are things different today? That's the question this chapter attempts to answer. People are supposed to learn from experience, but there are times when we merely continue to make mistakes.

Even our most distinguished citizens and "beautiful people" are not immune from society's compulsion to banish those whom it dislikes or tires of. For example, Robert Frost's life speaks volumes about love-hate, admiration-derogation, good-bad. Who doesn't remember him as the gallant old poet speaking words of praise and encouragement to the handsome president, John Fitzgerald Kennedy? Who didn't once wish that there could have been a time when the poet would sit down with us, would share his wisdom, would guide us through the certain travail ahead? And while most of us think about Robert Frost that way, there are others who also admire him — the literary critics, the professors of English, the poets — but who also think of him this way:

> So here the great man stood,
> fermenting malice and poems
> we have to be nearly as fierce
> against ourselves as he
> not to misread by their disguises. (Matthews, 1982, p. 51)

When the *New York Times Book Review* asked several distinguished authors to write about "My Most Obnoxious Writer," Harold Brodkey, a not inconsequential novelist himself, had this to say about Robert Frost:

> Robert Frost was esthetically illiterate, conceited, ruthlessly on the make — of course, that merely makes him an American poet — and a master of grotesque politics in his human attachments and in his getting ahead. This was in no clear way a necessity derived from his difficult position in the world of letters or from his moral sensibility in this beloved nation of shrewd men or from the rawness of nerves that goes with thought and the labor of expressing it. He was of a demonic vileness — I thought it showed in his face — a man devoid of moral judgment, as in his work, which consists mostly of morally blind statements, sly manipulations and shopkeepers' calendar apothegms. Perhaps he was what he was, if reasons are needed, because he knew his work was dull, and tinkling, both. (Brodkey, 1982, p. BR7)

There always is a dissatisfaction, a discontent with oneself if not others. Even the beautiful suffer the terror of banishment. Everyone encounters

---

reflects aspects of a later society — Clay's. Nonetheless, we must not forget that lepers and plagues can be comprehended only in terms of the world people lived in then.

banishment during a lifetime. But "monsters," particularly, encounter banishment. And "monsters" must be reckoned with even by people who have never thought seriously about mental retardation. Eugenics, euthanasia, sterilization, and old age transcend any field, or any profession, or any particular concern. *Everyone* has an interest in life, in general, and in his or her own life, most particularly. Everyone has an interest in death. It isn't that we, in mental retardaion, must know more about mortality than other people. It certainly isn't that we actually know more about mortality. Nevertheless, we're somewhat analagous to morticians when it comes to death, and obstetricians when it comes to life. Morticians comprehend no more than others about The Final Decree or life beyond the grave — if there is a final decree or if there is anything beyond the grave. But morticians are confronted with death so regularly that they must take it more seriously than the rest of us, and, for sure, they think about it more often than the rest of us, if for no other reason than the fact that death is their meal ticket. Of course, it doesn't seem possible for anyone to come to terms with living without coming to terms with dying.

So too obstetricians, when the subject is "life." Of course, obstetricians know how to deliver babies and have all the scientific facts about procreation, gestation, and newborns. But while they know everything about the science and technology of the birth process, they know nothing special about the miracle of birth — that is, they know no more than anyone else. But obstetricians think regularly about birth, and worry regularly about the lives of newborns, much more regularly than the rest of us. And people in mental retardation think and worry more about mortality than other people — because we are confronted with it more often, because we can't escape it, possibly because it too is our "meal ticket." We deal with fragile people usually, we deal with fragile minds by definition, and we deal with fragile dreams always. And so, while we have a great deal yet to learn about mortality — merely in the realm of that which can be learned by humans — we also have a great deal to teach, if we are smart enough to appreciate what we know, what we experience daily, and what others can learn from us. We have so much to teach that our lives need never be idle, our books never passive, our cups always filled.

Is banishment the product of a violent culture? This section is being written during the period when we traditionally celebrate the New Year. Newspaper pundits, TV commentators, and even the president of the United States dwell on the theme of the widespread and utterly senseless violence in the world. Although I cannot disagree with that conclusion, I am offended by the "evidence." In some fundamental way, the evidence is startling, disappointing, and depressing. To be sure, it illustrates that there is a problem — senseless murder. But there is also an insensitivity among those who shape and make the news. Time and again, we have heard and read about the violent attacks on the pope and the president of the United States. Time and again, we've heard and read about the murder of another president, or a rock idol. This is the evidence? Of course, we should mourn for the fallen Sadat and Lennon. Of course, we should cry when we remember the senseless murders of the Kennedy brothers, the Reverend King, the other martyred greats. We should be angered more than a hundred years later when we remember Booth's assassination of Lincoln. But such is not the compelling evidence that the world is going amuck, that governments are lunatic, that in the end unnecessary tragedy will fall everywhere on earth. Tragic as it is, Sadat's assassination is about the killing of one great world leader. Senseless as it is, President Kennedy's assassination is about the killing of one man, albeit a very powerful man. Those were special cases; not evidence that the world is going crazy, but simply reflections of the well-known fact that there are a few crazy people in the world. Most of us believe that life can be good—even with all of the suffering, with all of the dangers. There must be more to living than merely enduring it all.

Nevertheless, this society has yet to truly come to grips with the possibility that the *world itself* is going crazy. Otherwise, why do we continue to produce atomic weapons? Why does a Roman Catholic cardinal in the United States attempt to justify that work? Hydrogen bombs in the name of God? And powdered milk that kills thousands of Third World infants in the name of progress? We pollute our air, we befoul our streams, we destroy our wildlife, we poison our fish, we poison ourselves, we poison the world. Yet, we bemoan the senseless slaying of the great warrior as evidence of the madness abroad. Perhaps we should instead bemoan our own foolishness, our own needless destruction of this great planet.

We in the field of mental retardation, though no more qualified to fathom the mysteries of life and death, may nevertheless be more sensitive to those certainties. We in mental retardation may have more of a responsibility to *try* to fathom the unfathomable than those who don't experience daily the most serious of humanity's occurrences. Just as the doctor must *try* to know more about averting tragedy, those persons who devote themselves to this field must *try* to understand and deal with tragedies such as banishment and death. This is our special responsibility, our special burden, but also our special opportunity. In a way, some people in this field are more able to deal with the mortality puzzle than even the clergy. In a way, we see it in every one of our clients, in every one of their families. And because we experience it with so many people, we must try to understand it for ourselves (and in ourselves), and, consequently, we must try to understand it for everyone.

The Story of Frankenstein: As Told and Retold

Mary Shelley's (1831/1965) classic story of Dr. Frankenstein and the monster he created tells a much misunderstood tale. It is the story of a man banished from society, a man whose loneliness caused him to become a monster. In the current era, the story has been told and retold—in abridgements, in comic books, and in the films. The retold stories bear little resemblance to Shelley's. In the newer versions, the point is not that people can be made into monsters if they are banished from society, if their loneliness becomes an unremitting way of life. Rather, the point to the story of Dr. Frankenstein's monster has been distorted. There are ugly creatures in the world, this new version goes, that are everywhere—and so they must be discovered and routed out of decent society; they must be put away forever, or, better, killed.

Shelley tried to teach a primary lesson concerning the effects of loneliness on any human being. Hollywood twisted the story to teach another lesson—that people differ greatly, and that those who aren't like us (those who aren't more or less like Hollywood's one-dimensional celluloid people) do not deserve to live, much less be rehabilitated. Shelley tried to teach her readers that monsters are made, but that the "disease" can be prevented. Hollywood has tried to teach us that monsters are created from birth, that there is no cure and no amelioration for the "disease," that the only treatment is banishment or death.

Could the story of Dr. Frankenstein and his monster have been different? Yes, on all counts. We perseverate on the ugliness of the Elephant Man, on Shelley's monster, on the Hunchback of Notre Dame, and on the circus freak because appearances mean so much to us. I wonder if appearances mean so much to the animals in the forest or the fish in the sea. Possibly, but if so then they too share a limitation with humans—we cannot see or feel beyond that which can be seen with the eyes or felt by the hand. This story could have been infinitely different if humans were able to see beyond the surface of things, to feel beyond the skin of things, and to hear beyond the words and other noises.

All of us—Shelley included—seem victimized by the surface nature of human comprehensibility; we misunderstand things that are more complex than their mere appearances. Why is it that the most physically beautiful men and women are assumed beautiful in all aspects of their lives? Why is it that, in the real world and in the real manner of things, beauty is considered to be much more than skin deep, but we nevertheless evaluate it skin deep? Beauty gives the individual advantages (and disadvantages) in life that are almost impossible to deny. The beautiful woman is often popular regardless of her personality; the handsome man has ascribed to him characteristics that are sometimes burdensome to live up to.

Of course, there are exceptions. There was the misshapen scientist,

Charles Steinmetz, who helped to create General Electric. And there are other people with twisted bodies, pockmarked faces, swollen lips, or tortured speech who have become important in society. There are people for whom we might have predicted banishment, but instead, they held the reins of society during important times in its history. But those people are a rare exception to the rule: People who look too different, or behave too differently, or who see the world too differently, or whose visions about life itself are not easily appreciated, are often in some manner banished from society. When such people are young, they can be excluded from the public schools or placed in special schools. As they grow older, they can be banished to our various segregated institutions—be they mental hospitals, schools for retarded persons, jails, or other special compounds for the unwanted. As ordinary people become old, they, too, run the risk of exclusion from their lifelong homes and associations; they are placed in what are euphemistically called retirement villages or convalescent homes.

Could the story have been different? Perhaps. But the way people are, it really couldn't have been very different. Could the story be different for the next generation? Perhaps, but the way people persist on being, there doesn't seem to be much likelihood that the story will be different. There seems to be every probability that humans will continue to search for and root out the monsters amongst us. There seems to be every likelihood that humans will continue to use their eyes merely to see what's on the surface of life. Humans will continue to use their other senses merely to feel what's easy to find. And they will use their soul hardly at all. Humans invented monsters, and it seems to be an invention that will endure as long as humans endure. What of the mental retardation professional? Some people might consider that professionals—who today are given license to translate for the public the most ordinary phenemona—contribute more to the exacerbation than to the solution of this problem. Possibly, there are at least two ways to create monsters out of human beings. One is to banish them. Another is to construct a story so as to make them into something they do not want to be. Loneliness and untrue stories are mortal diseases. They are among the most significant etiological factors associated with mental retardation. Who is working on *those* cures? The answer to that question perhaps also answers why mental retardation resists cure. Monsters are monsters. Be they great in size, swift of foot, even bright—they are monsters. They may all be different, but they are all alike in one respect. Monsters are lonely.

Dangerousness: The Myth of the Monster

Once people are defined as monsters—whether they are the creation of a Dr. Frankenstein or the creation of a state and its doctors—there is no stopping further definition. Long before John Steinbeck's Lenny, mentally retarded people were "known" to have strong backs and weak minds; consequently, they could not be relied upon to act judiciously and safely. Society may be out of harm's way when the retarded person has a weak back to go with his weak mind, or when the gifted person has a strong back to go with his strong mind, but beware of a person with a strong back and a weak mind—or so the fright goes. Notwithstanding, once upon a time people who worked in this field didn't think about retarded people as dangerous. Years ago, when I made overnight visits to institutions, I would never lock my bedroom door—even when I slept in a dormitory with retarded people. But when I visit a university campus and remain overnight at the university's hotel or student union, I always lock my door at night. Quite simply, retarded people were not considered to be dangerous. That conception has changed.

In a paper I wrote concerning the unintended negative consequences to individuals who are unable to influence the kinds of stories that are told about them, I discussed an inservice training program at a state institution:

> I serve as President of the Board of Visitors of our region's developmental center. As part of their orientation and inservice training, employees there are required to enroll in a course on "the gentle art of self-defense." And from the looks of my mail, such courses are now the rage. For example, one such 30-hour program advertised as "nonabusive physical intervention," is designed "to teach control of aggressive outburst of behavior." It was created primarily for "direct care mental health and retardation workers, as well as psychiatric nurses, with quick and nonviolent solutions to such client behavior as biting, punching, kicking, choking, and the resistance of transport." The reader is informed that the course "will be thoroughly grounded in the principles of crisis intervention and team leadership." How ingenious! Who could have envisioned during one's innocence that combat training could be couched in such professionally appealing language? And for those who don't want or need the full dose offered by the 30-hour course, there is a 16-hour option, "designed to give the direct care force the ability to intervene effectively in an occasional problem situation." The last words of the program's originator insisted that, upon completion of the full program, each graduate will be able to protect himself and others from the following aggressive behaviors: punching, kicking, biting, choking, hair-pulling, being pinned on the floor, being choked on the floor, ankle and clothing grabs, flailing, and resisting transport. I'm not new to this work, and I don't get my kicks taking cheap shots at people who, for the most part, are as dedicated and decent as I aspire to be. Work with severely and multiply handicapped people is arduous. Work with aggressive and acting out clients is very difficult. But why do we have so many aggressive and acting out clients? And whatever the reasons for the inappropriate behaviors of severely handicapped people, what kinds of stories must we teach ourselves in order to prepare in such fiendish ways to deal with not only psychologically, but *by state definition*, physically

defenseless human beings? And does a state teach its employees about metal retardation when it inflicts such a course, such a story, on its hundreds of thousands of employees? Even when such courses "work," they tell untrue stories about the people connected with them. (Blatt, 1981, pp. 128-129)

Wolfensberger (1981a, p. 5) commented on both the content and impact of such training:

> It is commonly assumed that the various "holds" and other techniques which human service personnel are taught in order to restrain clients are harmless, but this is by no means the case. For instance, one of the techniques that has been taught to the personnel of state institutions for the mentally handicapped in New York was found to increase the likelihood that the client would suffer a fracture.
>
> One impact of all this is that it creates/perpetuates role expectations that clients will be violent. In turn, this probably contributes to negative attitudes and actual violence. Our interpretation of this sudden and phenomenal increase of interest in this topic, and the high attendance at events concerned with it, is that this is yet another way in which the path is prepared toward an increase in the prison population, the transfer of formerly institutionalized people into the prison system, and the rising consensus on "euthanasia" and genocide for severely devalued people.
>
> An example of this deplorable trend was the announcement of a workshop to be held in September, 1981, entitled "Approaches to the Violent Patient." The cover of the flyer that announced this workshop depicted what looked like a bayonet knife, with red drops of blood dripping off its tip. Hard as it may be to believe, the workshop featured five professors of psychiatry of the Harvard Medical School, plus one trooper of the Massachusetts State Police. The workshop offered a leisurely five and 3/4 hours of instruction at a tuition of $55, and could be taken for six hours of credit for the Physician's Recognition Award of the American Medical Association, and for continuing education credit for nurses and social workers.[4]

Mentally retarded people can be dangerous to their attendants and therapists, just as the world can be dangerous to retarded people. Is this perhaps a legitimate concern that has led to an evil practice? It also may be that we have now come full circle. The monster has been created, and today we are *teaching* the monster to "kill." Consider, for example, this excerpt from the May 15, 1982 *Philadelphia Inquirer* story entitled, "They Strike a Blow for Self-Confidence":

> As the man lunged toward her, Adele Fricker quickly pulled back in her wheelchair, put up one arm in self-defense and cocked the other so it was ready to strike.
>
> From her seated position, her best bet would be rigidly curling her fingers for a tiger claw to the groin of her attacker, or maybe a chop to the throat. Eyes wide and wild, she went for the tiger claw. The attacker retreated.

---

[4]From *Training Institute Publication Series (TIPS)*, *1*(4), p. 4, 5 by W. Wolfensberger (Ed.), 1981. Reprinted by permission.

> For Adele Fricker and her attacker, this encounter was practice, part of an unusual training program at the Moss Rehabilitation Hospital, 12th Street and Tabor Road, in the Olney section of Philadelphia.
> Called "Martial Arts for the Handicapped," the program is an effort to teach self-defense to people who feel particularly vulnerable on the street because of their disabilities.
> Each Wednesday for seven weeks, a group of 10 ambitious disabled people—some confined to wheelchairs, others suffering from cerebral palsy or weakened by multiple sclerosis or strokes—have been learning from a Philadelphian with a black belt in karate how to protect themselves with elbow jabs, quick punches and the tiger claw. (Kaufman, 1982, p. B1)

And so it goes! The above is a sample—I contend a representative sample—of the many "physical intervention" programs gaining acceptance among institutional leaders across the country. And what's good for the goose is good for the gander. What's good for attendants to control dangerous patients is good for patients to protect themselves from the dangerous larger society. And indeed, that larger society is violent:

> Violence in human services can be expected to be a reflection of violence in society generally. This means that we need to be alert not merely to the kind of violence that most people associate with street crime, but to "normative violence" or whatever we want to call it, which involves violent interactions as part of ordinary experiences and relationships of ordinary people. A number of recent surveys have concluded that there is now a remarkable degree of violence among people who date each other or who are lovers, even outside of marriage where a certain amount of violence has always been known to exist. Such violence ranges from the minor to the major. Surveys of undergraduates at a Minnesota college found that approximately 20% had been punched, slapped, or shoved by their dates or lovers. An Oregon survey put the figure at 25%. In Arizona, 60% of unmarried upper-class students had encountered some kind of violence while dating. (Wolfensberger, 1981a, p. 4)

The field of mental retardation may be in as great a state of disarray as the society of which it is a part. It might also be claimed that the field has never been in order. A case can be made that we *never* had a common purpose driven by a common philosophy—and that whatever bits of shared values existed hardly met the tests of decency and good judgment. At best, the field is in chaos; an ordinary man is called dangerous if he does dangerous things, but a retarded man is called dangerous merely because he is retarded. Possibly, there are people to discuss the chaos—to illuminate the situation, unravel the puzzles. But if there are such people, where are they, and why are they silent?

16.

Intelligence

NOWHERE IS THE Lie That Has Failed more destructive to the clinician and administrator of programs in mental retardation than when it is applied to questions about intelligence, the influence of inheritance and environment on it, and the possibility that a person can improve intellectually, that is, that intelligence is educable. This chapter returns to the theme of educability of intelligence. Various ideas concerning intelligence have gained currency, and, as noted throughout this book, many scholars have contributed those ideas. Adherence to one set of ideas rather than another entails serious consequences, as does adherence to the persistent—and unwarranted—assumptions about intelligence. And, as discussed in Chapter 8, there are heated controversies about this compelling question. In order to examine more closely the hypothesis that intelligence is educable, this chapter considers the conceptions fostered by Alfred Binet, Henry Goddard, Walter Fernald, Arthur Jensen, and other nativists and environmentalists. The chapter also considers an essay written by Marvin Pope, who himself was labeled mentally retarded, and who eloquently nailed down the lie that there are human lives without value—and the corollary belief that capability cannot ever be educated. The nature/nurture controversy, the educability of intelligence hypothesis, and the metaphors and controversies surrounding this concept we label "intelligence" have appeared throughout this book in different contexts. You will have already figured out for yourself how important the idea of the "intelligent person" is, especially in our technologically advanced, highly educated Western society—this despite the even "better" idea that life is too complex, that the relationship between heredity and environment is too complicated for even the "most intelligent person" to fathom, much less master.

Evolving Metaphors and Controversies on Intelligence: As Diety, Mystery, Threat, Hope

Enough in this book relies on the biographer's perception, wisdom, and honesty to suggest caution. Biographers pick over dead people as surely, if not as quickly, as undertakers. They may even work hard and honestly at their trade; but none can offer a complete picture; all engage in writing at least a bit of fiction — willingly or not; biography is necessarily a subjective enterprise.

With this caveat in mind, I turn in this section to the scholars — both historical and contemporary — who have explored the concept of intelligence, those who have been fascinated with the elusive search for answers to the "educability" question, on the one hand, and the search for programs and procedures to remediate inferior intelligence, on the other hand.

Alfred Binet and Theodore Simon were commissioned in 1904 by the French minister of education to find a practical way to identify children in the Paris schools who needed special education because of their retarded development (Gould, 1981). Until their work, there was no relatively inexpensive and uncomplicated way to measure a person's intelligence. Binet and Simon developed a series of short problems related to everyday life, such as counting and putting triangles, circles, and squares in their proper places. They grouped those tasks to make it increasingly difficult for the individual to succeed, so that individuals could be categorized according to a presumed mental age on the basis of the level of difficulty they could master. The tasks were designed in order to assess the individual's comprehension and ability to follow directions, make judgments, form evaluations, and make associations. The test went through several refinements, and, as noted earlier, mental age levels were later converted to intelligence quotients by Stern. As was also noted, these scales became popular with various other researchers who were looking for reliable and inexpensive methods to measure intelligence.

While Binet and Simon avoided equating the scales with the more general notion of "intelligence," others who used their work were not so inhibited. The person who may have been most responsible for bringing the Binet-Simon test to the United States was Henry Goddard (Gould, 1981). Goddard translated Binet's work into English and applied the scales to his various research endeavors — including his well-known but flawed study of the Kallikaks (see Smith, 1985). Goddard was the director of research at the Vineland Training School for the "feebleminded," and he was a mentor for Edgar Doll (creator of the Vineland Social Maturity Test), J. E. Wallace Wallin (creator of the first public school psycho-educational clinics), and others who were to become important figures in the field of mental retardaion. Goddard was convinced he was onto something important with his study of paupers and degenerates. He reported finding a "lowest" group of people who represented the progeny of an otherwise decent man who had had an unsavory relationship with a feebleminded barmaid during the Revolutionary War. Goddard and his research associates examined this soldier's legitimate as well as the illegitimate line of descendants (Goddard, 1912).

This work led Goddard to conclude that such people (the illegitimate descendants) presented a menace to the country. Furthermore, he postulated that many of the immigrants then flooding the United States posed a similar threat. In study after study, Goddard "proved" that the poor produce feebleminded children and that immigrants duplicate in their children their feeblemindedness and coarse manners. There were, however, many valid criticisms of Goddard's work, and scarcely 10 years after the Kallikak study, it was repudiated along with some of his other work. Notwithstanding, his public influence persisted, possibly to this day, in spite of the fact that Goddard reversed many of his earlier conclusions (Smith, 1985). By 1928, he admitted that mild mental retardation is not incurable, and that such individuals need not go to segregated institutions. But it was too late insofar as undoing the mischief that had been perpetrated (Gould, 1981).

It is sufficient to say that almost everything in the history of efforts to better define and measure intelligence — especially that history which reflects attitudes and practices in this country during the past 100 years — informs us that, almost since its beginning, we have been a nation "schizophrenic" in our racial, ethnic, and religious attitudes. While on the one hand we guarantee life, liberty, and equal treatment to all who come to our shores — regardless of color, religion, ethnicity — we should remember that we were once a "slave country." Further, we selectively limited immigration from those European countries that were not Anglo-Saxon or Nordic. For many years we cut off oriental immigration completely, and we have not yet decided whether women are fully equal to men.

As noted earlier, a number of our great political heroes, scholars, and scientists devoted themselves to "proving" the superiority of whites — and, conversely, the inferiority of foreigners, in general, and people of color, specifically. We have created a nation that guarantees schooling for everyone, and we believe in that right. Notwithstanding, it required a decision by the Supreme Court to legally guarantee the right of blacks to enroll in the same schools as whites. And while Public Law 94-142 is a reflection of this country's generosity, decency, and commitment to "education of all of the children of all of the people," that very law is also an admission that handicapped children are guaranteed schooling only because the federal government demands that it be made available. Furthermore, P.L. 94-142 is an admission that, without large federal subsidies, at least some of the states would find ways to ignore the educational needs of handicapped children, or, at the very least, would seek to mitigate the intent of that national law. At once, this law shows off America's best side and that side which we may yet find embarrassing. Evaluating our work and our purposes on behalf of the disenfranchised may appear to those willing to make the effort as a puzzle with no resolution, a task with no payoff.

Why all the activity in the area of intelligence—the research, the public laws, the lobbying, and even the data fudging by otherwise reputable scientists? This country was built from wilderness, was created by people who were judged by their capabilities more than by their pedigrees. For many generations, America was built and sustained by "go-getters," by people whose courage and intelligence saw them through the most arduous times. But what is left after the need to be courageous and independent diminishes? We could then worship capability and physical and mental skill. What built America was both the idea of a people conquering the wilderness and the actualization of that idea, thus concretizing the metaphor.

In the process, leaders and citizens alike experienced waves of resistance against immigrants, perceiving them as threats to the nation. What Jefferson, Lincoln, Goddard, and Fernald worried about remains worrisome today. And while politicians today are not as frank as Jefferson and Lincoln, they make their points, as Arthur Jenson and other ideological descendants of Goddard and Fernald make their points. Maybe these contemporaries should not be called "racists," but they believe that certain races are superior to others. Possibly, "racist" is the kindest judgment that will befall them. Suppose they're wrong? Suppose blacks are not intellectually or morally inferior to whites? Suppose intelligence is educable, and suppose the 40,000,000 functional illiterates in America could have learned to read, could have learned how to succeed better in this culture? Then it is not "merely" a question of racism. Then these ideological descendants of Goddard and Fernald will have to deal with their culpability in denying a large segment of people their rightful opportunities to grow and propser in this "land of opportunity." Then what may have been "merely" racism becomes irresponsibility, in the eyes of those who would judge leniently, and moral criminality in the eyes of those who would judge harshly.

Since the creation of the first institutions in this country, "intelligence" has remained a goal, a problem, and a controversy in our field. It's a goal because, by definition, those we deal with haven't enough of it. It's a problem because we have yet to figure out how to preserve it, much less educate it. It's a controversy because it's our most serious (and passionate) goal and problem. Some spend their lives studying the factors of intellect, while others spend their lives seeking ways to control and increase intellect. Unraveling the puzzle — our effort to comprehend what is nature and what is nurture — has been as unattainable as the goal to control intelligence and shape its development in people. Hence, around this concept we call "intelligence," we find virtually all of the most scandalous deceits in the field, as well as what some consider to be most of the opportunities. Nevertheless, in spite of a great deal of research and programmatic efforts (as well as frenetic activity and controversy), we are essentially where we were when Binet and Simon invented their test of intellect in the early twentieth century.

From the literature on mental retardation — or even from the daily newspapers — we know that the concept of intelligence is widely discussed, widely misunderstood (if only in the sense that otherwise informed people misunderstand it), widely invoked in the name of equality, democracy, and egalitarianism, and widely abused in the cause of racism. And as noted, the major scandals in the field of mental retardation have been, to an astonishing degree, connected to permutations of the nature/nurture issue. A partial roll call of such "embarrassments" might include:

1. Henry Goddard's doctored photographs of the Kallikaks;
2. Cyril Burt's fictitious collaborators and data;
3. Bernardine Schmidt's fictitious analysis, and, at least in part, fictitious study;
4. The legion of medical practitioners who claimed cures for people with Down syndrome (Benda and Turkel); enhancement of intellectual performance from certain drug therapies (e.g., glutamic acid) and surgical procedures (e.g., lobotomies, lobectomies, and other psycho-surgical techniques).

Notwithstanding both the good and fraudulent work, "intelligence" remains elusive and essentially unmeasurable (in part because we have not even achieved a common definition of it). Some worry about culture-free intelligence tests, while others seek to ban the use of tests entirely. Some claim the IQ test can measure innate potential, while others claim it measures little more than a level of professional racism. Some claim that intelligence is invariant, others claim it's educable, and still others claim the concept is meaningless. In important ways, the irony of the intelligence test is that it is as much a projective test — a sort of quantitative "Rorschach" as it is a "Binet."

Much has been written in support of and in derogation of the work of Cyril Burt and Rick Heber — two once-distinguished psychologists who were later disgraced (for much different reasons). Much has been written, pro and con, about Arthur Jensen (the nativist) and Harold Skeels (the environmentalist). Much has been written, and much has been ignored, concerning the work of scholars who have assumed polarized positions on the nature/nurture controversy. Burt was disgraced for alleged fudging or presenting nonexisting data. Heber apparently committed more financially oriented indiscretions. Skeels was once castigated and made the pariah, and years later Arthur Jensen found himself in similar circumstances. It almost appears as if those who insist on engaging in IQ controversy will get dirty—at least on the outside, and, so it seems, once in a while on the inside. The Harvard psychologist R. J. Herrnstein (1982) has claimed that the press and other media distort the controversy entirely in favor of the environmentalists. He has plaintively recounted the rigorous manner in which every unseemly element of Cyril Burt's life, time and time again, came out in the magazines and newspapers; on the other hand, he found it less than amusing that hardly a word was mentioned in those same journals and newspapers concerning Heber's fall from grace. Herrnstein has expressed concern about why the *New York Times* never asks a psychometrist to review books on the nature/nurture controversy, warning us that an antitesting bias has infected the media and many leftist organizations and their contributors. He has claimed that powerful pressure groups in politics, education, and the judiciary seek to contain the knowledge that science could bring to this controversy. There are anti-psychologists, egalitarians, sociologists, and other citizens who do not like testing—who do not like pitting white capability against black capability, the socially disadvantaged against the affluent. Of course, while Herrnstein's view must be examined seriously, environmentalists might make the same case of media neglect and distortion of *their* work. And so the controversy continues—fueled not only by the prejudices sustaining the principals engaged in the battle, but also by the prejudices of those who observe it, those who write about it, those who influence the larger society.

There is the story of the king who wanted to find the happiest man in his kingdom so he could wear his shirt and thus be happy too. Well, that happiest man was found, but he did not own a shirt. When he heard the king's story, the once-happy man became very sad—not because he needed to keep his shirt, but because he didn't have one to give to the king so as to make him happy. The shirt does not make the happy man, and the IQ score does not make the man intelligent. Everyone agrees on that. The disagreement has to do with the obverse question. Is it possible to examine the man, and because he is or isn't wearing a shirt, determine whether he is happy? Does the IQ score reflect intelligence? Or is there too small a relationship between the test score and the intelligence of the person? The story of the king and the happy man is also a projective test. One can read many things into it, derive many meanings and understandings from it, discuss it in many ways. What about the IQ test? Is the Binet as much a projective test as a measure of intelligence? Is a man born wise or stupid, or merely advantaged or not? Or could it be that there is no rule, no "reason" for human variation with respect to intelligence?

Persistently Recurring Assumptions

During the mid to late fifties, just after I began my career in college teaching, I became more and more worried about the icons of the field of mental retardation. My own dissertation (Blatt, 1956) gave little support for the idea that segregated special classes for mentally retarded children were inherently superior to other administrative arrangements for such children. My early work with Seymour Sarason offered little support for the idea that the then-labeled group, "cultural familial mentally retarded," inherited their retardation (Blatt, 1960). Later work with Sarason, creating what we then called a psycho-educational clinic, removed any vestiges of confidence in traditional teacher training programs (Sarason, Davidson, & Blatt, 1962). And efforts to find procedures and programs to stimulate educability, while never sufficiently successful to reject the hypothesis that intelligence cannot be educated, to this day remain at the core of the quest to "unravel" the mental retardation puzzle.

Notwithstanding these efforts to lay by the heels what is "known," what is assumed, and what needs yet to be understood in this field—and notwithstanding the considerably more impressive work of others toward a more comprehensible conception of the field—our leaders continue to harbor unwarranted beliefs concerning retarded persons, their families, what they get, and what they need. Indeed, persistently recurring assumptions we wrote about 25 years ago are, if anything, either more deeply ingrained than ever before or have been replaced by other equally intractable unwarranted assumptions. At the core of the myths, assertions, and silliness in the field is the question of human educability. It's as if mental retardation turned over its scholarship and practice to Harpo Marx, Dorothy Parker, Robert Benchley, Alexander Woolcott, Franklin P. Adams, George S. Kaufman, and the others from Algonquin Roundtable fame—with the command to bring sense and order to the field. It is as if we have a right to be surprised and chagrined when what we got in return were cruel wisecracks, a lot of back slapping and log rolling, and self-serving proprieties. If you are familiar with the Algonquin Roundtable *and* the leadership in mental retardation, you might be surprised when you compare the "under the surface" characteristics of the groups. You may conclude that the Algonquin

Hotel in New York City is the Willowbrook Developmental Center moved to a better neighborhood, and with higher toned clientele.

The most basic of the persistent assumptions is that people are generally bright or stupid, skillful or inept, good or bad. Relevant to this point is an intriguing paper by Ogden Lindsley in which he examined the puzzling and enigmatic individual referred to as the "idiot savant" (Lindsley, 1964b). Specifically, he looked at the life of Kiyoshi Yamashita, a Japanese artist who has been called the Van Gogh of the Orient, one whose pictures are sold for hundreds of thousands of dollars, but who has a measured IQ of 68 and who by all accounts has been judged to be mentally retarded.

Yamashita's artistic skills have developed to an extraordinary degree, despite the mental retardation "baggage" he carries. The idiot savant question has puzzled scholars in psychology and education for many years. But Yamashita isn't the first (nor will he be the last) retarded person who has extraordinary artistic or musical talents. Among others, Schaefer-Simmern (1948) has written accounts of the artistic capabilities of retarded people. And of course, the classic work of Scheerer, Rothmann, and Goldstein (1945) recorded examples of unusual special talents of retarded people. In a way, the inexplicable idiot savant, the now-maligned (but once attractive) notion of the defective delinquent, the puzzling accounts in our literature concerning discrepancies between in-school and out-of-school intellectual behavior, and the many assumptions, puzzles and arguments current to this day suggest that there's much we don't know, and, therefore, much to be learned. Possibly, "intelligence" is the most controversial, the most problematic, the most seriously argued, and the most essential concept in the field. Possibly, the concept that intelligence is modifiable – educable – defies too directly pessimism concerning the human condition. Who among us believes that human beings can "move mountains" – i.e., can change themselves, much less the world?

The Intelligent Voice of Experience

The advocate Robert Perske heard the following account and was kind enough to share it with me. Marvin Pope was a featured speaker at a 1982 meeting concerned with the misuse of diagnostic labels. I asked Mr. Pope for permission to reprint his statement here; shortly after receiving my request, in his own handwriting he sent gracious approval. Thinking back to the travails of May Seagoe in bringing Paul Scott's story to light, I am compelled to mention the otherwise unimportant fact that Mr. Pope's handwriting is legible and intelligent. Nevertheless, I fear that you will not believe that a mentally retarded man can write and think so well that "educated" people find his work interesting — even inspiring. It's only in retrospect that we believe the Helen Keller saga or the John Merrick saga — or, for that matter, the Albert Einstein or Leonardo saga. It's only in retrospect that any great accomplishment is believable. Else it would not be so great, so unbelievable.

I don't know if we should continue to label Marvin Pope as "retarded." I don't know why he refers to himself as "retarded." But even the wisest among us are victimized by our indoctrinations:

> Good morning. I am Marvin Pope and I live in a duplex apartment in a neighborhood called Plymouth Park in the City of Chesapeake . . . I am a client of the Chesapeake Supervised Apartment Program and have had my own apartment since September of 1981.
>
> My topic for this presentation is "labels." There are documented cases of people who have been labeled "genius" as children who, as young adults, have committed suicide because living up to the expectation of being a genius was just too much for them to cope with. There are documented cases of people who have been labeled "mentally retarded." What do these cases have in common? Labels. Because of the label, "genius," miracles were expected. Because of the label, "mentally retarded," nothing was expected. In both cases, labeling was the handicap.
>
> I am mentally retarded. That's what I've been told all my life.
>
> To hear it, makes me angry! I would like the general public to think of me as having a profound or a severe handicap. When I hear the term, "mentally retarded," I certainly don't think of myself that way. Yet Social Services has a thick file on me, labeling me "mentally retarded," because someone, when I was too young to help myself, decided my future.
>
> In the supervised apartment program, I have my P.O.R. (Problem Oriented Record) — you're all familiar, I know, with P.O.R.'s. My "needs" list isn't too long because I have my basic living skills, social skills — not too perfect, but who here is perfect? On the first line is a big zero — the words, "mentally retarded." What does it mean? It means don't expect too much.
>
> I work. In fact, I have several jobs. Sometimes I get fired. Sometimes I quit when the going gets rough. I can quit with just a slight twinge of guilty conscience because I can hide under the big safe umbrella that's labeled "mentally retarded."
>
> At this point I am learning to avoid "learned helplessness" that was created because I have lived with the label, "mentally retarded," through various placements of my life. Maybe I know — just maybe — I would be farther ahead today if my label didn't give society an excuse not to try harder with me during my school years. Maybe I know — just maybe — I would be farther ahead today if my label hadn't given me that excuse not to try harder. Maybe — just maybe — the only things that are labeled are clothes — not people.
>
> Thank you.

Marvin Pope is an intelligent voice of experience. But not all intelligent people are always intelligent. Some people are oblivious to the best in our society, and others to the worst. But still others are deliberately "blind"—by methodological intention, oblivious and insensitive to the real world. In a way, the "good" and "bad" about science is that it is blind to those matters in which more ordinary people find their passions. Science would have little place or skill to reckon the wisdom of Marvin Pope. Marvin Pope needs science less than science needs Marvin Pope.

17.

Life, Eugenics, Euthanasia, and Sterilization

THE NEXT TWO chapters will look at mental retardation as life and death, in terms of human mortality. These chapters will grope with those deep and unremitting—never satisfactorily answered—questions each one of us has concerning life, its meaning, and what lies beyond this Vale of Tears.

In this chapter, the American eugenic movement is reviewed—an effort that helped the nation create what is arguably the world's greatest agricultural system, but also that helped create a racist society. This chapter will also discuss euthanasia and sterilization—the right of the individual to life and the right of society to kill. Again we return to the questions: What is a human being? What are human beings entitled to—because they are humans? When does life begin? When can it be deliberately ended? Should it ever—under any circumstances—be deliberately ended? I will again draw parallels to Nazi Germany, as well as to anorexia and to the mental health movement. In the end the quintessential issue surfaces—freedom to live in ordinary society, freedom to live.

In this and succeeding chapters, you will read about deathmaking, about the effects of policies that are based on the belief that there are lives without value, and that these lives can be terminated—indeed, prevented. With this chapter begins a final summation of the most troubling practices and values in our field. As in Nazi Germany, there is indifference here. There is also the widespread belief that few wrongs have been committed against disabled people.

Eugenics

Wolf Wolfensberger (personal communication) has reflected on certain aspects of the Judaic-Christian roots to the modern understanding of mental retardation. As recently as 50 years ago, eugenicists declared that feebleminded people are not of much value to society, and referred to them as one of the so-called "dysgenic" classes, people who contribute negatively to the gene pool. In the 1800s, an institute of heredity was established in Boston. It gained sponsorship from such luminaries as Longfellow, the widow of the great educator Horace Mann, and Alexander Graham Bell. Later scientists such as Galton, Carl Pearson, and others worked mightily to promote genetic control of polluted genes among the masses. All of these efforts were to "better the race." As Wolfensberger noted, in 1903, the American Breeders' Association was founded in St. Louis by people who wanted to stay on top of this new science of genetics. It wasn't long before the Association formed the Eugenic Section, its purpose being to study the best practical means for cutting off defective germ plasm in the American population. Such philanthropic individuals as Mrs. E. H. Harriman offered financial support to these efforts, and eventually the Carnegie Institute of Washington gave its imprimatur and support to the program.

By the beginning of the second decade of this century, an international eugenics conference was held under the auspices of the Eugenics Education Society in London. Other countries soon joined this common effort to "improve the race." And their labors were not without success — enlisting religious as well as political groups to their cause. This was thought to be work of the highest ideal, devoted to human betterment, even as "a partnership with God and as a key to heaven." There was a time when it was believed that, with greater genetic control, the world would eventually be rid of idiots, imbeciles, other feebleminded persons, epileptics, the insane, psychopaths, chronic alcoholics, paupers, vagrants, persons likely to become public charges, beggars, people with tuberculosis or with other contagious diseases, criminals, people with low morals, polygamists, anarchists, prostitutes, and others not of good stock or moral worth. It was believed that someday the world would be rid of defectives, lunatics, delinquents, and dependents. At one time, society's goal was to achieve God's design on earth. Does human salvation lie in ridding the earth of its deviants? I prefer to believe the world is better today for having resisted (if not entirely rejected) those ideas. But I am troubled that there lingers yet deep and widespread feelings that it wasn't so much a case of giving up the dream as missing the opportunity. I am troubled that the philosophy, if not the practice, of human eugenics has strong representation in our culture; not the least reason here is the regular confirmation to farmers, dog fanciers, horse breeders, and others who know that genetic controls make for "better" corn, dogs, and horses. Why not people?

Topic of Cancer

For generations, retarded individuals have been viewed as dependent and unproductive burdens on society. The most optimistic view was of the "benign parasite"—if not a pathogenic curse, then at least an unwanted (and unnecessary) difficulty; it not a cancer, then an ugly tumor. That view is changing, but ever so slowly. And the positive perceptions have been evolving with little more speed among retarded persons themselves than among more ordinary citizens. There are reasons for this state of affairs.

Being retarded does not enhance one's self-perception. Being retarded makes the universe a segregated, punitive institution. Being the parent of a retarded person does not enhance one's pride in parenthood. Being the parent of a retarded person makes one wish that the world had either no long future or a very short memory. It can be said that being retarded is the intellectual equivalent of being black in a hostile southern town, being Jewish at the wrong country club, or being poor in the company of the rich. Being retarded, or being the parent of a retarded person, makes it difficult to be objective about matters concerning the mind—in the same way that few Jews assimilate while many remain "angry," in the same way that some blacks are called "Uncle Toms" while others are militant. But hardly any members of minority groups are truly unaffected by their experiences. For example, Walter Lippmann, a Jew, was essentially silent about the Holocaust throughout a period when his influence might have rallied Americans to rescue some of the victims. But like all "silent minority" members, he had his reasons—writing early in his career that uncritical allegiance to Zionism, and, implicitly, to "Jewishness," is deplorable regression to "tribalism."

For some people, the cancer of one's inheritance—be it racial, religious, or intellectual—is its denial. For others, it's the obsession with it. In a recent citation search of 10,000 items in special education, utilizing the Educational Resources Information Center (ERIC) system, I found that euthanasia and mercy killings were never mentioned. It is puzzling and distressing that the field of special education itself isn't taking a noticeable role, isn't making a noticeable statement, on an issue that has enormous implications for the very lives of its clients. About a dozen years ago, I did another literature search, utilizing one of the other computerized citation systems. Then, I could find no references to human abuse in connection with mental retardation. A dozen years ago "human abuse" was hardly known as a subject of interest, much less a field. Today, people are writing doctoral dissertations, if not taking advanced degrees, in such areas as child abuse.

Times change, but we refuse to learn from history. In 1929, Gosney and Popenoe wrote in their introduction to *Sterilization for Human Betterment*:

> The human race has developed through countless ages under the laws of heredity by the survival of the fittest. The weak and defective have perished. Only the physically strong and mentally alert could withstand the severe conditions of early life, reach maturity, and become the fathers and mothers of the next generation.
>
> Modern civilization, human sympathy, and charity have intervened in Nature's plan. The weak and defective are now nursed to maturity and produce their kind.
>
> Under Nature's law we bred principally from the top. Today we breed from the top and bottom, but more rapidly from the bottom. Today the most intelligent and efficient, the strongest strains of blood, as a rule, limit their children to a point that means the extinction of a family in a few generations. (p. v.)

The "evidence" for the above assertions was founded on the now discredited Kallikak study by Goddard, Dugdale's equally discredited Jukes study, and on the work of others not as well known but once influential in eugenics, sterilization, and other "social control" movements in this country.

And so I ask the question: Whom can you kill and *not* be accused of murder? A horse? Of course. Another animal? Of course, any animal. One can kill an animal and not have to suffer execution. One might "kill" a being who looks human, yet either doesn't act human or is near death, and this person would not suffer execution. There are serious debates on the rights of retarded people to survive (Affleck, 1977). There are even debates by theologicans concerning "death by choice" (Maguire, 1974). There are questions raised with ever increasing frequency concerning how far medical science should go in providing families with information concerning fetal characteristics (Smith, 1981). For example, the use of amniocentesis by older women is now an established medical practice. With ever increasing frequency, amniocentesis appears to be "useful" to certain families who want assurances concerning the sex of their unborn children or other characteristics of the developing embryo. There are distinguished doctors who, in our most prestigious medical journals, advise parents to participate in life (and death) decision making (Duff, 1981). There are various clinical positions concerning the rights of crippled, "grotesque," and retarded people—those a few still call freaks, and those who are always called "different" (Parrish, 1980).

Let me conclude by returning to the point that the cancer of one's inheritance is its denial. But it may also be said that the cancer of anyone's life is the denial of the right for people to be different, to live differently. To be an alien, to have to live in what seems to be becoming a world that cannot accommodate "strangers," is also a reflection of a society's sickness.

Free Will—To Live As Well As To Die

Nesbitt (1982) asked rhetorically, "If a parent can be entrusted with the right to decide where a child will go to school, cannot a parent . . . be entrusted with the right to decide when life-extending treatment fails to serve a child's best interests?" (pp. 262-263).

His answer:

> At first blush, this is an attractive method of handling the problems under discussion. It relieves both the courts and the legislature of grappling with the difficult moral issues these cases present. State interference with familial decision-making regarding life-extending treatment can be limited to those cases at the end of the spectrum, for example, a religiously motivated parental objection to a blood transfusion necessary to save an infant's life.
>
> This approach, however, is more properly characterized as an abdication rather than a solution. (p. 263)

Exactly so! Giving parents the authority to determine the life or death of their children is an abdication. Some would think it's a crime. If the parents feel that — for whatever reasons — they can't (or won't) care for their newborn, then they need not bring the baby home. They could "abdicate" by leaving the hospital without the baby, not by agreeing to kill the child. While the abortion issue is more complex, here too the mother could decide to "abdicate" after birth, not while the fetus is in utero (thus causing an abortion), and not with death to precipitate the separation. "Simply," the mother can give birth. "Not so simple?" you say. Nevertheless, it is a matter to ponder. In a 1983 case, the parents of "Baby Jane Doe" defended their decision to refuse life-sustaining surgery on their handicapped infant with the comment, "We love her very much, and that's why we made the decision we did." Children believe in Santa and fairy tales and all sorts of stories, and that's their charm. But adults who say that death is love should not be believed by even children. And adults who believe that incarceration is therapeutic and that killing is saving may cause more harm than good, much less express charm. But that question too is today one of the current debates. It's instructive to know that parents may decide to have treatment denied, but only while the infant is in the hospital. That same infant denied treatment one week later at home would cause criminal proceedings to be filed against the parents.

A newspaper headline announces that the parents of a child with Down syndrome refuse to permit the surgical repair of his damaged heart—an operation necessary to reduce his considerable suffering, possibly to enhance his chance for survival. Eventually, the highest court in that state rules that "even parents" have no right to deny life to their child (we might have said "especially parents"). An English newborn—but not so lucky—is injected with a lethal chemical. He too had Down syndrome, and he too had parents who didn't want him to live. But his doctor found a way to carry out the parents' wishes. What about the doctor? What about doctors who were once loved for healing? *He* was charged with murder, tried, but exonerated. And virtually every medical society in England applauded the verdict. Are mortal doses and pulled plugs to be the doctor's business? Such a legacy for future generations would turn the healer into destroyer, would make medicine the work of unwilling hires doing the dirtiest jobs imaginable, merely tolerated by some among us, hated and feared by others. The noble calling may well become the chore of the unable accomplishing the ungodly—for an unnecessary goal. A great teaching hospital permits yet another Down syndrome newborn to lie unattended and unfed in a crib for 14 days, until the baby dies of starvation. This infant also had parents who didn't want him to live, parents who had demanded that the hospital not intervene despite a congenital growth which, if untreated, prevented digestion. This unlucky baby was born in a teaching hospital whose legal counsel advised the medical staff that no court would rule against parents of a handicapped child who refused to have him treated—even when such treatment was necessary to save his life. And while this book was being written, newspapers reported that a microcephalic baby—born out of the artificially inseminated union of paid surrogate mother and disenchanted once-hopeful father—was for a while unwanted by both; sorry, it was all a mistake, a miscalculated decision. Life is also cheap in Western society. The moderns are not any further advanced morally than the ancients.

Eugenics, euthanasia, sterilization are the medical accommodations between life and death. The literature is replete with evidence that retarded people are sometimes systematically killed—either by denial of necessary treatment, or through active intervention (Duff & Campbell, 1973). Sterilization, colonization, rigid separation of the sexes, and other forms of eugenic control, have for generations been the means for preventing procreation among retarded individuals. Wolfensberger (1981b) has suggested that the field's preoccupation with "death making" and "life prevention" bears striking resemblance (at least in principle) to Hitler's preoccupation with killing and sterilizing Jews, Slavs, Gypsies, and—yes, of course—mentally retarded and mentally ill persons. For some people, mental retardation is an affliction worse than death. For others—for those who are so afflicted—it is life itself, however arduous. It is what one has, what one is. For some people, the "disease" of mental retardation means that one is not entitled to live. The sacredness of a human life, the guarantee that each life is valuable, does not hold according to those people; simply, there are those who do not believe that mentally retarded—particularly severely mentally retarded persons—are truly human.

What is a human being? There was a time when humanness meant that one was born from a human mother. That time seems to have long gone—not that most of us believe otherwise, but some of us (some of the most prominent among us) challenge such a claim. Does life begin at conception, during gestation, or only on delivery? Does it end when the doctor signs the official death certificate, or at internment, or when certain physiological signs no longer exist, or when a certain IQ isn't attained, or when a certain competency isn't demonstrated, or when a certain shade of skin isn't present? When? Or is life eternal? And for whom—the saved, the annointed, everyone? What is the definition of a human being? And what must we guarantee for each human being? We hear commentary that the human being is unique among all the animals in the universe. What is it that distinguishes the human from other animals? Free will. We have freedom to choose among that vast array of temporal options, freedom even to choose between heaven and hell.

For sure, while our religions teach us (and while our civil laws remind us) that the human being doesn't have the "right" to will his own demise (to kill himself), there is relative silence in the medical academy, as well as in the courts, as to whether certain human beings are entitled to the freedom to live—especially when those human beings cannot exercise their free wills to decide to live. It's all very complicated, but it's especially ironic that those who have difficulty controlling their own lives—elderly, poor, severely handicapped persons—are in greatest jeopardy insofar as society's concern in protecting their lives. In our society, it seems that people must again and again demonstrate their capacity to exercise free will in order to receive protection as human beings. Infants, severely retarded persons, old persons, and sick persons cannot expect that society will keep them from harm's way—exactly because they need protection. In this sense, ironically, society better protects those who don't need protection. The functional definition of "human being" is the ability to exercise free will. Because retarded people do not have that ability in abundance, their lives are jeopardized. Hitler threw people in concentration camps and, except for the strongest, took away their free will. In our society, we search out people who are weakened in mind or body or spirit—people who have lost or hardly ever had the will to choose—and then we do our mischief in the name of treatment, or even mercy. Reduce a man's free will, or find one who has lost it, and there you will find a candidate for extermination.

Wertham (1966) has described many merciless murders in his book, *A Sign for Cain*. What follows is an excerpt that may better clarify the euthanasia issue for the reader:

> Let us visualize a historical scene. Dr. Max de Crinis is professor of psychiatry at Berlin University and director of the psychiatric department of the Charité, one of the most famous hospitals of Europe. He is one of the top scientists and organizers of the mass destruction of mental patients. Dr. de Crinis visits the psychiatric institution Sonnenstein, near Dresden, to supervise the working of his organization. He wants to see how the plans are carried out. Sonnenstein is a state hospital with an old tradition of scientific psychiatry and humaneness. In the company of psychiatrists of the institution, Dr. de Crinis now inspects the latest installation, a shower-roomlike chamber. Through a small peephole in an adjoining room he watches twenty nude men being led into the chamber and the door closed. They are not disturbed patients, just quiet and cooperative ones. Carbon monoxide is released into the chamber. The men get weaker and weaker; they try frantically to breathe, totter, and finally drop down. Minutes later their suffering is over and they are all dead. This is a scene repeated many, many times throughout the program. A psychiatrist or staff physician turns on the gas, waits briefly, and then looks over the dead patients afterward, men, women, and children.
>
> The greatest mistake we can make is to assume or believe that there was a morally, medically, or socially legitimate program and that all that was wrong was merely the excesses. There were no excesses. Rarely has a civil social action been planned, organized, and carried through with such precision. It was not a "good" death, as the term "euthanasia" implies (from *eu*, "well," and *thanatos*, "death"), but a bad death, not a euthanasia but what may be called a dysthanasia. Often it took up to five minutes of suffocation and suffering before the patients died. If we minimize the cruelty involved (or believe those who minimize it), these patients are betrayed a second time. It was often a slow, terrible death for them. For example, a male nurse of one of the state mental hospitals described the routine he saw through the peephole of the gas chamber: "One after the other the patients sagged and finally fell all over each other." Others have reported that the dead gassed victims were found with their lips pushed outward, the tip of the tongue stuck out between them, clearly showing that they had been gasping for breath.
>
> The false term "euthanasia" was used by those who planned, organized, and carried out the action, and it is still being used now by those who do not know, or do not want to know, what really happened.
>
> The ancients meant by euthanasia the art and discipline of dying in peace and dignity. The only legitimate medicosocial extension of this meaning is *help* toward that end, with special emphasis on relief from pain and suffering. Euthanasia in this sense is the mitigation and relief of pain and suffering of the death agony by medication or other medical means. For the physician, that means a careful diagnosis, prognosis, and consequent action in relation to a special clinical state. As in any other medical procedures, this may involve a certain risk which requires the physician's best responsible judgment in the individual case. Whatever prob-

lems this may represent, they have no relation whatsoever to this massacre of mental patients. To confuse the two means to confuse humanity with inhumanity.[1]

Hitler came to power just over 50 years ago, when he assumed the German chancellorship on January 30, 1933. The weakened nation, unstable and economically out of control, looked for leadership and ideas. With Hitler, it found both in abundance. He set the people on a common course. But those within and without the land eventually learned that bargaining with evil misuses less the devil than those who would consort with him. We can learn from the Nazi parable. We too have set aside principles to exploit immediate opportunities. An analogy can be made between the German death camp and the mental retardation institution. Again, I emphasize that I do not compare the Nazi deeds to what retarded people experience here. Deeds are not being compared but rather basic principles. For example, ordinary German citizens of that era didn't kill anyone. Rather, they may be condemned for indifference to the killings they sensed were occurring or actually knew about. What reader doesn't know about Baby Doe and inhumane other practices?

There are *always* at least two arguments to face here. The first has to do with the bad institution—the Willowbrooks, Pennhursts, and all the others, those that bring Dachau to saliency. The second argument has to do with whether people should be institutionalized, even in excellent institutions. In theory, there could be a benevolent dictator of the United States—one who would make the people happy, even fulfilled. But *we* wouldn't have such a leader, however wonderful, however "good" for the people. It's like being forced to be in Lincoln Center or the Vienna Opera House. We would not give up our freedom even to hear the most remarkable music performed by the most remarkable musicians. So, there is the freedom issue—irrespective of the quality issue. The Willowbrooks of the world present immediate dangers to those incarcerated—genuine emergencies. But even if there were no immediate dangers, no emergencies, the freedom issue remains. While we discuss "life and death" issues, we must also remember what makes life worth living. Is anything more central here than being free—simply being free? Retarded people can live free, can have meaningful lives only if they are free. In this regard, they are no different from the rest of us.

---

[1] From *A Sign for Cain* (pp. 154-155) by F. Wertham, 1966, New York: Macmillan. Copyright 1966 by Frederick Wertham. Reprinted by permission of Macmillan.

Cadavers

Cadavers are lifeless remains. How important they are depends on one's aesthetic sensibilities as well as, possibly, one's religion, constitution, and family experiences. Whether the body is merely flesh and bones and will soon be dust in the ground, whether it is to be consumed by the earth or the fire, whether it can (or must not) be tampered with before it is laid to heavenly rest — or simply laid in the ground — are questions that mere mortals can't answer definitively, won't ever answer precisely, and we are probably better off because we're unable to answer. These questions are resolved by individual taste, custom, or religion. But most people certainly harbor the belief that they own their own bodies — at least during their lifetimes, if not for eternity. And furthermore, most people believe that one should have the choice as to whether his or her mortal remains are to go to the ground or the medical school. If one wants to donate kidneys, heart, whatever, to the organ banks, wonderful. But the choice is (or must be) the individual's — not one that another person can make for the individual, not one that society can make for the individual. That is, of course, if the individual isn't institutionalized — as a mental patient, as a pauper, or as someone who is caught with the "mental retardation" label.

Years ago, when I served as Director of the Massachusetts Division of Mental Retardation, Department of Mental Health, I became involved with the Boston area Cadaver Committee of its three medical schools. I learned then that, when a state school resident dies and neither family nor other interested parties are quick to claim the body, the deceased person is selected for medical study — probably in the same manner in which he was selected for institutionalization. In a sense, it's fitting because the person is treated in death as in life. Until I tried to put a stop to it — and I succeeded for but the briefest period of time — each involuntary corpse contributed one year of eternal life to society before being permitted to rest. Again, here is an irony of ironies. This person, given such short shrift from society, this person who owes so little to society, this person from whom society has exacted so much, now must give yet another year to the very people who stripped him or her of so much during his or her temporal life. Most of those people experienced lifetimes of sacrifice. Now their deaths must require further sacrifice. So much of this field is pornographic. That is, so much is about victims, degradation, and unnecessary suffering. "Mental retardation" has been the "in" dirty joke.

Are there still cadaver committees that snatch bodies from the state institutions? I don't know, but I suspect there are — in one form or another, with one disguise or another to keep the advocates tame. The importance of the cadavers to medical training is not germane. What is germane is the extent to which the medical community attaches importance to human value and dignity. Some things are even more important than education and science. Yes, some things are even more important than saving future lives, if such efforts are at the expense of degrading present lives. Humans can be degraded even after their mortal lives end.

The Concept of Starvation

Had the term "anorexia" not already been invented to designate the condition of those people who starve themselves — sometimes to death — anorexia might have been a suitable label for America's general revulsion with stupidity, maladroitness, and incompetency — with anything connected to what we generally understand to be mental retardation. Like the anorexic adolescent female, we have a ravenous egalitarian drive to make everyone equal, or better, to act as if everyone were equal. At the same time, we hate those who do not measure up to our conceptions of what is normal. And so, even while we loathe our meanness of spirit and narrow, bigoted views of what a human being can be, we are driven to starve ourselves of opportunities to enlarge variance in our lives. We shun those who are incompetent, infirm, palsied, different. We avoid those people as we try to avoid death itself; yet we know that to avoid them is to deny ourselves not only moral nourishment but the excitement and color that ultimately make life that much more worthwhile. Why do we do it?

Denying differences among people is one way of denying our mortality. Thus, denying differences gives us greater assurance that we are in control of life, that all is good with the world — that life can be lived that denies war, famine, pestilence, disillusionment, despair, and even death. Of course, the paradox is that (as with the anorexic adolescent) starving oneself of life's realities can kill — if not the body, then the soul. And the antidote? As with the anorexic, we must avoid starvation. People have a responsibility to themselves, if not to the society, not only to eat, which sustains the body, but to engage in experiences that sustain our conscience, our spirit, our ultimate sense of well being.

Many anorexic adolescents grow out of their torturous self-imposed starvation. Unfortunately, too many people who are anorexic about interacting with their fellow humans — difficult as well as joyous interaction — never grow out of that troublesome disease. Sadly, they die without ever knowing how rich their lives might have been. In our fruitless search for immortality, we sometimes neglect the good if imperfect lives we could lead. Like the anorexic, some of us have difficulty learning that — exactly because life always has its hazards, dangers, and problems — we can't live by always avoiding conflict and peril. To live, we sometimes must face genuine danger, and we usually must confront the real problems we have. Generally, problems do not go away by themselves. That's the substance of fairy tales; but even kings and presidents today cannot survive a fairy tale world—one in which they permit themselves to view living as painless, and all endings as happy. As Richard Hungerford said so eloquently, in the end happiness fails, fantasy fails. Fulfillment will come to the person who seeks to share responsibility, who seeks to be involved with the people and the issues of the time. That's the reality out of which one can achieve maturity, if not always happiness. Out of that reality, one gains wisdom.

It is not only the ordinary citizen who flinches at difficult problems, who has been infected with "anorexia oligophrenia." As discussed elsewhere in this book, the mental retardation establishment—The Family—avoids confrontation with the nasty problems associated with institutionalization (and its antidote, deinstitutionalization), and with abuse (and its antidote, compassion). Possibly, as the ordinary citizen seeks to avoid confrontation with mental retardation by denying its existence, the professional avoids it by fighting the wrong wars. On the one hand, thus, "everything" is different today as contrasted with two or three decades ago—we have more professionals with more degrees, we are spending more on our facilities and programs, there is more legislation designed to protect and enhance the lives of retarded individuals, and we have publicized needs more than ever before. On the other hand, little has actually changed. The mental retardation establishment has yet to win the war against institutionalization, against abuse and neglect, despite the fact that it has conquered its own dominion—its Family. As a profession, we are stronger and more widely respected than ever before. As a profession, we are organized, we are better paid, we are more entrenched. But it is possible that, while we may have won the professional war—that which is connected to our own lives, our own survival, our own welfare—we have not won the most important war—that which is connected to the lives of those whom we are reputed to serve. We have conquered those who would destroy the weakened profession. We have won a war for the Family. But to return to the original analogy, we are starving. We have yet to face the more compelling objective, the problems that became the basis for the creation and sustenance of our field. We have yet to fulfill our true mission.

Mental Retardation and Freedom

In a devastating critique of the psychiatric establishment, Szasz tore apart the troubling arguments of psychiatrists, psychologists, social workers, and para-professionals working in the mental health field, who wrote piously about "depriving persons of liberty in the mental hospital in order, ostensibly, to 'liberate' them" (1982, p. 765). On the one hand, such patients are described as "stuporous catatonics." On the other hand, they are presumed to have the capability to refuse medication, if they desire. Exposing the "naked emperor," Szasz simply quoted the mental health professionals' own words — which justify enchainment for the purposes of enhancing future freedom, which claim that the environment offering the greatest freedom available for certain mentally ill people is not the community, but rather, the community of specialists serving them in a closed asylum. Szasz noted that all of this may be accomplished only in institutions accredited by the Joint Commission on the Accreditation of Hospitals. Is it any wonder that institutionalized people have grave difficulties convincing their benefactors (the professionals), much less ordinary citizens, that they deserve to be free?

As I have said so often in this book, all people who are not dangerous to themselves or others deserve to be free, and furthermore, they deserve equal opportunities to learn, to develop, to live. Special evidence should not be required to guarantee that sort of freedom to anyone in our culture. If there is a burden in such a situation, it must be on those who would deny someone freedom.

In this chapter, I discussed the relationship between mental retardation and the eugenics movement, euthanasia, sterilization, free will, and death. *Those* are the genuine problems of life, and they are related to the overriding problem, the quintessential question — freedom. What is there to a life? Security, sustenance, and freedom. Freedom cannot thrive without sustenance in the form of food and shelter; but even the shelter and the tranquility are trivial without "food" for the soul, freedom. We rarely risk dying to be at peace with our neighbor. We rarely kill another human just to eat more. But we do both to be free.

One question often asked is, What does freedom mean to a retarded person? Is it comprehensible? Necessary? Desirable? For sure, freedom is not as tangible as food; nor does it necessarily make us feel as good as when we are at peace with ourselves and others. Would a retarded person die for freedom? This question defies accurate answers, not because it is asked of a mentally retarded person, but because of the nature of the question. Would you die for freedom? Yes, I think that a retarded person would die for freedom. I think that retarded people have died for freedom — as some have died because they weren't free. People die in different ways.

When people are enchained — either physically or psychologically — they may come to believe that their life is not worth living. While people kill themselves for many reasons, those reasons may be connected with a loss of hope that life will get better, a loss of belief that life has meaning. Elsewhere in this book I have remarked that there is no "psychology of mental retardation." Science has uncovered nothing that suggests a different psychology for mentally retarded persons. Mentally retarded people fall in love like other people fall in love, have the same fears and anxieties, harbor the same fantasies and aspirations, worry about the same demons. Mentally retarded people, too, seek to endure in this Vale of Tears; but when endurance is incomprehensible or inconceivable to them, they too may choose to kill themselves. Consequently, there's nothing about retarded persons that should lead us to believe that they think less of their freedom than do other people, or would be less inclined to fight for their freedom than other people. Retarded people too could be stirred to defend their freedom with their lives, or as happens with others from time to time, they could be enslaved. Mentally retarded people can give up their lives for their freedom, or they can accept their enslavement. But we have also learned that, without Moses, the children of Israel would have remained slaves. Without Lincoln, there may not have been an emancipation for years, if not decades. Without certain leaders, there may not have been a women's movement. And who knows but that there may be someone waiting at this moment, preparing at this moment, for a revolt of the idiots? "Mental retardation" has been a caged animal. And so have too many people been "caged animals."

18.

Mental Retardation and Mentality

SOME HAVE CATEGORIZED books such as *Christmas in Purgatory* (Blatt & Kaplan, 1966), *Revolt of the Idiots* (Blatt, 1976), and *The Family Papers* (Blatt et al., 1979) — books that described and interpreted institutional life — as journalistic exposés. Such books, some asserted, were possibly significant, possibly accurate, possibly even helpful to society, but nevertheless, they were journalism and not scholarship. Neither ungrateful for nor displeased with this assertion, I have nevertheless thought about it and finally struck upon an error with respect to the reasoning behind the assertion. If this were not an opportunity for me to make what I believe is an important point, I wouldn't bring the matter up now because it appears to be self-serving. What is journalism? Gathering and reporting the news. What is an exposé? Publicly disclosing a scandal or crime. I submit to you the idea that books like *Christmas in Purgatory* were not written by journalists earlier because in the minds of the journalists, mental retardation professionals, and ordinary citizens, there was no "news" in those institutions, there was no scandal or crime. There was no apparent need to expose evil — such as a prison warden abusing inmates, or a dishonest contractor using sand instead of cement on a building. In those cases, society needs exposés so wrongs can be righted. In the case of institutions, though, there were thought to be no wrongs. As in Nazi Germany, everything in the institution was right, was proper, was legal. What was there to expose? It would have been like writing an exposé of slavery in 1840. Again, what was to be exposed?

It isn't that many thousands of people didn't know about these human warehouses, the institutions, or about the beatings and solitary confinement of uncountable inmates, the sterilizations, the euthanasia, the unnecessary segregation, the debasement of human lives and the withering of spirit, or the denial of freedom. These were and are well known — as other practices were well known in Nazi Germany. Why weren't they reported? Why aren't they reported today? Is it because treating certain retarded human beings more poorly than certain animals are treated was (is?) nothing to be ashamed about, nothing to write or speak about? Then — and to some degree today — the problem was fixed on the inmate and not the caretaker. That is, it was thought to be in the nature of the condition — mental retardation — that certain people shuffled along dayroom floors naked and incontinent, that certain people *needed* to be beaten, drugged, isolated, or restrained, that certain people can as easily live in filth and degradation as in a decent and caring environment. Many thousands saw all of this, but, like the naked emperor, they learned and believed that the naked inmate was appropriately attired. Their eyes told them one thing, their brains another, and their souls still another. A discovery, not an exposé, was necessary. In a sense, no reporter could have writtent a book like *Christmas in Purgatory* because no reporter would have known enough — until it was first written by someone else, someone who could see that the emperor *was* naked, someone who knew and felt enough to make the discovery. And that's exactly what happened. You must prepare yourself to make discoveries about mental retardation, discoveries about the clients or pupils, and the therapists, doctors, or teachers. Don't be misled by people who would tell you there is little to learn, to discover. Think about the changes — the discoveries — of the last 20 years, and remember the many yet unresolved issues and dilemmas.

You must read about how death is made easy, and consider if it should be made easy. Consider how true *Christmas in Purgatory* is today. If there still is truth to that story, ask yourself why. Then try to work out what *you* can do to make it less a fact and more a tale from our past. How will you make the world better? What will you discover, invent, do?

Man's Faulty Memory

In his autobiographical work, *Look Homeward Angel,* Thomas Wolfe (1929) recounted the death of his favorite brother, Ben. He lies dying, and the family doctor admits that there isn't anyone — doctor, nurse, anyone — who can help him now. Ben is "drowning" from the flu that infected his already weak lungs. But not only Ben's unspent life grieves the family and drives the author to great depression. Ben's death reveals to each of them their common future, their common bonds, the common secret grief each shares. As Wolfe looks at Ben's shining eyes, already cast with the mark of death, as he sees the weakening heart struggle within the thin breast, he notices how each in the room observes life's miracle, and how the dark struggle always ends. And while one could think, "This is not everything, there must be more," the thought occurs that this *is* everything. Possibly, this is what it all means. In death as in life, you get what you see. Thomas Wolfe's eloquence describes a death one way. Those who stare too hard, too long, or too interestedly at mental retardation may describe death another way.

In this era of "computer worship," we tend to forget that the truly great marvel is the human brain itself. This wonderful instrument can also remember, if not like the computer then certainly sufficiently well to get along. The brain can fantasize, create something fresh and new, inflame mobs to kill, impassion others to build, and to seek ways to live together. Indeed, the brain is an awesome and wonderful instrument. Then why do human beings have trouble remembering their own mortality? It doesn't seem as if we should forget such serious business. But everywhere there is evidence that we do not seem to know we are going to die some day. William Saroyan, that extraordinary writer, said it perfectly just before he died in May, 1981: "Everybody has got to die but I have always believed an exception would be made in my case. Now what?" ("Saroyan. . .," 1981, p. A13). The "Now what?" question seems to be one that people want to avoid, even courageous people, even the very best among us. That's the way people are. It's not a complaint but an observation. But despite failing memory, while the unwavering preoccupations of humans are self-preservation and self-justification, always lurking near the soul (if not the heart) are two others—the "what now?" and "so what?" questions.

How many among us do remember our mortality, and also have faith in a life after death? There aren't many, and hence there aren't many who willingly face the reality of our mortality and the reality of a life that always involves unhappiness, disillusionment, pain, and broken dreams. For sure, most people do not want to make room for the reality of mental retardation. To the doctor, mental retardation is chronicity, the enemy of medicine—incurability. To the teacher, mental retardation is failure, the enemy of the pedagogue—a mean future. To the parent, mental retardation is death—the end of hopes, the end of ambition, the end of a family's line. Mental retardation hurts parents most of all. Lord, if your preachers can help anyone, let them help those parents.

People simply don't want to face their mortality. Similarly, mental retardation is very difficult to face. In so many ways, mental retardation is death—dead aspirations, no second chances, no ways out. In that sense, mental retardation is as serious an idea as any a person can have. Mental retardation is the study of life and death. In an introductory chapter for a book, mainly written by parents of handicapped children (Turnbull & Turnbull, 1978), I asked those parents how they could smile day after day, knowing what they know, knowing what we know:

> How can a man drive to work each morning, whistling, so content that when he stops for a red light he removes a speck of lint from his camel-hair coat? It doesn't seem natural, people content, so glad with the state of things, as if nothing will change, as if a thing done is done forever. Isn't there someone around to blow the whistle on this mess, to say, "Look here, you're going to die. Forget that speck of dust. Go to church. Quit your current life. Do something. Try to find out what it's all about. Admit that the jig's up, that maybe there never was a jig"?
>
> When the people discovered the Emperor really didn't have any clothes, they were satisfied. Their anxiety was relieved, their senses vindicated. And they were vexed with the Emperor for having subjected them to the embarrassing trick. Would they have been more compassionate if they had continued to look around and found that *they* didn't have any clothes either? Had they reached for that speck of lint a little less complacently, a little less automatically and absent mindedly, they might have realized there was no camel-hair coat, just the naked ape. Maybe that's why they were so easily taken in by the Emperor's hoax, because it was their own hoax. Maybe that's why they were so vexed with him, because they expected of emperors more than the everyday mortal hoax.
>
> Everybody pretends with you, but you know that you're going to tell a lot of lies during your lifetime to yourself and to others. To illustrate the lies with which we live, I want to discuss the biggest lie, the denial of one's mortality.
>
> We should examine the man whistling to work in his new Volvo. What's running through his head, in tune with the whistle and the sound of tires on pavement? Could these be his thoughts: Was the purchase of the radials a good deal? . . . His job? It's too boring. How can he get more money? Or better radials? Those are the big problems he's thinking about.
>
> Why is it that dying is one of the two most difficult ideas to think about, or to talk about? Because it is the most difficult idea to remember. We keep forgetting it's going to happen to each of us. We can't believe it, and that, too, is the problem. Dying is unbelievable. That's why living is the other most difficult idea to think about. Living, too, is unbelievable.
>
> What can be done? Not much, except to stop the hand wringing, and to face facts. What are the facts? There aren't any. The one most fearful, most hopeful question people have—the question which only humans can ask, which in itself by its asking separates a human from other animals—is not answerable, nor can it ever be answerable by humans. Therefore, face life. The point is, one will never truly comprehend life's mysterious puzzles, but one should so arrange his life that he spends time struggling to understand the mysterious, even that which will never be understood. It isn't enough for a human being to escape the unknown or the difficult, to crowd the important questions and ideas out of his mind with ques-

tions of new tires or the widths of old ties. One shouldn't purge his system of that which a human being must face up to. One risks his life not when he faces hard problems, but when he denies seeking to understand the puzzle of his existence.[1]

Remember and don't be misled. Remember, humans are mortal. There is an end to wealth, as there is an end to pain and earthly despair. The only thing certain about temporal life is that everything ends, everything is lost, nothing can be saved except one's soul — and, of course, that too is arguable. So remember.

Try to conceptualize the important differences between what occurs when a family decides it's time to let a loved one go and when a state legislature regularizes the painful exception to the laws of God, if not always those of society. I raise again the correlates between the Holocaust and our brutal institutions of the past. Of course, *nothing* compares to the Holocaust — not Willowbrook, not Pennhurst, not war. Nevertheless, I draw the comparison. I hope that these last chapters — which are so preoccupied with death and destruction, revolt and execution, will spur you to think further about what occurs when one's very life is a matter for debate, when one's existence is out of his or her control, and when one's freedom is controlled by the state.

A celebrity dies. The story later comes out that the family took advice from the doctor and decided not to continue life-saving efforts. The doctor is reluctant to advise on such matters, given the mandate to prolong life, even the life for which there is no hope of recuperation, even the life for which there is no respite from agony. Eventually, however, the doctor either straight-forwardly advises termination or casts commentary in such a way as to give advice while not giving advice.

Not everything about euthanasia is incomprehensible. Not everything is mean or wicked. But it is difficult to grasp what's happening around you when an elderly parent is at death's door, or a misshapen baby is at life's entry. The ordinary person — and, to a large extent, the ordinary professional — is perplexed, confused, indecisive, and angry about such confrontations. Advances in medicine — advances in technology and the basic sciences — have created unsolvable problems, have presented us with dilemmas that involve neither happy circumstances nor satisfactory options. The law is of little help with such matters. In fact, sometimes the law regularizes and sanctions that which would otherwise be the rare exception, that which might better be left ambiguous. It's one thing to anguish about a loved one's life or death. It's another thing to codify the decision, to regularize what

---

[1]From "On the Bill of Rights and Related Matters" by B. Blatt, 1978. In R. Heinich (Ed.), *Educating All Handicapped Children* (pp. 5-6), Englewood Cliffs, NJ: Educational Technology Publications. Copyright 1978 by Educational Technology Publications. Reprinted by permission.

should never be other than the extraordinary exception. Even then such a decision should be troubling, should evoke anguish and pain.

I ask you to examine these questions. At the very least, they're important enough to wrestle with, even when resolution is not guaranteed. Some are so important that they require our involvement whether or not our presence in the situation sheds light or offers amelioration. To paraphrase Groucho Marx, people aren't supposed to forget significant events in their lives, but in mortality's case we make an exception.

Regularizing Death

Those who write in (or about) the field of mental retardation must, if they concentrate on the important issues and problems, inevitably write about death as well as life, despair as well as hope. Witness the following editorial in the April 27, 1982 issue of the *New York Times,* which captured the euthanasia craze and the beginning evidence of a society going "crazy," in a way that may make this one of the most serious if not more important editorials published by that venerable newspaper. But it is also possible that, as with so many other important statements, this one too went unnoticed or insufficiently understood.

Private Death
There is a baby girl in a New York hospital with the kind of birth defects for which there is no help. Her parents, doctors and nurses are waiting for nature to take its course, but so far nature has not been kind. Meanwhile, they look for a place in which she can live in warmth and peace. When she sickens, as is inevitable, no extraordinary means will be used to save her; when she dies, her friends will know as much relief as grief. But for the few months that are her life she will have been treated with courtesy, acknowledged as a human being.

Another baby was born two weeks ago in Indiana. He had an incomplete esophagus, which is operable, and Down's syndrome, the consequences of which are impossible to estimate at birth. Nature took its course very quickly—he died in six days—but with considerable help. At his parents' request, the infant wasn't fed. The decision, the family lawyer said, was "a private matter."

Why private? Had that baby been normal, his death by starvation would have been a public concern. But because he had been inadvertently robbed of perfection, he was deliberately robbed of life. His flaws somehow canceled out his rights.

Two county courts and the Indiana State Supreme Court appear to have agreed—they declined to force his parents to feed "Infant Doe." But if children have a chance to live, shouldn't they get it, whether or not their parents are willing? And if they haven't a chance, like that little girl in a New York hospital, shouldn't they be allowed to leave this world in their own good time?

Whether to carry a fetus to maturity is still, and should remain, a woman's choice. But once born, a child is no longer part of another human being; he is a part of society and entitled to its protection. Their undoubted anguish explains the decision made by Infant Doe's parents, but not the courts' refusal to intervene. The death of Infant Doe is not "a private matter."[2]

In the Sunday, April 11, 1982 issue of the *New York Times*, an article on the same question appeared, this an "update" on an earlier story about a twin who was killed so that the other twin could live. This was made possible by a new technology—one that permits parents to choose to destroy an abnormal fetus while permitting the normal one to live. Previously, the parents would have chosen to abort both of the fetuses the mother was carrying. Is this a triumph for modern technology or a defeat for humanity?

Surgical Death
One boy twin was developing normally in the 40-year-old mother's womb. The other, tests showed, had Down's Syndrome, which often results in severe retardation. Dr. Thomas D. Kerenyi and Dr. Usha Chitkara, operating at the Mount Sinai Medical Center in Manhattan, inserted a long needle into the heart of the abnormal fetus and destroyed it. The other twin later was born normally.

The procedure—the first such surgery to succeed in the United States—was described by the doctors in January 1981. The parents were not named. Some physicians criticized the procedure as "misuse of medicine."

The surviving boy is "now over a year old and developing perfectly normally," Dr. Kerenyi reports. The mother has no regrets, he says, feeling that "if we didn't do it, she wouldn't have this child now—she would have been forced to abort them both."

Dr. Kerenyi says that most physicians who got in touch with him supported the surgery. He has since counseled a medical team in the South on the procedure, he says, but "unfortunately they were not successful"—both twins were lost. (p. 37)

It's one thing when a doctor, with concurrence from the family, stops "treating" an old and hopelessly ill patient who is in excruciating pain. I make no public judgment about either the motives of the family or the morals of the doctor. But it's another thing when a state legislature endorses euthanasia. In the first instance, the decision is made—rightly or wrongly—about a single individual, by people who presumably love that individual, and the decision is carried out by a physician who presumably examined every other alternative before agreeing to "give up." In the first instance, the decision is presumably an informed one, based on love and concern for the patient, and not for society's convenience. The decision surely represents an exception in the lives of the participants, even in the life of the doctor who faces death regularly, and the decision is accomplished only after great anguish. When a state passes a law to regularize death, however,

---

[2]From "Private Death," 1982, *New York Times*, April 27, p. A22. Reprinted by permission.

then the exception becomes the rule. When a state promotes death, then we are no longer dealing with mercy killings, but genocide. You must decide how far a state can go before it is a "killer," rather than "protector" of the citizens. The quintessential example is Nazi Germany.

Possibly never in history was there a state like Nazi Germany in promoting death, regularizing it so as to make it common, and administering it to such a degree that it was efficient. Contrast the involvement of German citizens in making death during the Holocaust and the fact that many Americans today have never seen a dead person. Nobody—except a person with bizarre needs—enjoys seeing dead people. Notwithstanding, avoiding death means also avoiding a fundamental truth that each of us must face. The point here, though, is that Americans don't see death, even at the cost of rushing Grandma to the hospital to die rather than permitting her to remain in her own bed to die.

In Nazi Germany, many thousands were involved in making death. What can we learn from the Holocaust? If we learn from the Holocaust that it happened to 13 million people, we will have learned a great deal. If we learn from the Holocaust that it happened in these ways to these people, and in those ways to those people, then we will have also kept faith with the pleas of the millions who perished, who as they were led away pleaded, "Remember, do not forget us, do not forget what happened." But there is more to learn from the Holocaust. It isn't enough to remember the details of what happened. Why did it occur? Can it occur again? Will it occur again? It isn't even enough to learn about *the* Holocaust. We must learn about holocausts in general, so that we can recognize one wherever we see it, even when it is in a different form, in a new disguise. Just like the mediocre fourth-grade teacher who teaches the children the map of Syracuse, New York, it's not enough to teach about *the* Holocaust. We must be like the better fourth-grade teacher who teaches about maps, so that wherever we are we will be able to read and understand maps. We must learn about holocausts, so that wherever we are we will be able to read and understand holocausts. The *regularized death*—whether it is in Hitler's Germany and intended for the purpose of killing Jews, or in California, for the purpose of freeing from life old, terminally ill, or handicapped persons—must be recognized in the different settings in which it occurs, across time and place. Not that the monstrousness of one equals the other, or that the enormity of one equals the other. But they are related—in principle, if not in details. I write this with trembling hand, because I know that such comparisons diminish, if not trivialize, the unique and utter evil of the Holocaust. But I ask you to lay aside your annoyance with such comparisons, and instead, force yourself to uncover the relationships. As Bruno Bettelheim (1960, p. 262) remarked: "Auschwitz is gone, but as long as this attitude remains with us, we shall not be safe from the indifference to life at its core." It is in terms of this attitude that the Holocaust in Germany is intimately related to the human warehouses in the United States.

One lesson that may be learned from the Holocaust is that skills and values are discrete characteristics. Consider the story of the infamous Dr. Joseph Mengele, the death maker at Auschwitz. According to an account of someone there, this evil man delivered a baby from one of the camp's inmates, paying scrupulous attention to modern medical procedures. A few minutes after the delivery, however, he gave the order to send mother and child to the crematorium (Bettelheim, 1960). Skills are not values, and education is no substitute for virtue; the value of a human life cannot be determined by the application of science or the wisdom of scientists.

A second lesson to be learned from the Holocaust has to do with the unbelievability of horror. I worry greatly, and for good reasons, about making comparisons between what occurred in Nazi Germany and what is occurring in our institutions. Indeed, in terms of the deaths accomplished, the pains inflicted, and the horrors perpetrated, there are no valid comparisons. Such examinations, however, uncover at least one striking similarity: The institutional establishment today makes strenuous efforts to downplay the seriousness of their problems (Blatt et al., 1979) just as revisionist historians deny that the Holocaust ever occurred. People don't want to believe in the possibility of raw, unrelieved, senseless evil.

This brings us to the third lesson to be learned from the Holocaust, the lesson that can be learned anywhere were it not so difficult for most people to face—our mortality. Now, some forty years after the Holocaust, we are quickly forgetting it ever happened. We spend our lives on earth denying our mortality, so why should we spend even a moment admitting the senseless slaughter of millions? Why should we spend even a moment seeing that there are old people who die according to a plan, and that there are people of all ages whose lives are deliberately not fostered? Regulated death is neither popular among the people nor mentionable among polite society. It's gauche. Consequently, when *Christmas in Purgatory* (Blatt & Kaplan, 1966) was published, there was a hue and cry from across the land that the story was untrue, that the pictures were doctored, or that (as one venerable state commissioner of mental health remarked) the pictures were 50 years old. The original "good news" about *Christmas in Purgatory* was that it simply wasn't true. The good news today about *Christmas in Purgatory* is the bad news that it was true. In that sense, we have made progress.

With respect to the Holocaust, the "good news" coming from people such as Robert Faurisson, a professor at the University of Lyon in France, is that it never happened (Dawidowicz, 1980). The gas chambers were a lie, the genocide was a lie, the only things gassed in Auschwitz were the lice. Auschwitz was a rumor. The lie was the problem, not the event. On a much lesser scale, the same reasoning has been applied in mental retardation. The denial of what once occurred in our large institutions (and which to some degree continues) is related to the denial of the Holocaust. "Where is the proof?" demand the commissioners, on the one hand, and the historical revisionists, on the other. So we are forced time and time again to lay out the proof—year after year, decade after decade, so that even proof becomes less believable. The big lie isn't accomplished because it resembles truth, but because it is so blatant, so insistent, so unadorned and unembarrassed. Just as people deny the Holocaust, people deny *Christmas in Purgatory*, deny Kraeplin and the legion of those who gave personal testimony to the horrors of Willowbrook, Pennhurst, Belchertown, Partlow, and the many others.

In Nazi Germany, it seemed to make sense to kill Jews. In another culture, it seems to make sense to kill elderly or retarded persons. Everything seems to make sense. Everything has a purpose. Everything has a justification and an explanation. Or does it?

If killing life or spirit doesn't make sense, possibly we in this field should inaugurate something like the Passover Sedar—much different, of course, but exactly like it in one fundamental way. Each year at a certain time, we in this field might gather together with family, colleagues, and friends. Then, we could together read and discuss a prescribed tract that would recount those bitter days when people were tortured and bruised of body and spirit. Lest we forget, we must deliberately work to remember. Lest we even fleetingly consider the Nazi officer, Klaus Barbie, who justified the death camps on the grounds that Hitler solved a 6.5 million person unemployment problem, we must remember that evil means can never justify any goal. Isn't there even a joke about the man who kills his parents and then pleads for the court's mercy on the ground that he is an orphan? Remember.

Permutations on Death

What follows is the plea of a physician who, himself, is dying from amyotrophic lateral sclerosis (ALS), commonly known as "Lou Gehrig's disease." The disease was advanced when it was noticed by his colleagues. At that time, David Rabin was in every sense a valued member of the Vanderbilt Medical Center community. He had friends and colleagues galore, people who counted on him—and vice versa. It was the warmest and most decent environment he had ever known. Then it all changed. He now had a fatal disease, and even his closest friends (mostly doctors) didn't know what to make of it, didn't know how to help, didn't know how to deal with him. So they shunned him.

Do not ignore relationship between terminal illness and mental retardation. The relationships are more than simply metaphorical. It is ironic that Rabin's experiences may be substituted for the person with severe or moderate mental retardation, without changing even the obvious situations connected with Rabin's capability and status:

> It has been three years since my first symptoms suggested a diagnosis of amyotrophic lateral sclerosis (ALS).
> I turned 45 in January 1979. I was then director of endocrinology at the Vanderbilt Medical Center, and my research in the areas of metabolism and reproduction was flourishing. I was supremely happy with my wife and family; we traveled often and enjoyed an active and varied social life. . . . In June of 1979 I noticed some stiffness in my legs. Within two short weeks I discovered quite by chance that my reflexes had become pathologically brisk. When I could no longer dismiss fasciculation as mere "restless legs" and it became clear that there were no sensory symptoms, the diagnosis of ALS reached my consciousness despite every attempt at denial.
> Let me share some of the reactions of my professional colleagues, beginning with an account of the behavior of my personal physician. To confirm the diagnosis, I traveled to a prestigious medical center renowned for its experience with ALS. The diagnostic and technical skills of the people there were superb, and more than matched the reputation of the institution. The neurologist was rigorous in his examination and deft in reaching an unequivocal diagnosis. My disappointment stemmed from his impersonal manner. He exhibited no interest in me as a person, and did not make even a perfunctory inquiry about my work. He gave me no guidelines about what I should do, either concretely—in terms of daily activities—or, what was more important, psychologically, to muster the emotional strength to cope with a progressive degenerative disease.
> . . . The only thing my doctor did offer me was a pamphlet setting out in grim detail the future that I already knew about too well. He asked to see me in three months, and I was too polite or too cowed to ask him why—what benefit was there for me to make the journey again? I still recall that the only time he seemed to come alive during our interview was when he drew the mortality curve among his collected patients for me. "Very interesting," he said. "There's a break in the slope after three years." When, a few months later, I read an article by him in which he emphasized the importance of a compassionate and supportive role for the physician caring for the patient with ALS, I wondered whether he had been withdrawn because I was a physician.
> By the fall of 1979 I was walking with a limp; I countered the queries I received in every corridor by saying that I had "a disk." This was not threatening to my colleagues, who proffered advice on how to deal with it and regaled me with their own back problems. I was still a full member of the fraternity, in excellent standing. By early 1980, however, the limp was worse, and I now held a cane in my right hand. The inquiries ceased and were replaced by a very obvious desire to avoid me. When I arrived at work in the morning I could see, from the corner of my eye, colleagues changing their pace or stopping in their tracks to spare

themselves the embarrassment of bumping into me. This dramatic change in their behavior occurred when it became common knowledge that David Rabin had ALS. I state with total conviction that my colleagues never meant to hurt me. On the contrary, I was *of* Vanderbilt, and they grieved for me, yet were unable to express their grief.

As the cane became inadequate and was replaced by a walker, so my isolation from my colleagues intensified. I recognize that my own behavior and personality may have contributed to the situation: I am gregarious and, I believe, warm with people; I also value my independence. I did not call a press conference to announce that I had ALS; I did not raise a banner asking for help; rather, I continued to do my work insofar as I was able. Did that put them off? Did they reason, "He wants to pretend that everything is normal, so let's play his game"? How often, as I struggled to open a door, would I see a colleague pretending to look the other way? On the other hand, why was it so natural for the nonphysicians—the technicians, the secretaries, the cleaning women—to rush to open the door for me, even if it was the door to the men's toilet? I can only guess that my colleagues thought it would embarrass me if they offered help. How wrong they were, and how distorted their reasoning—accepting help is preferable to sustaining a fracture.

One day, while crossing the little courtyard outside the emergency room, I fell. A longtime colleague was walking by. He turned, and our eyes met as I lay sprawled on the ground. He quickly averted his eyes, pretended not to see me, and continued walking. He never even broke his stride. I suppose he ignored the obvious need for help out of embarrassment and discomfort, for I know him to be a compassionate and caring physician. . . .

Some of my close relationships with fellow physicians have also deteriorated since my illness. For a friend to maintain interest and empathy for a week or a month was relatively easy; to show sustained concern over three years required a commitment of quite a different order. I have received relatively few telephone calls or letters from the scores of colleagues I have met in more than 20 years of academic life: former fellows and students, fellow members of study sections, faculty members at numerous medical schools where I have lectured. I hear indirectly about their concern; however, the definitive step of writing me a letter of support is more than the majority can manage. Why this deafening silence? Perhaps it is because we, as physicians, are the healers. We dispense treatment, counsel, and support; and we represent strength. The dichotomy of being both doctor and patient threatens the integrity of the club. To this fraternity of healers, becoming ill is tantamount to treachery. Furthermore, the sick physician makes us uncomfortable. He reminds us of our own vulnerability and mortality, and this is frightening for those of us who deal with disease every day while arming ourselves with an imagined cloak of immunity against personal illness. . . .

This account is not intended as a litany of complaint but as a call to physicians to express the compassion they feel toward sick colleagues. It is also meant to draw attention to our frequent inability as physicians to deal with members of our profession who no longer fit the mold of the compleat healer. Toward these ends, I would like to make some concrete suggestions. First of all, do not ignore your colleague. Greet him. Inquire about his health. Offer him support if he is physically handicapped. Don't assume that he prefers seclusion. Ask to visit him. Don't hide behind the false morality of "respecting his privacy"; if it is inconvenient he will tell you.

Secondly, be conscious of the family and extend your support to them. Make a point of asking how your colleague's spouse is feeling and how he or she is coping. The spouse and the children are suffering at least as much as the victim and need support, encouragement, and acknowledgment of their travail. Do not expose the wife to the "premature-widow syndrome," as some physicians do who encounter my wife and never mention my name or inquire about me at all.

Thirdly, bear in mind that the absence of a magic potion against the disease does not render the physician impotent. There are many avenues that can be helpful for the victim and his family. I am often surprised and moved by the acts of kindness and affection that people perform. Fundamentally, what the family needs is the sense that people care. No one else can assume the burden, but knowing that you are not forgotten does ease the pain.[3]

The link between medical ethics, terminal illness, and handicapped people is reified in the following commentary by Jerome Newton. A physician who directs a school health department, Newton has been critical of P.L. 94-142. Of course, I too have been critical of certain features of Public Law 94-142. Moreover, I am critical of a society that *needs* such a law to guarantee education for its handicapped children. There, the similarity ends, however. I might even take issue with Dr. Newton's conclusion concerning the "least restrictive environment," as well as whatever it is he finds onerous insofar as severely handicapped individuals are concerned:

> Uncritical support of P.L. 94-142, Education for Handicapped Children Act, is not only bad politics, it is also bad pediatrics and bad education.
>
> The June 1982 isue of *News and Comment* states that "the highest possible appropriations must be provided" and that "no reduction in current authorized levels of funding is acceptable." In taking this position the Academy is stating that simply spending more money is the only action necessary to meet the school needs of handicapped children. In reality the problem is much more complex. The Academy should selectively seek the continuation of some and the modification of other aspects of the law.
>
> The due process provision and civil rights guarantees are essential to help individual parents and physicians deal with the bureaucracy of school districts. On the other hand, the "least restrictive environment" provision is ruinously expensive, unworkable, and should no more be a legal or legislative issue than should extreme and lengthy life support in terminal illness.
>
> The only effect of the individual educational plan has been to require school districts to hire people to write them; the handicapped student does not benefit.

---

[3]From "Compounding the Ordeal of ALS: Isolation from My Fellow Physicians" by D. Rabin, P. Rabin, and R. Rabin, 1982, *The New England Journal of Medicine, 307*(8), pp. 506-509. Reprinted by permission.

On the other hand, involvement of other agencies and professionals must be strengthened. Present provisions are not sufficiently explicit; there are many handicapped children not receiving available services simply because the need for them is not recognized by educators.

Finally, the emphasis on the most severely handicapped receiving priority services is, obviously, the result of political lobbying, not a rational medical-educational decision. This issue needs to be addressed and modified.[4]

A passage from Mishna, one of the primary volumes of Jewish religious commentary, may provide critical insight to the reader:

> Why did God originally create only one person? . . . . It is to inform us of the greatness of the Holy One, blessed be He. For human beings mint many coins from the same die, and they all look the same. But the King of all Kings, the Holy One, blessed be He, formed all people in the mold of the first person, and not a single one resembles any other one. (Sanhedrin 4:5)

All human beings are created from some primary source, but all human beings are different. We are all the same. We are all different. No two look and act alike, but everyone is alike in a fundamental way. And what is that fundamental common charactristic that all humans share? We are all human. And as human beings, we are all equally valuable. Those who "believe," know that each of us was created from a single person. Those who do not "believe" nevertheless know that each of us evolved from common phenomena. We all live. We all die. What happened before our lives began and what happens after our lives terminate are the mysteries. But we *know* that all human beings share a common ancestry and destiny. Essentially, that may be the most important story to comprehend from the Bible — whether it's from the Old Testament or the New Testament, whether one looks at the King James Version or the Koran. There are variations in words, variations in emphases, variations in who is important and who isn't important. Notwithstanding, our heritage leads to an inescapable conclusion: All people are similar in that they share a common beginning, a certain end, and equality in the eyes of an almighty being; at the same time, all people are different — in ways that are important in the eyes of humans, but not in the eyes of God.

Even scientists agree that, after all is said and done, people are people. Even nativists agree that, after all is said and done, human beings are human beings regardless of variation in intelligence and other characteristics. And yet, even with such widespread agreement, we continue to "study the

---

[4]From "P.L. 94-142 — No Law is Perfect" by J. Newton, 1982, *American Journal of Pediatrics* (News and Comment), *33*(8), p. 1. Reprinted by permission.

problem." Organizations examine the problems of aging for example; and indeed, specialists called gerontologists develop environments and programs specifically for elderly people. What's so terrible about that? Nothing, but everything. While specialists develop unique environments for elderly people, they also ponder questions concerning when to stop treatments, when to offer the individual a "death with dignity." Other organizations solicit members to join up in the event that some day members will need "help" in achieving a "painless" or "inexpensive" demise. Parents have made conscious decisions not to permit certain surgical procedures that would keep their babies alive. And some doctors support such decisions—doctors and their own medical societies! Regulations prepared by the Reagan administration to prevent infanticide of retarded newborns was decried by nine medical groups—including the American Academy of Pediatrics (*New York Times*, March 20, 1983).

Such issues have engendered the formation of seemingly unlikely coalitions. If historians later view the seventies as the apex of the liberal movement, and the eighties as the beginning of a long period of reaction, they may also ponder the teaming of the conservative "right-to-lifers" and liberal "advocates." On the Baby Doe issue, for example, such unlikely partnerships as the National Right to Life Committee and the Association for Retarded Citizens have nervously allied to protect the lives of all newborns. And while most liberals have supported the so-called Handicapped Coalition, many also support Parent Choice with respect to abortion and the Baby Doe issue. Conversely, advocates for disabled people have been on the sidelines with respect to the abortion issue, and indeed, many are sympathetic to so-called parent rights and choice. Handicapped people themselves, like others in society, often press for the right to have abortions as a way of leading responsible and independent lives. There are other uneasy, if not altogether strange, alliances. Handicapped people are angry about the tinge of charity connected to the benefits they are given; so too is the "New Right" angry about people "on the dole"—too much charity for those who would be better off if they worked for their keep. It is perhaps not surprising that in a society where "single issue" groups predominate, unusual coalitions are forged.

The issues around which these coalitions form are by no means trivial; they are in fact questions of life and death. But whose life? Although retarded and other handicapped people are not considered in the same category as animals, they are more likely to be deprived of their lives than the rest of us. Though human beings, they have been judged to be of cheaper quality. So, while people in Western civilization may be "equally valuable," some seem to be *more* "equally valuable." Thus, some are more likely to enjoy the privilege of dying a natural death than others—others who are less gifted, less intelligent, less valuable.

Is there more to a life than what we see in an obituary? Somehow, those newspaper characterizations seem inadequate. By temporal standards, the ordinary person gets few if any lines—often at the expense of the bereaved family (who must pay for these, as one pays for any advertisement), or of the deceased (whose life is necessarily given short shrift, both because newspapers have other business and families have other needs for their resources, especially at such times). Even famous, rich, or powerful people receive no more than a column or two, once in a while with a picture, usually of bygone days. Can a person's life be summed up in an obituary? Of course not. Then, how can it be summed up? Not well, ever. Not passably, usually. The flower of youth is usually portrayed as if by one who paints by the numbers. The triumphs of a lifetime seem small under the glare of harsh retrospection. The explanations that had once sufficed later appear to be excuses. And a coherent philosophy wrought from life's travails and successes becomes incoherent to those who later attempt to unravel the mess. If left to the analyses of third- and fourth-hand observers, the summation of most lives concludes with the notation that there was once a good person, or an average person, or a silly person, or a silent person, or a person we didn't know well, if at all. In the end, the obituary does not matter. In the end, people are people. In the end, rich and powerful people lie down next to poor and weak people. The professor and the resident of the state institution are not companions in life, but in death they become not such strange bedfellows. No one is great enough to escape mortality. Only the rarest individual is great enough to escape the common ignominity of the human being—out of sight, out of mind. We all know this. And we all know that this knowledge shouldn't depress us. Rather, the common bond all humanity shares makes each individual stronger and more permanent—immortal, in a way. The common bond links together not only one generation but all generations to all others, past and future.

Long, long ago, it seems, people understood the reasons for life, for death, for pain, for the "unfairness" of it all. They knew that nothing is unfair; everything is planned. People once believed in a grand design, in a benevolent as well as angry Lord. Long ago, people had answers for the vexing questions of life, for the vicissitudes of living. Even without total comprehension, there was total acceptance among the faithful. Today there is science, but also disaffection, also alienation and despair. But the human being can turn a stone into a statue, paint into a masterpiece, despair to hope. It has also been said that the Lord has mysterious ways.

19.

Living Well Together is the Best Revenge for the Past

"A VICTOR'S JUSTICE," was Hermann Goring's conclusion. Many Nazis went to their graves unrepentant. In their eyes, they weren't wrong. They had merely lost. Of the many profound tragedies of the Holocaust was the widespread agreement among the Nazis that they were right all along, that given the opportunity they would *do it all again*.

What are the convictions of contemporary American institutional administrators? Do they believe they were right, and would they do it all again if they had the opportunity? What are the convictions of contemporary physicians? Would there be more nontreatment of severely handicapped newborns if certain laws and risks did not proscribe against it? What are the convictions of the public with respect to euthanasia? After all, there are those who think it is humane to put sick animals to sleep so they won't suffer. And there are those who think of themselves as humane who think of severely retarded people as little different from animals. And what about the anti-vivisectionist who would put a dog to sleep but who is unsure about severely retarded persons? These questions begin to get at the future for disabled and other vulnerable people in our society.

Will disabled people themselves revolt? Is a revolt necessary to ensure their rights? Or, do the reforms of the past two decades sufficiently guarantee better lives for disabled people in the coming decades? These and other questions will be addressed in this recapitulation of the issues, problems, and directions in the field.

I will conclude the book with a vision of what the next hundred years may bring. We should look ahead to better days for all people.

A "Revolt of the Idiots" Movement

In 1976 I wrote a story depicting a peaceful revolution by retarded inmates. *Revolt of the Idiots: A Story* (Blatt, 1976) is about a fictional institution inhabited by fictional characters who act out a drama. But, as I asked in the prologue to the book: What is fiction? While it is said (and believed) that truth is stranger than fiction, can you who have lived through wars, institutional scandals, and a world gone insane deny that fiction may most adequately portray certain truths? The point of *Revolt of the Idiots* is that not until the inmates, themselves, decided to do something about their own lives and destinies did the world change in any substantial way. Especially the state and its institutionalizers should know that people who have the courage to endure can find the resolve to revolt. Such a revolt was never attemped before. It probably was hardly ever thought of before. Out of the ranks of those who are unwanted, unlettered, and uneducable, there need to be leaders. Out of the ranks of those who are enslaved, leaders must rise to lead the inmates from slavery to freedom. Because few outsiders would risk everything to free them, if a revolt ever actually occurred, this would have to be *their* revolt; and most of them would need to be a part of it or it would not work. The inmates would have to plan their exodus as if they alone mattered. As the protagonist in the story proclaimed:

We can count on no other people. We are our destiny.

What does that mean again, Adam?

It means that we are human beings who have rights. It means that we have to fight for those rights because other people alone can't fight for us. They can help, but we must do the real work. It means that, if we really believe that we should be free citizens, it will happen. If we don't, it will never happen. (Blatt, 1976, p. 150)

In this story, it came to pass that the inmates won their freedom. And in the real world? In the real world, revenge for the suffering and the injustice may be found where we create decent lives for all people. In the real world, living well together is freedom. And that is the best revenge for the past. It might also be said that, whether a creation of people or God, whether temporal or heavenly, living well together as free people is the rarest of rare gifts.

People want to live well together and to fit into society, into the group, into the organization. Some people have an easy time fitting in while others don't. It is presumed that some people don't fit in because there is something wrong with them (e.g., they are mentally retarded). Others don't fit in because there is something wrong with society (e.g., they are blacks or women). In a fundamental way, however, whenever a person doesn't fit in, there is something wrong with society. This is not an easy problem to overcome — because it is so pervasive — embedded in the very fabric of the culture. It is a systemic problem, not a local or situational one. There is the story of the poor man who couldn't afford necessary surgery, so he offered the doctor a few dollars to touch up his x-ray. Of course, that doesn't work. Likewise, cosmetic attention to serious societal problems won't work.

Years ago, Frank Garfunkel and I concluded that there is a profound difference between the individual who does not "fit" and the group that does not "fit" (Blatt, 1981). For thousands and thousands of years, women were treated by the male-dominated society as individuals who *could not* fit into certain roles such as that of the doctor, the engineer, the minister, or the athlete. Of course, every now and then, a woman so surpassed her male counterparts that she was admitted into the medical fraternity, the engineering school, or the ministry. Until relatively recently, however, women did not "fit."

For hundreds of years in this country, blacks were thought of as inferior. Not until the civil rights movement was there the serious suggestion that individual blacks are *not* the problem, but society *is* the problem and that it *isn't the individual blacks* who don't "fit," but that *blacks as a group* don't "fit."

Retarded individuals have always been in the "no-fit" category. If the child who was not toilet trained hoped to enter the public school, then the child needed to be toilet trained. It wasn't until the reforms of the seventies that society began to take more seriously the idea that its *schools* too must change, that there are good reasons not to impose toilet training as a requirement for school entrance. It isn't that retarded children, or any children, shouldn't be toilet trained but rather, that it should not be a criterion for going to school. And so we came to understand better the idea that we needed to deal with clinical and policy issues. Moreover, we came to understand better that while retarded people need to be toilet trained, or black people need to be better educated, or women need to learn more physics, society too must change. Society must offer greater opportunities to those groups who "don't (and wish to) fit" so they may learn the ways and skills of the dominant culture — so they *do* "fit." Furthermore, society must not conclude merely that *each* individual woman candidate for admission to the medical school is different from the male candidate. Rather, society must acknowledge that women *as a group* are different from men as a group; and society must examine those differences not only in terms of the weaknesses they may present but also in terms of their strengths.

As I near the end of this volume, I turn again to the preoccupation of many of these pages: What will it take to "change the world"? If the world is to change, individuals must change. If the world is to become better, I must become better. Gentleness, kindness, and magnanimity are the characteristics of people who would strive to change the world. But there's more. It is necessary to listen to the truth from any person (not only from professional colleagues) and from anywhere (not only from prestigious journals or favorite commentators). To change the world, to take advantage of the alternatives before us, we must develop a tolerance for the ideas that others put forth. We must be willing to listen to many people—not only to those whose credentials endow them with authority, or those who write with the imprimatur of a great publisher, or those who lecture from the podium of a great university. We must listen to truth wherever it is—even when it emanates from the mouths of innocent children, or from uneducated laborers, or from the victims themselves—the idiots.

Returning to the previous discussion of Robert Frost, Anthony Hecht (1982) recounted his reaction to the *New York Times* book review of the final volume of Thompson's *Biography of Robert Frost*. He remembered that the reviewer was so revolted by the unseemly aspects of Frost's character that he "declared that if he had known earlier what sort of man Frost actually was, he would have left any room the poet entered" (p. 3). I too remember vividly reading that particular review and the subsequent letters to the editor about the review, Frost, and the book itself. But my remembrance today dwells on something else I felt at the time. Almost everyone—the reviewer, the letter writers, those who disdained Frost, and those who admired him—seemed compelled to comment on Frost's vanity, selfishness, mischief. The biography appeared to have engendered license to defame the poet. But as I read the "assassinations" of Frost's character and stability, I returned again and again to a comment someone wrote in one of those letters to the editor, something like, "How could that terrible old man have written such beautiful poetry?" I thought about *this* comment, which should have been made but was never evoked: "How could such a wonderful poet, a person who has brought enormous pleasure and fulfillment to so many of us, have done such silly and cruel things?" The elements of Robert Frost's life illustrate the elements of anyone's life. In understanding his life is the key to understanding those among us who are "different" as well as those who disappoint us. The proper question, the best question, the question that does not defeat but that encourages us to endure and perhaps triumph over adversity and injustice is always the question that asks: "Why did this good person go wrong?" or "Why does this good society ignore that evil?" People are people, and Robert Frost was in a fundamental sense no different from the rest of us. The lesson to be learned from his life, the most important lesson to be learned from anyone's life, is less how the evil in him permitted good to escape, and more the lesson connected with how the good in him permitted alienation and cruelty to occur. If a "Revolt of the Idiots" movement is to take place, it won't be because we will have decided that mentally retarded people aren't retarded, or that mentally retarded people are as eloquent as the rest of us, or that mentally retarded people have as much to contribute to society as many of us. Rather, it will be because we have realized that people with less obvious capabilities are nevertheless people, essentially no different from the rest of us. We will have discovered that such people are as human as any of us, and must not be banished, psychologically or physically. The lesson to be learned from Robert Frost's life, or from anyone's life who disappoints us, is why (and under what conditions) good people disappoint us. When we look for the good in people we will find ways to make the world better. We will even learn about goodness from the criminal, stability from the unstable, and intelligence from the unintelligent. From that group of seemingly indolent expatriates on the French Riviera during the years between the two Great Wars, we can also learn that living well is the best revenge. Live well good people! As for the rest of us, we should work to make it happen.

A Recapitulation

In this book, I have tried to say that the field of mental retardation is, itself, unimportant. But it offers opportunities to examine the most important issues facing the human race. It isn't that secluding retarded people is wrong, but that secluding people is wrong. Or sterilizing them. Or ending their life. In that sense, mental retardation is both the most trivial and most important field.

In this book I have attempted to discuss some fundamental problems of society and their relevance to the field of mental retardation. Consequently, I have tried to speak to students in all disciplines, including those who do not ordinarily read textbooks on mental retardation. I have tried to deal with both fundamental problems of society and the elemental principles of the field. Hyperbole abounds in this field; and we live in a world where foolishness is disguised as wisdom, hyperbole as revelation. Our exaggerations make us more foolish, but even our wisdom often drives us to deep troubles. And yet, there is something touching—silly and frail—very human and touching about the activity and frenzy in the field of mental retardation. As a field, we are searching for something, groping to be better, but we don't know what "better" is. We also are unsure of our values. Thus, we neither know where to look nor what to look for.

Once upon a time, people aspired to leave the world a better place.

Once upon a time, that was the lesson young children were expected to learn, older children were expected to practice, their parents were expected to teach and live by, and their grandparents were expected to model and be judged by. That lesson once enjoyed greater popularity than it does today, but it has an inspiring history. So we ask again: How does one go about changing the world? Better, how does one leave the world a better place than how he or she found it? It's a very old ideal, at least as old as ancient Athens, whose citizens pledged:

> We will ever strive for the ideal and sacred things of the city both alone and with many; we will revere and obey the city's laws; we will transmit this city not only not less, but greater, better, and more beautiful than it was transmitted to us.

What follows are some ideas that summarize the values embedded in this book:

1. *You are the beginning context.* To change the world, you must change. To inspire others to change, you must change yourself. You can lay the blame for evil on the callous society, a confused bureaucracy, or a mean adversary. Your censure may even hit right targets; but if blaming other people and other institutions permits you to avoid personal confrontation with the problems we face in society, then you too contribute to the evil. Before the world can change, I must change.

2. *You must remember what each of us tries hard to forget—our mortality.* Of course, each of us knows that people die; but most of us live as if it simply won't happen to us. As William Saroyan remarked before his death, when he knew he was mortally ill—when he realized that it would happen to him too, "Now what?" You shouldn't live your life without ever asking that most serious of all questions: "Now what?"

3. *People are people.* Each human being is fragile, interdependent, at times, silly, at times even wonderful, often weak when it doesn't matter, and sometimes strong when it does matter. People are people. Those among us who understand that idea have strength that others don't share. Those among us who understand that idea understand that we too are capable of being the parents of a severely retarded child; we, like everyone else, draw the cards of life.

    People are people. As alluded to earlier, there's a saying among special educators that unexceptional people spend their lifetimes seeking ways to become exceptional, and exceptional people spend their lives seeking ways to become unexceptional. The ordinary want to be extraordinary, and the extraordinary want to be ordinary. The ordinary person dreams of becoming rich and famous, and the rich and famous person has romantic memories of an anonymous life when he or she could walk the streets unnoticed, eat a meal uninterrupted, do without fanfare the simple things that now mean so much—because those are excactly the things now denied. But there's another way of looking at these personal flights from reality. Everyone is fleeing from his or her own reality—not only the ordinary person looking for eminence, or the eminent person demanding to be left alone. Everybody is fleeing from the same things—the small and great irritations each of us must experience simply by living, the unhappiness each of us must face at some time during our lives, the disappointments even great people have. And we flee from our certain mortality. The grass is never greener on our side; that's why the grass is always greener on the other side. Human beings can no more escape their condition than zebras can escape their stripes. People are people.

The disease of professionals is that we tend to deny this truth. We tend to think we are different from our clients, that we will never have the problems they have, that we will never face the dilemmas they face, that our children will be the smartest and the best, that our lives will be beautiful. The disease of consumers is that they tend to believe the professionals. In the end, nevertheless, people are people. In the end, we share the same destiny; and in the end, we have much in common. It is crucial for our leaders to realize this sameness. Far more important than intelligence, personality, or skills, is magnanimity—the willingness to bend over backwards in dealing with those who would follow the person who would lead. There is always the "glass half empty"—"glass half filled" decision to be made. This is the most important decision to be made about people. We can improve the world immeasurably if we would but look for the best in each other. When we are tempted to ask how this terrible or stupid person was able to accomplish some good, we should better ask how someone who has achieved something marvelous could have been so terrible or stupid. We should be more surprised than we are in the face of human stupidity, and more expectant than we are of human accomplishment.

4. *Education is serious stuff.* Socrates was sentenced to drink hemlock because the leaders of Athens didn't like his curriculum. Socrates died for education. There should be those among us who would at least want to live and work for it. At least, to work for it. Of course, education isn't everything. It's not even enough, although many people believe it's enough. Notwithstanding, this society doesn't suffer from an overabundance of learning and wisdom. Better schools will not prevent all the problems we now have and will not solve all of those problems that cannot be prevented; but the institutions of education will better serve our efforts to improve this world than the institutions of ignorance.

5. *Despite the need to improve our schools and other educational programs, we are an educated people.* On the other hand, we must not be arrogant about what has been accomplished. Especially in our dealings with other cultures, we must learn to use our knowledge and technology more wisely, more generously, and more decently. But also, we must work harder to understand non-Western cultures and their peoples.

6. *What is the role of the teacher, the doctor, and other practitioners in the helping professions?* Is it to decide whether a person can learn or not, to decide whether the patient will get better or not, to decide who will be treated and who will die? No, their roles should always be sharply focused on healing the sick person, teaching the ignorant person, stilling the hurt of the distraught person, and bringing cheer to the despondent person. The job of the human service professional is not merely to observe whether a person can or cannot change, but to facilitate, to realize, to make change come true. Our job is not to test the "Educability Hypothesis," but to make it come true, to demonstrate that capability is educable.

7. *Educability is a two-edged sword.* We should deal with our clients as if they *will* learn, as if they *will* be healed, as if their physical, emotional, and intellectual health *will* be restored. We must serve our clients because they are entitled to receive our help. Anne Sullivan accepted the responsibility to teach Helen Keller not because she expected Helen to eventually attend Radcliffe College or because she expected Helen to become a world-famous inspiration to people in every walk of life. The "miracle" of the Anne Sullivan-Helen Keller saga was exactly that no one expected things to turn out so marvelously well. By definition, that's the ingredient required for a miracle. The paradox of the Anne Sullivan-Helen Keller saga, the paradox of any miracle, is that it must be unexpected. Anne Sullivan necessarily had other reasons for assuming responsibility for Helen, or there would have been no miracle, no story, no demonstration of educability. Educability is a two-edged sword: Even if educability cannot be empirically verified, the clinician must behave as if it has been verified.

8. *Bands play not only at the Mardi Gras but also at funerals.* So, we must be careful about what bandwagon we jump on. Once upon a time, the preferred treatment setting for handicapped individuals was segregation. Today, it is mainstreaming. I believe in mainstreaming. But you owe it to yourself, as well as to those you serve, to know which bandwagon you've jumped on—or you may find yourself going to the cemetery rather than to the festival. You must also be aware that the final paralysis may result from the tug between popular, if uninformed, advocacy, and corrupt, often poisonous, authority.

9. *Most people revere their freedom more than their very lives.* Some insist that evidence is needed to justify deinsitutionalization. Did Lincoln require evidence to free the slaves? No. He needed only the belief that all people in this country who were neither dangerous to themselves or others deserved to be free. Did anyone ever willingly give up his or her life to improve reading scores in a class, or to enhance a group's vocational aptitude? No. But every day, all over this globe, people lay down their lives rather than submit to physical or political enslavement. The battle to evacuate institutions, or to integrate handicapped children in the public schools, is being fought on behalf of freedom for these people rather than improved clinical conditions and opportunities. The prepotent issue in this century will not be on the "right to treatment" but on each persons' inalienable "right to freedom."

10. *Technology is not the answer, though it involves interesting and useful methods.* Often, it takes a lot of artillery to kill crab grass. Often, the artillery can go as wrong as it goes right. Technology may be a good solution for some problems, but it's rarely connected with the significance of the problem. Chesterton wrote an engaging and powerful essay called, "Music with Meals," in which he argued that people don't need to justify listening to music. People don't need to make a case for music as an aid to digestion. Conversely, people *do* need to make a case for technology. While listening to music can be its own reward, the elevator is important only for those who want to go to the fourth floor. I worry about a technology that continues to produce electric can openers (which make people useless), electric egg beaters (which make technology frivolous), and bicycle and rowing machines going nowhere (which make us silly).

11. *We must learn more from history.* We must learn lessons from Nazi Germany. Given the choice to take their children home from institutions or leave them to be killed, some parents came for the last time to bid their goodbyes. What does this mean? Today, we still debate whether the rights of children transcend parental authority. We must struggle to better understand the lesson to be learned from Itard's (1932/1962) *Wild Boy of Aveyron.* Is it that a wild boy, a mentally retarded child, can be made educable, or is it that *all* people are educable? We must also better comprehend the lesson from Rousseau's (1762/1961) *Emile.* Is it that the child is noble, or that *all* people are noble?

12. *What does the Biblical version of the brimming cup mean?* To make the world better is to transform the empty to the brimming cup. How can we transform an empty life to a full life? Bigger isn't necessarily better; that is, more isn't necessarily better. The empty caldron is not the good life; that small, full brimming cup is the good life each person seeks.

But there is a seeming contradiction. Our lives are full when the corn has been picked, when the work is completed. But for the barn to overflow, the field has to be barren. So too throughout our lives. There will be necessarily empty places, as it is equally certain that there will be times when there seems to be too much. Some places are empty because the harvest has just been taken, and it's time for both land and laborer to rest. But other places are barren because they have been neglected, and, thus, may always be barren. Some places are filled because there is greed. Others are filled because there is hope and there is responsibility to care for family and neighbors. The brimming cup has little to do with the size of the cup or the temporary nature of its contents. It is all in the mind and, for sure, in the soul.

13. *It doesn't matter who fishes or who cuts bait, who rows the boat or who cooks the fish*, as long as there is someone to do each important job in the community. The concept of community requires that there is a genuine place for everyone in the life of the group.

14. *Giving people facts can change their behavior.* If people are told the truth, they will not go off the deep end. They might even do something positive to corrrect the problems, or mitigate them, or at least understand them better.

15. *Stories can kill people, so we must be careful about the stories we tell.*

16. *There are sufficient resources in our society to serve all of the people.* There always was, there is now, and there will probably always be a significant discrepancy between what is needed to satisfy all of the people and what we have to satisfy them. Hard times merely require us to work harder, to be more thoughtful, to substitute our hard work and wisdom for dollars (which we don't have enough of) or additional workers (which in this society only dollars can purchase).

17. *We must work hard to deprogram our lives.* Too many of us live rigidly segmented lives—where our work is separated from our recreation and, thus, where our work becomes drudgery and our recreation becomes escape. Once, long ago, there were people who didn't need to flee the workplace because it satisfied their needs, which went well beyond the mere need to earn a living. Once, work and life were intertwined.

18. *Mental retardation is an invented disease whose cure lies with those who invented it—civilization itself.* In at least that way, mental retardation is both very trivial and very important, both curable and incurable.

19. *There are individuals who do not fit, and groups who do not fit.* The women's movement was once on the individual-no-fit train, but is now on the

group-no-fit train. As long as mental retardation is on the individual-no-fit train, it will continue to be perceived as a clinical problem, and consequently there will always be retarded people who will never fit. The field of mental retardation can learn from the women's movement, the civil rights movement, and other minority movements.

20. *I am sympathetic to liberal goals, but it seems that what works more often than not are conservative ways.* I am also sympathetic to creative (if not outlandishly imprudent) objectives, but it seems that the prudent pursuit of even outlandish objectives probably offers the best chance to succeed.

21. *Those of us in this field must work harder.* We seem to be guided by a law of inertia—it's either too early or too late to do something about a problem, it's either his fault or her fault, and "I have my own problems." Possibly, that may be why the more things change in this field, the more they remain the same. But there's an aura, a feeling that things are changing. Possibly, it's because things today remain the same *differently* from how they remained the same before. Everyone is for deinstitutionalization, but we have institutions. Everyone is for mainstreaming, but children are segregated in the schools. Everyone is for reforming diagnostic procedures, but children are still selected for special programs because they have low IQs. We have bureaucratized our values and codified our advocacy and good intentions. We must remember the biblical admonition not to offer wild animals for sacrifice. Sacrifice must cost something. We must offer things we will miss. We must give valuable things. Of course, the most valuable sacrifice to a cause is the offering of oneself. Work. Work. Work.

The Conquest of Mental Retardation

Science enjoys and deserves an honored place in human affairs. But while a multiplication table is either true or not, and while an atom has a finite valence, the group home is "true" only in a certain psychological-social context; and one person's religion is another's oppression. While science unravels some puzzles, it muddles others. Science can do little to solve the fundamental puzzles inherent in mental retardation. Science is a mixed blessing. It invents things both to destroy as well as to cure people. At the same time, science may stifle creativity. For example, the great scientist, Thomas A. Edison, was regarded by other scientists of his day as a tinkerer, a technician, someone who created interesting gadgets (Hounshell, 1980). Even in science, those who are different pay a special price for the "privilege."

Science is also a mixed blessing because it can misdirect us as well as set us on proper courses. Science is something real and useful, but it is also fantasy and mischief. Consider the question of curability of mental retardation. Consider that there was a time when psychiatrists were asked to vote whether homosexuality is a mental condition. Such a consideration certainly sheds a different light on the nature of the concept of "cure." I have discussed changes in definitions of mental retardation, which have been determined by the vote of members of professional committees. I have discussed the proposition that mental retardation means different things in different communities. What does all this add up to? I am not certain, but I am certain that these phenomena have little to do with science. Then, the prepotent questions: What is the place of science in the field of mental retardation? How will mental retardation be cured, if it can be cured? How can we conquer mental retardation? By science? Yes and no. Science may help, but science will create new problems for us as we solve old ones. Science not only uncovers truths, but it enlarges ignorance. That is, the more we learn and discover, the more we realize we don't know. All to the good? Of course. But conversely (and paradoxically), the very capability of science to reveal both truth and ignorance causes us to overestimate its power and importance. Science can't do everything. It can't conquer mental retardation.

How, then will mental retardation be conquered? The beginning step in conquering mental retardation lies in how we conceptualize human beings. Are all human beings equally valuable? If so, then we must decide that all of us will do with less so that each of us has a fair chance to live as decently as human beings are meant to live. If so, then we will conquer mental retardation. If the answer is no—if all human beings are not equally valuable, then the pragmatic solution to the "problem of mental retardation" is easier, but the price we pay will be greater. The price is a loss not only of decency and morality of the individual, but also that of the culture. And if we decide to pay that price (to protect a second car, or a second television set, or anything that's truly discretionary in our lives), we must also be willing to give away what some claim to live by—our morality and decency. The biblical command "We are our brothers' keepers" has perhaps seen better days. The Golden Rule, too, has perhaps seen better days. When we give up those guides by which decent individuals claim to live, we may be giving up everything that makes life worth living. The choice is not only whether we can conquer mental retardation. The choice is whether we can conquer selfishness. Our choice may be between the good, if imperfect, society and a society in which no decent person wants to live.

In this book, I have attempted to show that one thing wrong with research in mental retardation is that while a plethora of data is ground out with merciless insistence, there is a paucity of ideas. Many people are doing research, but too much of it is trivial, and little of it addresses serious problems. It is not that the researchers themselves are not serious. For that matter, it is not that the researchers are incompetent. Rather, they don't seem to study problems in mental retardation. Of course, some will claim that this is an overstatement.

There appears to be yet another problem, one alluded to by Gould (1980) in his book of essays on natural history. He reminds us of Newton's well-known aphorism—the modest admission that if he had accomplished something worthwhile, it was by standing on the shoulders of giants. But Gould also reminds us that it wasn't Newton who first articulated the idea that science progresses when we capitalize on the work of our elders. Possibly, as long ago as the twelfth century, Bernard of Chartres offered that same observation. Who will deny that there is much to learn from our predecessors? Rhetorical as the question may seem, many in the field of mental retardation practice—if not believe—differently. The modern aphorism might read: "If I don't see, never you mind, my subscribers don't read. Publish. Publish. I will stomp on the backs of my forebears, especially those who disagree with me." Today, it seems that too many things need to be reinvented. It seems that what is old is irrelevant or erroneous. And it seems that what is new is, by definition, important—however trivial, however transitory it may be.

So, scholars in the field have at least two serious problems—an absence of purpose to solve problems in mental retardation, and a lack of interest in capitalizing on what has already been discovered. Consequently, it is a rare pleasure to read works such as Gould's, for here is a person who is able to communicate his ideas without the jargon that enslaves most scholars. Further, Gould is able to examine the issues in relevant historical contexts, which helps students to realize that many great discoveries are made by different and unrelated scholars at approximately the same time. As Gould suggested, "Most great ideas are 'in the air,' and several scholars simultaneously wave their nets" (1980, pp. 47-48). Gould examined scientific contributions in historical and personal contexts, making such discoveries real for the reader. Readers shouldn't always have "fun," but neither should they be bored and annoyed to distraction or indifference.

Possibly, in the grand scheme of archival literature, there is a place for studies that report on the number of marbles that fall in certain holes under certain provocations. But there's more to science than that, in spite of the fact that our archival journals rarely let that particular cat out of the bag. I contend that it is also important for people in mental retardation to know that Samuel Gridley Howe's wife, Julia Ward Howe, wrote "The Star Spangled Banner" while both were at an educational conference in Washington, DC. It's also important to know that when Henry David Thoreau graduated from Harvard College, he wanted to be a teacher at the School for the Blind in Watertown. But he didn't have the proper credentials, so he was rejected for the position. That knowledge may be more important to professors of special education than to professors of English literature. I suggest that students devote time to the works of the better communicators and explainers of scholarship, the Stephen J. Goulds of the world, as well as to professional journals. Part of the science fantasy in mental retardation is that science not only cures but educates. At best, science reveals certain phenomena. There is something beyond science that is required to comprehend phenomena.

The Amnesia of Mental Retardation

Where mental retardation is concerned, there are perhaps more histories than memories, of which there are precious few, and hardly a true and interesting one. There are more cornerstones than remembrances of why the buildings were built, what the vision promised, if there had even been a vision at the dedication. In our field, there are more heroes than victories; but more defeats than villains. We may have forgotten more than we should have remembered, more than was good for us. It is a special amnesia. It might be claimed that the conquest of mental retardation—its cure—will be achieved as we recover from our special amnesia. We tend to have amnesia when it comes to remembering mental retardation, as we have amnesia when it comes to death and pain. Possibly it is because of this amnesia that even people who make their living using words— communicators such as writers, teachers, or politicians—encounter difficulties in discussing the problem. Sometimes their words on this subject are so subtle as to be misunderstood or entirely incomprehensible. A vagueness usually accompanies embarrassment. Metaphors are often substituted for more precise understandable language. When it comes to mental retardation, conceptual clocks run either slow or fast, and sometimes not at all. And yet, like death itself, it's unmentionable in polite society. In a sense, mental retardation is not unlike the ambulance. In most ordinary communities, ambulance sirens are heard once in a while. In ordinary communities, people usually stop for a moment, listen to the shrieking siren, think a private thought or two, and go back to their business. In the retirement community, ambulances are heard very frequently, sometimes hour after hour. What do the people there think about when those piercing sounds intrude into mundane activities or pleasant reveries? You might expect that the interruption would evoke different thoughts. But that's probably not the case. Even in the retirement community, where everybody should be acutely aware that each person is mortal, if not at death's door at the moment; even there, a person has probably developed skill in returning quickly to business or daydreaming. The bells toll, but are not understood — and not by accident. A can is jarred loose from the shelf and falls harmlessly. Life too has its jars and jiggles; but ask the people in California if there is a difference between a jiggle and an earthquake. There is, but not to them. That's why people still find San Francisco one of the great places to live in America. If we can forget the difference between a jiggle and an earthquake, if we can forget the San Francisco earthquake, we can find ways to forget about mental retardation — and life's other unpleasantries.

The thought of mental retardation causes people to have amnesia. That is, those who have a retarded child sometimes want to forget it, or forget their own fragile links to the child, as well as to all other human beings. Those who don't have a retarded child want to forget the possibility that they might have such a child. "It can't happen to me (to us)" is a delusion harbored by most of us. Why? A life gets better, there is always a tomorrow with a rainbow, Americans always move upward and onward. Judy Garland and Mickey Rooney are forever young. Or, "Happiness First, All Else Will Follow"; this was the motto — and probably still is the motto — of a once-famous institution for retarded persons. Hungerford reminded us that the reality of life insures that, if we live long enough, there will be disillusionment, despair, war, famine, depression. Amnesia causes us to forget unpleasantness. The amnesia of mental retardation is the obverse of our continuous links with happiness, with health, with accomplishments, with cheating death. "I won't die" is the secret covenant we make with our destiny. "Sure, I know that people die, but I will escape the terrible decree." Mental retardation is a terrible decree.

The field suffers from another form of amnesia; for want of a better designation, let's call it "cultural amnesia." Here, I refer to the widespread belief that everything worthwhile has been invented during our lifetimes, and for the most part, has been invented within the last few years. We choose to ignore our uncommon histories. But in some respects mental retardation is one of those fields that hasn't changed during the years; and, for that matter, to some extent it has changed for the worse, and not for the better. Didn't someone once say that what's new isn't true and what's true isn't new?

We in this field have chosen to ignore or forget our rich history, traditions, and the wisdom accumulated through the decades. What are the points emphasized in this book? That insofar as clinical practice is concerned, intelligence is educable. That insofar as clinical practice is concerned, examination (or evaluation, or diagnosis) must always be connected with treatment (that which is attempted on behalf of the client). That there must be advocates who work on behalf of retarded persons as they would work on their own behalf. Itard, Seguin, Montessori, and Binet himself were all staunch believers in the idea of educability. They and a throng of others long ago articulated the principle that a diagnosis that goes nowhere means nothing but mischief. Insofar as advocacy is concerned, for thousands of years people were instructed to love their neighbors as themselves, to do unto others as they would have others do unto them, and to be our brothers' keepers. Notwithstanding, the educability hypothesis remains debatable at best, the clinical ethos is misunderstood or ignored, and the concept of advocacy and its ideals have enjoyed more hopeful days. And so, the field suffers from two kinds of amnesia: the denial of our mortality, and the ignorance of our history. If we have improved along these lines at all, it might be in the sense that we at least recognize the amnesia from time to time, whereas in the past we did not want to know about it.

The Next Hundred Years

In our field, the problem with prophesy is that if it is optimistic, it is heresy; if it is pessimistic, it is predictive—self-fulfilling. Either way, while prophets are merely pretentious, prophesy is usually mischievous. While one need not be a Nostradamus to make predictions, we should be reminded that one also need not be Superman to think he can fly. Earlier, I attempted to make an analogy between religion and mental retardation. I return to that analogy in this section. It's been said that prophesy and hyperbole characterize religion. The quintessential example is achieved when the two are combined. Consider the embarrassment suffered by the Seventh-Day Adventists that moment on October 22, 1844, when the faithful learned that the Lord did not return to earth according to the calculated vision of William Miller.

We too in the field of mental retardation have had, as the Adventist would say, our "Great Disappointments." We have heard the hyperbole that the instituiuon will save society, or that the institution will destroy society, or that the special class is the only way, or that the special class is no way. Prophesy and hyperbole are not unique to religion. Therefore, I avoid offering here pictures of the future. What follows is less a calculation of what will be than it is my understanding of what could be, of what should be. Please keep this disclaimer in mind. I too will try to keep it in mind. To say that the world is changing rapidly is to say the obvious. To say that the world is changing mightily may also be obvious; but it isn't helpful. Consequently, I have chosen to try to be helpful, even if wrong.

People are exceedingly optimistic. They pontificate about the future society but are not certain about tomorrow's world. Indeed, the eminent futurists of our age—Kahn, Toffler, and others—appear to have been hardly more accurate than our star economists. Notwithstanding, they are important to listen to, not because they should be believed, but rather because they are believable; not because they always tell the truth, but rather because the good ones try not to lie. They tell plausible and interesting stories. I look at the futurists and try to connect their prophesies with a vision concerning handicapped individuals in the new society.

Herman Kahn (Kahn, Brown, & Martel, 1976) worried that the Congress of the United States had become so sophisticated that it was no longer able to see (much less solve) problems. Along the same vein, Toffler (1980) observed that the country is becoming more and more decentralized, even though the federal government appears to be more forceful and integrated than heretofore. This shift from federal to local and state autonomy and responsibility has been called "The New Federalism." It has been most forcefully articulated by Ronald Reagan and the White House staff. The New Federalism—the decentralization of government—also seems to be a national mood, and in the minds of many, in the national interest. The most compelling question—the one yet to be tested—is whether the states are now (or ever can be) in a position to effectively take over responsibility for current federal programs on behalf of handicapped, poor, and other people in need. The federal government has attempted to reduce taxes and to reassign priorities to defense and other "national interests" while reducing its influence on financial and programmatic supports for handicapped citizens. The federal deficit is enormous, and one reason for reducing federal initiatives on behalf of handicapped persons is to reduce that deficit. The truth is, however, that such a reduction would not make a blemish, let alone a dent, in that deficit. Where the shift in human service responsibility will lead the nation is difficult for anyone to predict, but it's safe to say that many people are worried about the federal pullback on resources and services to special population groups. The guesses of the best of experts remain simply that—guesses. That too must be remembered.

Sellin (1978) was brave enough to speculate about the lot of retarded persons and their families in the year 2000. He was hopeful, though I cannot understand why. Possibly, it is because he saw greater interdependence among the people, a rediscovery of traditional values, and greater reluctance to grow merely for the sake of growing. But for whatever the reasons, Sellin held the optimistic view that the world will be better by the year 2000. He had more specific predictions, too, interpreting the advent of advocacy as a positive sign. And now that people seem to have accepted advocacy with equanimity, the concept of the retarded person as citizen may actually be endurable. Sellin also interpreted the emerging ideology of "normalization" in the same vein—not merely as a new rhetorical vogue, but as a regularized part of the American value system. He found noteworthy the emergence of such new practices as alternative schools, community control of services, and expanded work opportunities for retarded adults. Insofar as medical prevention and amelioration is concerned, Sellin saw as encouraging the continued efforts of various agencies to further develop early detection programs. Sellin made few predictions concerning education; and what he did say has been ignored or actually obliterated since the advent of the Reagan administration. And, as might be expected, most of his predictions for the future concerning the economics of mental retardation and legislative gains and needs are now (but a few years after publication of his book) either obsolete, trivial, or irrelevant—whereas once they were compelling concerns. For example, to characterize Public Law 94-142 as a "blockbuster," would today be to exhibit naiveté about the current federal effort (reinforced by national mood) to erase much of its scope and impact. Sellin's optimistic predictions may be a good way to illustrate the futility of discussing the future. So much for precision in the social sciences.

What will the earth be like in a hundred years? Will there be an earth in a hundred years? If so, would we today recognize it? Will it be a fine world? But what is "fine"? Each person has a different vision of paradise. For some, it's a palace; for others, it's a log cabin in the woods. Nobody actually knows what the Messiah will bring. Few will even admit to knowledge about the more mundane world we inhabit. Few dare to predict the future society. But astrologers predict the future. Most people don't take them seriously, yet it isn't because they're always wrong. Street corner prophets predict the future, predict the end of the world. They too aren't taken seriously. Palm readers, and those who see tomorrow from tarot cards and crystal balls, are outside the fringe of respectability, and are never listened to by people on the "inside," people who are supposed to know. There are the gypsies of the world, and there are those who shape society. But it isn't that the gypsies are never right, and that the politicians and economists or even scientists are always right. It's one thing to predict what will happen when two parts of hydrogen combine with one part of oxygen. It's another thing to predict what the rate of inflation in the United States will be next year, let alone in ten years. In the former category, school children can be correct. In the latter, a legislator's batting average is probably no higher than that of the astrologer. Those who would make predictions should comprehend that their visions are necessarily distorted. And furthermore, the greater the discrepancy there is between present reality and future vision, the greater the probability of error. In the modern age, we less often build on the current foundation than create anew, or try to.

What follows are my plausible stories—plausible not because I put together the bits and pieces of current life and followed a construction of evidence to lead to true answers. Really, what I end with is less prediction than wish, much less prophesy than plea. Notwithstanding, there is certainty in these predictions, the certainty that comes from the conviction that there is no roadblock so formidable as to prevent this vision from coming true. As with so many other discussions on "what will happen. . . ," what follows are descriptions of "what can happen" *if* people work together to make it happen. What is not yet clear is what kind of future people want. There are always good and bad stories.

Today, three-quarters of the world starves while the remainder may have more than they need but nevertheless strive for yet more. In the United States, few people starve; nevertheless, too many live in relative poverty, while too many have more than they need and waste more than they should. Here in the United States, those who live in luxury have enlisted the throngs to work yet harder to make life yet easier for them. Here in the United States, we are moving away from a more equitable distritubion of resources and away from a more equitable distribution of responsibilities. Consequently, unless there is a serious disruption in the way things are going in the United States, in a hundred years there could be two identifiable classes: a small rich class, and a large poor class. Also, unless there is a shift in social policy, in a hundred years there could be a third group of people in America—classless and stateless, neither participating citizens nor quite human. This will be a new category of people—individuals who either were born into the pariah class, or lived long enough in it to become members. During the mid-twentieth century, our scholars in mental retardation created the term "surplus population." This term has been useful for categorizing people in institutions, and more recently for indicating what happens to old or otherwise unwanted people. But we in this society don't know what "surplus" truly can mean in a society run amok in its own narcissism, selfishness, and worship of youthfulness and affluence. In a future society, it is possible that we will create camps for millions of people who were born defective, who became defective, or who are now useless in terms of the "common good." There are several "attractive" reasons for fostering such a program in the twenty-first century:

- It would root out of the culture those people who materially contribute little or nothing to it.

- It would stimulate the creation of yet another major service industry.

- It would stimulate the expansion of many contiguous industries such as construction, manufacturing, food processing, wholesaling, and service professions.

- It would insure ordinary families against the catastrophic responsibilities of caring for a severely retarded child or an aged incontinent mother.

What is a dream? What is a nightmare? For every vision, there's an antivision. For every future, there could have been another future. And so too here. During the next hundred years, people can realize that there is no greater good than that which a parent gives to a child, or a child to a parent. During the next hundred years, people can realize that life is enriched to the degree that there is variance and color in it. It is exactly that difference between us which makes life interesting, not what we have in common. During the next hundred years, people can realize that there will not be sufficient resources to care as we have in the past for those whom we designate as handicapped, aged, or unneeded. We will either have to embark upon a systematic form of euthanasia to destroy the "surplus population," or we will have to change our policies on the treatment of such people. During the next hundred years, we will either learn to live better with one another, distribute our goods more equitably to one another, and care better for those in need, or we will destroy one another. But remember, good reader, poets write more compelling prose than poetry; and those who would predict the future are more persuasive than reliable.

Will there be enough for everyone in a hundred years? There will be enough if we are smart enough, and especially, good enough. We will have to share more reasonably and more decently. Will there be enough to care for handicapped and aged citizens? Yes, but the rest of us will have to discover that enrichment lies in keeping families together, in keeping communities together, in doing good for other people. We will have to prick our conscience often enough, and confront each other's behavior now and again. Something valuable accrues to your account when you serve others, but also when you enlist the service of others. Will there be room for all the elderly citizens? Yes, if we remember that some day we too will be elderly. And if we are strong and good enough to act decently when moral imperatives are at odds with mortal passions and vanities.

How does one begin to end a book whose last section is supposed to be less a summary than a vision of the future? A writer isn't supposed to prattle about the difficulty of the craft; but endings are never easy, and good endings of books are always difficult to pull off. What comes to mind here is something I wrote several years ago—less poetry than dialogue and again, less vision than prayer:

"What is Man?"
"One who knows he exists."
"That's Descartes."
"Descartes is Man."
"Can Man endure?"
"First, he must think, so he can be."
"Is that enough?"
"No, to endure, Man must feel."
"How can he improve?"

"He must invent."
"What is his most important invention?"
"Ideas."
"But, Man has so few ideas."
"Because he is violated."
"Then, how should Man meet violence?"
"With other than violence."
"How will I know what I am?"
"When you know what you are not."
"And, then will I know?"
"Yes, if you don't fool yourself."
"How will I know of the cosmos?"
"When you cease the struggle to understand."
"How can I know without understanding?"
"That is the only way to know of the cosmos."
"What must I resist?"
"What everyone else seems to do."
"What, then, would I learn?"
"What no one else knows."
"When everything is gone, what is left?"
"You."
"Then, what do I have?"
"Everything or nothing."
"But, there is an interconnection."
"Are you asking if a man is alone?"
"No, I'm saying he is not."
"Then, you are wrong."
"A man is not unrelated!"
"But he is unique."
"He is not an island."
"But he is even less a carbon."
"I sense an unfriendliness."
"No, it is independence you feel."
"Whose?"
"Yours, if you seize it."
"What is the essence of life?"
"Inner reality."

"Which is?"
"Hidden truth."
"Then, what is truth?"
"False truth or true truth?"
"THE truth."
"Honest explanation."
"Independence risks everything."
"Dependence nothing, for there is nothing."
"Too many problems."
"And many solutions."
"How do I begin?"
"Analyze things."
"To learn about them?"
"To learn about yourself."
"What should I look for?"
"Your vulnerability."
"Which is?"
"What you will try to overlook."
"How will I know when my path is honest?"
"When you walk alone."
"What is the danger then?"
"That others may follow you."
"Who will our leaders be?"
"Those who have learned to listen."
"Then, how will they lead?"
"By following their people."
"What will it require?"
"Independence."
"The leaders'?"
"And the peoples'."
"Who will follow this kind of leader?"
"Those who will be free not to."
"Who will obey?"
"Those who are independent."
"Then, what is the world?"
"Each person."
"All people together?"

"No, each one counted separately."
"Where is the world going?"
"Look at its past."
"What will we learn from it?"
"That we learn nothing from it."
"Don't we learn from history?"
"Only that we have not learned from history."
"Then, we are doomed to relive it again and again."
"Or, to begin to learn from history."
"How, then, have we planned?"
"Poorly."
"One hears that there is virtue in not planning."
"False virtue, for any road will take you to your goal."
"You are too negative about the past."
"Or too optimistic for the future."
"But you find so little that has been good."
"Because I feel it can become better."
"When will it?"
"When the enslaved are free."
"Why?"
"So I will be free."
"Whom do you mean?"
"Anyone who does not harm, yet remains enchained."
"Possibly for his protection?"
"Possibly merely to enslave him."
"Who are some examples?"
"All those whom we separate without cause."
"Name some."
"All those at New Hope times all those at other New Hopes."
"Define a New Hope."
"A New Hope is. . ."
"Yes?"
"Impossible to define."
"And you would set inmates there free?"
"So we can be free."
"Where will they go?"
"Where we go."

"But they will need help."
"Who doesn't?"
"But you said each man is alone."
"And you said he isn't."
"Then, what is the riddle?"
"First, let's find the answer."
"Which is?"
"Only a free person can be responsible for other free people."
"And the riddle?"
"Why does being free cause one to give up freedom,
to insure his freedom,
and enlarge his respect for freedom?"
"Eureka!"
"Those who are enslaved cannot contribute to others."
"And, no one is completely free until all who should be are free."
"That's why leaders must follow their people."
"And the people must be free to choose leaders."
"And, to be free, a man must have self-respect,
which requires relationships with others,
that reinforce his freedom and dependence,
which again answers the riddle."
"Therefore, you call for a New Man."
"Is there another way?"
"From where will he arise?"
"Obviously, from the ranks of the enslaved."[1]

---

[1] From *Revolt of the Idiots: A Story* (pp. 140-143) by B. Blatt, 1976, Glen Ridge, NJ: Exceptional Press. Copyright 1976 by Exceptional Press. Reprinted by permission.

References

Affleck, G. (1977). The right to survive. *Mental Retardation, 15,* 52.
Anderson, A. R., & Moore, O. K. (1960). Autotelic folk-models. *Sociological Quarterly, 1,* 203-216.
Ashmore, R. D. (1975). Background consideration in developing strategies for changing attitudes and behavior toward the mentally retarded. In M. J. Begab (Ed.), *Behavior toward the mentally retarded and society.* Baltimore: University Park Press.
Atkinson, T., Brown, K., Giambetti, A., Lichter, S., McCord, W., Mlinarcik, S., Searl, S., & Taylor, S. (1981). *Title XIX and deinstitutionalization: The issue for the 80's.* Syracuse, NY: Syracuse University, Center on Human Policy.
Beré, J. (1981, October 3). Corporate philanthropy. *New York Times,* p. 27.
Berg, A. S. (1978). *Max Perkins, editor of genius.* New York: E. P. Dutton.
Bernard, K. (1982, February 22). The first step to the cemetery. *Newsweek,* p. 15.
Bettelheim, B. (1960). *The informed heart.* Glencoe, IL: Free Press.
Biklen, D. (n.d.). *Detour from equality: The supreme court interprets public law 94-142.* Unpublished manuscript.
Biklen, D. (1977). *The elementary school administrator's practical guide to mainstreaming.* Syracuse, NY: Human Policy Press.
Biklen, D. (1983). *Community organizing.* Englewood Cliffs, NJ: Prentice-Hall.
Binet, A. (1909). *Les idées modernes sur les enfants.* Paris: Ernest Flamarion.
Birch, H., & Richardson, S. (n.d.). The functioning of Jamaican school children severely malnourished during the first two years of life. (Reprinted from *Nutrition, the Nervous System and Behavior,* Pan-American Health Organization, Scientific Publication, *251,* 64-72.)
Blatt, B. (1956). *The physical, personality, and academic status of children who are mentally retarded attending special classes as compared with children who are mentally retarded attending regular classes.* Unpublished doctoral dissertation, Pennsylvania State University, University Park.
Blatt, B. (1960). Some persistently recurring assumptions concerning the mentally subnormal. *The Training School Bulletin, 57,* 48-59.
Blatt, B. (Project Director). (1963). *The education of handicapped children in Rhode Island.*

Providence, RI: Legislative Commission to Study the Education of Handicapped Youth.
Blatt, B. (1966). *Intellectually disfranchised: Impoverished learners and their teachers*. Boston: Commonwealth of Massachusetts, Division of Mental Hygiene.
Blatt, B. (1967). A hypothesis of theories and methods in special education. In J. Helmuth (Ed.), *The disadvantaged child* (Vol. 1). Seattle: Special Child Publications.
Blatt, B. (1968). Markings in the pioneer career of J. E. Wallace Wallin. *Journal of Education, 151,* 111.
Blatt, B. (1970a). A concept of educability and correlates of mental illness, mental retardation, and cultural deprivation. In N. R. Bernstein (Ed.), *Diminished people: Problems and care of the mentally retarded*. Boston: Little, Brown.
Blatt, B. (1970b). *Exodus from pandemonium: Human abuse and a reformation of public policy*. Boston: Allyn & Bacon.
Blatt, B. (Project Director). (1971). *Massachusetts study of educational opportunities for handicapped and disadvantaged children*. Boston: Massachusetts Advisory Council on Education.
Blatt B. (1972). Review of *Mental subnormality in the community: A clinical and epidemiologic study* by H. G. Birch, S. A. Richardson, D. Baird, G. Horobin, & R. Illsly. *Exceptional Children, 38,* 439-440.
Blatt, B. (1973). *Souls in extremis: An anthology on victims and victimizers*. Boston: Allyn & Bacon.
Blatt, B. (1975). Toward an understanding of people with special needs. In J. M. Kauffman & J. S. Payne (Eds.), *Mental retardation: Introduction and personal perspectives*. Columbus, OH: Charles E. Merrill.
Blatt, B. (1976). *Revolt of the idiots: A story*. Glen Ridge, NJ: Exceptional Press.
Blatt, B. (1977). Issues and values. In B. Blatt, A. Ozolins, & R. Bogdan (Eds.), *An alternative textbook in special education: People, schools and other institutions*. Denver: Love.
Blatt, B. (1978). On the bill of rights and related matters. In R. Heinich (Ed.), *Educating all handicapped children*. Englewood Cliffs, NJ: Educational Technology Publications.
Blatt, B. (1979a). Bandwagons also go to funerals: Unmailed letter 3. *Journal of Learning Disabilities, 12*(3), 8-11.
Blatt, B. (1979b). Bandwagons also go to funerals: Unmailed letter 4. *Journal of Learning Disabilities, 12*(6), 7-8.
Blatt, B. (1980). Rediscovering the nineteenth century. *Exceptional Parent, 10*(3), 52-53.
Blatt, B. (1981). *In and out of mental retardation: Essays on educability, disability, and human policy*. Austin, TX: PRO-ED.
Blatt, B. (1982). *In and out of the university: Essays on higher and special education*. Austin, TX: PRO-ED.
Blatt, B., Bogdan, R., Biklen, D., & Taylor, S. (1977). From institution to community: A conversion model. In E. Sontag (Ed.), *Educational programming for the severely and profoundly handicapped*. Reston, VA: Council for Exceptional Children, Division of Mental Retardation.
Blatt, B., & Garfunkel, F. (1969). *The educability of intelligence: Pre-school intervention with disadvantaged children*. Washington, DC: Council for Exceptional Children.
Blatt, B., & Kaplan, F. (1966). *Christmas in Purgatory: A photographic essay on mental retardation*. Boston: Allyn & Bacon.

Blatt, B., & Ozolins, A. (1981). The university of scholarly deeds. *The Syracuse Scholar, 2*(2), 41-52.
Blatt, B., Ozolins, A., & McNally, J. (1979). *The family papers: A return to purgatory.* New York: Longman.
Blom, G. E. (1981, January). *Heather's story: Psychotherapy and the practice of the least restrictive alternative.* Issue paper, Michigan State University, Lansing.
Board of Education of the Hendrick Central School District, Westchester Co. v. Rowley ex rel. Rowley (458 U. S. 176, 1982).
Bogdan, R., & Ksander, M. (1980). Policy data as a social process: A qualitative approach to quantitative data. *Human Organization Journal of the Society for Applied Anthropology, 4,* 302-309.
Bogdan, R., & Taylor, S. (1982). *Inside out: The social meaning of mental retardation.* Toronto: University of Toronto Press.
Boyer, E. L., & Hechinger, F. M. (1981). *Higher learning in the nation's service.* Washington, DC: Carnegie Foundation for the Advancement of Teaching.
Braddock, D. (1981). Deinstitutionalization of the retarded: Trends in public policy. *Hospital & Community Psychiatry, 32*(9), 607-615.
Brodkey, H. (1982, August 29). My most obnoxious writer. *New York Times Book Review,* Sec. 7, p. BR7.
Brunvand, J. H. (1981). *The vanishing hitchhiker.* New York: Jeffrey Norton.
Brutten, M., Richardson, S., & Mangel, C. (1973). *Something's wrong with my child: A parent's book about children with learning disabilities.* New York: Harcourt Brace Jovanovich.
Budoff, M. & Orenstein, A. (1983). *Due process in special education: On going to a hearing.* Cambridge, MA: Ware Press.
Burt, C. (1957). The inheritance of mental ability, Bingham Lecture. *American Psychologist, 13,* 1-15.
Carver, J. N., & Carver, N. E. (1972). *The family of the retarded child.* Syracuse, NY: The Center on Human Policy and Syracuse University Press.
Cassell, E. J. (1982). The nature of suffering and the goals of medicine. *The New England Journal of Medicine, 306*(11), 639-645.
Cassileth, B. (1982). After laetrile, what? *The New England Journal of Medicine, 306*(24), 1482-1484.
Certo, N., Haring, N., & York, R. (1984). *Public school integration of severely handicapped students.* Baltimore: Paul H. Brookes.
Chatterjee, P. (1975). Decision-support system: A case study in evaluational science. *Journal of Applied Behavioral Science, 11*(1), 62-74.
Clark, L. H., Jr. (1982, February 2). The business of business isn't charity. *The Wall Street Journal,* p. 31.
Clarke, A. M., & Clarke, A. D. B. (1965). *Mental deficiency: The changing outlook.* New York: Free Press.
Clay, R. M. (1909). *The medieval hospitals of England.* London: Methuen.
Coffey, H. S., & Wellman, B. L. (1936). The role of cultural status in intelligence changes of preschool children. *Journal of Experimental Education, 3,* 192-202.
Cruickshank, W. (Ed.). (1971). *Psychology of exceptional children and youth* (3rd ed.). Englewood Cliffs, NJ: Prentice-Hall.

Dawidowicz, L. (1980). Lies about the holocaust. *Commentary, 70*(6), 31-37.
Doll, E. A. (1935). *The Vineland social maturity scale: Manual of questions.* Vineland, NJ: Vineland Training School.
Dubos, R. (1981). *Celebrations of life.* New York: McGraw-Hill.
Duff, R. S., & Campbell, A. G. N. (1973). Moral and ethical dilemmas in the special care nursery. *New England Journal of Medicine, 289*(17), 890-894.
Duff, R. S. (1981). Counseling families and deciding care of severely defective children: A way of coping with "medical Vietnam." *Pediatrics, 67*(3), 315-320.
Dugdale, R. L. (1877). *The Jukes.* New York: Putnam.
Edgerton, R. (1967). *The cloak of competence.* Berkeley: University of California Press.
Farber, B. (1959). Effects of a severely mentally retarded child on family integration. *Monographs of the Society for Research and Child Development, 24*(Whole No. 71).
Farber, B. (1960). Family organization and crisis: Maintenance of integration in families with a severely mentally retarded child. *Monographs of the Society for Research and Child Development, 25*(Whole No. 75).
Foner, P. S. (Ed.). (1967). *Helen Keller: Socialist years, writings and speeches.* New York: International Publishers.
Goddard, H. H. (1912). *The Kallikak family: A study in the heredity of feeblemindedness.* New York: Macmillan.
Good Housekeeping family health & medical guide. (1980). New York: Hearst Books.
Goodenough, F. L., & Maurer, K. (1940/1961). The relative potency of the nursery school and the statistical laboratory in boosting I.Q. *The Journal of Educational Psychology,* 541-549. Reprinted in J. J. Jenkins & D. G. Paterson (Eds.), *Studies in individual differences.* New York: Appleton-Century-Crofts.
Goodman, W. (1981, December 6). Irving Kristol: Patron saint of the new right. *New York Times Magazine,* pp. 90, 190, 200, 202-203, 206-207.
Gordon, E. W., & Ullman, M. (1956). Reactions of parents to problems of mental retardation in children. *American Journal of Mental Deficiency, 61,* 158-163.
Goshen, C. E. (1967). *Documentary history of psychiatry: The source book on historical principles.* New York: Philosophical Library.
Gould, S. J. (1980). *The panda's thumb: More reflections in natural history.* New York: W. W. Norton.
Gould, S. J. (1981). *The mismeasure of man.* New York: W. W. Norton.
Gould, S. J. (1982, February). In praise of Charles Darwin. *Discover,* pp. 20-25.
Graney, B. J. (1980). Hervey Backus Wilbur and the evolution of policies toward mentally retarded people. Dissertation Abstracts, International, *40,* 6229A. (University Microfilms No. 80-13, 376).
Green, F. C. (1955). *Jean-Jacques Rousseau: A critical study of his life and writings.* Cambridge: Cambridge University Press.
Greenfield, J. (1972). *A child called Noah: A family journal.* New York: Holt, Rinehart & Winston.
Grossman, F. K. (1972). *Brothers and sisters of retarded children: An exploratory study.* Syracuse, NY: Syracuse University Press.
Grossman, H. J. (Ed.). (1977). *Manual on terminology and classification in mental retardation* (rev. ed.). Washington, DC: American Association on Mental Deficiency.
Grossman, H. J. (1983). *Classification in mental retardation.* Washington, DC: American Association on Mental Deficiency.

Hearnshaw, L. (1980). *Cyril Burt, psychologist.* Ithaca, NY: Cornell University Press.
Heber, R.F. (1959). Manual on terminology and classification in mental retardation. *American Journal of Mental Deficiency, 64*(2), 399-400.
Hecht, A. (1982, February 7). The making of a writer: Masters of unpleasantness. *New York Times Book Review,* p. 3, 25.
Herr, S. S. (1979). *The new clients: Legal services for mentally retarded persons.* Washington, DC: Research Institute on Legal Assistance, National Legal Services Corporation.
Herrnstein, R. J. (1982, August). I.Q. testing and the media. *Atlantic,* pp. 68-74.
Hertz, J. H. (Ed.). (1964). *The pentateuch and haftorahs* (2nd ed.). London: Soncino Press.
Hounshell, D. A. (1980). Edison and the purse science ideal in 19th-century America. *Science, 207,* 612-617.
Hungerford, R. H. (1950). On locusts. *American Journal of Mental Deficiency, 54*(4), 415-418.
Hungerford, R. H. (1946). Peace on earth. *Occupational Education, 4*(3), 49-51.
Hungerford, R. H. (1949). On brotherhood. *Occupational Education, 6*(6), 125-130.
Hutchinson, E. F. (1982). Wheelchairs. *The Exceptional Parent, 12*(1), pp. 7, 60.
Ingelfinger, F. J. (1980). Arrogance. *New England Journal of Medicine, 303*(26), 1507-1511.
Irving, J. (1981). *The hotel New Hampshire.* New York: E. P. Dutton.
Itard, J. M. G. (1932/1962). *The wild boy of Aveyron* (G. Humphrey & M. Humphrey, Eds. and trans.). New York: Century. (Paperback edition, Appleton-Century-Crofts, 1962)
Jensen, A. R. (1973). Let's understand Skodak and Skeels finally. *Educational Psychologist, 10*(1), 30-35.
Justice at the ready. (1982, June 2). *New York Times,* p. A20.
Kagan, J. (1972, December). *Cross cultural perspectives on early development.* Paper presented at the annual meeting of the American Association for the Advancement of Science, Washington, DC.
Kahn, H., Brown, W., & Martel, L. (1976). *The next 200 years: A scenario for America and the world.* New York: William Morrow & Co.
Kanner, L. (1949). Problems of nosology and the psychodynamics of early infantile autism. *The American Journal of Orthopsychiatry, 19,* 416-426.
Kanner, L. (1964). *A history of the care and study of the mentally retarded.* Springfield, IL: Charles C Thomas.
Kaufman, M. (1982, May 15). They strike a blow for self-confidence. *Philadelphia Inquirer,* pp. B1-B2.
Keller, H. (1903). *The story of my life.* New York: Doubleday.
Kemper, J. S., Jr. (1981, December 22). Reagan's voluntarism: The ten percent solution. *The Wall Street Journal,* p. 20.
Kilpatrick, W. H. (1914). *The Montessori system examined.* Boston: Houghton Mifflin.
Kolstoe, O. (1972). *Mental retardation: An educational viewpoint.* New York: Holt, Rinehart & Winston.
Kraepelin, E. (1962). *One hundred years of psychiatry.* New York: Philosophical Library.
Kronenberg, H. M. (1982). Looking at genes. *New England Journal of Medicine, 307*(1), 50-51.
Lemaitie, J. (1907). *Jean-Jacques Rousseau.* London: William Heinemann.
Lemkau, P., Teitze, C., & Cooper, M. (1941). Mental hygiene problems in an urban district. *Mental Hygiene, 25,* 624-646.

Lemkau, P., Teitze, C., & Cooper, M. (1942a). Mental hygiene problems in an urban district: Second paper. *Mental Hygiene, 26,* 100-119.
Lemkau, P., Teitze, C.,& Cooper, M. (1942b). Mental hygiene problems in an urban district: Third paper. *Mental Hygiene, 26,* 275-288.
Lemkau, P., Teitze, C., & Cooper, M. (1943). Mental hygiene problems in an urban district: Fourth paper. *Mental Hygiene, 27,* 279-295.
Lewis, J. F. (1973). The community and the retarded: A study in social ambivalence. In G. Tarjan & R. K. Eyman et al. (Eds.), *Sociobehavioral studies in mental retardation* (Monograph No. 1). Washington, DC: American Association on Mental Deficiency.
Lindsley, O. R. (1958). Intermittent grading. *The Clearing House, 32*(8), 451-454.
Lindsley, O. R. (1960). Characteristics of the behavior of chronic psychotics as revealed by free-operant conditioning methods. Reprinted from *Diseases of the Nervous System,* Monograph Supplement, *21*(2), 66-78.
Lindsley, O. R. (1964a). Direct measurement and prosthesis of retarded behavior. *Journal of Education, 147,* 62-81).
Lindsley, O. R. (1964b). Can deficiency produce specific superiority—The challenge of the idiot savant. *Exceptional Children, 31*(4), 225-231.
Long, K. (1977). *Johnny's such a bright boy, what a shame he's retarded.* Boston: Houghton Mifflin.
Luther, M. (1959). *What Luther says* (Vol. 3). St. Louis: Concordia.
Luther, M. (1967). *Luther's Works* (Vol. 54). Philadelphia: Fortress Press.
MacMillan, D. L. (1977). *Mental retardation in school and society.* Boston: Little, Brown.
Maguire, D. C. (1974, January). Death by chance, death by choice. *Atlantic,* pp. 56-65.
Mambort, T., Thomas, E., Few, R., Magin, P., & Torge, H. (1981, March). *Community acceptance: A realistic approach.* Montgomery County Board of Mental Retardation & Developmental Disabilities.
McCandless, P. (1979). "Build! build!" The controversy over the care of the chronically insane in England, 1855-1870. *Bulletin of the History of Medicine, 53*(4), 553-574.
McCue, J. D. (1982). The effects of stress on physicians and their medical practices. *New England Journal of Medicine, 306*(8), 458-463.
Milgram, N. A. (1969). The rational and irrational in Zigler's motivational approach to mental retardation. *American Journal of Mental Deficiency, 73,* 527-532.
Montessori, M. (1964). *The Montessori method.* New York: Schocken Books.
Montessori, M. (1967). *The absorbent mind* (C. A. Adyai, trans.). Madras, India: Kalakshetia Publications.
Moore, O. (1960). *Yale-Hamden Hall responsive environments project: Scientific evaluation.* Unpublished manuscript.
Moore, O. (1961). *A field demonstration at the Woodrow Wilson rehabilitation center.* New Haven, CT: Yale University Press.
Moore, O. (1982). The clarifying environments program: 1960-1980. In B. Holzner & J. Nehnevajsa (Eds.), *Organizing for social research.* Cambridge, MA: Schenckman.
Nazzaro, J. N. (1977). *Exceptional timetables: Historic events affecting the handicapped and gifted.* Reston, VA: Council for Exceptional Children.
Neel, J. V. (1981). Genetic effects of atomic bombs. *Science, 213,* 1205.
Nesbitt, J. B. (1982). Terminating life support for mentally retarded, critically ill patients: The prosecutor's perspective. *The Journal of Legal Medicine, 3*(2), 245-265.

New York State Department of Mental Hygiene. (1955). *A special census of suspected referred mental retardation.* Onondaga County Study, New York.
Newton, J. (1982). P.L. 94-142—no law is perfect. *American Journal of Pediatrics, 33*(8), 16.
Osborne, D. (1982, February/March). State of siege: Can the Democrats mastermind the great escape? *Mother Jones,* pp. 22-31.
Ostroff, E. (n.d.) *Humanizing environments: A primer for the Massachusetts Department of Mental Health.* Boston: Massachusetts Department of Mental Health.
Parrish, M. (1980, October 6). The quality of mercy. *New West,* pp. 13-24.
Payne, J. S., & Patton, J. R. (1981). *Mental retardation.* Columbus, OH: Charles E. Merrill.
Perkinson, H. J. (1980). *Since Socrates: Studies in the history of western educational thought.* New York: Longman.
Perske, R. (Ed.). (1977). *Improving the quality of life: A symposium on normalization and integration.* Arlie, VA: National Association for Retarded Citizens.
Pines, M. (1982, August 31). Down's syndrome masked by surgery. *New York Times,* p. C2.
Plato (1937). *Phaedo.* In B. Jowett (trans.), *The dialogues of Plato.* New York: Random House.
Poll on alumni values stirs debate in ivy league. (1982, June 2). *New York Times,* p. B6.
Posner, B. (1966). Five days as a retarded laundry worker. *Rehabilitation Record, 7*(3), 1-5.
Private death. (1982, April 27). *New York Times,* p. A22.
Rabin, D., Rabin, P., & Rabin, R. (1982). Compounding the ordeal of ALS: Isolation from my fellow physicians. *The New England Journal of Medicine, 307*(8), 506-509.
Richardson, S. A. (n.d.). Ecology of malnutrition: Non-nutritional factors influencing intellectual and behavioral development. (Reprinted from *Nutrition, the Nervous System and Behavior,* Scientific Publication No. 251, Pan American Health Organization)
Rimland, B. (1964). *Infantile autism: The syndrome and its implications for a neural theory of behavior.* New York: Appleton-Century-Crofts.
Robinson, N. M., & Robinson, H. B. (1976). *The mentally retarded child: A psychological approach* (2nd ed.). New York: McGraw-Hill.
Rosen, M., Clark, G., & Kivitz, M. (1976). *The history of mental retardation: Collected papers* (Vols. 1 & 2). Baltimore: University Park Press.
Rosenhahn, D. L. (1973, February 9). On being sane in insane places. *Medical World News,* pp. 17-19.
Rousseau, J. (1961). *Emile* (B. Foxley, trans.). New York: E. P. Dutton. (Original work published in 1762)
Rutter, M., Tizard, J., & Whitmore, K. (Eds.). (1970). *Education, health, and behavior: Psychological and medical study of childhood development.* New York: Wiley.
Saenger, C. (1957). *The adjustment of severely retarded adults in the community.* Albany: Interdepartmental Health Resources Board.
Sarason, S. B. (1959). *Psychological problems in mental deficiency* (3rd ed.). New York: Harper.
Sarason, S. B. (1976). Community psychology and the anarchist insight. *American Journal of Community Psychology, 4*(3), 243-261.
Sarason, S. B. (1981). *Psychology misdirected.* New York: Free Press.

Sarason, S. B. (1982). *The culture of the school and the problem of change* (2nd ed.). Boston: Allyn & Bacon.

Sarason, S. B. (1985). *Psychology and mental retardation: Perspectives in change.* Austin, TX: PRO-ED.

Sarason, S. B., Davidson, K., & Blatt, B. (1962). *The preparation of teachers: An unstudied problem in education.* New York: Wiley.

Sarason, S. B., & Lorentz, E. (1979). *The challenge of the resource exchange network.* San Francisco: Jossey-Bass.

Sarason, S. B., Zitnay, G., & Grossman, F. K. (1971). *The creation of a community setting.* Syracuse, NY: Syracuse University Division of Special Education and Rehabilitation.

Saroyan to be cremated. (1981, May 19). *Syracuse Herald Journal,* p. A13.

Schaefer-Simmern, H. (1948). *The unfolding of artistic activity.* Berkeley: University of California Press.

Scheerenberger, R. C. (1982). *Public residential services for the mentally retarded: 1981.* National Association of Superintendents of Public Residential Facilities for the Mentally Retarded.

Scheerer, M., Rothmann, E., & Goldstein, K. (1945). A case of "idiot savant": An experimental study of personality organization. *Psychological Monographs, 58*(4).

Schonell, F. J., & Watts, B. H. (1956). A first survey of the effects of a subnormal child in the family unit. *American Journal of Mental Deficiency, 61,* 210-219.

Schultze, G., & Williams, G. D. (n.d.). *What's right with public education in New York State: Resource manual.* Albany: New York State Educational Conference Board.

Seagoe, M. V. (1964). *Yesterday was Tuesday, all day and all night: The story of a unique education.* Boston: Little, Brown.

Sequin, E. (1855, January 23). State of New York report #33 in assembly. *4th Annual Report of the Trustees of the New York State Asylum for the Idiots.*

Seguin, E. (1976). Idiocy and its treatment by the physiological method. In M. Rosen, G. Clark, & M. Kivitz (Eds.), *The history of mental retardation: Collected papers* (Vol. 1). Baltimore: University Park Press. (Original work published in 1864)

Sellin, D. F. (1979). *Mental retardation: Nature, needs, and advocacy.* Boston: Allyn & Bacon.

Shahn, B. (1965). *Haggadah.* London: MacGibbon & Kee.

Shelley, M. (1965). *Frankenstein.* New York: New American Library, Signet Books. (Original work published 1831)

Sigelman, L., Roeder, P. W., & Sigelman, C. K. (1981). Social service innovation in the American states: Deinstitutionalization of the mentally retarded. *Social Science Quarterly, 162*(3), 503-515.

Silberstein, R. M., & Irwin, H. (1962). Jean Marc-Gaspard Itard and the savage of Aveyron: An unsolved diagnostic problem in child psychiatry. *Journal of the American Academy of Child Psychiatry, 1,* 314-322.

Skeels, H. M., & Harms, I. (1948). Children with inferior social histories; Their mental development in adoptive homes. *Journal of Genetic Psychology, 72,* 283-294.

Skeels, H. M. (1966). Adult status of children with contrasting early life experiences. *Monographs of the Society for Research in Child Development, 31*(3, Serial No. 105).

Skodak, M., & Skeels, H. M. (1949). A final follow-up study of one hundred adopted children. *Journal of Genetic Psychology, 75, 85-125.*

Slezak, Z. (1981, October 14). [Acting Commissioner of State of New York Office of

Mental Retardation and Developmental Disabilities in correspondence to Senator William T. Smith.]

Sloan, W., & Stevens, H. A. (1976). *A century of concern: A history of American Association on Mental Deficiency, 1876-1976.* Washington, DC: American Association on Mental Deficiency.

Smith, J. D. (1981). Down's syndrome, amniocentesis, and abortion: Prevention or elimination? *Mental Retardation, 19*(1), 8-11.

Smith, J. D. (1985). *Minds made feeble: The myth and legacy of the Kallikaks.* Rockville, MD: Aspen Systems.

Smith, J. O., & Arkans, J. (1974). Now more than ever: A case for the special class. *Exceptional Children, 40*(7), 497-502.

Stern, W. (1914). *The psychological methods of testing intelligence* (G. Whipple, trans.). Baltimore: Warwick & York.

Stern, W. (1971). Bibliographie Jerusalem: Anlaesslich der gedenfeiern. Unpublished manuscript.

Steel, R. (1980). *Walter Lippmann and the American century.* Boston: Little, Brown.

Streissguth, A. P., Landesman-Dwyer, S., Martin, J. C., & Smith, D. W. (1980). Teratogenic effects of alcohol in humans and laboratory animals. *Science, 209,* 353-361.

Surgical death. (1982, April 11). *New York Times,* p. 37.

Szasz, T. (1970). *The manufacture of madness: A comparative study of the inquisition and the mental health movement.* New York: Harper & Row.

Szasz, T. (1973). *The second sin.* Garden City, NY: Anchor Press.

Szasz, T. (1982). The psychiatric will: A new mechanism for protecting persons against "psychosis" and psychiatry. *American Psychologist, 37*(7), 762-770.

Terman, L. M. (1925). *Genetic studies of genius.* Stanford, CA: Stanford Univrsity Press.

Toffler, A. (1980). *The third wave.* New York: Bantom Books.

Torrance, E. P. (1980). Japanese attitudes on giftedness and creativity. *The Education Digest, 45,* 29-32.

Tredgold, A. F., & Soddy, K. (1956). *A textbook on mental deficiency* (9th ed.). Baltimore: Williams & Wilkins.

United Nations Declaration on the Rights of Disabled Persons. Adopted December 9, 1975.

Untold story of coast immigration center unfolds. (1981, September 13). *New York Times,* p. 84.

Wallin, J. E. W. (1917). *Problems of subnormality.* Yonkers-on-Hudson, NY: World Book.

Wertham, F. (1966). *A sign for Cain.* New York: Macmillan.

Wieck, C. A. (1980). *The cost of public and community residential care for mentally retarded people in the United States.* Thesis, University of Minnesota, Minneapolis.

Wilson, D. C. (1975). *Stranger and traveler: The story of Dorothea Dix, American reformer.* Boston: Little, Brown.

Wolf, T. H. (1973). *Alfred Binet.* Chicago: University of Chicago Press.

Wolfe, T. (1929). *Look homeward angel.* New York: Charles Scribner's Sons.

Wolfensberger, W. (Ed.). (1973). *A selective overview of the work of Jean Vanier and the movement of l'Arche.* Monograph No. 1. Toronto: National Institute on Mental Retardation.

Wolfensberger, W. (1975). *The origin and the nature of our institutional models.* Syracuse, NY: Human Policy Press.

Wolfensberger, W. (1980). The definition of normalization: Update, problems, disagreements, and misunderstandings. In R. J. Flynn & K. E. Nitsch (Eds.), *Normalization, social integration, and community services.* Austin, TX: PRO-ED.

Wolfensberger, W. (Ed.). (1981a). *Training Institute Publication Series (TIPS), 1*(4), p. 4, 5.

Wolfensberger, W. (1981b). The extermination of handicapped people in World War II Germany. *Mental Retardation, 19*(1), 1-7.

Wolfensberger, W. (1982). *A position statement on a Christian approach to the sexuality of mentally retarded people.* Unpublished manuscript. Syracuse University, Division of Special Education and Rehabilitation.

Zigler, E. (1969). Developmental versus difference theories of mental retardation and the problems of motivation. *American Journal of Mental Deficiency, 73,* 536-556.

Zober, M. A. (1978, July). *Residential setting for mentally retarded persons: A review of the literature that assesses policy related residential characteristics and personal adjustment.* Newton Upper Falls, MA: Massachusetts Association for Retarded Citizens.

Index

Abendberg (Switzerland), 37, 39
Aberdeen (Scotland), 74
Accountability, 215–217
Adams, Franklin P., 315
Administrative mental retardation, 70, 74–75
Advocacy, 208–211
Algonquin Roundtable, 315–316
American Association on Mental Deficiency, 38–39, 68–69, 71, 77, 91, 118–119, 127, 188, 213, 229
American Breeders' Association, 320
American Psychological Association, 53, 77, 156
Amnesia, 362–364
Amniocentesis, 131
Amyotrophic lateral sclerosis (ALS), 342–345
Anorexia, 329–330
Anti-Poverty Act, 227
"Apology" (Socrates), 28–30
Architects, 201–202
Aristotle, 14, 31
Arrogance, 290–291
Aspirations
  bureaucratization of values, 238–240
  elusive opportunity, 242–243
  goals and means, 235–238, 241–243
  mortality and, 241–242
  See also Paradoxes
Association for Persons with Severe Handicaps, 211
Association for Retarded Citizens, 177, 213, 347
Association of Medical Officers of American Institutions for Idiots and Feebleminded Persons, 38–39
Asylum for the Deaf and Dumb (Hartford, CN), 40
Augustine, *Saint*, 31
Autism, 124
Autobiographies, 102–110
Auto-education, 47

Babinski, Josef Francois Felix, 50
Balbiani, 50
Banishment
  causes of, 298–303
  dangerousness and, 305–308
  Frankenstein's story, 304–305
Bankers, 202–204
Barbie, Klaus, 342
Bell, Alexander Graham, 320
Benchley, Robert, 315
Bere, James F., 113–114

Bernard of Chartres, 361
Bettelheim, Bruno, 196, 340-341
Biklen, Douglas, 84, 113, 196
Binet, Alfred, 13, 17, 19-20, 22, 27, 49-52, 154, 289, 309, 310, 363
Biography of Robert Frost (Thompson), 352-353
Board of Education v. Rowley, 231
Bogdan, Robert, 106-107
Bonaterre, 33
Booth, John Wilkes, 303
Brenda, Clements, 155
British Journal of Statistical Psychology, 56
Brodkey, Harold, 301
Brown, George W., 39
Brown v. Board of Education, 228
Brunvand, Jan Harold, 141
Builders, 201-202
Bureaucratization, 238-240
Burt, Cyril, 20, 50, 55-56, 151, 156, 313-314

Cadavers, 328-329
Caldwell, Erskine, 263
Carnegie Institute of Washington, 320
Carver, John, 92-95
Carver, Nellie, 92-95
Casa del Bambini, 47
Caston, Don, 196
Cattell, James McKeen, 50
Center on Human Policy (Syracuse, NY), 182-183, 211
Chaerephon, 29
Charcot, Jean Martin, 50
Charity, 113-114
A Child Called Noah (Greenfield), 97-99
Children's Hospital (Paris), 35
Chipman, Alida, 104-106
Chitkara, Usha, 339
Christianity, 140-141
Christmas in Purgatory (Blatt), 185, 212, 333-334, 341-342
Chromosomal disorders, 130-132
Citizenship, 233
Civil Rights Act, 227

Civil Service Act, 226
Clarifying Environment, 144-146
Clark University, 52
Classification
  educational and psychometric, 132-133
  by etiology, 117-132
  by special characteristics, 133-135
Classroom variation, 270-272
Clinical teaching, 273-274
Clinicians, 283-287
Communicable disease, 244
Communitization/institutionalization controversy, 158-169
Community Organizing (Biklen), 113
Community perspectives, 87-89
Comparison, 139-141
Connecticut School of Imbeciles (Lakeville), 39, 43
Controversies
  cure/permanence, 155-156
  institutionalization/communitization, 158-169
  on intelligence, 310-315
  nature/nurture, 150-155
  normalization/mainstreaming, 158-169
  pathology/variance, 157-158
Cooperative Research Act, 226
Council for Exceptional Children, 91, 188, 213
Crick, Francis Harry Compton, 125-126
Crime, 75-76
Cultural amnesia, 363-364
The Culture of the School and the Problem of Change (Sarason), 188-189
Cure/permanence controversy, 155-156

Dangerousness, 305-308
Darwin, Charles, 238
Death
  permutations on, 342-348
  private, 338-339

INDEX / 385

regularizing, 338-342
surgical, 339
See also Euthanasia
Decision making, 215-217
A Declaration on Human Rights and Responsibilities, 265-266
de Crinis, Max, 326
Defective delinquency, 76
Definitions, 15, 67-72
Deinstitutionalization, 179-188
Department of Education (U.S.), 226
Department of Health and Human Services (U.S.), 240
Department of Justice (U.S.), 240
Dessau (Ger.), 23-24
Diagnosis
 ideals of, 257-258
 labels in, 316-318
Dialogues (Plato), 34
Diary of a Mongoloid (Seagoe), 102-106
Differentiation of people, 8
District of Columbia Institution for the Deaf, 225-226
Dix, Dorothea, 40, 42-43, 140
Doll, Edgar, 289, 311
Dominant inheritance, 127-128
Doren, G.A., 39
Down, Langdon, 130
Down syndrome
 etiology of, 117-118
 euthanasia in, 240, 323-324
 intelligence and, 313
 personal narrative of, 102-106
 surgical death and, 339
 telling stories about, 141-142
 treatment of, 130-132
Dubos, R., 110, 116-117
Dugdale, R.L., 322
Dye (IQ researcher), 53-54

Edison, Thomas A., 359
Educability hypothesis, 7-8, 16, 27, 57-58
Education Department (U.S.), 226
Education of All Handicapped Children Act (Public Law 94-142), 57, 60, 168, 177, 222-227, 277, 311-312, 345-346, 366
Educational goals, 274-276
Educational Resources Information Center (ERIC), 321
Educational retardation, 132-133
Einstein, Albert, 10, 317
Elementary and Secondary Education Act, 227
Elementary School Administrator's Practical Guide to Mainstreaming (Biklen), 196
Elephant Man, 304
Eliot, T.S., 140
Emile (Rousseau), 25, 103, 164, 357
Emotional factors, 124
Endocrine disorders, 122
Endogenous
 conditions chromosomal disorders, 130-132
 dominant inheritance, 127-128
 genetics in, 125-127
 polygenic inheritance, 127
 recessive transmission, 128-130
Enumerology, 66-67
Environmentalism, 31, 154
Epidemiology, 73-74, 78
ERIC system, 321
Esquirol, Jean Etienne Dominique, 35
Ethics (Maimonides), 34
Etiological classification, 117-132
Eugenics, 320-321
Euthanasia, 323-328, 338-342. *See also* Death
Exodus from Pandemonium (Blatt), 215
Exogenous conditions
 emotional factors, 124
 endocrine disorders, 122
 gestational disorders, 122-123
 infection, 119-120
 malnutrition, 123
 prematurity, 122-123
 toxic agents, 120-122
 trauma, 120
Expectations, 146-147
Experts' views, 90-91

Explanations
  by comparison, 139-141
  professional attempts at
    expectations, 146-147
    insufficient childhood learning, 144-146
    prosthetic supports, 147-148
    storytelling, 141-143
    what's wrong, 138-139

Facility development, 201-202
"Family" conspiracy, 211-215
The Family of the Retarded Child (Carver), 92-95
The Family Papers (Blatt), 184-185, 212, 333
Family views, 91-99
Farber, Bernard, 96
Faurisson, Robert, 341
Fere, Charles, 50
Fernald, Walter E., 115, 309, 312
Fetal alcohol syndrome, 121
Feurstein, Reuben, 130-131
Ford, Henry, 26
Frankenstein, 304-305
Free will, 110-111, 323-328
Freedom, 263-265, 330-332
Freud, Sigmund, 140
Froebel, 46
Frost, Robert, 82, 140, 301, 352-353

Gallaudet College (Washington, D.C.), 226
Galton, Sir Frances, 50, 320
Galvani, 33
Garfunkel, Frank, 351
Garland, Judy, 363
Genetics, 125-127
Gestational disorders, 122-123
Gilhool, Thomas, 206-208
Goals, 263-265
Goddard, Henry, 20, 26, 27, 50, 52, 115, 151, 309, 310-311, 312, 313, 322

Golden Rule, 256-257, 360
Good Housekeeping Family Health & Guide, 115-116
Gordon, Ira, 54
Goring, Hermann, 349
Gould, Stephen J., 150-155, 361-362
Governmental role, 82-85, 189-190
Greenfield, Josh, 97-99
Grossman, Frances, 95-96
Guatemala, 147
Guggenbuehl, Johann Jakob, 37-38, 39
Guthrie, Robert, 130

Haggadah, 16
Hall, G. Stanley, 53
Handicapped Coalition, 347
Harriman, Mrs. E.H., 320
Health and Human Services Department (U.S.), 240
Hearnshaw, L.S., 55-56
Heather's Story (Blom), 182
Heber, Rick, 313-314
Hecht, Anthony, 352
Hereditary conditions. *See* Endogenous conditions
Herr, Stanley, 206-208
Herrnstein, R.J., 51, 314
Hill, Grace, 104
Hillel, Rabbi, 256
Hiroshima, 121
The History of the Care and Study of the Mentally Retarded, (Kanner), 23
Hitler, Adolph, 249, 327
Hobson v. Hansen, 229
Hospice des Incurables Bicetre, 35-36
The Hotel New Hampshire (Irving), 298
Howe, Julia Ward, 361
Howe, Samuel Gridley, 21, 27, 39-40, 41, 42, 43, 361
Human Ecology Forum, 182
Humanizing Environments: A Primer (Ostroff), 182
Humphrey, George, 33
Humphrey, Muriel, 33
Hunchback of Notre Dame, 128, 304

Hungerford, Richard, 13, 19, 20-23, 30, 206, 274-276, 330, 363

Ideals
  Golden Rule, 256-257
  of placement and treatment, 258-263
  of testing and diagnosis, 257-258
Les Idees Modernes sur les Enfants (Binet), 19
Idiocy, and Its Treatment by the Physiological Method (Seguin), 35
In and Out of Mental Retardation (Blatt), 215
Incidence, 72-75, 78
Industries
  as advocates, 208-211
  bankers, 202-204
  builders and architects, 201-202
  decision-making in, 215-217
  "family" conspiracy in, 211-215
  lawyers, 206-208
  merchants and manufacturers, 202-204
  organized labor, 202-204
  politicians' roles, 204-206
  research and treatment, 198-201
Infection, 119-120
Inherited conditions. *See* Endogenous conditions
Inservice training, 306-307
Inside Out (Bogdan and Taylor), 106-107
Institute for the Human Environment (San Francisco), 201
Institution for Feebleminded Youths (Columbus, OH), 39
Institutionalization/communitization controversy, 158-169
Intelligence
  diagnostic labels in, 316-318
  metaphors on, 310-315
  recurring assumptions on, 315-316
Intelligence Quotient
  in defining retardation, 68-69
  discovery of, 51-52
  in mental testing, 156
  and social justice, 75
  validity of, 314-315
Intermediate Care Facilities for the Mentally Retarded, 183
Interstate Commerce Act, 226
Irving, John, 298
Itard, Jean-Marc-Gaspard, 10, 17, 22, 27, 33-34, 35, 43, 46, 48, 99, 103, 154, 289, 357, 363

Jacob's syndrome, 132
Jefferson, Thomas, 312
Jensen, Arthur, 20, 51, 55, 156, 309, 312, 314
Jervis, George, 155
Jesus Christ, 14, 31
Johnson, Lyndon, 190
Joint Commission on the Accreditation of Hospitals, 331
Jones, James, 263
Joyce, James, 140
Judaism, 140-141
Justice Department (U.S.), 240

Kagan, Jerome, 146-147
Kahn, Herman, 364-365
Kamin, Leon, 55
Kanner, Leo, 124, 155
Kaufman, George S., 315
Keller, Helen, 13, 17, 18-19, 89, 103, 149, 164, 317, 356
Keller, Helen Bass, 103-104
Kennedy, John Fitzgerald, 56-57, 190, 301, 303
Kennedy, Robert, 303
Kerenyl, Thoms D., 339
Kerlin, I.N., 39
Kilpatrick, William H., 47
Kinesthetics, 47
King, Martin Luther, 20, 303
Kirk, Sam, 27, 51, 52, 53, 54, 56, 154
Knight, Henry M., 39, 43
Kristol, Irving, 221-222

Ladd, George Trumbull, 52-53
LaGuardia, Henry, 22
Larry P. v. Riles, 229
Lavoisier, Antoine Laurent, 33
Lawyers, 206-208
Learning insufficiencies, 144-146
Legislation, 222-227. *See also* specific laws
Leonardo da Vinci, 317
Lincoln, Abraham, 303, 312, 332
Lindsley, Ogden, 147, 316
Lippmann, Walter, 150
Litigation, 227-232
Locke, John, 32, 46
Longfellow, Henry Wordsworth, 320
Look Homeward Angel (Wolfe), 334-335
"Lou Gehrig's disease", 342-345
Louis XVI, 32
Lowell, Robert, 140
Luther, Martin, 13, 14, 17, 23-25, 26

Mainstreaming/normalization controversy, 158-169
Malmö Conference, 99-102
Malnutrition, 123
Mann, Horace, 40, 320
Mansfield (CN) Training School, 43-44
Manual on Terminology and Classification in Mental Retardation, 71, 118-119
Manufacturers, 202-204
Marx, Groucho, 338
Marx, Harpo, 315
Marx, Karl, 238
Medicaid (Title XIX), 183
Medical practitioners, 283-287
Memorial to the Legislature of Massachusetts, 42-43
Memory, 334-338
Mengele, Joseph, 341
Mental Orthopedics (Binet), 20, 49
Mental testing, 156
Merchants, 202-204
Merrick, John, 128, 317

Metaphors
 on intelligence, 310-315
 on retardation, 82
Meyerson, Lee, 88
Miller, William, 364
Mills v. Board of Education of the District of Columbia, 228
The Mismeasure of Man (Gould), 152
Mobilization of professions, 188-190
Mongolism. *See* Down syndrome
Montesquieu, 33
Montessori, Maria, 22, 27, 46-48, 52, 154, 166, 363
Montgomery County (OH), 182
Moore, Omar K., 144-146, 271
Moral goals, 235-238, 242-243
Morel, Benedict Augustin, 46
Mortality, 241-242, 334-338
Mosaicism, 131
Moses, 14, 332
Moss Rehabilitation Hospital (Philadelphia), 308
Murphy, Ed, 106
Murphy, Gerald, 263-264
Murphy, Sarah, 263-264
Myers, Edward, 289

Nader, Ralph, 216, 235, 238-240
Nagasaki, 121
National Defense Education Act, 227
National Institute on Mental Health, 213
National Right to Life Committee, 347
Nativism, 31, 154
Nature/nurture controversy, 150-155
Nesbitt, J.B., 323
Neurofibromatosis, 128
New Haven State Teachers College, 92-95
New York Asylum for Idiots (Syracuse), 39
Newton, Isaac, 26, 361
Newton, Jerome, 345
Nirje, Bengt, 99-102

Noah, 14
Nondysjunction, 131–132
Normalisation, 48, 158–169
Normative teaching, 273–274
Nurture/nature controversy, 150–155
Nutritional deprivation, 123

Occupational Education Curriculum, 274–276
Office of Education (U.S.), 213
Organized labor, 202–204

Pagaste (Northern Africa), 31
Paradoxes
  communicable disease, 244
  inevitability of, 250
  sexuality, 245–248
  withholding treatment, 248–250
Parent Choice, 347
Parents' movement, 176–179
Parker, Dorothy, 315
Pathology/variance controversy, 157–158
Paton, Allen, 263
Pauling, Linus, 130
Pearson, Carl, 320
Pennsylvania Association for Retarded Children v. Commonwealth of Pennsylvania, 228–230
Pennsylvania Training School, 39
People First, 211
Pereire, Jacob Rodrigue, 32–33
Perkins Institution for the Blind, 40
Perkins, Maxwell Evarts, 263
Permanence/cure controversy, 155–156
Perske, Robert, 316
Personality characteristics, 134–135
Perspectives
  of experts, 90–91
  family, 91–99
  of mentally retarded, 99–110
  metaphors, 82
  societal, 82–85
  of strangers
    in the community, 87–89
    in the schools, 89–90
    in the workplace, 86–87
Phenylketonuria (PKU), 129–130
Philanthropy, 113–114
Physical characteristics, 134
Pinel, Philippe, 33, 35, 289
PKU. *See* Phenylketonuria
Placement, 258–263
Plato, 10, 14, 17, 27, 28, 30–31, 34
Political forces
  citizenship, 233
  legislation, 222–227
  litigation, 227–232
  politics, 232–233
  See also Socio-cultural forces
Politicians, 204–206
Polygenic inheritance, 127
Pope, Marvin, 309, 316–318
Posner, Bernard, 86–87
Practitioners
  arrogance of, 290–291
  medical, 283–287
  psychological, 288–289
  teachers and professors, 270–283
Predictions, 364–372
Prematurity, 122–123
Presidential Task Force on Private Sector Initiatives, 83
President's Committee on Employment of the Handicapped, 86
President's Committee on Mental Retardation, 73
President's Committee on "National Employment of the Physically Handicapped Week", 226
Prevalence, 72–75
Private death, 338–339
Professors, 277–283
Prometheus, 10
Prosthetic supports, 147–148
Psychiatry, 140–141, 288–289
Psychological Problems in Mental Deficiency (Sarason), 288

Psychologists, 288-289
Psychometric
  retardation classification of, 132-133
  incidence of, 74-75

Quasimodo, 128

Rabin, David, 343-345
Radiation poisoning, 121
Reagan, Ronald, 83, 220, 227, 347, 365, 366
Recessive transmission, 128-130
Religion, 140-141
Research, 198-201
Responsive Environment, 144-146
Retarded people's views, 99-110
Revolt of the Idiots (Blatt), 333, 350-353
Richards, James B., 40
Rimland, Bernard, 124, 155
Rooney, Mickey, 363
Roosevelt, Franklin Delano, 18, 238
Rousseau, Jean Jacques, 10, 13, 17, 25-26, 32, 33, 46, 60, 103, 357
Rowley, Amy, 231

Saenger, G., 96-97
Salem (MA), 45
San Antonio Independent School District v. Rodriguez, 228
Santayana, George, 186
Sarason, Seymour, 7, 51, 55, 95, 106, 154, 188-189, 201, 289, 315
Saroyan, William, 335, 354
Schmidt, Bernardine, 313
School perspectives, 89-90
Scott, Paul, 102-106, 316
Scripture, Edward Wheeler, 52-53
Seagoe, May, 102-106, 316
Seguin, Edouard, 27, 34-37, 39, 40-41, 43, 46, 47, 289, 363
Self-perception, 321-323
Sellin, D.F., 365-366

Services
  deinstitutionalization, 179-188
  mobilization of professions, 188-190
  parents' movement, 176-179
  special education, 176-179
Sexuality, 245-248
Shelley, Mary, 304-305
Shockley, William B., 112
A Sign for Cain (Wertham), 326-327
Simon, Theodore, 19-20, 50, 51-52, 310
Sinclair, Upton, 140
Singer, Isaac Bashevis, 197
Skeels, Harold, 27, 38, 51, 52, 53-55, 154, 156, 314
Skinner, B.F., 147
Sloan, William, 289
Social justice, 75
Social selection, 31, 154
Society
  view of, 82-85
  zero-sum, 219-222
Society for the Psychological Study of the Child, 50-51
Socio-cultural forces
  legislation, 222-227
  zero-sum society, 219-222
  See also Political forces
Socrates, 27-30, 60, 355
Sokoloff, David, 201
Southbury (CN) Training School, 43-44
Southern Connecticut State College, 92-95
Special education, 176-179
Starvation, 329-330
State Institution for the Feebleminded (Jacksonville, IL), 39
Steinmetz, Charles, 304-305
Stern, Louis William, 51-52
Stevens, Wallace, 140
Storytelling, 141-143
Strauss, Alfred A., 289
Sullivan, Anne, 18, 103, 149, 164, 356
Surgical death, 339
Szasz, Thomas, 189, 331

Taylor, Elizabeth, 89
Taylor, S., 106-107
Tay-Sachs disease, 129
Teaching
  educational goals in, 274-276
  ideal qualities in, 272-273
  methodology studies of, 270-272
  normative vs. clinical, 273-274
  professors' roles in, 277-283
Technical means, 235-238
Terman, Lewis, 27, 50
Testing, 257-258
Thompson, Polly, 18
Thoreau, Henry David, 220, 361-362
Thurow, Lester C., 220-222
Toffler, 364
Toxic agents, 120-122
Training
  as industry, 198-201
  inservice, 306-307
Trauma, 120
Treatment
  as industry, 198-201
  as moral dilemma, 258-263
"Trisomy 21", 131
Tuberous sclerosis, 128
Turkel, Henry, 155

United Nations Declaration on the Rights of Disabled Persons, 266-267
Universities, 277-283

Values, bureaucratization of, 238-240
Vanier, Jean, 167
Variance/pathology controversy, 157-158
Vineland Training School, 53, 311
Vocational Rehabilitation Act, 227
Voltaire, Francois Marie Arouet, 23, 32, 33

Wallin, J.E. Wallace, 27, 52-53, 289, 311

Watson, James Dewey, 125-126
Weikart, 51
Wertham, F., 326-327
White, Marian Rose, 107-110
Wilbur, Charles T., 39
Wilbur, Hervey W., 27, 39, 40-41, 42, 43
The Wild Boy of Aveyron (Itard), 33, 99, 103, 164, 357
Willowbrook cases, 229
Wilson, Woodrow, 53
Withholding treatment, 248-250
Wolfe, Thomas, 334-335
Wolfensberger, Wolf, 129, 166, 179-180, 210, 247, 289, 307, 320, 324
Woolcott, Alexander, 315
Workplace perspectives, 86-87
Wyatt v. Stickney, 229-230

XYY syndrome, 132

Yamashita, Kiyoshi, 316
Yesterday was Tuesday, All Day and All Night (Seagoe), 102-106

Zero-sum society, 219-222
Zigler, Edward, 2899